# Western Political Thought

## From The Ancient Greeks to Modern Times

Second Edition

Shefali Jha

Pearson

*Editor—Acquisitions*: Kaushal Jajware
*Senior Editor—Production*: G. Sharmilee



ISBN 978-93-528-6934-3

First Impression, 2019
Eighth Impression, 2022
**Ninth Impression, 2023**

Published by Pearson India Education Services Pvt. Ltd,
CIN: U72200TN2005PTC057128.

Head Office: 1st Floor, Berger Tower, Plot No. C-001A/2, Sector 16B,
Noida - 201301, Uttar Pradesh, India.
Registered Office: 7th Floor, SDB2, ODC 7, 8 & 9, Survey No. 01 ELCOT IT/ ITES SEZ, Sholinganallur, Chennai 600119, Tamil Nadu, India.
Phone: 044-66540100,
Website: in.pearson.com, Email: companysecretary.india@pearson.com

*Compositor*: In-house
Printed in India at Shree Maitrey Printech Pvt. Ltd., Noida

# Western Political Thought

Second Edition

# *About Pearson*

*Pearson is the world's learning company, with presence across 70 countries worldwide. Our unique insights and world-class expertise comes from a long history of working closely with renowned teachers, authors and thought leaders, as a result of which, we have emerged as the preferred choice for millions of teachers and learners across the world.*

*We believe learning opens up opportunities, creates fulfilling careers and hence better lives. We hence collaborate with the best of minds to deliver you class-leading products, spread across the Higher Education and K12 spectrum.*

*Superior learning experience and improved outcomes are at the heart of everything we do. This product is the result of one such effort.*

*Your feedback plays a critical role in the evolution of our products and you can contact us –* reachus@pearson.com. *We look forward to it.*

*For My Mother*

# CONTENTS

# PREFACE TO THE SECOND EDITION

I have often wondered at the nature of the hyper-political times we seem to live in. The news about the world, whether of my immediate national context, or from more distant parts, predominantly is about political events; this makes me want to be able to make sense of the importance of politics in our lives all the more. The use of political power to bring about change is a constant motif of our time. Whether it is through the capture of the power of the state, or through the mobilization of large groups of people into a movement, the political domain has become the medium of change and evolution of the world as we know it.

Are the problems that confront us today of such a scale that they cannot be addressed except by organizing collectively? We also have to be careful about maintaining autonomy at some level, whether it is in the case of a cultural association or a sports association or a University. Whose idea of change is to be allowed to become politically effective and why? The dominant political idea of a representative democracy—which is multicultural and inclusive, egalitarian and socially just— is being challenged by the idea of majoritarianism. As this has set forth a cascading number of political conflicts, the question then arises, 'How do we resolve these issues?'

This second edition of *Western Political Thought* is an attempt to include in its reach the political ideas of some of the more recent thinkers. These thinkers certainly draw on the classics of western political thought like the writings of Marx, Rousseau, Locke and Aristotle; however, they also extend our understanding of the political in several ways. Rawls, for instance, shows us that if the idea behind democracy is that of cooperation between free and equal citizens, then our acceptance of democracy as a form of government requires us to abide by certain other specific principles. Gramsci argues that democratization entails fundamental social change which cannot come about without political mobilization. And feminist political theory claims that the central ideas of western political thought—justice, individual liberty, equality, community, democracy—need to be re-examined in the light of how they apply to the position of women.

Several of the chapters of this book have emerged out of my teaching of political thinkers to my students. I remain grateful to my students for their interest as well as their questions, which have enabled me to think more deeply about the arguments of the political philosophers. If students have been one mainstay of the development of the book, the other resource has been access to libraries. Here I must acknowledge both the Central Library of Jawaharlal Nehru University as well as the W.A.C. Bennett Library of Simon Fraser University for providing me access to some of the material on which these chapters are based. I would also like to thank both my editors at Pearson, Kaushal Jajware and Jubi Borkakoti, without whose constant encouragement, I would not have managed to find time from my University duties to finish this edition.

Shefali Jha

# PREFACE TO THE FIRST EDITION

The year 2009 began with a deluge of stories and analyses of the economic meltdown affecting almost each and every country in the world. News of shrinking economies, millions of jobs being lost, soaring unemployment rates, and governments trying different measures to stimulate their economies dominated the media. This only highlighted the important role that governments play in managing the welfare of their citizens. Why is it that in times of crisis we expect the government to bail us out, yet at other times, we want the government to stay out of our affairs? What does this assume about the relationship between us and the government?

States, in order to ensure the welfare of their population, not only have to administer their own territories, but sometimes have to decide about intervening in the affairs of another country. When the citizens of a country are accused of 'terror strikes' against the citizens of another country, can the government of the first country excuse itself by claiming these citizens to be non-state actors? Whether it is the case of what happened on 26 November 2008 in Mumbai, or on 11 September 2001 in New York, states are held accountable not only for the well-being of their citizens, but also for their actions. So states are not only to look after the welfare of their citizens, but also to exercise control over their population. Not only are they to control the actions of their citizens with respect to each other, but also with respect to other countries and other peoples. The twin governmental objectives of control and welfare are linked to one another. Without control, there will be no welfare, that is, control or disciplining by the state is always justified on the basis of its benefits or advantages for the members of the state.

What happens, if, as it did happen in 2009, the head of a regime of a sovereign country is sought to be arrested by an international body? When the International Criminal Court issued an arrest warrant against the president of an independent country in early 2009, for crimes against his own people, demonstrations erupted in that country. Should not only the people of a country have a right to decide if its leaders have committed crimes against them? What if the people are so deeply divided that their government can act with impunity towards one section of them? We are back to the question of the relationship between people and their government or their state.

It is clear that these political questions are not yet resolved, even though the institutions of the state and government have been with us for a long time. Long ago, in human history, groups of people organized themselves into political communities and states and governments emerged. To live subject to the rules made by those wielding political power now seems to be an inescapable part of our lives, but we continue to ask questions about the structures of political power in different societies.

The significance of government and that of our relationships with each other in terms of power makes significant the activity of political thought, thinking systematically about these questions of politics. No wonder that we do have with us a long-standing tradition of thinking about political issues—a well-developed and rich tradition of political thought. It is a tradition that has often been mined for arguments in support of, or against, alternative political arrangements. Many great thinkers are seen as part of this tradition because not only do they refer to one another in their work, but their writings are taken to have developed a common language for the discussion of political problems.

Some of the thinkers belonging to this tradition of Western political thought do share a common spatial and temporal framework. Plato and Aristotle were, for instance, addressing political questions emerging from the practices of Greek city-states. Hobbes, Locke and Rousseau are seen as having created the social contract tradition in responding to similar changes taking place in their societies as the feudal world slowly transformed into an emerging modernity. Between the Greeks and the moderns, we look at examples of Christian political thought, as well as at Machiavelli. Our last four thinkers include two from the Utilitarian tradition, Bentham and Mill, and two German thinkers, Hegel and Marx; these thinkers are linked not only by belonging to similar schools of thought, but also by experiencing similar changes in their countries. But what is our justification for placing Aristotle and Marx, divided by so many centuries and analysing such different societies, in the same tradition of political thought? Not only does Marx refer to Aristotle in his writings, but many of his concepts show an Aristotelian influence.

Finally, if we have agreed on the identity of this tradition of Western political thought, how do we link this tradition with our concerns today?

Many of the problems that we face today are understood as deriving from our political arrangements, and if these political arrangements could be understood more adequately, and modified or changed, we might be better off. The Western tradition of political thought may be just one tradition of political thought, but it is an important tradition. In addressing the political problems or concerns of their day, the thinkers belonging to this tradition, constructed the political subject with certain attributes—the attributes of reason and independence—and incorporated those human beings who apparently lacked these attributes differently into the state. The Western tradition of political thought developed a specific political theory of how rational and independent subjects were related to the state. When we look at how they used this theory to address their political issues, we become more self-conscious or reflexive about the terms in which we understand our own political investigations.

That is why, in many parts of the world, including in India, one of the ways in which students of political science learn to think about political issues and about political ideas is by going through the works of Plato, for instance, or those of Rousseau or Marx. In their attempt to understand the ideas of these thinkers, students look for commentaries on their writings. This reader on Western political thought has been written for undergraduate students of political science in India who are just beginning their study of Plato's *Republic* or Hobbes' *Leviathan* or Hegel's *Philosophy of Right*. The reader is meant to assist them in their effort to comprehend and understand the classics of Western political thought.

Putting together this reader for students, I would like to acknowledge my own debt to my teachers, both at Jawaharlal Nehru University, and at the University of California, Los Angeles, who taught and introduced me to the discipline of political thought. It is their lectures and seminars that engendered and sustained my interest in this area of political science. I would also like to thank the students, both at Miranda House, and at Jawaharlal Nehru University, who attended my classes in Western political thought, and whose interventions often helped me with interpretive issues. I am grateful to the staff of the Jawaharlal Nehru University Library, New Delhi, the Nehru Memorial Museum and Library, New Delhi, and the Georgetown University, School of Foreign Service Library at Doha, Qatar, for providing me with all the material that helped me to write this reader. I would like to thank my editors at Pearson Education, specially Kamini Mahadevan, Debjani M. Dutta and Sukanya Chakrabarti, without whose insistence, encouragement and hard work, this book would not have been produced. Finally, I thank my family for their constant and patient support of my work.

# ABOUT THE AUTHOR

Shefali Jha teaches political science at Jawaharlal Nehru University. She has taught courses in Western Political Thought both to undergraduate students at Miranda House, University of Delhi, and to postgraduate students at the Centre for Political Studies, Jawaharlal Nehru University. She did her doctoral work on Hegel's concept of freedom at the University of California, Los Angeles. Her interests lie in the areas of political philosophy, feminist political theory and constitutionalism and democracy.

# Introduction

## READING CLASSICAL TEXTS OF POLITICAL THOUGHT: METHODOLOGICAL ISSUES

In 1950, there were seventy-three sovereign countries in the world; by 1968, within a span of less than twenty years, some forty-nine newly independent nations had been added to the map of the world.[1] Therein lies the root of our attraction, some might even say, the root of our fatal attraction, for politics. Containing the tantalizing and enticing whiff of the new, politics enlarges our sense of self. Through politics, we can create new stories, or new worlds that we can now investigate. The Age of Discovery, with all its excitement of finding new lands, may be over, but with politics, the reaching out to the new remains an ever present possibility. In politics, this newness is not like the sudden disclosure of a new planet which had always existed as part of a solar system, instead it is the creation of something that did not exist before, by us, through our political action. The European Union is new, the Islamic Republic of Iran is (was) new, the women's movement is new, and so on, with the assumption being that these political entities are not just new, but new and 'better' for many of us.

Politics seems to be one of the significant markers of human creativity, and in societies where this creativity often seems to bear fruit, as in a modernizing society, thinking about politics is a central concern. This book, however, is not only about political thinkers from modernizing societies; it also ranges over what political thinkers from the distant past said about politics, how they defined politics and what they took its main features to be. Did they, in their classic works, also talk about the transformative or creative role of politics?

A conversation with voices from the past is what an engagement with the history of political thought is. But why should we care about what was said about political institutions and political power in the past—the new political institutions the creation of which was advocated in the past—when the past is long gone? And it's not even our past—why make so much effort, in studying the history of Western political thought, to recover the meaning of voices from someone else's long gone past?

Well, we might be curious about that past. The past is a legitimate object of enquiry, pace the discipline of history. We read Plato and Aristotle to fulfil our antiquarian interests. We are curious about the Greek city-states of the pre-Christian era; we want to know about Athenian democracy and Spartan oligarchy and *Republic* and *Politics* help to satisfy that curiosity.

But we are not historians. We are political scientists trying to get our bearings amidst the intense political conflicts of today. We might not have much interest in the ancient Greeks; we puzzle instead, over the reasons for conflict in our societies, and we investigate ways of managing or resolving this conflict. How do we answer then, the question of the relevance of a work of political philosophy that was written in another time and place, to current politics? Have you at sometime come across an individual so immersed in her reading of Plato's dialogues not because of any desire about Greece, but because, she says, reading Plato helps her to make sense of modern politics. *Republic* helps her to better comprehend the political arrangements of her own world; but how can a book about ancient Greek constitutions also be a book about contemporary politics? Or, to put it in slightly different terms, why are courses in the history of political thought part of the curriculum of a degree in political science in so many parts of the world?

In answering the question of why do we, or why should we, study the history of Western political thought, we find that we are led to address the problem of how do we study a tradition of political thought. These two questions are inextricably linked, and in considering one, we cannot but probe the other. So, how do we recover the meaning of what was said by these voices from the past? We have to first understand what it is that they said, to interpret the meaning of their words, before we can use their writings to either increase our knowledge of the past, or to better understand our own present-day conditions. Let me start, then, with the problem of methodology: how should we study the political thought of a particular thinker?

## THE TEXTUAL METHOD

Let us take a well-known text, for instance, Hobbes' *Leviathan*. How do we understand the meaning of what is written in this book? For a long time, the answer to such questions was provided by the textual method. The textual method has been described as insisting that given 'the autonomy of the *text* itself as the sole necessary key to its own meaning,...the *text* itself should form the self-sufficient object of inquiry and understanding'.[2] To understand the meaning of the *Leviathan*, we only have to read it again and again, or if necessary, we should read it along with the corpus of Hobbes' other writings. If the meaning of some passage in the *Leviathan* is unclear to us, we take the help of some other passage in the same work, or at the most, in some other book written by Thomas Hobbes. A study of political thought becomes, then, a systematic perusal of certain classic texts.

This method of studying the Western tradition of political thought came under attack, in the 1960s, by the members of the 'Cambridge school' who argued that since meaning can only emerge in a context, when we ignore the context by insisting on the autonomy of the text, what we do is to surreptitiously introduce our own context as a frame in which to put what the text says.[3] We take the historical text to be answering our questions. So it's not as if we have really respected the autonomy of the text; because meaning requires context, what we have done is to illegitimately frame the text in our context instead of its own context.

According to these critics, this has led to the canon of classic texts being taken to be providing answers to a number of set questions, like 'what is justice', or 'what is the relationship between the citizen and the state', or as I asked earlier, why is there conflict in human communities and how can we manage it, and so on. As each thinker is understood to be responding to these same 'enduring' and 'abiding'[4] questions, as important to us as to him, the discipline of political thought becomes a comparison of these answers given by different historical figures. Let's look at a couple of examples: when we find Aristotle, discussing in the first few books of *Nichomachean Ethics*, the centrality of the concept of choice to the concept of moral action, and J.S. Mill, many centuries later, in *On Liberty*, making freedom of choice essential for the development of our moral and mental faculties, we take both philosophers to be grappling with the same issue, thus committing the fallacy of a liberal (mis)reading of Aristotle. Here is another, starker example: you might have come across a commentary on Plato in which he is presented as the first communist. To interpret Plato on property with allusions to Marx as if both these philosophers were dealing with the same (eternal) problem of property and power—is that not to make a serious interpretive error?

The assumptions underlying the textual method are blamed for the following exegetical problems. When it is presupposed that a political philosopher is trying to answer a certain set question, the meaning of everything she wrote is sought to be fitted in the framework of a doctrine, and any inconsistencies or contradictory statements of the philosopher are just ignored, instead of being taken as clues that the thinker might be trying to do something other than answer some 'universal' question. Critics have further argued that this textual method also leads us into making the mistake of conflating 'the retrospective significance of a given historical work' with 'its meaning for the thinker himself'.

## THE SOCIAL CONTEXT METHOD

The textual approach was sought to be replaced by the social context method in the study of political thought. The contextual method holds 'that it is the *context* "of religious, political, and economic factors" which determines the meaning of any given text, and so must provide "the ultimate framework" for any attempt to understand it'.[5] If we apply this methodological principle to our earlier example, it follows that before reading *Leviathan*, we must know that in writing it, Hobbes was trying to intervene in the raging debate between the king's faction and the parliamentary faction in England in the first half of the 17th century. When *Leviathan* was published in 1651, the English civil war had just come to a close, with the English king, Charles I, being executed in 1649. For the next eleven years, no king was allowed to take the throne. It was in these turbulent times that *Leviathan* was written, and unless we are aware of this political context, no number of readings of *Leviathan* will help us to understand its meaning.

*Leviathan* was a response to pressing political questions or political problems of the day. If we are unaware of these problems of 17th century English politics, we will take *Leviathan* to be answering our political concerns, and in this manner, completely misunderstand its meaning. Political philosophers of the past must not be taken to be addressing our political concerns; their political concerns are different, of their own time. We must not see the history of political thought as a series of different answers to the same questions; the questions themselves are different, these different questions emerging from specific historical circumstances.

In order to study political thought then, we require knowledge of history. We must place the writings of the political philosopher we are studying in the economic, social and political context in which she was writing. If ideas are 'responses to immediate circumstances' then we must know the nature of the society in which the thinker was writing. It is the use of the contextual method that allows a scholar like Macpherson, for instance, to read the work of Hobbes and Locke in the context of a changing economic system, and to interpret it as the work of 'bourgeois' thinkers.[6] What the historical context is, may however, also be a matter of interpretation: we are familiar with Tully's criticism of Macpherson for misinterpreting Locke's conception of property by not seeing that the property that Locke was concerned to defend against the state was the property of the religious Dissenters, and not that of the 'bourgeois' rich. For Tully, to use 'the "rise of capitalism" as the governing framework [context] for interpreting seventeenth-century political thought',[7] is to ensure misinterpretation of thinkers like Hobbes and Locke. Looking at the text in context is also a matter of interpreting the context correctly. If we use modern categories to interpret the context, rather than the text, it is as if we are committing the same error. We cannot claim to be moving beyond the text to the context when we seek to understanding the historical context in our present-day categories. We have to read the past in its own terms.

When the textual method was attacked in the name of 'the context', its proponents began to fear for the classics. If the text was going to be reduced to its context, what need was there to read the classic texts? In their campaign to save the text, the advocates of the textual method began shifting the battle lines of the methodological debate. No one believed any longer (that is, if someone ever had) the 'absurd notion' that the classic texts 'are self-sufficient objects of inquiry, which can be understood in isolation'. Having accepted that 'we have to read even a great text in its context', what was still pointed out was that—'but we have to understand what its author understood that context to be, not insert it into some context constructed by our scholarship'.[8] The question now was—how was the context to be understood? What should we mean by 'the context' became the new point of debate.

## ALTERNATIVE APPROACHES

Although the textual method has been accused of committing the 'most mistakes' or leading to the 'worst misunderstandings' of a text, it is not as if the contextual approach, as we just saw above, does not have its own pitfalls. It is true that the contextual method makes us aware that we always approach a text with certain presuppositions. It is, as if, to guard against these presuppositions, that the contextual method warns us to situate the text in its own context. Many leading scholars of the art of interpretation have, while agreeing that meaning can only exist in context, however pointed out that it is humanly impossible to completely bracket our own presuppositions and our own questions. If it is true that contextualizing is an essential component of understanding, that understanding cannot take place without a context, then it is equally true that we cannot remove our own context from the picture. Hans-Georg Gadamer, an exponent of modern hermeneutics, for instance, argued that successful interpretation of meaning takes place through a 'fusion of horizons': a mingling of our own horizon with the horizon of the text makes it possible for an earlier text to have meaning for us.[9]

If it is the context of the text that makes it what it is, it is our context which makes us what we are. We learn to think and reason within a certain tradition, and the assumptions or presuppositions of this tradition mediate our grasp of what is written in the text. Instead of seeing these assumptions as hampering our understanding of the past, Gadamer believed that it is through these assumptions that we think, interpret and understand at all. We always bring our own questions to bear on the past; this does not imply that we read the canon of political philosophy as repositories of 'timeless truths' or 'ageless wisdom' but it does mean that we read Machiavellli's *Discourses* not only because we want to know more about 16th century Florence, but because we want to use this book to increase our understanding of ourselves and of our political situation. In which way do these works of political thought add to our self-knowledge is a question that remains to be answered.

Gadamer believed that all human beings were part of an 'effective history', part, that is, of the same historical process. It is this shared belonging to the same historical process that allows our horizon to fuse with that of the past. In that sense, our presuppositions are not, as long as we are also aware of the text's specific historical context, a hindrance to the understanding of the text, but actually an entry into the meaning of the text. What needs to be clarified here is whether this applies to those belonging to a particular tradition, lets say that the past and present of the people of the West forms one continuous history, or whether members of a different tradition, let's say the people of Kenya and Tanzania, are also part of this same history, and will therefore have an entry point into the meaning of the Western tradition of political thought. (Did the previous era of globalization—the colonization and the labour migrations of the late 19th and early 20th centuries—ensure one history for the world?) If they are not part of the same history, then how do they understand the work of an alien tradition, or do they misunderstand it? Moreover, when meaning is a variable determined by the fusing of two contexts, that of the writer and that of the reader, does it follow that for readers in different historical times, the meaning of the same text would be different—this conclusion seems to take us as far away as possible from the 'autonomy of the text' methodological thesis.

For members of the Cambridge school, on the other hand, going down the 'fusion of horizons' road of interpretation is to end up in a blind alley of misunderstanding and misinterpretation. Remember, their main criticism of the textual method was that it allows us to frame a historical text anachronistically in our contemporary context. These scholars disagree with Gadamer that we should not try to bracket our own presuppositions because they allow the text to speak to us. This will lead, they argue, to a completely instrumental view of the text which they want to counter not with the idea of the autonomy of the text but with the idea of the autonomy or integrity of a socio-historical slice of time. (Would it follow that the categories of 17th century English political thought would be as alien to a 21st century English reader as to an Indian reader?)

The Cambridge school insists, then on the significance of the text's historical context; where the social context approach goes wrong is in ignoring the most important historical context of a text—its linguistic context. In different historical periods, a certain political language is dominant, and we have to become familiar with this political discourse before we can interpret a particular text from that time.

The contextual method has thus been faulted by the Cambridge school for throwing the baby out with the bathwater. As one critic puts it, while 'a study of social context may *help* in the understanding of a text', 'the fundamental assumption of the contextual methodology, that the ideas of a given text should be understood *in terms of* its social context, can be shown to be mistaken, and to serve in consequence not as a guide to understanding...'[10] If the meaning of the text is produced wholly by the social context, then why should we read the text at all? Often you will find yourself being exhorted not just to read about Hobbes but to read Hobbes himself. But if the meaning of *Leviathan* can be reduced to its context, then why do we bother with *Leviathan* itself?

If we reduce the text to the social context, then we will, Skinner argues, lose the point of what is being said in the text. Skinner tries to replace the central concept of the 'social context' with his conception of the 'linguistic context'. Again, what is the linguistic context of a text? For every philosopher in question, a certain language of politics is available to him in which he understands the political questions of his day. For instance, when Locke used the word 'trust' or the phrase 'government by consent', these words had a specific meaning at that time, which we must know in order to decipher the meaning of these terms in Locke's writings.

When we become familiar with the dominant political conceptions of a particular time, only then can we also understand the original contribution of a political philosopher, because we can see then how he deviated from the dominant political ideas. As has famously been shown in the case of Machiavelli, it was Machiavelli's use of the term 'virtu', a dominant idea of Renaissance Italy, with a completely different meaning given to it by him, which ensures that today we still read Machiavelli and leave the many others who also wrote advice books for princes in 15th–16th century Italy to specialist historians.

For Skinner, to understand a statement is to know more than its meaning; it is to also grasp the illocutionary force[11] of that statement. It is knowledge of the linguistic context—how words were used at that time—that allows us to grasp the illocutionary force of an utterance. By making these statements political thinkers were not just saying something, they were doing something, since 'to make a statement *is* to perform an action'. Given this theory of linguistic action or of speech acts, the meaning of their statements must include the use they wanted to make of the statements and this can only be revealed by knowing the linguistic context of the time.

## CONCLUSION

We have looked at four positions on the interpretation and relevance of 'political writing in past time'. Briefly, and simplistically, if the textual method's advice is to read and reread the text carefully and we will find it answering our questions, the social context method asks us instead to make the economic and social context of the work a priority, using modern categories to interpret that historical context. For Gadamerian hermeneutics, our reading of the text must be informed by a true intermingling of contexts. For the Cambridge school, when we interpret a 16th century text through a familiarity with its linguistic context, keeping our own presuppositions out, we realize that the writer is using political terms with meanings specific to that time. Coming back to the question of why we study the history of political thought, this does not mean that it is an irrelevant exercise, that the text has no relevance for us. It is its difference—how the political concerns of that time were different—that makes the text relevant to us, not the fact that its author was asking the same questions about politics as us. 'The classic texts, especially in social, ethical, and political thought, help to reveal—if we let them—not the essential sameness, but rather the essential variety of viable moral assumptions and political commitments.'[12] Approaching the texts in this way, 'knowledge of the history of such ideas can then serve to show the extent to which those features of our own arrangements which we may be disposed to accept as traditional or even "timeless" truths may in fact be the merest contingencies of our peculiar history and social structure'.[13] Such a consciousness allows us to develop a critical perspective with respect to our own society and to see what can be changed in it. Instead of seeing the history of political thought as a series of mistakes, as a series of unsuccessful attempts to answer our questions—we cannot use Plato's organic conception of the state to defend individual rights; we cannot use Rousseau's conception of direct democracy in contemporary large nation-states—we can use the work of earlier political thinkers to query our contemporary institutions—the centrality of labour in our lives, the overriding concern with consumption and therefore with production, and the modern bureaucracy as such an integral part of the contemporary democratic state.

Is that how the work of earlier political philosophers is used in contemporary political theory? What are we to make of a political theorist, like Martha Nussbaum for example, making self-consciously Aristotelian arguments to throw light on contemporary political arrangements? Political theory today abounds with Aristotelians, Lockeans, Hegelians and Nietzscheans. In terms of method, how are we to interpret someone calling himself a Lockean today? Does that person read the *Two Treatises on Government* to understand how different our politics is, or does he read it in terms of a common political language between the past and the present? When a theorist argues for more attention to Hellenistic philosophy today on the grounds that 'the writings of modern writers as diverse as Descartes, Spinoza, Kant, Adam Smith, Hume, Rousseau, the Founding Fathers of the United States, Nietzsche, and Marx, owe in every case a considerable debt to the writings of Stoics, Epicureans, and/or Skeptics, and *frequently far more* than to the writings of Plato and Aristotle',[14] is she claiming that the linguistic context of any modern political philosopher, whether it is Nietzsche or herself, is partly inherited from the past? Where does the linguistic context of any philosopher come from? Nussbaum argues for the importance of both 'the historical and the literary context', pointing out that even though Roman writers like Cicero were greatly influenced by the Greek Stoics, their own work has to be understood to be 'standing in an intimate relation to Roman history and politics'.[15] The influence of the philosophical tradition of the past is always refracted by the theorist's own historical situation. The same questions would arise for those of us who are from India, or China, or Africa, reading the canon of Western political thought.

Just because in this book, a series of thinkers are chronologically arranged in successive chapters, we should not take this to mean that each of these thinkers has provided us with successively better designed new political institutions, since some of these political institutions seem to be based on opposing ideals. Nor are we to take the later writers as providing us with a better approximation of the general idea of politics. In fact, they provide us with radically different conceptions of politics, or we can say that they make us familiar with radically different ways of legitimizing political power. It is interesting to see the reasons given to legitimate political rule changing over time. If at an earlier moment, political rule was linked to the idea of the development of virtue, at another later moment, it begins to be legitimated by the idea of its protection of individual liberty. If, in earlier times, the language of virtue was used to discuss political institutions, later this discussion comes to be couched in the language of liberty and the rights of the individual. This change in the political concepts justifying political authority also led to a questioning of the harmony between an individual's interests and the interests of others. Virtue talk assumed the priority of the public good for the fulfilment of an individual's private interests; but the language of rights seemed to construct the public good as the sum of individual interests.

Politics brings about change; if our goal is human happiness or human welfare, we can use politics as an instrument to change things in that direction. In ancient Greek political thought, for example, the political community was to be organized to create virtue amongst its citizens because that was seen as the road to happiness. Individuals needed to be part of a community to lead happy lives; the community can only exist if its members behave virtuously; for the community to be sustainable over time, its members' virtue must be continuously encouraged. The community seems to depend on something—its members' sense of virtue—that it itself plays a role in creating. The community which is organized politically in the right manner will be able to create virtuous citizens. In Greek political thought, however, as we will see later in the chapter on Plato, we also find a conception of virtue leading to happiness not through the political community but because virtuous individuals have healthy souls. But the legitimating principle of political authority remains its link to virtue.

We find the legitimating principle of political authority changing over time. The goal remains individual happiness, but virtue does not get us there; instead, this role is taken over by individual rights. We ensure a greatest chance of happiness for individuals in that regime which is best at protecting individual rights—political authority is legitimated by the idea of individual rights. Do we study the history of Western political thought, then, to see how the legitimating principles of political order change? There was a time in the history of the West when happiness was seen as an attribute of another world, of life after death, and in that case, nothing much could be expected from politics. If happiness was available only in union with God, and that too after death, then all aspects of the human world, including politics, counted for nought. A variation on this way of thinking is to argue that when people are dying of poverty and disease, and happiness is equated with domination, hedonism and consumerism, then happiness is not of much value, and politics in the service of this kind of happiness is also not worth the effort. This is not to claim that the human world can never match the value (happiness) of the so called heavenly world, but that what we have made of the human world so far makes it imperative for us to create something else, something different, something new. These changes in the history of Western political thought make us aware of or clearer about, what counts as a defensible view of human happiness today, and how is it related to the organization of political power.

In answering the question of how is, or why should the business of political design be relevant to human concerns, political thinkers from the past help us to look anew at how we think of this question today. In fact, one suggestion has been, as we saw, that it is because they provide us with a snapshot of different ways of organizing our collective life that they are useful to us. To believe that our present was unfolding in the past, or that our present was contained in the past and therefore the past has inexorably led up to our present, is not the same as maintaining that the whole purpose of the past was to lead up to our present. The last proposition belongs to a teleological conception of the historical world, and holding on to it would lead us to make the unjustifiable claim that it was the goal or intention of earlier political thinkers, in writing their 'great works' to solve our contemporary political problems. They were grappling with their own political problems, given to them by their own circumstances, and they grasped these problems in their own concepts. These conceptual grids are taken by some to have changed radically over time, although others argue that some of these political concepts have travelled through time.

What I have tried to do in this chapter is to show how debatable these questions still are—how do we study the history of political thought; why do we study it at all; what is it a study really of ? Before you start your reading of Plato or Rousseau, or as you study them, you should think about these three questions and try to work out your own answers to them because these answers will affect your interpretation and understanding of the meaning of their writings. I am not asking you to get bogged down in methodological issues, which seem to have become the bane of social scientists, but to keep some of these issues in mind.

## NOTES

1. Adam Przeworski, Michael E. Alvarez, Jose Antonio Cheibub, Fernando Limongi, *Democracy and Development: Political Institutions and Well-Being in the World 1950–1990*, Cambridge: Cambridge University Press, 2000, p. 36.
2. J. Tully, *Meaning and Context—Quentin Skinner and his Critics*, Polity, 1988, pp. 29–30, (emphasis in original).
3. Q. Skinner, J.M. Dunn, and J.G.A. Pocock are loosely said to belong to the Cambridge school because while teaching at Cambridge University, they shared similar positions on historical interpretation.
4. See L. Strauss and J. Cropsey (eds.), *History of Political Philosophy* (3rd edition), Chicago: University of Chicago Press, 1987, p. xiii.

5. J. Tully, *Meaning and Context—Quentin Skinner and His Critics*, Polity, 1988, p. 30, (emphasis in original)
6. C.B. Macpherson, *The Political Theory of Possessive Individualism*, Oxford: Oxford University Press, 1962.
7. J. Tully, *An Approach to Political Philosophy: Locke in Contexts*, Cambridge: Cambridge University Press, 1993, p. 127
8. See N. Tarcov and T.N. Pangle, 'Leo Strauss and the History of Political Philosophy', in L. Strauss and J. Cropsey, *History of Political Philosophy*, pp. 913–914.
9. See the 'Introduction' in Robert J. Dostal (ed.), *The Cambridge Companion to Gadamer*, Cambridge: Cambridge University Press, 2002.
10. J. Tully, *Meaning and Context: Quentin Skinner and his Critics*, Polity, 1988, p. 59, (emphasis in original).
11. For a discussion of the relationship between the illocutionary force of a sentence and its meaning, see Q. Skinner, Chapter 7 in *Visions of Politics–Vol. I – Regarding Method*, Cambridge: Cambridge University Press, 2002.
12. J. Tully, *Meaning and Context—Quentin Skinner and His Critics*, Polity, 1988, p. 67.
13. *Ibid.*, p. 67.
14. M.C. Nussbaum, *The Therapy of Desire—Theory and Practice in Hellenistic Ethics*, New Jersey: Princeton University Press, 1994, p. 4, emphasis mine.
15. M.C. Nussbaum, *The Therapy of Desire—Theory and Practice in Hellenistic Ethics*, p. 7.

# ONE

# The Greek City-State: Democratic Institutions in Athens

One of the claims made in the introduction to this book was that in order to avoid misinterpreting the ideas of a thinker, we have to place that thinker in his or her historical context. We have to be aware of the social and political conditions that the thinker is responding to. Since, in the next few chapters, we are going to study the political thought of the philosophical threesome of Socrates, Plato and Aristotle, which has dominated for so long the study of Greek moral and political philosophy, we need to have a look at their historical context.

Socrates and Plato were Athenian citizens and even though there were times when they were severely critical of the social and political institutions of classical Athens,[1] to understand their works, we must have some idea of how those institutions functioned. Aristotle was not an Athenian citizen, but he spent more than half of his life there, first studying with Plato, and then setting up his own school and teaching there. The Athenian city-state formed the backdrop for the political thought of all three philosophers.

Ancient Greek history is usually divided into the following four periods: the Mycenaean period (1600–1100 BCE), the 'Dark Ages' (1100–700 BCE), the Archaic Age (700–480 BCE) and the Classical Age (480–320 BCE) We begin our story around 800–700 BCE when the so-called Dark Ages were ending and the Archaic Age was beginning in Greece, with the rapid establishment of hundreds of Greek city-states. By 750 BCE, the Greek peninsula was suffering from the effects of a population explosion, and many city-states of the Greek peninsula began sending out colonies to settle down in nearby coastal areas. First, the Aegean coast of Asia Minor was colonized, followed by the southern coast of the Black Sea. Then, to the west, colonies were settled on the coast of Albania and southern Italy, in Sicily, on the southern coast of France, and even in north-eastern Spain.

Greek colonies were also found in Egypt and Libya. 'By the 6th century, Hellas had become a cultural and linguistic area much larger than the geographical area of Greece. Greek colonies were not politically controlled by their founding cities, although they often retained religious and commercial links with them.'[2] Some of the famous modern cities of the Mediterranean coast have their beginnings as new settlements of the Greek city-states, for instance, Marseilles (Massilia), Naples (Neapolis) and Istanbul (Byzantium). By the classical era, there were certainly more than 1,500 city-states in this region, even if some were little more than modern towns. Each city-state or *polis* consisted of the main city surrounded by an agricultural hinterland. Each city-state formed a separate and independent political unit.

The age of archaic and classical Greece was not only the age of the spread of the Greek city-states all over the Mediterranean coast, but it was also an age of transition in, and consolidation of political institutions in these city-states. Originally, each Greek city-state was ruled by a king, called the *basileus,* but gradually, by about 700 BCE, the *basileus* was replaced in most Greek city-states by groups of three men, called *archons*. The *archon eponymous* functioned like a chief magistrate, the *polemarch* was the head of the armed forces and the *archon basileus* performed religious duties.[3] In Athens, these three officials were elected from the ranks of the nobility for a term of ten years, but by 683 BCE, their term had been reduced to just one year. Gradually the number of *archons* in Athens increased to about nine. After finishing their term, these *archons* became lifetime members of a body called the Council of Areopagus which was responsible for the city's government. The government of Athens in the 7th century was thus in the hands of the aristocracy, in the form of the nine *archons* supported by the Council of the Areopagus. In most of the other city-states as well, kingship was replaced by oligarchic forms of government. Oligarchy, that is, rule by the few, usually the noble born, and the rich and wealthy, was the dominant form of government in the Greek city-states.

## DEMOCRACY IN ATHENS

We said earlier that there were as many as 1,500 city-states at this time; yet, the city-state of Athens has received more historical attention than any other. There are several reasons which justify this concentrated attention. First of all, Athens was much larger than most other city-states, both territorially and in terms of population. In the 5th century, Athens is supposed to have had as many as 50,000 citizens, whereas Sparta, with the next largest citizen body, had only 10,000 citizens. Many Greek city-states had a citizen body of only about 400 to 900 citizens. Attica, with Athens at its centre, covered a territory of 2,650 sq. kms, whereas the average Greek city-state had a territory of only 50 to 100 sq. kms. The region of Boeotia, just north of Attica, for example, with about 2,600 sq. kms, contained several poleis.[4] Politically too, Athens was an anomaly in Hellas given that from about 500 BCE to around 300 BCE, except for two brief interruptions, Athens remained a democracy. For 200 years or so, with hardly any real break, the city was under democratic institutions and these institutions must have influenced Athenian life a great deal.

Did the flowering of culture in Athens at that time—in the form of the great philosophers like Plato and Socrates, the celebrated dramatists, like Aeschylus, Euripides, Sophocles and Aristophanes, and beautiful art—have something to do with its democratic practices? It has been pointed out that when the other Greek city-states, from the 8th to the mid-6th centuries, were establishing colonies, Athens was quiet; during the 7th and 6th centuries, Athens had no poets to boast of, except Solon; and there is no record of any visits of the famous 6th century Ionian philosophers to Athens. Suddenly, in the 5th century, Athens was at the forefront of everything. Did this have to do with the establishment of democratic institutions by Cleisthenes in 508/507 BCE? Soon after democracy was firmly established in Athens, the Greco–Persian wars began and Athens helped the Ionian Greeks to throw off their recently acquired Persian yoke. The Persian king, Darius, sent a large army to Greece which was defeated by a much smaller Athenian force at Marathon in 490 BCE. In 480 BCE, a large Persian fleet of over 1,200 ships, sent by Xerxes, Darius's son, was defeated by the Athenian navy, off the coast of the island of Salamis. In 478 BCE, Athens established the Delian League under its leadership, ostensibly to protect the other Greek city-states, since skirmishes with Persian forces continued sporadically for another three decades, till the peace of Callias was finally declared in 449 BCE, when Persia accepted the independence of the Greek city-states of Asia Minor.

Did Athens's increase in power in the 4th and 5th centuries have to do with its new form of government? Questions such as these as well as our modern interest in democracy draw our attention specifically to the city-state of Athens. We began our discussion of the Athenian *polis* by referring to the argument that much of Western political thought is a response to Athenian democracy. This claim is often repeated: 'The history of political thought in the West is largely the history of warnings about the hasty, greedy, and intemperate courses on which the masses are likely to embark if they ever get power in their hands.'[5] If it is not just Plato and Aristotle who were reacting to Athenian democracy, but the entire tradition of Western political thought, then it seems all the more important for us to have some idea of this democratic regime.

When was democracy first established in Athens? This question continues to be debated extensively by historians. Many scholars take Cleisthenes's reforms of 508/507 BCE to be definitive, but some insist that Athenian democracy can only be said to be established much later with the reforms of Ephialtes and Pericles in the period 460–452 BCE. Sidestepping this debate we can only note that there seem to be at least four important moments in the development of democracy in Athens: Solon's economic reforms of the late 6th century, Cleisthenes's reorganization of the tribes in the early 6th century, the reforms of 462–460 BCE associated with Ephialtes and Pericles and finally, the changes of 404–403 BCE.[6] We can examine each of these transitions briefly.

Usually, accounts of Athenian democracy begin with Solon, who was appointed the *archon eponymous* in Athens in 594 BCE. Solon is said to have started the story of Athenian democracy by undertaking some major economic reforms. As soon as he became the *archon*, Solon cancelled all outstanding debts and forbade any creditor from selling anyone who was in his debt, into slavery. In Attica which had an agrarian economy, poorer farmers who had taken loans from a richer neighbour to make ends meet were forced to mortgage their land to their creditor when they were unable to repay their loans. These debt-ridden farmers became the *hektemorioi* or tenant farmers bound now to pay one-sixth of their land's produce to their creditor. Many of these *hektemorioi* had by the 7th century, finding themselves unable to even pay the sixth part of the produce to the creditor, been forced to sell their families and themselves as slaves to the creditor.[7] When Solon decreed the cancellation of all debts and the return of their lands to the *hektemorioi*, and abolished all forms of debt-slavery, he took a major step towards reducing the stark inequalities that existed in Attica. Some fragments of Solon's poems are still extant, in which he describes himself as freeing the land and liberating the farmers.[8]

This, however, did not mean that the differences between the rich and the poor disappeared. To Solon also goes the credit of formalizing the Athenian population into four property classes: At the top were the *pentakosiomedimnoi* or the 'five hundred measure men', who obtained, every year, at least 500 measures of produce from their land. One measure or *medimnos* was approximately equivalent to 38 kgs or 50 litres. The next class was made up of the *hippies* whose estates produced between 300 and 500 measures annually, and who were able to provide a horse and be cavalrymen in times of war. They were followed by the *zeugitai*, with 200–300 measures, who could pay for their own armour and who became infantrymen during war. The last class was made up of the *thetes*, who could only produce less than 200 measures from their land. The *thetes* were manual labourers and did not pay taxes. It is estimated that more than half of the citizen population of the city-state of Athens was made up of *thetes*.[9] What

Solon did was to allow Athenian citizens from all four classes to participate in Athenian political institutions, unlike before, when political activity in Athens was only the preserve of the nobility, or of the wealthy.

To counteract the power of the nobility in the Areopagus, Solon decreed that the *archons* would no longer be purely from the members of the nobility; the nine *archons* could now be chosen from the first two property classes of the *pentakosiomedimnoi* and the *hippies*. Solon is also said to have established a new political institution, the *boule,* to advise the *archons*. Membership to the *boule* was open to the first three Athenian classes. Solon also increased the importance of another pre-existing advisory body, the *ekklesia,* by enacting a law that every Athenian citizen, including the *thetes,* could sit in the *ekklesia* where they would vote on governmental policy. Solon also reformed the judicial system. Whereas, earlier, the *archons* and the Areopagus performed all judicial functions, Solon now allowed members of all property classes to be included as jurors in a new system of courts. Any citizen could appeal to these new courts against the decisions of the *archons*.

Solon's democratic reforms became the foundation on which later statesmen, who wanted to introduce democratic laws, based their policies. His reforms withstood the tyranny of Peisistratus, who was a younger associate of Solon, and who, presenting himself as the champion of the people, ruled as a tyrant, first from 559 to 556 BCE and then from 546 to 528 BCE. Even as a tyrant, however, Peisistratus kept the Solonian constitution in place. Finally, his sons were overthrown by Cleisthenes, who retained some of Solon's changes and who is considered, due to his own revisions to the constitution in 508/507 BCE, to be the real founder of Athenian democracy by most scholars. Like Solon, the first thing that Cleisthenes did was to modify the social structure of Attica. Bypassing the earlier four Ionian tribes which had been based on kinship, Cleisthenes reorganized the people of Attica into ten new tribes based on *demes,* or place of residence. Attica was divided into 139 *demes*; these *demes* were classified as belonging to the coast, to an inland area, or to the city. The *demes* or localities of the coast were divided into 10 groups or *trittyes* and the same was done with the inland and the city *demes*. One group or *trittyes* of *demes* from each region was assigned to one of the 10 new tribes. So each of the ten tribes was made up of three *trittyes* and through the *trittyes* of anywhere from six to twenty-one *demes*. Thus, the new tribes were dispersed over the entire geographical area of the *polis*. It was on the basis of these new tribes that the membership of citizens from all over Attica to Athens's central political institutions was organized. 'This was the first systematic attempt to establish binding institutional links between the centre and the periphery and incorporate all of Attica formally within the Athenian *polis*. The result was less the restructuring of an old political community than the creation of a new one'.[10] Thus, Cleisthenes was the one responsible for integrating all the people who lived in Attica into one political community. By opening the highest political offices to all citizens, he made them feel that they were all a part of the same body. We will come to know more about his political reforms when we discuss the political institutions of Athenian democracy, in the next section. The following description of Athens's main political organs will incorporate both Cleisthenes's reforms as well as some of the changes made by later democratic leaders.

## POLITICAL INSTITUTIONS OF ATHENIAN DEMOCRACY

Let us look more closely at some of the central political institutions of democratic Athens. At the forefront was the *ekklesia*, which it was the right and duty of every male Athenian citizen, who was over 20 years old, to attend. Citizenship was restricted to free born Athenian males, and out of a population of about 300,000 in Athens, not more than 50,000 would have been citizens. The quorum of the *ekklesia* was set at 6,000, and it met about 40 times in a year, which means that there was a session of the *ekklesia* after about every nine days. Of the 40 annual meetings, at least 10 were extremely important. Each such session was called the main meeting or the *ekklesia kyria*, 'in which there was always a vote of confidence for the officers of the state, discussions on the price of corn which was set by the state, the taking up of matters related to defence as well as to the confiscation of the property of various persons by the state'.[11] About a century after the reforms of Cleisthenes, when democracy was restored in Athens after the oligarchic coup failed in 403 BCE, payment was also introduced for attending the meetings of the *ekklesia* and each citizen was paid around three *obols* (approximately one day's earnings for manual labour) for attending.

Five days notice had to be given for a scheduled meeting of the *ekklesia*. Along with this notice, a placard announcing the proposals to be discussed at the meeting had to be put up in the *agora* (marketplace). On the day of the meeting, some police officers would descend on the marketplace with long ropes, dipped in red colouring, in their hands. With these ropes they would try to herd in all the citizens who were delaying going to the assembly. If a citizen got red colour on his clothes, he would be fined for attending the meeting late. The citizens at the assembly voted on the laws being proposed, or the policy being decided. A proposal would be announced, say, a proposition to increase the garrison of the allied city of Byzantium. After the proposal was introduced, the herald would ask loudly, 'Who wishes to speak?' After that, it was open to anyone and everyone to come up to the *bema* (podium) to put forth his views on the matter at hand, 'When it is something to do with the government of the country that is to be debated, the man who gets up to advise them may be a builder or equally well a blacksmith or a shoemaker, merchant or ship owner, rich or poor, of good family or none.'[12] The Athenians saw free speech as integral to the proper functioning of their democracy. Not only was Athenian democracy based on *isegoria*—an equal opportunity to speak given to all citizens, irrespective of their status—but democracy in Athens also allowed *parrhesia*—frank and critical speech—to all its citizens.[13] Whenever an important motion was being discussed in the assembly, there would usually be many speakers, both supporting and opposing the motion. Soon there would be a demand for closure through a vote and voting would take place by a show of hands. This is how important issues of war and peace, treaties with other city-states, as well as matters of domestic policy were decided by the Athenian citizens. Decisions of the assembly were recorded and published, and the more important ones were even carved in stone tablets, several of which have survived.

There were many mechanisms set in place to ensure that the citizens took the proceedings of the assembly seriously. The rules demanded that speakers stay on the subject at hand, and not slander anyone. Breaking this rule meant having to pay a penalty. There was also the interesting mechanism of *graphe paranomon,* which was a suit, or an accusation against a bill or proposal which was contrary to the law. If the assembly passed this accusation against any leader or against any of its members, that person would have to pay a fine. It was important that the deliberations of the assembly were conducted carefully, especially since it was an extremely powerful body. Along with passing laws and policymaking, the assembly also had the power to hear charges of *eisangelia,* which was an accusation of crimes against the state. At each *ekklesia kyria,* any citizen could bring charges of treason against any official or a private citizen. To bring these charges, no prior permission from the *boule* was needed. In the later years of Athenian democracy, from 403 BCE to 322 BCE, the Assembly prosecuted some 30 generals on charges of *eisangelia.*[14]

The second important political institution in Athens was the *boule* or the council, which was permanently in session throughout the year, and which was responsible both for preparing the agenda of each session of the assembly, as well as for implementing the decisions taken at these sessions. The council consisted of 500 citizens, with 50 citizens (all over 30 years of age) being assigned to it every year from each of the 10 tribes. Each group of 50 from a particular tribe acted as a standing committee or *prytaneis* of the *boule* for 36 consecutive days. This group of 50 was responsible for the work of the *boule* for those days. On each of those 36 days, one out of those 50 would be chosen by lot to become the chairman of the *boule* for that day, and would preside over its meetings on that day. If there was a meeting of the *ekklesia* set for that day as well, then he would also preside over that meeting. No citizen could serve on the *boule* more than two times in his lifetime. Anyone wanting to be a member of the *boule* had to be approved first by his *deme*. The *demarch* or head of the *deme*, who himself was chosen by lot for a year's term, together with the *deme's* assembly which met at least once a year, would consider his *demesmen* for membership to the *boule*. If there were more candidates than the *deme's* allocation, then the members of the *boule* from that *deme* were chosen by lottery. Membership to the council was, however, restricted to the first three property classes.

The *boule* set the agenda of the assembly. Mostly, no proposal could be discussed in the *ekklesia* unless it had already been vetted and debated in the Boule. The draft proposals or probouleumata of the *boule* were 'either in the form of recommendations or simply as open questions for the assembly to decide on'.[15] Decisions taken at the assembly were recorded as decisions of the *boule* and the assembly, for example in the form of 'Resolution of the *boule* and the Demos'.

The *boule* was helped in its executive functions by magistrates, and there were as many as 600 of them in Athens, each appointed for an annual term. The most important magistrates were the ten generals or the *strategoi*, appointed annually; one from each tribe. Each tribe selected its own general and there was no bar on repeated appointments of the same person for generalship. Pericles, for example, was a *strategoi* continuously from 443 BCE to 429 BCE. Since Athens was almost always at war, the *strategoi* were very important officials. About 90 other magistrates were also elected, including the most important financial officers and some religious functionaries. The other 500 magistrates—the superintendents of the market and of weights and measures, those responsible for the maintenance of roads and for cleaning the streets, those in charge of the prisons, the record keepers, etc.—were chosen by lottery, and usually worked in committees of ten, with one member from each tribe. One particular magistracy could be held only once in a lifetime, and all magistrates had to submit to an audit of their *euthynai* (accounts) on leaving office. Under this procedure, auditors looked at the accounts of the funds under the officer, and brought charges of corruption, if any. If the officer was convicted, he had to pay back 10 times the amount that he had defrauded.

Like the assembly, the Athenian court system allowed for a maximum of participation by the citizens. The courts were known as the *dikasteria* and the jurors who served in them were the *dikasts*. Under Cleisthenes's reforms, every year 6000 Athenian citizens aged 30 or over were chosen and registered as a pool of jurors. These 6,000 were chosen by lot from those willing to stand, 600 being selected from each tribe. The majority of the jurors, after the introduction of pay for the *dikasts* in 451 BCE, actually came from the poorer classes. The courts ranged in size from 201 to 501 jurors to even larger sizes depending on the kind of case being heard. There were basically 10 kinds of courts differentiated by the type of offences they could hear. Each of these 10 courts was assigned 600 *dikasts*, and on the days on which one particular kind of court was in session, the *dikasts* assigned to it would turn up at dawn, and the court would begin as soon as the required number of jurors had turned up. These courts were in session for about 200 days in a year. At each session, the petitioner and the defendant were assigned an equal amount of time to make their case; there were no lawyers in the Athenian system. The jury heard both sides but did not deliberate. The members of the jury would, after listening to both sides, cast their vote anonymously.[16]

Finally, the nine archons and the Areopagus continued from earlier times, but their powers were much curtailed. From 487/486 BCE, the *archons* began to be chosen by lot from a list of 500, put forward by the tribes, and this made their position weaker. They were left with some judicial duties and the Areopagus, of which they still became members after their year was over, became a body with mainly religious duties. By the reforms of 460–452 BCE, the Areopagus lost its powers of the scrutiny of and control over office holders, such powers being transferred to the assembly. The archonship was also opened to the *zeugitai* class in 457 BCE.

## THE SOCIOLOGICAL BASIS OF ATHENIAN DEMOCRACY

It has often been pointed out that when, in a population of 250,000 to 300,000, about 80,000 to 100,000 were slaves, 25,000 were *metics* or resident aliens with no political rights, not to mention all the Athenian women who were not given any rights, and only up to a maximum of 50,000 Athenian males were considered citizens, it is difficult to call such a system democratic. The non-participation of the majority of the population cancels out the active participation and self-rule of a minority of the population. Even if we accept that Athens was a democracy in comparison with the form of government prevalent in other city-states, the received opinion is that it was slavery that was the basis of this ancient democracy. Both Hannah Arendt and the Marxists, for example, agree on this one fact, although one views it positively and the other negatively. For Arendt, since the slaves did all the work, ordinary Greek citizens could remove themselves from the sphere of production and devote their energies to politics, the life of action. Labour confines us to the realm of necessity; the slaves made it possible for Athenian citizens to do something more reflective of human freedom, that is, political action. Marx and Engels decried this same fact;

the slaves did all the work and the citizens, specially the richer ones, reaped all the fruits thereof. For Marx and Engels furthermore, it is labour that expresses all human creativity, and so the Greeks lost out not only because of inequality, but also because they were idle.

Against both these positions, E.M. Wood puts forward her interesting thesis that it was the ordinary peasant citizens and the craftsmen citizens who formed the basis of Athenian democracy. Wood convincingly shows how the ordinary Greek citizen was a farmer or craftsman, who had to do his own manual work himself. When Solon came to power in 594 BCE, many of the farmers were, as we have already seen earlier, in debt-bondage to large landowners, and Solon laid the foundations of Athenian democracy by his one sweeping reform of abolishing debt-bondage. Wood suggests that debt bondage be interpreted not only as bonded labour because of unpaid debts, but as many other forms of tributary labour as well. Due to this reform, by the 5th century, the Athenian land tenure system was characterized by a mass of small independent producers.[17] These small farmers who lived in the villages of Attica, did own one or two slaves, but that did not enable them to earn their living without doing any work themselves. These citizen farmers and craftsmen had to work quite hard at cultivating their farms, or at their crafts, to support their families. They also had to find the time to attend the meetings of the assembly and the sessions of the courts. One of the reasons why payment for attending the assembly was introduced in later years, both for the *dikasts* as well as assembly members, was because, for these ordinary citizens, taking a day off from work to fulfil their political duties meant a loss of their earnings. It was to encourage these small farmers to be part of Athenian democracy that payment was introduced. 'The Athenian countryman had a close and direct relationship with the city, he voted in its assembly, bought and sold in its markets, took part in its religious festivals, sued in its courts, had the same political rights and obligations—including that of military service—as the urban population.'[18]

Here we must also point out the bearing of the Athenian citizen army on the kind of democracy that existed in Athens. If every citizen in Athens could attend the *ekklesia* and discuss and vote on matters of state, every citizen over 18 years of age was also to serve in the army. The Athenian army was a citizen army. Those who fought for Athens—and we have to remember that Athens was almost always at war—were citizens, and not the slaves or the women. We have seen earlier that Solon's classification of Athenians into different property groups foregrounded a citizen's ability to serve in the army. Those who could provide a horse were the cavalrymen of the army, belonging to the *hippies* class and citizens of the *zeugitai* class, who could provide their own armour, were the *hoplites* or the infantrymen of the army. The *thetes,* who were the poorer citizens, who made up more than half of the citizen-population of the city-state, had not the resources to be either cavalrymen or infantrymen. Instead, they manned the *triremes* or the ships, which formed the backbone of the Athenian navy. If 9,000 Athenian hoplites fought against the Persians at Marathon, the sea battle of Salamis in 480 BCE saw the use of 180 Athenian *triremes*, with at least 200 men being needed to man each *trireme*. Athens ran the Delian League on the basis of its all powerful navy, and this navy would not have been able to function without the ordinary rowers of the *triremes*. If these rowers, comprising of *thetes*, were the basis of the might of the Athenian empire, they had to have a say in the decisions of this empire, which they did through their role in the assembly and the *dikasteria*. It was during these years that Athens became so powerful that its imperial behaviour sparked off a war with Sparta in 459 BCE. The second Peloponnesian War between Sparta and Athens lasted for nearly 30 years, from 431 BCE to 404 BCE, ending in Athens's defeat, for which it was its democratic regime that was held responsible.

So, according to many scholars, including Wood, it is not true to say that politics in Athens was the preserve of the rich and that democracy was a pure sham. There really was wide spread participation in politics, irrespective of one's class position. Irrespective of one's 'ancestry, education, or wealth', that is, in spite of not belonging to 'the old and new upper classes',[19] any Athenian male citizen could express his opinion at any given time, on any subject. Politics, in Athens, however, was the preserve of men. Women were cloistered and kept indoors. It is said that a girl would not recognize her grown-up brother because women and men occupied, and grew up in different spaces in the house. Women looked after the home and the men looked after the affairs of the city. Athenian men lived a public life, spending all their time in the *gymnasia* (exercise halls), the *agora* and in the *ekklesia* with other men. The private sphere was looked down upon, and even the emotion of love or *eros* denoted, not a relationship between a man and a woman, but a homosexual relation between an older man and his younger male lover. Homosexuality was acceptable in Greece, and women were seen as necessary only for child-bearing.

Now that you have some idea of what the Athenian city-state looked like, in terms of its social structure and its political organization, this might help you to better understand the writings of Plato and Aristotle, and the reported dialogues of Socrates. These thinkers were obviously responding to the practice of democracy in Athens. Socrates's insistence on speaking his mind on any and every occasion mirrors the democratic practice of *parrhesia*. Plato is famous for comparing a democratic assembly to an out of control 'great beast' in *Republic*, and Aristotle's very definition of political rule as a continuous alternation between ruling and being ruled in turn captures the status of Athenian men as citizen-subjects.

## NOTES

1. For the argument that much of Western political thought is basically an attempt to contain the shock of Athenian political democracy, see Jennifer T. Roberts, *Athens on Trial: The Antidemocratic Tradition in Western Thought*, Princeton: Princeton University Press, 1994.
2. http://www.crystalinks.com/greeksocial.html.
3. The term 'anarchy' literally means 'no *archon*'.
4. Greg Anderson, *The Athenian Experiment: Building an Imagined Political Community in Ancient Attica, 508–490* BCE, Ann Arbor: University of Michigan Press, 2005.
5. Jeremy Waldron's 'Precommitment and Disagreement', in Larry Alexander (ed.), *Constitutionalism: Philosophical Foundations,* Cambridge: Cambridge University Press, 1998), p. 282.
6. See Kurt A. Raaflaub, Josiah Ober, and Robert W. Wallace (eds), *Origins of Democracy in Ancient Greece,* Berkeley: University of California Press, 2007, pp. 163–167.
7. John Thorley, *Athenian Democracy*, 2nd edition, London: Routledge, 2004, p. 10.
8. Kurt A. Raaflaub, *The Discovery of Freedom in Ancient Greece,* Chicago: University of Chicago Press, 2004, pp. 45–46.
9. See John Thorley, *Athenian Democracy*, pp. 13–14.
10. Greg Anderson, *The Athenian Experiment*, p. 40.
11. John Thorley, *Athenian Democracy*, p. 33.
12. Plato, *Protagoras* in *Plato: The Collected Dialogues Including the Letters,* edited by Edith Hamilton and Huntington Cairns, Bollingen Series LXXI, Princeton: Princeton University Press, 1987, p. 317.
13. See Arlene W. Saxonhouse Chapter 4 in *Free Speech and Democracy in Ancient Athens*, Cambridge: Cambridge University Press, 2006.
14. Jon Elster, 'Accountability in Athenian Politics' in Adam Przeworski eds, *Democracy, Accountability and Representation*, Cambridge: Cambridge University Press, 1999, pp. 268–70.
15. John Thorley, *Athenian Democracy*, p. 31.
16. David L. Stockton, *The Classical Athenian Democracy*, Oxford: Oxford University Press, 1990.
17. Ellen M. Wood, *Peasant, Citizen and Slave: The Foundations of Athenian Democracy*, London: Verso, 1989.
18. Ellen M. Wood, *Peasant, Citizen and Slave: The Foundations of Athenian Democracy*, London: Verso, 1997.
19. Kurt A. Raaflaub, *The Discovery of Freedom in Ancient Greece*, p. 276.

## READING LIST

Anderson, Greg, *The Athenian Experiment: Building an Imagined Political Community in Ancient Attica, 508–490* BCE, Ann Arbor: University of Michigan Press, 2005.

Finley, M.I., *Politics in the Ancient World*, Cambridge: Cambridge University Press, 1983.

Raaflaub, Kurt A., *The Discovery of Freedom in Ancient Greece*, Chicago: University of Chicago Press, 2004.

Raaflaub, Kurt A., Josiah Ober and Robert W. Wallace (eds), *Origins of Democracy in Ancient Greece*, Berkeley: University of California Press, 2007.

Roberts, Jennifer T., *Athens on Trial: The Antidemocratic Tradition in Western Thought*, Princeton: Princeton University Press, 1994.

Saxonhouse, Arlene W., Chapter 4 in *Free Speech and Democracy in Ancient Athens*, Cambridge: Cambridge University Press, 2006.

Stockton, David L., *The Classical Athenian Democracy*, Oxford: Oxford University Press, 1990.

Thorley, John, *Athenian Democracy*, 2nd edition, London: Routledge, 2004.

Wood, Ellen M., *Peasant, Citizen and Slave: The Foundations of Athenian Democracy*, London: Verso, 1989.

## CENTRAL THEMES

1. **The theory of Athenian 'exceptionalism'**: Out of the hundreds of city-states that existed in classical Greece, why is it that the city-state of Athens has attracted so much scholarly attention? Which features of the Athenian *polis* continue to draw our modern imagination and why?
2. **The political institutions of Athenian democracy**: Between the 5th and the 3rd centuries BCE, Athenian democracy operated through a set of political institutions which were modified and strengthened during these 200 years. How did the Assembly, the Council and the Courts function? What were the democratic features of these institutions?
3. **The Athenian social structure**: The scholarly debate about the strengths and shortcomings of Athenian democracy is based, to a large extent, on claims about the participation of different social groups in Athens in the Assembly, the Council and the Courts. What is your understanding of the social structure of Athens, and of its impact on Athenian democratic institutions?
4. **The importance of warfare in Athenian politics**: The Persian wars, and the Peloponnesian wars had a major impact on Athenian history. Should the role of Athenian citizens in their democratic institutions be understood in complement with the manning of the Athenian army and navy by these same citizens? How are the effects of war to be understood in the story of Athenian democracy?

# TWO

# Plato (427–347 BCE): Justice and Reason

Plato was born in 427 BCE in Athens, in one of its oldest and most distinguished families. As we saw in the last chapter, these were troubled times for Athens, which was suffering mounting losses in the second Peloponnesian War. Pericles died in 429 BCE, after leading Athens in the war for two years. Athens's first overwhelming reversal came in 413 BCE, when its fleet was destroyed at Syracuse, and it was finally defeated by Sparta in 404 BCE. Both in 413–412 BCE and in 404–403 BCE, the democratic government of Athens was overthrown by oligarchic factions, which ruled for short periods. In 404–403 BCE, when Athens experienced a second year of civil strife, and the so-called 'tyranny of the 30' backed by Sparta, established itself, Plato was invited to join the oligarchy, since some of the '30 tyrants' were his relatives. Plato refused to have anything to do with this government. When the democrats came back a year later, they began a wave of revenge punishments. These included judicial proceedings against Socrates and his subsequent execution, in 399 BCE. In shock and disgust at the death of his teacher, whom Plato revered as the wisest man in Athens, Plato left Athens and began his travels in Greece, Egypt and Italy. Plato returned in 387 BCE to Athens where he founded the Academy. After 20 years of running the Academy, he was invited, in 367 BCE, to the city-state of Syracuse in Italy to act as a political advisor. He made another trip to Syracuse in 361 BCE, but on both occasions his experience was an unhappy one and he had to flee from its ruler, Dionysius II. Except for these years, he mostly stayed in Athens, busy with his writing and teaching at the Academy. It is interesting to read about Plato's life in his own words in his *Seventh Letter*.[1]

As we have already mentioned, the death of Socrates had a great impact on Plato. Plato considered himself to be Socrates's student, and he had great respect and admiration for his teacher. Socrates influenced him to such an extent that most of his dialogues are written as conversations between Socrates and other notable citizens of Athens. Socrates is the main protagonist of Plato's dialogues. In fact, since Socrates did not leave any writings of his own, much of what we know today about Socrates, is through the Platonic corpus.

## SOCRATES AND THE EUDAEMONIST AXIOM

Socrates, who was probably born in 470 BCE and died in 399 BCE, lived when Athenian culture was at its zenith. Not only was he a contemporary of Pericles, he also lived during the time of the great Athenian dramatists, Sophocles and Euripides, whose plays we still read today. Just as their tragedies focused on human dilemmas, similarly Socrates was responsible for turning the philosophic gaze away from natural philosophy to moral philosophy. Whereas Ionian philosophers like Thales and Anaximander were interested in investigating the composition of nature, Socrates insisted that philosophers should pay attention to questions of human conduct, such as how human beings could live good lives. This was the central question bequeathed by Socrates to his followers.

'In the development of Greek thought', Socrates is said to be 'the first to establish the eudaemonist foundation of ethical theory.'[2] Socrates did this through his 'Eudaemonist Axiom' that 'happiness [*eudaimonia* in Greek] is desired by all human beings as the ultimate end of all their rational acts'.[3] If the goal of human life is *eudaimonia* or happiness, what kind of life should individuals live, in order to be happy? 'Do we all wish to do well in the world?...since we all wish to do well, how could we do well? If we had plenty of good things, eh?...if we had plenty of good things, we should be happy and do well'.[4] To be happy, to live the good life, do we need the goods of 'wealth, health, handsomeness, other bodily blessings, good birth and power and honour in one's country, temperateness, uprightness, bravery, wisdom and good fortune'?[5] Socrates's answer was that it was actually a life of *arête* (virtue) that was essential for happiness. Socrates believed that everything had a specific function or goal. The function of a knife, for instance, is to cut things. To perform its function well, a thing needs a special quality or virtue. For example, to be able to cut well, the knife needs to be sharp, that is, the excellence or virtue of a knife consists in its sharpness. Analogically, if the goal of human beings is to live well or happily, they also need specific virtues or excellences in order to achieve this goal.[6]

For much of the Greek tradition, happiness was not so much a state of mind, as a certain kind of activity which was constitutive of it. In the Greek word *eudaimon*, '*eu* means well and *daimon* means "divinity" or "spirit".

To be *eudaimon* is therefore to be living in a way that is well favoured by a god'.[7] This is why 'well-being' or 'flourishing' are often 'proposed as less misleading translations' of *eudaimonia*. Thus, according to Socrates, happiness, that is living a good life, means acting virtuously.[8] For Socrates, virtue is related to happiness, not merely in an instrumental fashion. Happiness is not merely a consequence of virtue; something which is opposed to virtue cannot also achieve happiness for us. Socrates believed that happiness means acting virtuously: 'Virtue is the only constituent of happiness... virtue *is* happiness, the whole of it.'[9] Thus, happiness is virtue. Moreover, Socrates held that non-moral goods like health and wealth were not irrelevant for happiness. As long as they were conjoined with virtue, a healthy life and physical comfort could increase our happiness.[10]

If the answer to the question, 'How can I live well or make myself happy?' is, 'By being virtuous', then we have to ask, 'What is virtue?' What is interesting is that by making happiness dependent on virtue, Socrates seemingly forestalled the conflict between one person's happiness and another's. If being virtuous means being oriented to the interests of others, then the same virtuous action would make the doer of that action, as well as others, happy. The Greeks believed that the capacity for the four cardinal virtues—courage, wisdom, justice and temperance—was given to everyone because it is necessary for social life. One of the Greek myths that Plato relates in the *Protagoras,* was that when human beings were created, they were made weaker than animals and therefore, had to try to live together in order to be able to deal with the stronger animals. 'They sought therefore to save themselves by coming together and founding fortified cities, but when they gathered in communities they injured one another for want of political skill, and so scattered again and continued to be devoured. Zeus therefore, fearing the total destruction of our race, sent Hermes to impart to men the qualities of respect for others and a sense of justice, so as to bring order into our cities, and create a bond of friendship and union.'[11] The virtues, being required for any collective endeavour, become necessary for individual happiness. This was the customary way of linking virtue with individual happiness. What we have to see is whether for Socrates, too, this was the route through which virtue became happiness or living well.

In Plato's dialogues, various notable citizens of Athens invariably encounter Socrates, who poses questions to them regarding the nature of virtue. One of these questions was whether virtue is one thing or many. Socrates believed in the unity of all virtue, claiming that a courageous man would also be wise, just and temperate. All the virtues went together. From the idea of the unity of virtue, follows the other Socratic principle: that virtue is knowledge. If a wise man cannot but be brave, this implies that we are cowardly only because of our ignorance. If we knew about the value and the meaning of virtue, we would not act immorally. Having given us these hints about virtue, Socrates went on to ask questions about the acquisition of virtue or, rather, about the acquisition of knowledge of virtue.

## THE SOCRATIC ELENCHUS

How did Socrates find out the answers to these questions about virtue? The distinctive Socratic method of investigation of moral questions has been termed the 'Socratic Elenchus', which means cross-examination. Socrates was (in)famous for stopping anywhere on the streets of Athens, in the marketplace or at somebody's house, and beginning a discussion on the meaning of beauty, truth or virtue. Such a discussion would usually begin with Socrates asking others their definition of, say, beauty. Subsequently, Socrates would ask his interlocutor to explain the meaning of the different aspects of his definition and through this cross-examination, get him to accept that there was an inconsistency in his definition of beauty, and thereby move the argument forward.

> The basic structure of a typical elenchus is simple. Socrates asks a question, either a request to be told what some virtue is (for instance, "What is bravery?"), or some other question about a virtue. The interlocutor affirms some proposition p in answer to Socrates' initial question; under Socrates' questioning he agrees that he also believes q and r; and he discovers, under further questioning, that not-p can be derived from q and r; hence he finds that his beliefs commit him to p and not-p. Finding himself in this situation, he is 'at a loss' (*aporein*) about what to believe.[12]

The Socratic method of investigation was dialogic and knowledge of what is beauty or love was sought to be gained through this dialogic process. The dialogic process was so important to Socrates that he refused to put his thoughts down in writing. 'The historical Socrates did not write. He did not write because he believed that the real value of philosophizing lay in the responsive interaction of teacher and pupil, as the teacher guides the pupil by questioning to become more aware of his own beliefs and their relationship to one another... Books lack the attentiveness and responsiveness of true philosophical teaching.'[13]

No wonder, then, that we have to depend on Plato's writings to become familiar with Socratic ideas. Our most familiar image of Socrates is drawn from Plato's many dialogues. According to Christopher Rowe,

> [The Socrates] who is the main speaker in most of Plato's dialogues [has] certain marked distinguishing features: he is drawn to beautiful young men and

> adolescent boys, while he himself is, by usual standards, remarkably ugly; he knows nothing, but can outsmart anyone he meets; in spite of saying he knows nothing, he goes on saying and evidently believing a number of extremely odd things ('no one goes wrong willingly', 'all the virtues are one', 'all desire is for the good', and so on); he specialises in question-and-answer, but is usually the questioner;...he can drink anyone under the table, but never gets drunk; he is courageous, hardy, typically goes barefoot; and so on.[14]

Scholars disagree over whether and when in his dialogues, Plato moved away from Socrates's teachings and begin to develop his own philosophical position. For Gregory Vlastos, the Platonic dialogues are populated by not one but two Socrates, and only one of them is the historical Socrates. In his early elenctic dialogues, Plato gives us a picture of this dialogic Socrates. However, from *Republic*, Book II onwards, a different Socrates begins to appear. Vlastos has listed 10 differences between these two Socrates:

> Whereas the Socrates of the early Platonic dialogues seeks knowledge elenctically but keeps avowing that he knows nothing, the Socrates of the later Platonic dialogues seeks demonstrative knowledge and is confident of finding it. The earlier Socrates' method of philosophical investigation is adversative: he pursues moral truth by refuting theses defended by dissenting interlocutors. The later Socrates is a didactic philosopher, expounding truth to consenting interlocutors. The earlier Socrates' conception of philosophy is populist, that of the later Socrates is elitist. The later Socrates has an elaborate political theory while the earlier one has no such theory.[15]

Is either of the two Socrates of the Platonic dialogues the real Socrates? Vlastos's position is that the Socrates of the early dialogues is the historical Socrates, and till the time when these early dialogues were written, Plato believed in the Socratic method of elenchus. In his middle period, Plato began to give up many of Socrates's beliefs, and the new Socrates of the middle and later dialogues represents Plato's own turn away from the historical Socrates. Vlastos's position is contested by Rowe for whom Plato remained deeply Socratic till the end, and therefore continued to use Socrates as the main speaker even in his later dialogues. For Rowe, Plato remains Socratic in his focus on rational knowledge as leading us to virtue.[16]

## PLATO'S POLITICAL THEORY

Plato is the only one among all the political philosophers we will read about in this book, to have left us all his writings in the form of dialogues, 35 of which are extant or still available to us.[17] Some scholars of Greek political theory, like Vlastos, believed as we just said, that Plato's thought changed radically by the time he wrote the middle dialogues, like *Republic*. Other commentators have argued for a unity in Plato's philosophical position, reflected in a continuity especially between his early and middle dialogues.[18] It is pointed out, that though Plato never speaks in his own voice in the dialogues, and the *dramatis personae* is always someone other than Plato—Socrates, Gorgias, Cephalus, Glaucon, Alcibiades and so many others—the author is always Plato. 'It is in the entire writing that the author speaks to us, not in the remarks made by individual speakers.'[19] As the author, Plato may have deliberately constructed his early dialogues as aporetic, not only to give us a picture of the historical Socrates, but also in order to use these early dialogues to create a setting for his own philosophical position in *Republic*.

We should also consider why Plato spent so much of his creative energy in composing the dialogic form to express his philosophical positions. Plato's dialogues all have different settings and are usually presented as recountings, as a result of which, a major role is played by the narrator's memory. In *Symposium,* for instance, the person remembering the dialogue and recounting it to his friend, has actually heard it from another friend, in whose memory the dialogue has stayed for twenty years or so. One wonders whether all these features are a part of Plato's political analysis. In another instance, when Plato makes the port of Piraeus the setting of the conversation on justice in *Republic,* in our interpretation of the same, are we to consider the fact that Piraeus was the base of the democratic opposition against the 30 tyrants of 404 BCE, that Polemarchus was the main financial backer of this democratic opposition, and that it was at the temple of Bendis (the goddess whose celebration brings Socrates to the Piraeus in *Republic*), that the decisive battle took place in which 'the 30' were defeated by the democratic faction?[20]

We left Socrates debating questions of happiness and virtue, and of the knowledge of virtue, and we might now ask what such questions have to do with political philosophy? 'The art concerned with the soul I call the political art',[21] states Socrates in *Gorgias*. For Socrates, just as knowing how to make a body healthy is an art, namely, the art of medicine; and being able to guide ships from one harbour to another is an art, namely the art of navigation; similarly, the knowledge of how to make someone virtuous is an art. Socrates sees himself as practising the political art of making his fellow citizens virtuous: 'I think that I am one of very few Athenians, not to say the only one, engaged in the true political art, and that of the men of today I alone practice statesmanship.'[22] Here, Socrates is responding to the accusation that he is apolitical. Plato never portrays Socrates making a speech in the *Ekklesia*. In that sense, Socrates's conversations were always private; in the houses of friends or in the marketplace. Since virtue, by harmonizing the happiness of a group of people, is the foundation of any collective life, then, by focusing his discussions constantly on virtue, was not Socrates engaging in political enquiry? By convincing everyone that they must never indulge in acts of injustice, Socrates was teaching them the elements of citizenship.[23]

Trying to make his own sense of the Socratic questions of *eudaimonia* and *arête,* Plato's answers are given more in terms of politics. Plato turned the questions of individual happiness and individual virtue into one of their relationship with different political arrangements. Whether we organize our political institutions in the form of a democracy or an aristocracy; how this will impact the ability of individuals to gain knowledge of virtue and to live virtuous lives—these seem to be Plato's questions, not Socrates's. If virtue leads to, or is happiness, and virtue is constituted of justice, courage, temperance and wisdom, we have to, for example, not merely be convinced about not doing injustice, but to find out what justice exactly is. Plato will begin to examine the idea of justice, in *Republic,* by pointing to its political dimension.

Plato's *Republic,* which he wrote in his middle age, is used all over the world, to introduce political science undergraduates to Plato. *Statesman* and *Laws,* written by Plato when he was much older, are other important dialogues for students of political philosophy. But I would like to begin this discussion with two of Plato's early dialogues, *Apology* and *Crito.* Both these dialogues cover Socrates's trial and punishment, and the two poles of Plato's political philosophy are clearly revealed here. Plato's mature political position of *Republic* seems to be prefigured in these early dialogues.

*Apology* is a dialogue between Socrates and his accusers. Charged with leading Athenian young men astray with his discussions, Socrates explains that all that he was doing was trying to find out for himself the truth of the proclamation of the Delphic oracle that Socrates was the wisest man of Athens. This is the first principle of Platonic philosophy: One's individual reason is the final authority over oneself. Plato shows us Socrates refusing to accept the authority of the oracle, a semi-divine entity, and going about asking people questions about what they know, to find out whether they are wiser than him. Socrates says that he first sought out the poets and the artisans, for such persons were traditionally seen as knowledgeable individuals in Athens, but he was not satisfied with their answers. Religious knowledge, in the form of the oracle, had already been considered as insufficient by him. During his trial, when he is offered forgiveness on the condition that he will cease to have his infamous discussions, Socrates categorically refuses. The life of reason, by which Plato means a life of individual questioning and of seeking for the truth, is the only life worth living. As Socrates says in his own words, 'Gentlemen,...so long as I draw breath and have my faculties, I shall never stop practising philosophy and exhorting you and elucidating the truth for everyone that I meet...I spend all my time going about trying to persuade you, young and old, to make your first and chief concern not for your bodies nor for your possessions, but for the higher welfare of your souls, proclaiming as I go, wealth does not bring goodness, but goodness brings wealth and every other blessing, both to the individual and to the state'. Towards the end of his defence, we find Socrates saying that 'to let no day pass without discussing goodness and all the other subjects about which you hear me talking and examining both myself and others is really the very best thing that a man can do, and that life without this sort of examination is not worth living'.[24] Here, Socrates is linking virtue with both 'private' and 'public' good as well as claiming that knowledge of virtue can only be achieved through a rational discussion conducted with others.

What happens in *Crito*? Here we see Socrates in jail, waiting for his execution. His friend, Crito, comes to visit him and tells him of a plan for his escape. His friends will spirit him out of jail, out of Athens, and he can live the rest of his life in exile in another city-state. Again, Socrates categorically refuses and explains his decision in the following manner. Whatever he is, he says, is because of his native city which has nourished him both physically and intellectually. In return, he has certain obligations to his city, to his political community, one of them being speaking out against any unjust practices of the city. Socrates accepts that an individual's reason develops by participating in the life of the city, and yet, that an individual's reason can be used to judge the practices of the community. If one has not spoken out against an unjust law when it was applied to others, and not tried to change it, one has no right to run away when the unjust law is applied to oneself. This is the other pole of Plato's political philosophy: the importance of the political community to an individual's moral and intellectual development and the almost 'sacredness' of one's obligations to it. Personifying the laws, Plato has them reproach Socrates in the following way:

> Socrates...although we have brought you into the world and reared you and educated you, and given you and your fellow citizens a share in all the good things at our disposal, nevertheless by the very fact of granting our permission we openly proclaim this principle, that any Athenian, on attaining to manhood and seeing for himself the political organization of the state and us its laws, is permitted, if he is not satisfied with us, to take his property and go away wherever he likes...if any one of you stands his ground when he can see how we administer justice and the rest of our public organization, we hold that by so doing he has in fact undertaken to do anything that we tell him... anyone who disobeys is guilty...because, after promising obedience, he is neither obeying us nor persuading us to change our decision if we are at fault in any way. And although all our orders are in the form of proposals, not of savage commands, and we give him the choice of either persuading us or doing what we say, he is [and you are] actually doing neither.[25]

These two aspects of Plato's thought, as represented in *Apology* and *Crito*, both early dialogues, come together uneasily in *Republic*. Which kind of city (political community) is it that develops our rationality (our ability to know virtue) and what is the extent of our obligation to it? To answer this question, Plato constructed *Republic* as a dialogue between Socrates and his friends, ostensibly on a specific virtue, that of justice. Returning to Athens after witnessing a religious procession at Piraeus, the harbour, Socrates and company are stopped by Polemarchus and invited to his house where they engage in a discussion of justice. As in the earlier dialogues, Socrates's method is first to examine existing conceptions of justice. Only when he has shown that the knowledge of justice of Polemarchus, Thrasymachus, Glaucon and Adimantus is rife with contradictions, does he give us his own conception of justice. He sets out to meet Glaucon's challenge to prove that justice is the 'fairest of goods', that which is good not only because of its consequences but which is good in itself (see Box 2.1).

### Box 2.1

**THE CHALLENGE TO SOCRATES ON JUSTICE:**

They say that to do injustice is, by nature, good; to suffer injustice, evil; but that the evil is greater than the good. And so when men have both done and suffered injustice and have had experience of both, not being able to avoid the one and obtain the other, they think that they had better agree among themselves to have neither; hence there arise laws and mutual covenants; and that which is ordained by law is termed by them lawful and just. This they affirm to be the origin and nature of justice; it is a mean or compromise, between the best of all, which is to do injustice and not be punished, and the worst of all, which is to suffer injustice without the power of retaliation; and justice, being at a middle point between the two, is tolerated not as a good, but as the lesser evil, and honoured by reason of the inability of men to do injustice. For no man who is worthy to be called a man would ever submit to such an agreement if he were able to resist; he would be mad if he did. Such is the received account, Socrates, of the nature and origin of justice.

Now that those who practise justice do so involuntarily and because they have not the power to be unjust will best appear if we imagine something of this kind: having given both to the just and the unjust power to do what they will, let us watch and see whither desire will lead them; then we shall discover in the very act the just and unjust man to be proceeding along the same road, following their interest, which all natures deem to be their good, and are only diverted into the path of justice by the force of law.

*Republic, Book II*

Socrates says he will answer the question of who is a just individual by describing what justice is in the city. The question of the just individual is the same as the Socratic question of the virtuous individual, since justice was, as we saw earlier, one of the four cardinal Greek virtues. But Plato offers us an interesting twist here: To find out about the virtuous individual, we have to examine the just political community, thus, moving from moral philosophy in the direction of political science. Here, the dialogic quality of *Republic* comes to an end and a long monologue begins on what justice is, in the city. First, Socrates explains how a city comes into being. The first political community, he says, is established when a farmer, a craftsman, a blacksmith, and other such like individuals get together. None of these men can efficiently fulfil all their needs by themselves. Therefore, it is more sensible if they each specialize in their own tasks and exchange goods and services with others, to fulfil their various requirements. As their needs increase and cannot be fulfilled internally, the members of the community turn aggressive and begin to prey on other communities. This is when the need arises for another specialization: the guardians. It is the guardians who will defend the city against external attacks and also maintain internal law and order. Plato's full blown city, containing the three classes of the farmers and the craftsmen, the auxiliaries or soldiers, and the philosophers, is built, then, on the twin principles of interdependence and specialization. The philosophers and the soldiers, together called the guardians, depend on the farmers for their food and other material needs. The farmers depend on the guardians for protection and guidance. The farmers have the ability to do the work of production, the soldiers are those with military skill, and the philosophers are the ones with the most developed reasoning powers.

The Athenians believed that they were autochthonous, children of the soil they lived on, and not the descendants of ancestors who came from other lands. It was this illusion that Plato was playing on in his myth of the metals in *Republic*.[26] Plato makes Socrates ask the guardians to spread this 'noble lie' among the farmers of the Callipolis, or the ideal city: that the earth was their mother, and as children of the earth, they were born with some metallic component in their bodies. Some were born with gold in their bodies (those meant to be philosophers), others with silver (those meant to be auxiliaries), and some with brass (those meant to be farmers). This 'noble lie' would serve two purposes. It would make everyman believe that he was part of a bigger family with all the other members being his brothers, and it would also lead everyone to accept their station in life as natural, as suited to the qualities they were born with.

This is also where Plato's theory of the individual psyche fits in. Here we find Plato fleshing out a conception of human nature that underlies the concept of virtue and justice. After all, if making individuals virtuous is an art, then as in the other arts, the practitioner of this art must also know the nature of her material, in this case, human nature. Plato begins by saying that 'the same forms and qualities are to be found in each one of us that are in the state',[27] because the state is made up, after all, of individuals. For Plato, just as the city contains three groups, a person's soul, which is always superior to his body, is also made up of three elements. The lowest element consists of the appetites, which is followed by the spirited part of the soul, and the highest element is the rational part of the soul. Plato names 'that in the soul whereby it reckons and reasons the rational, and that with which it loves, hungers, thirsts, and feels the flutter and titillation of other desires, the irrational and appetitive.'[28]

Our appetites are often in conflict with our reason. Plato believed that our reason is able to control our unruly appetites with the help of the spirited part of our soul. 'When his desires constrain a man contrary to his reason [and] he reviles himself and is angry with that within which masters him, and that as it were in a faction of two parties the high spirit of such a man becomes the ally of his reason.'[29] Every individual must keep his appetites and spirit under the control of his reason. Plato also believed that in some individuals the appetites were dominant, in others, spirit and in a few individuals, reason. Those individuals who lived for their appetites should farm, the spirited ones should be auxiliaries, and the ones who lived for reason should be philosophers. This was not a caste system, because Plato clearly stated that a child with the potential of becoming a farmer could be born to a philosopher and vice versa. For Plato, children show their potential as they go through the educational system, and according to their capabilities, they should receive further training. Although there is some controversy about whether Plato advocated a state-run educational system for the children of all the classes, or only for those of the guardians, it seems reasonable to believe that he wanted all children to be educated in schools run by the state, since he believed that it is through this education that they learn what justice is. After about 12 years of compulsory education in music and gymnastics, only some of them are given military training. After two years of military training, a second division takes place, and again, only a few of the 20 year olds go ahead into a rigorous programme of mathematics, geometry, astronomy and dialectics.

Plato's conception of justice, then, flows from his vision of the political community. Justice, he shows, is that which serves the common interest. Even a den of thieves requires principles of justice if it is to sustain itself. In any common endeavour, there must be a fair distribution of the fruits of that endeavour, if the project is to continue, and it is the principles of justice that will define what this fair distribution is. A state is a common effort by a number of individuals. Hence, every state requires principles of justice as its foundation. The individual members of any state must be convinced that their state is a just state, and they must follow the principles of justice of their particular state.

Having convinced us of the centrality of justice, Plato gave us his specific principles of justice, which have to do with the earlier mentioned ideas of interdependence and specialization. For a successful political community, the functions of production, protection and statesmanship are to be adequately fulfilled. Therefore, justice requires that some individuals take up farming, others become soldiers and some others become philosopher-rulers. Plato imagined a community in which some individuals, those in whom the appetites are dominant, have an aptitude for farming; others, with more than usual spirit, become soldiers; and a few who live for reason, become philosophers. In this manner, the principles of justice ensure that not only is the common interest served, with individuals fulfilling their obligations to the political community, but that the happiness of these individuals is also served because of the harmony between what they do, what they get, and their individual psyches. It is important to remember here, that Plato specified that the producing class gets to enjoy the benefits of private property and family life. This class lives the life of the appetites, so it is part of Platonic justice that not only does it do the work of production, but it also enjoys the fruits of wealth and emotional fulfilment in a nuclear family. The guardians, whose appetites are weak, have no interest in the above, so they get to live in common barracks and have common meals with no family life. This is also part of Platonic justice.

So, now we know how responsibilities and rewards will be distributed in a just city. What about the original Socratic/Platonic question of who is a just/virtuous individual? A just individual is one who does his job, and does not interfere in another's work; one who does not take more than his share, and does not take another's share. 'To do one's own business and not to be a busybody is justice.' Justice 'is this principle of everyone doing his own task'. Justice is when 'no one shall have what belongs to others or be deprived of his own'. It is 'the having and doing of one's own and what belongs to oneself'.[30] A farmer will be just, if he does the work of production and does not try to involve himself in political decision making. An auxiliary will be just, if he fulfils his military function and does not hanker after wealth. Platonic justice confines the life of reason to the philosophers. Plato also claims that when an individual's soul is in harmony, that is, when his reason, spirit and appetite are in the right relationship to each other, he will not overstep his bounds. 'Each of us, also in whom the several parts within him perform each their own task—he will be a just man and one who minds his own affair.'[31] Such a man 'will not embezzle any deposits entrusted to him, nor will he indulge in theft or betray his comrades or his state'.[32] Thus, justice means not only sticking to one's own job, but also being fair. Justice, thereby, prevents any harm coming to the state. If what we pronounce to be injustice is that which 'works the greatest harm to one's own state', then justice becomes whatever is good for the state. Here, Plato is showing us the good consequences of justice.

Yet, just a little later we find Plato claiming 'the truth of the matter' to be that justice is something 'not in regard to the doing of one's own business externally, but with regard to that which is within and in the true sense concerns one's self, and the things of one's self. It means that a man must not suffer the principles of his soul to do each the work of some other and interfere and meddle with one another'.[33] This has led some commentators to accuse Plato of using the idea of justice to refer only to something intrapersonal (see Box 2.2). Justice, here, is only a relationship to the self, and has nothing to do with interpersonal relations. The concept of the ideal state is just an analogy for Plato; a story with no independent meaning of its own.

### Box 2.2

**PLATO ON THE JUST INDIVIDUAL:**

But in reality justice was such as we were describing, being concerned however, not with the outward man, but with the inward, which is the true self and concernment of man: for the just man does not permit the several elements within him to interfere with one another, or any of them to do the work of others,- he sets in order his own inner life, and is his own master and his own law, and at peace with himself; and when he has bound together the three principles within him, which may be compared to the higher, lower, and middle notes of the scale, and the intermediate intervals—when he has bound all these together, and is no longer many, but has become one entirely temperate and perfectly adjusted nature, then he proceeds to act, if he has to act, whether in a matter of property, or in the treatment of the body, or in some affair of politics or private business; always thinking and calling that which preserves and co-operates with this harmonious condition, just and good action, and the knowledge which presides over it, wisdom, and that which at any time impairs this condition, he will call unjust action, and the opinion which presides over it ignorance.

*Republic, Book IV*

Other scholars, taking the story of the ideal state much more seriously, point out that if the Socratic concept of virtue points to the link between the happiness of an individual and the happiness of others, the Platonic concept of justice specifies this link as a distribution of work and benefits. Such a just distribution leads to the happiness of all. Plato has been lauded down the ages for his insight, that the concept of justice, by leading to the happiness of all, becomes an essential requirement for any stable political community. His specific conception of justice, however, has often been criticized as organic and inegalitarian. For instance, terming it as a conception of functional reciprocity, according to which each member of a city 'has a right to those, and only those, socially distributable benefits, which will maximize his contribution (his work or function)',[34] Vlastos accuses Plato of sacrificing the interests of the individual in the name of justice in the city. Defending Plato's conception of justice, other scholars argue, that if Plato is interpreted as wanting to show that justice as a virtue leads to happiness—'Plato's interest [is] how to make a city virtuous and happy'[35]—then Plato would not have thought of benefits as entitlements only in compensation for contribution. Not regarding the individual members of the political community 'only or primarily as contributors, but rather as subjects whose well being matters',[36] Plato used the distributive principle that of citizens receiving whatever goods they are capable of benefiting from. 'Citizens are not benefited in compensation for their contribution. The relationship between contribution and benefit is actually the reverse of compensation: you contribute what you do because of the goods you have received, but you received the goods you did because of your ability to benefit from them, and not by the contribution you made.'[37]

## PLATONIC RATIONALISM

So far, we have concentrated on one central aspect of Platonic political philosophy, which is the importance of the political community, focusing on justice. When we examine Plato's conception of the philosopher–rulers more carefully, we come across the other pole of Plato's philosophy: the importance he gave to reason. Let us first examine Plato's advocacy of the coming together of philosophy and politics in the form of the philosopher kings and queens, in greater detail (see Box 2.3).

**Box 2.3**

**PLATO ON THE NEED FOR UNITING POLITICAL POWER AND KNOWLEDGE:**

Until philosophers are kings, or the kings and princes of this world have the spirit and power of philosophy, and political greatness and wisdom meet in one, and those commoner natures who pursue either to the exclusion of the other are compelled to stand aside, cities will never have rest from their evils—nor the human race, as I believe—and then only will this our State have a possibility of life and behold the light of day.

*Republic, Book V*

Influenced by the Socratic dictum that virtue is knowledge, Plato believed that political ills and injustice can be eradicated, if knowledgeable people are put at the helm of a city-state's politics. The philosophers are knowledgeable because they are the ones who undergo the educational process. Thus, they are the only ones who have knowledge of the ideas of the good, justice, beauty, truth, courage and the other moral attributes.

Plato called these ideas Forms. He believed that each entity that exists in our world is an imperfect copy of the Form of that thing existing in a transcendental realm. These Forms can be 'seen' only by those with a rational mind. The philosophers can see the Form of justice; therefore, they can ensure that justice in the city-state matches that Form as much as possible (see Box 2.4).[38]

**Box 2.4**

**PLATO ON THE GOOD AS THE OBJECT OF KNOWLEDGE:**

Now, that which imparts truth to the known and the power of knowing to the knower is what I would have you term the idea of good, and this you will deem to be the cause of science, and of truth in so far as the latter becomes the subject of knowledge; beautiful too, as are both truth and knowledge, you will be right in esteeming this other nature as more beautiful than either; and, as in the previous instance, light and sight may be truly said to be like the sun, and yet not to be the sun, so in this other sphere, science and truth may be deemed to be like the good, but not the good; the good has a place of honour yet higher.

*Republic, Book VI*

Not only do the philosophers have the right kind of knowledge, they are best suited for the job of ruling because they have no private interests. Plato did not allow his guardian class anything private. Plato argued that it is easier for an individual to go against the common interest, not for his own sake, but for the sake of his family. To avoid this possibility, Plato disallowed the guardians to have a family. None of the guardians were to know which of the children they collectively lived with were born from their own flesh. They were to consider themselves the parents of all the children, and similarly the children would think that they have many mothers and fathers. The guardians were not to live in individual houses but in common barracks and to own no personal property except perhaps a few articles of clothing, etc. Their basic needs for simple food and clothing were to be met by provisions produced by the farmers.

Of the guardians, the philosophers are best suited to rule because reason is dominant in their soul. This brings us to the issue of Plato's rationalism. The most important aspect of Plato's philosophy is his rationalism. For him, reason ruled the world, not god. For the Greeks, even the gods had to follow the rational laws of nature, and were punished if they transgressed these laws. Human beings have the capacity to understand this rational order, if they develop their intellectual capacities by training in mathematics and dialectics. For Plato, the goal of human life was a life of reason. A rational individual spends his life contemplating and accepts no authority save his own reason.

What is reason? How does an individual gain knowledge of the rational order? Unlike in *Crito,* Plato no longer seems to believe that one's reason develops in the midst of one's political community, even if it is a just city. The philosopher can only gain knowledge by removing himself from the political community. This message comes across in *Republic,* in Plato's analogies of the cave and of the divided line. The cave is a metaphor for the illusionary world of politics, and only those few who are able to get out of the cave are able to use their reason to gain knowledge. Similarly, the divided line separates the world of becoming, that is, the world of politics and of change, from the world of being, and it is only by transcending the world of becoming that one can use one's reason to gain knowledge of the Forms. Knowledge of the Forms, rather than rhetoric, is political knowledge. We can refer here to the 'ship of the state' simile used in *Republic,* where Plato construes the Athenian *demos* (people) as the hapless owner of a wayward ship, and where the ship operates as a representation of the state. The ignorant and indisciplined sailors, who are the ship's crew, are like the Athenian politicians who use their rhetorical powers to persuade the ship-owner (*the demos*) to let his ship (*the polis*) be under their charge, even though they have no knowledge of navigation (statecraft). They laugh at the navigator, who actually knows how to guide the ship, because he is gazing at the sky and the stars. Plato reminds us, that 'the true pilot must give his attention to the time of the year, the seasons, the sky, the winds, the stars, and all that pertains to his art if he is to be a true ruler of a ship'.[39] At the beginning of the chapter, we noted that Socrates turned the philosophic gaze downwards from the heavens (nature) towards human beings on earth. Here, Plato seems to be discounting that because his philosopher, who has political knowledge, 'remains after all "a thinker on things in the sky"'.[40] The development of reason no longer takes place in dialogic interaction with other members of the community, but in the contemplation of something that already exists outside the community, that is, the Forms. No longer do true definitions of moral concepts appear in public discourse. What is interesting in *Republic* is that on the one hand, Plato is contemptuous of the elements of a private life, like private property, a family, etc., all of which according to him, denotes selfishness. A philosopher is meant to be devoted to the public good and must stay away from the private life. On the other hand, the philosopher's method of gaining knowledge—contemplating the good—seems very private. Of course, the individual has to fulfil his obligations to the political community. The philosophers must turn from their quest for knowledge to reform the community, but their knowledge is no longer indebted to the community. We seem to have arrived at a paradox, here, regarding the concept of virtue: It remains, for Plato, essential for the community, but gaining knowledge of virtue is now, to a large extent, divorced from a life in the community (see Box 2.5).

## Box 2.5

**PLATO'S VIEWS ON THE DEMOS:**

Imagine then a fleet or a ship in which there is a captain who is taller and stronger than any of the crew, but he is a little deaf and has a similar infirmity in sight, and his knowledge of navigation is not much better. The sailors are quarrelling with one another about the steering—every one is of opinion that he has a right to steer, though he has never learned the art of navigation and cannot tell who taught him or when he learned, and will further assert that it cannot be taught, and they are ready to cut in pieces any one who says the contrary. They throng about the captain, begging and praying him to commit the helm to them; and if at any time they do not prevail, but others are preferred to them, they kill the others or throw them overboard, and having first chained up the noble captain's senses with drink or some narcotic drug, they mutiny and take possession of the ship and make free with the stores; thus, eating and drinking, they proceed on their voyage in such a manner as might be expected of them.

Him who is their partisan and cleverly aids them in their plot for getting the ship out of the captain's hands into their own whether by force or persuasion, they compliment with the name of sailor, pilot, able seaman, and abuse the other sort of man, whom they call a good-for-nothing; but that the true pilot must pay attention to the year and seasons and sky and stars and winds, and whatever else belongs to his art, if he intends to be really qualified for the command of a ship, and that he must and will be the steerer, whether other people like or not-the possibility of this union of authority with the steerer's art has never seriously entered into their thoughts or been made part of their calling. Now in vessels which are in a state of mutiny and by sailors who are mutineers, how will the true pilot be regarded? Will he not be called by them a prater, a star-gazer, a good-for nothing?

*Republic, Book VI*

The philosophers use their knowledge of virtue to demand that the practices of their community need to be reformed radically. Take the case, for example, of gender relations: Plato states, first of all, that in terms of reason, the relevant difference is not between men and women, but between some men and women and other men and women. Since some women have reason dominating their souls just as some men do, these women can become philosopher-queens after the requisite training in dialectics. If women are to be philosopher-rulers, they must also get the same early education in gymnastics and music. (One can imagine the reaction to Plato's idea that young Athenian women were to exercise naked in public just as young Athenian men did, given that Athens was an extremely patriarchal society with women living in secluded quarters.) Plato also points out, that those women, who are meant for a life of philosophy, cannot waste their time rearing children and doing housework. Plato's proposals regarding gender relations were radical (see Box 2.6), as were his plans for revamping the Athenian educational system. Similarly, Plato's idea that philosophers must rule, went against the democratic politics of the day. All these proposals show Plato's reason standing in judgement on Athenian social and political customs.

Box 2.6

**PLATO ON THE ABILITY OF MEN AND WOMEN TO DO THE SAME THINGS:**

You agree then, I said, that men and women are to have a common way of life such as we have described—common education, common children; and they are to watch over the citizens in common whether abiding in the city or going out to war; they are to keep watch together, and to hunt together like dogs; and always and in all things, as far as they are able, women are to share with the men? And in so doing they will do what is best, and will not violate, but preserve the natural relation of the sexes.

*Republic, Book V*

## PLATO'S LATER POLITICAL DIALOGUES

Plato's political thought is often divided into three periods: the early Socratic dialogues, the middle period, and the later political dialogues like *Statesman* and *Laws*. The radical edge of Plato's political theory of *Republic* is said to be lost in *Laws* which opens with a conversation between three men: an Athenian stranger, Clinias from Crete and Megillus from Sparta, who are discussing the founding of a Greek colony in Magnesia in southern Crete. Socrates is completely missing from this dialogue, in which the Athenian stranger is asked by the others to lay out his proposals for the social and political structures of the new colony. The new colony is to be settled by a small number of male citizens (only 5,040), and they are to live there with their families, their slaves, as well as with *metics* and other visiting aliens. The male citizens are to be gentlemen farmers while handicrafts and trading are to the occupations of the *metics*. The citizens are to be divided into twelve tribes and into four property classes.

In terms of political structure, the highest body is the Nocturnal Council, consisting of the wisest men of Magnesia. Below it is another small body, called the Guardians of the Laws, 10 of whose members are also part of the Nocturnal Council. Below that is an executive council of 360, as well as the assembly, which was attended by all citizens. Most of the public offices are filled by election, although, a small number are also filled by lottery. The rich are strictly fined for not attending the assembly. There is also a scrutiny that every official has to undergo at the end of his tenure.

This seems a far cry from the philosopher kings and queens of *Republic*, who were such embodiments of reason that there could be no question of making them accountable to the rest of the political community. However, one can see the remnants of the idea of the rule of reason in the Nocturnal Council and in the body known as the Guardians of the Laws. Political decision making is still in the hands of the wise. Although there is private property and families, excessive wealth is not allowed and everybody sits down to meals together. Another remnant from *Republic* is Plato's advocacy of public offices for women as well. It can be argued that *Laws* should not be interpreted as a text in which Plato gives up his theory of Forms and of the rule of philosophy. *Laws* reveal, instead, a modification of those positions to make it possible to administer not an ideal state, but a practicable state.

## MOVING BEYOND PLATO

Every criticism is an interpretation, and we have already seen how fraught with pitfalls the interpretive task is. Are we decided on our interpretation of Plato? Was he mainly a political thinker, or was he basically doing philosophy with an emphasis on epistemology and ethics? One has to go no further than Aristotle to look for hard-hitting criticism of many aspects of Plato's thought. Of the many criticisms that Aristotle makes in Book II of *Politics*, and which have been further developed by others later, let us pause by just a few. Plato's political theory was tainted with elitism. Political decision making in Plato's ideal state was in the hands of a few philosophical rulers. No doubt, Plato was certain that these rulers would always be oriented towards the common good. However, he was so strongly elitist that not only did he believe that the vast majority of human beings simply lack sufficient reason to decide important things for themselves, he also considered them incapable of judging the adequacy of the decisions of their rulers. By using the idea of reason to put individuals into different categories, Plato was also attacking the democratic institutions of Athens. Plato has been sharply criticized by Karl Popper for using 'the *theory of (unchecked) sovereignty*' of the philosopher rulers to undermine the idea of an accountable government.[41] For other critics, philosophy as a form of political knowledge became, in Plato's hands, a means of suppressing politics itself. For these critics, Plato's proposal that the vast majority of the denizens of the ideal city unquestioningly follow the regulations of the philosophers also undermined his own project of developing their moral selves. In all these different ways, then, Plato is being accused of undermining his own fundamental value of justice.

Focusing on reason as a human attribute and on the role of reason in human life is valuable, but Plato went wrong, critics charge, not only in restricting reason to a few, but also in developing, when describing the reason of these few, a concept of a totally ungrounded reason. For Plato, reason has nothing to do with either human experience or our emotions and passions. This is no longer seen to be an adequate conception of reason and it fails to capture the process of the development of human reason. The political repercussions of seeing reason as the opposite of interests, passions, emotions or experience can also be unsettling. Given all these problems, although the idea of reason remains a central category for political thought, later philosophers, beginning with Aristotle, give us a different picture of how human beings can use reason to arrange their affairs.

## NOTES

1. Edith Hamilton and Huntington Cairns (eds), *Plato: The Collected Dialogues Including the Letters,* Bollingen Series LXXI, New Jersey: Princeton University Press, 1987, pp. 1574–98. Scholars disagree over whether *Seventh Letter* is authentic, that is, whether it was really written by Plato himself. One position is that whether or not it was written by Plato, the events it describes in Plato's life are true. For the controversy over *Seventh Letter* see George Klosko, *The Development of Plato's Political Theory,* 2nd edition, Oxford: Oxford University Press, 2006.
2. Gregory Vlastos, *Socrates, Ironist and Moral Philosopher,* New York: Cornell University Press, 1991, p. 10.
3. *Ibid.,* p. 203.
4. Plato, *Euthydemus* in *Plato: The Collected Dialogues including the Letters,* edited by Edith Hamilton and Huntington Cairns, pp. 392–94.
5. *Ibid.*
6. As Socrates asks in *Gorgias,* is not 'the goodness of anything, whether implement or body or soul or any living thing...due to the presence of some excellence?' Edith Hamilton and Huntington Cairns (eds), *Plato: The Collected Dialogues Including the Letters,* p. 289.
7. Richard Kraut, *Aristotle: Political Philosophy,* Oxford: Oxford University Press, 2002, p. 53, n 4.
8. See Martha C. Nussbaum, *The Fragility of Goodness: Luck and Ethics in Greek Tragedy and Philosophy,* Cambridge: Cambridge University Press, 2001, p. 6.
9. Gregory Vlastos, *Socrates, Ironist and Moral Philosopher,* p. 208.
10. Let us construct a Socratic dilemma: If the only way to get a clean water-connection is by lying, then we have to forgo the clean water, since to be virtuous is our paramount concern. But what if we could get the clean water without lying? Should we, then try to get such a clean water-connection (a non-moral good, but not contrary to virtue) to enhance our happiness?
11. Edith Hamilton and Huntington Cairns (eds), *Plato: The Collected Dialogues Including the Letters,* New Jersey: Princeton University Press, pp. 319–20.
12. Terence Irwin, *Plato's Ethics,* New York: Oxford University Press, 1995, p. 17.

13. Martha C. Nussbaum, *The Fragility of Goodness*, Cambridge: Cambridge University Press, 2001, p. 125.
14. Christopher Rowe, 'Socrates in Plato's Dialogues' in Sara Ahbel-Rappe and Rachana Kamtekar (eds), *A Companion to Socrates*, Oxford: Blackwell Publishing, 2006, p. 159.
15. Gregory Vlastos, *Socrates, Ironist and Moral Philosopher*, pp. 48–49.
16. Christopher Rowe, 'Socrates in Plato's Dialogues', in Sara Ahbel-Rappe and Rachana Kamtekar (eds), *A Companion to Socrates*, pp. 168–169.
17. The exact chronological ordering of Plato's dialogues is contentious, but here is an example of how the more important of his dialogues are often divided: The early dialogues are said to consist of *Apology, Crito, Laches, Charmides, Euthyphro, Hippies Minor, Ion,* and *Protagoras*, followed by the *Lysis, Cratylus, Euthydemus, Gorgias, Hippies Major, Menexenus, Meno, Phaedo,* and *Symposium*. The middle dialogues include *Republic, Parmenides, Theaetetus,* and *Phaedrus*. The later dialogues are made up of *Timaeus, Critias, Sophist, Statesman, Philebus,* and the *Laws*. See Terence Irwin, *Plato's Ethics*, p. 12.
18. For the debate between the 'development' and the 'unity' viewpoints, see George Klosko, *The Development of Plato's Political Theory*, 2nd edition Oxford: Oxford University Press, 2006, pp. 24–29.
19. As quoted in Malcolm Schofield, *Plato: Political Philosophy*, Oxford: Oxford University Press, 2006.
20. Malcolm Schofield, *Plato: Political Philosophy*, p. 47.
21. Edith Hamilton and Huntington Cairns (eds), *Plato: The Collected Dialogues Including the Letters*, p. 246.
22. *Ibid.*, p. 302.
23. See Dana Villa, *Socratic Citizenship*, New Jersey: Princeton University Press, 2001, pp. 31–41.
24. Edith Hamilton and Huntington Cairns (eds), *Plato: The Collected Dialogues Including the Letters*, pp. 15–16 and 23.
25. *Ibid.*, pp. 36–37.
26. See Edith Hamilton and Huntington Cairns (eds), *Plato: The Collected Dialogues Including the Letters*, p. 659.
27. *Ibid.*, p. 677.
28. *Ibid.*, p. 681.
29. *Ibid.*
30. *Ibid.*, p. 675.
31. *Ibid.*, p. 684.
32. *Ibid.*
33. *Ibid.*
34. Gregory Vlastos in Rachana Kamtekar, 'Social Justice and Happiness in the *REPUBLIC*: Plato's Two Principles', in *History of Political Thought*, Vol. XXII 2; Summer 2001, p. 192.
35. R. Kamtekar, p. 205.
36. *Ibid.*, p. 216.
37. *Ibid.*, p. 215.
38. We are familiar with the claim, that the idea of justice exists in our minds; that our mind creates or constructs the idea of justice through a process of

abstraction. For Plato, the philosophers copy the idea of justice in their minds from the Form of justice.

39. See Morag Buchan, *Women in Plato's Political Theory*, Routledge, 1999.
40. See David Keyt, 'Plato and the Ship of State', in Gerasimos Santas, *The Blackwell Guide to Plato's Republic,* Malden: Blackwell Publishing, 2006, p. 198.
41. Karl R. Popper, *The Open Society and Its Enemies*, Vol. II, 5th edition (revised), London: Routledge, 1966, p. 121.

## READING LIST

Ahbel-Rappe, Sara and Rachana Kamtekar (eds), *A Companion to Socrates*, Oxford: Blackwell Publishing, 2006.

Barker, E., *Greek Political Theory: Plato and His Predecessors*, New York: Routledge, 1977.

Hamilton, Edith and Huntington Cairns (eds), *Plato: The Collected Dialogues Including the Letters,* Bollingen Series LXXI, Princeton: Princeton University Press, 1987.

Irwin, Terence, *Plato's Ethics*, New York: Oxford University Press, 1995.

Klosko, George, *The Development of Plato's Political Theory*, Oxford: Oxford University Press, 2006.

Kraut, Richard (ed.), *The Cambridge Companion to Plato,* Cambridge: Cambridge University Press, 1992.

Santas, Gerasimos, *The Blackwell Guide to Plato's Republic,* Malden: Blackwell Publishing, 2006.

Schofield, Malcolm, *Plato: Political Philosophy*, Oxford: Oxford University Press, 2006.

Villa, Dana, *Socratic Citizenship*, New Jersey: Princeton University Press, 2001.

Vlastos, Gregory, *Socrates, Ironist and Moral Philosopher*, New York: Cornell University Press, 1991.

## CENTRAL THEMES

1. **The use of justice to fit the individual into the community:** Plato seems to argue that in human life, most substantial results are due to collective effort, and sustained collective effort is not possible without some norms of justice being in place. What is the conception of justice that he unfolds? Does he use his conception of justice to mitigate the conflict between individuals and the community?
2. **Reason and experience in a theory of knowledge:** Reason is said to be the lynchpin of Plato's philosophic vision. The rational structure of the cosmos can be recreated by human beings in their social universe when they follow the light of reason. Do you think that Plato's conception of reason can be used in a theory of social reform?
3. **Democracy and the rule of philosophy:** It is quite clear from Plato's writings that he had a jaundiced view of Athenian democracy. What do you think of

Plato's warning that democracy often descends into a rule of demagogues, or, in modern parlance, populist rule? In trying to mitigate the ills of the democracy practised in his times through his conception of the rule of philosophy, what is it that Plato missed?

4. **Women and politics:** Plato said that men and women were different by nature, but their natural differences were, unlike the differences between farmers and guardians, irrelevant to their political roles. What problems do you find with Plato's theory of the political equality of men and women?
5. **The public and the private:** In Plato's times, Athenian men spent most of their day in public spaces–in the gymnasia, the *agora*, the *ekklesia* and the academies. Plato took this association with the public to another level when he condemned the institutions of private property and the family for the Guardians. What was Plato's purpose in denying the pleasures of property and of family life for the Guardians? In Plato's conception, are there any private aspects of life, for instance in how knowledge of the Good is gained, for those who are most closely associated with political decision making?

# THREE

# Aristotle (384–322 BCE): Moral Action and the Best Constitution

Someone once said that in philosophy one can either be a Platonist or an Aristotelian. It is a difficult choice to make, especially in political philosophy. If the Platonic principle of combining philosophy with politics translates, as we saw in the previous chapter, into an anti-democratic regime, then is it not preferable to go with the Aristotelian definition of political rule as ruling and being ruled in turn? On the other hand, what is one to do with Aristotle's staunch belief in natural hierarchies and his exclusion of slaves and women from his principle of political rule?

This fundamental difference between Plato and Aristotle is surprising, given that Aristotle was Plato's faithful student and remained at the Academy till Plato's death in 347 BCE. Aristotle was not an Athenian; he was born in Stagira near Macedonia. His father was a physician and Aristotle's early interests were in medical and biological studies. Aristotle's father was the physician of the king of Macedon, Amyntas III, who died in 370/369 BCE. Amyntas III was succeeded in 359 BCE by Philip with whom Aristotle is said to have had close personal ties.[1] Aristotle is also said to have tutored Philip's son, Alexander, for a few years. When Aristotle was seventeen, in 367 BCE, he left Stagira for Athens to study under Plato. He stayed at the Academy for twenty years, leaving Athens after Plato died in 347 BCE and the Academy acquired a new head not to Aristotle's liking. After some years in Asia Minor, Aristotle moved to Pella, the capital of Macedonia, to become Alexander's tutor for six years from 342 to 336 BCE. He returned to Athens in 335 BCE to set up his own school, the Lyceum. Like many other Greek city-states, Athens had, by then, become a Macedonian protectorate, but after Alexander's death in 323 BCE, the Athenians rebelled and declared war against Macedonia. Since Aristotle was associated with Alexander, he had to flee from Athens and died in exile in 322 BCE.

Aristotle was a prolific writer, composing texts on a wide variety of subjects. His early work, *Protrepticus,* was soon followed by *Metaphysics, Physics, Rhetoric, Poetics, Eudemian Ethics, Politics, Nichomachean Ethics, De Anima* and *De Interpretatione,* as well as many other texts. The transition from antiquity into the middle ages, however, saw the domination of neo-Platonism in philosophy, probably because the emerging Catholic Church found Platonism more conducive to its doctrines and actively tried to suppress competing philosophical schools. This, along with the fact that none of Aristotle's works—except a couple of books on logic—survived into the middle ages, meant that Aristotle was almost lost to the Western tradition till all his other works were translated into Latin in the 12th and 13th centuries. It was only between 1240 and 1280 that new translations of *Politics* and *Nichomachean Ethics* became available. Not only were Aristotle's own works translated, but certain commentaries on Aristotle by the widely read Arab scholars ibn Sina (980–1037) and ibn Rushd (1126–1198) were also made available in Latin. In fact, the teaching of Aristotle in the Universities of Paris and Oxford was often mediated through the commentaries of these two Arab philosophers.[2]

Aristotle's early works, like *Protrepticus,* show the stamp of Plato, but soon enough, his differences from his teacher became more apparent. Many of these differences flow from Aristotle's rejection of Plato's method of practising philosophy. Plato had searched for truth in the super-sensible world of the Forms, trying to remove himself from everyday human life. For Aristotle, a philosopher had to not ignore but investigate the *phainomena* (appearances) and *endoxa* (beliefs, what we believe, what we say) of everyday life. Plato rejected 'both the evidence of sense perception and the data of shared language and belief', while Aristotle sought to work with these appearances to show that many of the seeming contradictions in the world of appearances worked themselves out when philosophy investigated them properly. The resolution of the contradictions implies that truth lies in the world of appearances itself, and not in some transcendental world of the Forms. If the Forms represent the truth, then the Forms are contained in the appearances themselves. Even if some of our ordinary beliefs turn out to be false, many of the more basic and universal ones contain the truth.[3] Thus, Aristotle spent a lot of time gathering information about these *phainomena.* He and his students are supposed to have compiled information on 158 constitutions of his time. Of these, unfortunately, only the *Athenian Constitution* is extant. Aristotle is said to have used these empirical details about different political arrangements to write *Politics,* his theoretical treatise on political science. It also followed that Aristotle was much less contemptuous both of practical knowledge and of the social and political practices of contemporary Athens. Aristotle's differences from Plato are also highlighted when one examines the former's moral theory in *Nichomachean Ethics*. Given the intellectual disagreement between the two, it is not surprising that Aristotle spends the first six chapters of Book II of *Politics* criticizing Plato's theory in *Republic* and *Laws*.[4]

## A THEORY OF MORAL ACTION

Disagreement there may be between the two philosophers, but the questions that Aristotle struggled to answer were the questions he inherited from Socrates and Plato. What kind of goods are required for human beings to flourish and what kind of political community is it which can best provide these goods? A human being's goal is to live a life of *eudaimonia,* in other words, to flourish. Aristotle is to be credited for fleshing out the idea of *eudaimonia*. Whereas for Socrates and Plato, to live well was to live virtuously, Aristotle seems to have analytically distinguished between a well-lived life and a virtuous life by defining *eudaimonia* independently of virtue. *Eudaimonia* refers to 'the full normal functioning of a thing relative to the capacities specific to its natural kind'.[5] The purpose of anything, its end, is to use its capacities to its fullest. That is when it can be said to flourish. A knife, for instance, as we said before, is defined by its capacity to cut. When it is used for cutting and it cuts well, it can, as it were, be said to flourish. Sharpness is the quality or virtue which enables the knife to cut well. Human beings, like other things, are creatures with specific capabilities. These capabilities allow us to function in certain ways. A well-lived life, a flourishing life, is one in which we are able to use our capabilities to function in ways specific to us as humans.[6] For example, human beings are capable of speech and reasoning. The faculty of practical reasoning, when conjoined with the virtue of *phronesis* (practical wisdom)—which it needs if it is to be exercised properly—enables us to live a well-functioning life instead of a dysfunctional one. So the virtues, by allowing our capabilities to be used well, get linked to the well-functioning or well-lived life.

'The science of the good of man is politics', and politics is concerned with 'how to realize their good for a body of men', states *Nichomachean Ethics*.[7] *Nichomachean Ethics,* both in its beginning and at its end, makes a crucial reference to *Politics,* thus presenting itself as a kind of introduction to *Politics*. *Nichomachean Ethics* is concerned with the good life for a human being and how virtue is a component of this good life. Politics is the science of the good or happy life for a group of persons and if virtue is—as we saw in the previous chapter—essential to this goodness or happiness, a discussion of virtue becomes our prolegomenon to politics. In the *Nichomachean Ethics,* Aristotle adds a significantly new dimension to an already existing ethical theory by prefacing his theory of the moral virtues with a long discussion of what is it that we mean when we say that someone is acting morally.

In *Nichomachean Ethics,* instead of beginning with a discussion of a specific virtue—like justice, which is the focus of Plato's *Republic*—Aristotle provides us first with a general theory of moral action. Before we can know what each virtue is—and Aristotle's list is much longer than the usual Greek one—we have to know what it is to act morally. Before we can know what moral action is, we must understand what we mean by action. Aristotle's theory of moral action is derived from a general theory of animal and human action. In the process of explaining moral action, the question of what is it about us that makes it possible for us to be moral is also answered. Aristotle believed that all action was characterized by 'its object-directedness and its responsiveness not to the world *simpliciter* but to the [actor's] own view of it'.[8] In that sense, all action, rational or non-rational, is intentional. Here we see Aristotle discounting Plato's view of most human beings as being in the clutch of 'brutish' involuntary desires.

In *Nichomachean Ethics,* we find that the first thing that Aristotle says about morality, in Book II, is that the realm of morality includes only those areas in life in which things can be otherwise (see Box 3.1). For instance, moral criteria do not apply to nature. A stone when thrown upwards will always fall down, so we cannot say either that the stone acts morally or that it acts immorally in always falling down. The realm of human affairs, however, is the realm of things that can be otherwise, so moral criteria do apply in this sphere.

**Box 3.1**

**THE DOMAIN OF MORALITY IS ONE OF CHOICE:**

From this fact it is plain that not one of the Moral Virtues comes to be in us merely by nature: because of such things as exist by nature, none can be changed by custom: a stone, for instance, by nature gravitating downwards, could never by custom be brought to ascend, not even if one were to try and accustom it by throwing it up ten thousand times; nor could file again be brought to descend, nor in fact could anything whose nature is in one way be brought by custom to be in another. The Virtues then come to be in us neither by nature, nor in despite of nature, but we are furnished by nature with a capacity for receiving them and are perfected in them through custom.

*Nichomachean Ethics, Book II*

In Books II and III of *Nicomachean Ethics,* Aristotle gives us an extended definition of moral action. Moral action is very important to understand because moral development is the goal of human life. 'Virtue, then, is a state of character concerned with choice, lying in a mean, i.e., the mean relative to us, this being determined by a rational principle, and by that principle by which the man of practical wisdom would determine it.'[9] For it to be said of someone that he has morally excelled himself in his actions, Aristotle writes, it is necessary that this person must be in a certain condition when he so acts: 'in the first place he must have knowledge, secondly he must choose the acts, and choose them for their own sakes, and thirdly his action must proceed from a firm and unchangeable character'[10] (see Box 3.2).

**Box 3.2**

**THE DIFFERENT ELEMENTS OF VIRTUOUS ACTION:**

Again, the cases of the arts and the virtues are not parallel: because those things which are produced by the arts have their excellence in themselves, and it is sufficient therefore that these when produced should be in a certain state: but those which are produced in the way of the virtues, are, strictly speaking, actions of a certain kind (say of Justice or perfected Self-Mastery), not merely if in themselves they are in a certain state but if also he who does them does them being himself in a cer tain state, first if knowing what he is doing, next if with deliberate prefer ence, and with such preference for the things' own sake; and thirdly if being himself stable and unapt to change.

*Nichomachean Ethics, Book II*

In these passages, Aristotle is pointing to at least three different aspects of what it is to be moral. First, in order for us to be able to say that someone has acted morally, that someone must have intended, in his action, to have acted morally. The actor must have intended to bring about some good for others. If an individual has acted in a way beneficial to others, but under compulsion, or without any understanding of what he is doing, he cannot be called moral. Moral acts must always issue from a choice, and so volition is essential to a definition of morality. This coupling of morality with intentionality and volition is explicit in Aristotle's limited analogy of moral philosophy with the art of medicine. Just as medicine is a therapeutic art which heals the body, moral philosophy provides therapy for the soul. However, while a sick patient can heal his body by merely following the doctor's orders without really understanding them, philosophical therapeutics only work, according to Aristotle, if the person seeking to make his moral self better, understands the process of philosophical reasoning and actively participates in it.[11] For Aristotle, 'ethical *logoi* [argument] are unlike medical treatment, in that they involve a reciprocal discourse in which the pupil is not ordered around by an authority figure, or manipulated by coercive tactics, but is intellectually active for herself'.[12] Here, Aristotle seems to be going back to the spirit of Socrates, rejecting Plato's didactic model of moral teaching in *Republic*.

Let us get back to volition as an attribute of moral action. What is volition, then? To choose to do something is not to do it impulsively, but to do it after some deliberation. 'Choice will be the deliberate desire of things in our own power.'[13] Volition is deliberate choice and the process of deliberation is also important. This process of deliberation points to the second feature of moral action for Aristotle: To be moral, an individual must not only have the strength of will, but also the faculty of right judgement. Aristotle gave the name *phronesis* to this faculty of right judgement. Even after deliberation, if we lack *phronesis*, we might choose a course of action that will actually harm others. In such a case, our actions cannot be called moral even if we did not intend the harm.

The third aspect of Aristotle's theory of moral action has to do with character. By doing the right action repeatedly, that is, by forming good habits, we can build a character, which will result in right actions (see Box 3.3). Once we spoil our character by doing immoral acts, that becomes our second nature and it makes us 'choose' to do further bad acts. Just as the stone cannot but fall down, we become unable to make choices inconsistent with our character. However, although moral criteria do not apply to the movement of the stone, we can be blamed for our bad character because we created it by choosing to act immorally over a long period of time.[14]

**Box 3.3**

**ONE'S CHARACTER IS ALSO A MATTER OF ONE'S CHOICES:**

Furthermore, it is wholly irrelevant to say that the man who acts unjustly or dissolutely does not wish to attain the habits of these vices: for if a man wittingly does those things whereby he must become unjust he is to all intents and purposes unjust voluntarily; but he cannot with a wish cease to be unjust and become just. For, to take the analogous case, the sick man cannot with a wish be well again, yet in a supposable case he is voluntarily ill because he has produced his sickness by living intemperately and disregarding his physicians. There was a time then when he might have helped being ill, but now he has let himself go he cannot any longer; just as he who has let a stone out of his hand cannot recall it, and yet it rested with him to aim and throw it, because the origination was in his power. Just so the unjust man, and he who has lost all self-control, might originally have helped being what they are, and so they are voluntarily what they are; but now that they are become so they no longer have the power of being otherwise.

*Nichomachean Ethics, Book III*

Now that we know the form of virtuous action, we have to realize this virtuous action in a body of men. This takes us to the realm of politics. The science of ethics and that of politics are closely related because both are practical sciences. Aristotle distinguishes between three forms of knowledge based on their ends: the contemplative sciences, like natural philosophy and mathematics, have theory as their end; the practical sciences have good action as their end; and the productive sciences, like the useful arts, or *techne*, like weaving and shipbuilding, have the creation of an object as their end.[15] Although sometimes Aristotle makes an analogy between politics and the productive sciences, calling politics an art with legislation as its product, mostly he sharply distinguishes political science as a separate kind of practical knowledge with good action as its end. Good action needs both *phronesis* and good character. *Phronesis* becomes political science when applied to a collection of men.

## FROM MORAL THEORY TO POLITICAL PHILOSOPHY

When Alasdair MacIntyre began one of his books with the claim that '[a] systematic history of Aristotelianism would be an immense undertaking populated by a great variety of rival Aristotles',[16] he was obviously pointing to the radically different interpretations of Aristotle available to us today. One of the things of direct interest to us, which has hinged on these rival interpretations, is the very order of the books of *Politics*. *Politics* consists of eight books. Those commentators who see more of a certain kind of continuity between Plato and Aristotle insist on reading them as they are traditionally ordered; but those who (beginning with Werner Jaeger in the 20th century) see Aristotle as moving away from Plato, consider Books VII and VIII to have been written earlier with Book II, and Books IV–VI to have been written in Aristotle's later anti-Platonic period.[17] Werner Jaeger's magnum opus on Aristotle, translated into English in 1934 as *Aristotle: Fundamentals of the History of his Development*, set off an acrimonious debate among scholars over the dating of the different books of the *Politics*. For Jaeger, Books VII, VIII and II, on the ideal constitution, belong to Aristotle's early period. He sees these three books as closely connected not only to *Eudemian Ethics*, but also to Aristotle's even earlier Platonic tract, *Protrepticus*. Jaeger also added Book III to this early period. Books IV–VI are said to have been written much later and finally, Aristotle is said to have added Book I to introduce the whole set of books. Jaeger's theory has been rejected by W.D. Ross who believes that all of *Politics* comes from the last period of Aristotle's life. In its conclusion, *Nichomachean Ethics* states that the work of writing a treatise on politics still remains and Ross uses this to argue against Jaeger's early dating of parts of *Politics*. In this controversy over the dating of the different books of *Politics*, what scholars are also fighting over is the nature of Aristotle's theory. Were there two Aristotelian theories, an early idealist one replaced by a latter empirical political theory, or is Aristotelian theory to be taken as a whole with both an idealist and an empirical component? For our purposes the eight books of *Politics* can be categorized as follows: Book I: from the household to the city; Books II, VII and VIII: of ideal constitutions; Books III and IV: citizenship and constitution defined, kingship, aristocracy and the polity presented as good constitutions; and Books V and VI: of perverted constitutions. Instead of foregrounding Books II, VII and VIII, in this discussion we will focus mostly on Books I, III and IV.

Now that we are entering a discussion of *Politics*, we have to see how Aristotle uses his conception of morality to support the political principle of ruling and being ruled in turn that he comes up with in his political treatise. *Politics* faithfully follows the plan laid out for it in the last chapter of *Nichomachean Ethics*. Book I of *Politics* begins by clearly distinguishing the political association from the family on the grounds that while the family is an association of unequals, and is held together by relationships of hierarchy and subordination, the political community or the *polis*, on the other hand, is a community of equals, and the principle of rule suited to it is that of a statesman and not that of a kingship. 'It is a mistake to believe that the statesman [*the politikos*, who handles the affairs of a political association] is the same as the monarch of a kingdom, or the manager of a household, or the master of a number of slaves.'[18] The absolute type of kingship is a form of government in which a single person is the final decision maker on every issue. This type of kingship corresponds to paternal rule over a household. Just as paternal rule is kingship over a family, similarly, this type of kingship may be regarded as paternal rule over a *polis*. This idea of paternal rule over a *polis* goes against the principle of equality that is fundamental to the idea of a *polis*. Aristotle sees nothing wrong in having paternal rule in a family because he believes that the three relationships that constitute a household—that between a husband and his wife, between parents and their children and between the master and his slaves—are unequal relationships. The husband is superior to the wife, the parents to the children and the master to his slaves. Therefore, it is only just that that the husband/master rule over the household. The political community is not a large household for Aristotle. Between the household and the political community, there is a difference not of degree but of kind. 'But [besides rule of the sort exercised by their ruler over persons in a servile position] there is also rule of the sort which is exercised over persons who are similar in birth to the ruler, and are similarly free. Rule of this sort we call political rule; and this is the sort of rule which [unlike rule of the first sort] the ruler must begin to learn by being ruled and by obeying'[19] since '[a] state aims at being, as far as it can be, a society composed of equals and peers [who, as such, can be friends and associates].'[20]

Not only is the political community an association of equals, but, Aristotle tells us, in Book I of *Politics*, it is also the highest kind of association (see Box 3.4). It has that status because not only does it meet the needs of subsistence, defence and sociability, but it also makes its citizens moral. The ethical development of its members is its primary purpose and it is this criteria that Aristotle uses to distinguish the *polis* from other subsidiary associations: '...a *polis* is not an association for residence on a common site, or for the sake of preventing mutual injustice and easing exchange... the various institutions of a common social life—marriage connections, kin groups, religious gatherings, and social pastimes...are the business of friendship. It is therefore for the sake of good actions and not for the sake of social life, that political associations must be considered to exist.'[21]

It is also this purpose that allows us to make sense of Aristotle's claims that man is a political animal, or that the state is a natural association. Man

**Box 3.4**

**THE STATE IS AN ASSOCIATION NOT MERELY FOR LIVING BUT FOR LIVING A GOOD LIFE:**

Nor was civil society founded merely to preserve the lives of its members; but that they might live well: for otherwise a state might be composed of slaves, or the animal creation: but this is not so; for these have no share in the happiness of it; nor do they live after their own choice; nor is it an alliance mutually to defend each other from injuries, or for a commercial intercourse: for then the Tyrrhenians and Carthaginians, and all other nations between whom treaties of commerce subsist, would be citizens of one city; for they have articles to regulate their exports and imports, and engagements for mutual protection, and alliances for mutual defence; but [1280b] yet they have not all the same magistrates established among them, but they are different among the different people; nor does the one take any care, that the morals of the other should be as they ought, or that none of those who have entered into the common agreements should be unjust, or in any degree vicious, only that they do not injure any member of the confederacy. But whosoever endeavours to establish wholesome laws in a state, attends to the virtues and the vices of each individual who composes it; from whence it is evident, that the first care of him who would found a city, truly deserving that name, and not nominally so, must be to have his citizens virtuous; for otherwise it is merely an alliance for self-defence; differing from those of the same cast which are made between different people only in place: for law is an agreement and a pledge, as the sophist Lycophron says, between the citizens of their intending to do justice to each other, though not sufficient to make all the citizens just and good: and that this is fact is evident, for could any one bring different places together, as, for instance, enclose Megara and Corinth in a wall, yet they would not be one city, not even if the inhabitants intermarried with each other, though this inter-community contributes much to make a place one city. Besides, could we suppose a set of people to live separate from each other, but within such a distance as would admit of an intercourse, and that there were laws subsisting between each party, to prevent their injuring one another in their mutual dealings, supposing one a carpenter, another a husbandman, shoemaker, and the like, and that their numbers were ten thousand, still all that they would have together in common would be a tariff for trade, or an alliance for mutual defence, but not the same city. And why? not because their mutual intercourse is not near enough, for even if persons so situated should come to one place, and every one should live in his own house as in his native city, and there should be alliances subsisting between each party to mutually assist and prevent any injury being done to the other, still they would not be admitted to be a city by those who think correctly, if they preserved the same customs when they were together as when they were separate.

It is evident, then, that a city is not a community of place; nor established for the sake of mutual safety or traffic with each other; but that these things are the necessary consequences of a city, although they may all exist where there is no city: but a city is a society of people joining together with their families and their children to live agreeably for the sake of having their lives as happy and as independent as possible: and for this purpose it is necessary that they should live in one place and intermarry with each other: hence in ail cities there are family-meetings, clubs, sacrifices, and public entertainments to promote friendship; for a love of sociability is friendship itself; so that the end then for which a city is established is, that the inhabitants of it may live happy, and these things are conducive to that end: for it is a community of families and villages for the sake of a perfect independent life; that is, as we have already said, for the sake of living well and happily. It is not therefore founded for the purpose of men's merely [1281a] living together, but for their living as men ought; for which reason those who contribute most to this end deserve to have greater power in the city than those who are their equals in family and freedom, but their inferiors in civil virtue, or those who excel them in wealth but are below them in worth.

*Politics, Book III, 9*

is a *zoon politikon* (political animal) because it is only by living in a political community that he realizes his true nature, which is to become a moral being. Similarly, the state is an association natural to man because it is essential for the completion of his nature. According to Aristotle, men are born with the potential of becoming moral, but this potential can be actualized only under the right social conditions. The most important of these social conditions is being a member of a political community. It is for this reason that the state is supposed to complete the nature of men (see Box 3.5).

The goal of human life is to live well. We saw in the earlier section that according to Aristotle, to live well is to live as a moral person—something that requires deliberation and choice. In the words of an important contemporary Aristotelian philosopher, if a man is going to live well, he must have 'a sense of shame about shameful things and a striving towards fine things'. Nussbaum identifies this complex combination of shame of bad actions and striving toward good as the feeling of self-respect. She goes on to show how marked the difference of opinions is between Plato and Aristotle regarding the social conditions of self-respect. 'It should be

Box 3.5

**THE STATE IS A NATURAL ENTITY:**

Hence it is evident that a city is a natural production, and that man is naturally a political animal, and that whosoever is naturally and not accidentally unfit for society, must be either inferior or superior to man: thus the man in Homer, who is reviled for being "without society, without law, without family." Such a one must naturally be of a quarrelsome disposition, and as solitary as the birds. The gift of speech also evidently proves that man is a more social animal than the bees, or any of the herding cattle: for nature, as we say, does nothing in vain, and man is the only animal who enjoys it. Voice indeed, as being the token of pleasure and pain, is imparted to others also, and thus much their nature is capable of, to perceive pleasure and pain, and to impart these sensations to others; but it is by speech that we are enabled to express what is useful for us, and what is hurtful, and of course what is just and what is unjust: for in this particular man differs from other animals, that he alone has a perception of good and evil, of just and unjust, and it is a participation of these common sentiments which forms a family and a city.

*Politics, Book I*, 2

stressed here that the issue between the two is not the issue of individualism… [Aristotle] will insist that although the good may be objective, the choice of the good must come from within and not by dictation from without. All reflective men might choose the same good life; but what makes each of them a good man is that he is the one who chooses it. It will not count as a good life for him unless it is a life chosen by his own practical reason.'[22]

It follows, then, that the *polis* can make its citizens moral only by giving them the right to make political decisions. It is important to make political decisions because the state is the largest community which is united by impersonal ties. It will not do to take decisions at the level of the family, because the family is a set of personal relationships. Morality requires that one is able to be impartial between one's own interests and the interests of others who are not related to one personally. For Aristotle, then, there cannot be any question of not participating in politics, of letting others—no matter how wise they are—take all the political decisions, because unless one's own acts are the result of one's own deliberate choice, one cannot be moral. The purpose of the *polis* cannot be realized without allowing all citizens a share in judicial and deliberative office. All citizens must sit in the *Ekklesia*, the principal assembly, and be members of the Dikasteria, the courts. In that sense, Aristotle was much closer to the democratic traditions of his day, since, in the heyday of Athenian democracy, citizenship entitled one to precisely these privileges, and all adult Greek males both of whose parents were Greek were entitled to these rights of citizenship. This was what Aristotle meant by his idea that all citizens, by turn, participated in ruling and in being ruled (see Box 3.6).

We have tried to show how Aristotle's emphasis on moral autonomy determines his conception of politics. This relationship is encapsulated well in the following passage from one of Nussbaum's later works:

> [...]Aristotle's interest in stability in political life is tempered by his concern for other social values, such as the autonomy of individual choice and civic vitality. Among the available conceptions of the *polis* he does not opt for one that would seek to maximise stability and unity by turning over all choice-making to a single person or a small group. Against Platonic efforts to eliminate conflict and instability through minimising the legislative engagement of separate wills, Aristotle defends a conception of the city as a 'plurality', an association of 'free and equal' citizens who rule and are ruled by turns.[23]

**Box 3.6**

**POLITICAL RULE IS RULE OVER EQUALS:**

But there is a government of another sort, in which men govern those who are their equals in rank, and freemen, which we call a political government, in which men learn to command by first submitting to obey, as a good general of horse, or a commander-in-chief, must acquire a knowledge of their duty by having been long under the command of another, and the like in every appointment in the army: for well is it said, no one knows how to command who has not himself been under command of another. The virtues of those are indeed different, but a good citizen must necessarily be endowed with them; he ought also to know in what manner freemen ought to govern, as well as be governed: and this, too, is the duty of a good man.

*Politics, Book III*, 4

## THE POLITY AND ARISTOTLE'S CLASSIFICATION OF CONSTITUTIONS

In Socrates, virtue seemed to have two aspects. It not only brought happiness to the individual, but it also safeguarded the community. Many of Aristotle's admirers, including Nussbaum above, seem to imply that in his emphasis on virtuous action as a safeguard to the community, Plato weakened the conception of virtuous action,[24] a failing which was rectified by Aristotle. So far, in our discussion of Aristotle, we have also concentrated on his analysis of the conditions in which individuals can be said to act virtuously. What about the second aspect of virtue? Does Aristotle also discuss the consequences of individuals practising virtue for the political communities of which they are part? A political association, the citizens of which are virtuous, is, Aristotle argued, most stable because there is justice in this society. Aristotle's discussion of the just and stable *polis* is introduced in *Politics* as part of his analysis of the 'best' form of government, called the polity.

Aristotle's analysis of the merits of the polity is part of his discussion on how constitutions should be classified. A constitution is, for Aristotle, a way of distributing deliberative and judicial office, that is, the rights of citizenship. Two principles can be used to classify constitutions: a) whether legislative and judicial office is concentrated in the hands of one, the few or the many, and b) whether those who hold these offices are performing their function keeping the common good in mind. These two principles give us three good constitutions, namely, monarchy, aristocracy and polity, and three perverted forms, namely, tyranny, oligarchy and democracy. Aristotle does not stop here; in keeping with his eye for variation in the world, he goes on to list about five different types of kingship, five types of democracy, four types of oligarchy and several kinds of polities and tyrannies. Democracy, for Aristotle, is the least bad of the perverted constitutions, and the peasant-based democracy is much better than the extreme democracy in which there is no respect for the law.

In Books III and IV of *Politics*, Aristotle pulls together several arguments to build up his case for the polity being, from among the three good constitutions, the best one. The polity is the constitution in which judicial and deliberative office is widely distributed and in which the many rule in the common interest. The polity also follows the principle of the sovereignty of the law, ensuring that the citizens are taking decisions through their deliberations and not in the form of arbitrary decrees. Aristotle's belief that it is the many that are collectively wiser than the few or than even the one wisest man made him discount a monarchy or aristocracy as better than the polity. The many, taken together, having more moral prudence than the one wise person, must be placed at the helm of political affairs.

> There is this to be said for the Many. Each of them by himself may not be of good quality, but when they all come together it is possible that they may surpass—collectively and as a body, although not individually—the quality of the few best... when there are many [who contribute to the process of deliberation], each can bring his share of goodness and moral prudence; and when all meet together the people may thus become something in the nature of a single person, who—as he has many feet, many hands, and many senses—may also have many qualities of character and intelligence.[25]

This passage from *Politics* has been considered to have given birth to Aristotle's 'doctrine of the wisdom of the multitude'.[26] The wisdom of the multitude consists in their common deliberation: 'Deliberation among the many is a way of bringing each citizen's ethical views and insights to bear on the views and insights of each of the others, so that they cast light on each other, providing a basis for reciprocal questioning and criticism, and enabling a position to emerge which is better than any of the inputs and much more than an aggregation or function of those inputs.'[27]

Thus, the wisdom of which the multitude is capable emerges only when they get together. Since the polity allows the many to rule after collective deliberations, it is the wisest constitution.

If the many, taken as a whole, contribute most to the possibility of good actions, which is the end of the state, then it is only just that they get the rights of citizenship. Justice, for Aristotle, does not mean arithmetical equality with everybody counting as one. It is instead, a principle of proportionality with only those counting as equal who are equal with respect to some relevant criteria; it is only these persons who should get equal treatment. Since the many make the most contribution to the goal of the state, it is amongst them that citizenship rights should be equally distributed. Such a constitution is a just constitution and so the best constitution.

Some scholars have gone so far as to assert that it is not the *polis* generally, but a specific *polis*, the polity, which is posited by Aristotle as man's *telos* (goal). '...[T]he political regime appropriate to the 'natural *polis*' of *Politics* Book I and to the '*polis* of our prayers' of Book VII is, in certain analytically important ways, to be understood as a democracy'.[28] Since Ober goes on to describe this best regime as an aristocratic democracy which matches Aristotle's description of a polity, we can claim Aristotle to be arguing that the polity is our *telos*. This would also fit in with what, for Aristotle, is the distinguishing feature of human beings: speech and deliberative judgement. Both speech and deliberative judgement come into play properly only in a polity. 'Speech is the mark of man's political nature because speech is the medium in which politics takes place... Speech, for Aristotle, is not just the unanimous chanting of accepted truths about justice: it is a matter of conversation, debate in the *ekklesia*, articulate discussion...'[29] If it is the polity which is the final goal of all human endeavour, then obviously it must be the polity which is the best constitution.

Aristotle goes on to describe different aspects of the polity. Sociologically speaking, the polity is characterized by the predominance of the middle class. In Book I, Aristotle tells us that compounds or wholes like the state must be analysed into their parts, if they are to be understood, and he breaks up the state into its constituent units of the households. But the population of a state can also be broken up into other categories: according to occupational groups like farmers, mechanics, labourers, soldiers and priests, or according to social classes like the rich, poor and middle classes. Aristotle states, quite clearly, that while the rich only know how to rule and be masters, the poor only know how to be ruled and be slaves, and it is the members of the middle class who know both how to rule and be ruled. Since the middle class is in a majority in the polity, the polity best approximates the idea of a *polis* as a community of friends and equals, which, as we have seen earlier, is part of Aristotle's definition of a *polis* (see Box 3.7).

Box 3.7

**THE RICH ONLY KNOW HOW TO RULE AND THE POOR ONLY KNOW HOW TO BE RULED:**

In every city the people are divided into three sorts; the very rich, the very poor, and those who are between them. If this is universally admitted, that the mean is best, it is evident that even in point of fortune mediocrity is to be preferred; for that state is most submissive to reason; for those who are very handsome, or very strong, or very noble, or very rich; or, on the contrary; those who are very poor, or very weak, or very mean, with difficulty obey it; for the one are capricious and greatly flagitious, the other rascally and mean, the crimes of each arising from their different excesses: nor will they go through the different offices of the state; which is detrimental to it: besides, those who excel in strength, in riches, or friends, or the like, neither know how nor are willing to submit to command: and this begins at home when they are boys; for there they are brought up too delicately to be accustomed to obey their preceptors: as for the very poor, their general and excessive want of what the rich enjoy reduces them to a state too mean: so that the one know not how to command, but to be commanded as slaves, the others know not how to submit to any command, nor to command themselves but with despotic power.

A city composed of such men must therefore consist of slaves and masters, not freemen; where one party must hate, and the other despise, where there could be no possibility of friendship or political community: for community supposes affection; for we do not even on the road associate with our enemies. It is also the genius of a city to be composed as much as possible of equals; which will be most so when the inhabitants are in the middle state: from whence it follows, that that city must be best framed which is composed of those whom we say are naturally its proper members. It is men of this station also who will be best assured of safety and protection; for they will neither covet what belongs to others, as the poor do; nor will others covet what is theirs, as the poor do what belongs to the rich; and thus, without plotting against any one, or having any one plot against them, they will live free from danger: for which reason Phocylides wisely wishes for the middle state, as being most productive of happiness. It is plain, then, that the most perfect political community must be amongst those who are in the middle rank, and those states are best instituted wherein these are a larger and more respectable part, if possible, than both the other; or, if that cannot be, at least than either of them separate; so that being thrown into the balance it may prevent either scale from preponderating.

*Politics, Book IV, 11*

For all these reasons, the polity is also the most stable constitution: 'It is clear that the middle type of constitution is best... It is the one type free from faction; where the middle class is large, there is least likelihood of factions and dissension among the citizens'[30] This link between justice and stability is also clearly put forward by Aristotle in the later books of the *Politics,* in which he discusses injustice as the prime cause of revolution and instability in societies.

The polity, then, being the most prudent *polis,* the most just and the most stable *polis,* approximating most closely the very definition of a *polis,* and fulfilling most the function of a *polis,* is the best constitution.

In this brief foray into Aristotle's political theory, we have referred on and off to his 'political naturalism', that is, his conception of a 'natural' *polis*. Aristotle's political naturalism is part of his teleological way of thinking. Since Aristotle's teleological principles, like his moral theory, greatly influence his conception of politics, we need to have some understanding of Aristotle's teleology.

## ARISTOTELIAN TELEOLOGY

Teleology is central to Aristotle's theory of explanation. Aristotle begins by talking of the four different kinds of causes in his theory of explanation—the material cause, the efficient cause, the formal cause and the final cause.[31] Take for instance, the example of a stone sculpture: The shape of the sculpture will be the consequence of the kind of stone used (material cause), the technique and tools the sculptor uses in working on the piece of stone (efficient cause), the idea of the statue that the sculptor has in his mind (formal cause), and the sculptor's purpose in making the sculpture (final cause). Similarly, consider the case of the development of a seed into a plant: The chemical make up of the seed is the material cause of development; watering and fertilizing it at regular intervals is its efficient cause; its formal cause is the relationship between the growing seedling's different parts and the final cause is the seed's goal of becoming a plant.

Now, the issue is that while Aristotle does 'suggest that a full understanding of anything requires a grasp of all four causes,' he also states that it is the final cause that provides the real explanation of any phenomena. Let us look at the following contrast drawn up by Aristotle:

> Why should we suppose that nature does act "for" something and because it is better? Why should not everything be like the rain? Zeus does not send the rain in order to make the corn grow; it comes of necessity. The vapour that has been drawn up is bound to cool, and having cooled, to turn into water and come down.[32]

Does it rain because the purpose of rain is to make the corn grow, or does it rain because of the cooling of the water vapour? It is quite clear that for Aristotle, nature cannot be understood as a system of efficient causation alone. Nature is a purposive system; there is teleology in nature. To put it in Ackrill's words, Aristotle 'aims at providing a teleological explanation in terms of the good which some organ or process brings to the animal or plant and also a non-teleological explanation in terms of the necessary materials and movements which bring about those organs or processes... However, Aristotle's teleological convictions go rather further than this. For he holds that... the natural movements that terminate in there being this or that organ, this or that animal, are for the sake of that organ or animal, and so can be *properly* and *primarily* explained only by reference to their "end".' (Italics mine.)[33]

In Aristotelian metaphysics, although natural substances are compounds of matter and form, it is their form which is their source or cause of moving or of being at rest. It is their form which is their internal source of movement or change, which guides them to the end which is specific to their natural kind. A thing is said to exist by nature if it has this internal principle of change; if the impulse driving it towards its end or goal is internal to it. Thus, Aristotle distinguishes between a statue, which is an artefact, and an olive plant, which is a natural thing. The form of a statue exists outside of it, in the mind of the sculptor, whereas the form of the olive plant, that which causes the olive seed to strive towards its goal or *telos* of becoming an olive tree, is internal to it.[34]

In this context, to say that man is a political animal by nature, or that the *polis* exists by nature, must mean that a natural impulse in human beings leads them to form political communities. Ants and bees live in organized groups by nature. Their nature, an inner drive, leads them to form large groups that serve a common purpose. In that sense, ants, bees, wasps and cranes are 'political' animals. But man is more of a political animal than a bee. Man's capacity to speak and reason allows human beings to 'reflect on and choose [their] common task, and to pursue it, in cooperation with others, with greater intelligence than is possessed by any other animal...'[35] 'Calling human beings "political animals" refers not to our highly general desire to escape isolation and form social ties of some form or other, but to our more specific desire...to live in a community in which we can lead a richer and more complex life than is available in the household.'[36] This more complex life is necessary for the full realization of all our natural capacities.

In the case of a *polis*, thus, if the families and clans and villages coming together to form it are its material cause, what these families do to maintain their collective subsistence and security is its efficient cause, the constitution of a *polis* is its formal cause, and the purpose of there being a *polis*—the moral development of its members, the full realization of our natural capacities—is its final cause. According to teleological principles, one knows the nature of something by finding out the end towards which it is striving. All living things strive towards an end. What is the nature of a human being? What is the goal that a human being strives towards? For Aristotle, the fact that human beings can speak shows that they have reason, which, in turn, shows that they have the capacity to be moral. Their goal of becoming moral beings can only be achieved in a rightly organized *polis*. Everything that human beings do can be explained by reference to this goal of moral development. It is their *telos* of moral development which causes the coming together of human beings into a political community and the further development of that community. Here we see Aristotle's teleology bringing together his concepts of individual virtue and the state.

If a natural object is capable of something—for instance, if a mango seed is capable of becoming a mango plant under the right conditions—it only makes sense to call the natural order rational if these capacities and conditions go together for the most part. For Aristotle, nature may not be a moral system but it most certainly displays a rational ordering. In the human world, however, we have to consider why these conditions seem so difficult to establish, if human beings are naturally born with certain capacities. Why is it that some groups of human beings are successful in establishing these conditions, while others fail miserably, when all human beings are born with the same capacities and capabilities? These are the interesting questions that Aristotelian teleology raises when applied to human beings. We have to consider how to undertake an analysis of the factors which determine whether or not the conditions required for moral development will be fulfilled.

## PROBLEMS IN ARISTOTLE'S POLITICAL THEORY

Like Plato, Aristotle considered reason to be the hallmark of a human being, and like his teacher, he thought that not all human beings had the same amount of reason. Plato had claimed that some men and women were more rational than other men and women. Aristotle, however, believed that all Greek men were more rational than all women and all non-Greek 'barbarians' of either gender. Some of us might be prepared to consider the Platonic claim of differential reason but most of us would reject the Aristotelian version of it outright. Aristotle himself points to the human capacity of language as a mark of human rationality; but if women and barbarian slaves can use language as effectively as Greek males, why does he consider them to be deficient in reason? Even in Aristotle's time, there were a few Athenian centres of philosophy which took in women students. As for slavery, the Sophist dictum that all slavery was conventional had been around for a long time. Yet, we find Aristotle unable to move beyond the dominant prejudices of his time with respect to women and slaves.

Aristotle's tendency to stay close to the traditions of his society is often presented as a mark of his realism or conservatism. This is also what makes Aristotle, unlike Plato, stay closer to the democratic traditions of Athens. But even here, a problem crops up. Earlier we saw that Aristotle prefers the polity as the best form of government because of his overriding concern to develop the moral autonomy of citizens. Nussbaum goes as far as to say that his concern for autonomy trumps any concerns for stability. If that is so, it is perplexing to read, in *Politics,* the long section on how different constitutions are to be preserved. Aristotle gives us many reasons for why any constitution becomes unstable, that is, is overtaken by stasis, the most important being the prevalence of injustice. He also discusses the causes as well as the remedies of stasis in specific constitutions. For instance, Aristotle presents us with several ways in which a tyrant can preserve his form of constitution—tyranny—which include establishing an espionage system to prevent conspiracies against his rule, exiling any citizen who seems to be gaining in wealth and/or popularity and can be a possible competitor, imposing extremely high taxes on the people to prevent them from having any time for anything else, and so on.[37] If Aristotle's overriding concern is with the moral autonomy of the individual members of a state, then why does he give such advice? Perhaps we are misreading Aristotle here. Maybe we should see Aristotle as a political scientist who is showing us how tyrants actually behave in order to maintain their rule rather than advising tyrants how to do so. Still, the sections on how to forestall stasis in different constitutions sit uneasily with the earlier books of *Politics.*

Aristotle has also been criticized for separating the 'parts' of a state from its 'conditions' and then denying the status of citizenship to these 'conditions'. In Book IV of *Politics,* we find Aristotle stating that the many parts of the state include the farming class, the mechanical class, the marketing class, the agricultural labourers, the defence forces, the authority which determines what is just, the rich and the magistrates. Later, however, in the so called more Platonic Book VII, Aristotle, after claiming that, '[i]n the state, as in other natural compounds, the conditions which are necessary for the existence of the whole are not organic parts of the whole system which they serve',[38] points out that mechanics, shopkeepers and those engaged in farming cannot be considered as parts of the state. He further advocates the vesting of the constitutional powers of the state—the military and the deliberative powers—in the same set of persons, but at different stages of their lives. The same persons who when young, perform military duties, are to, when more mature, perform the deliberative functions. In addition, 'the persons who exercise these powers must also be from the propertied classes,' [39] and it is the senior members of these classes alone who will occupy the priestly offices. This extremely restrictive conception of citizenship then, comes in for much criticism.

There may be disagreement over the kinds of groups to whom Aristotle limits the right to take part in political deliberations, but the link between virtue and politics is unambiguous in Aristotle. In later political theory, this connection between the political sphere and the well lived-life will become problematic.

## NOTES

1. R. Kraut, *Aristotle: Political Philosophy*, Oxford: Oxford University Press, 2003, p. 7.
2. J. Marenbon, *Later Medieval Philosophy (1150-1350): An Introduction*, London: R & KP, 1987.
3. M.C. Nussbaum, *The Fragility of Goodness*, Cambridge: Cambridge University Press, 2001.
4. There are many commentators who, on the other hand, claim a strong continuity between the theories of Plato and Aristotle. We will refer briefly to the relationship between Plato and Aristotle again when we begin our discussion of *Politics*.
5. F.D. Miller, Jr., *Nature, Justice and Rights in Aristotle's Politics*, Oxford: Clarendon Press, 1995, p. 18.
6. M.C. Nussbaum, 'Human Functioning and Social Justice: In Defense of Aristotelian Essentialism', in *Political Theory*, XX (2), May 1992, pp. 220–223.
7. Aristotle, *The Nichomachean Ethics*, translated by W.D. Ross, in Richard McKeon (ed.), *The Basic Works of Aristotle*, New York: Random House, 1941.
8. M.C. Nussbaum, *The Fragility of Goodness*, Cambridge: Cambridge University Press, 1986, p. 276.
9. Aristotle, *Nichomachean Ethics*.
10. *Ibid.*
11. M.C. Nussbaum, *The Therapy of Desire: Theory and Practice in Hellenistic Ethics*, Princeton: Princeton University Press, 1994.
12. *Ibid.*
13. Aristotle, *Nichomachean Ethics*, Book III.
14. Aristotle, *Nichomachean Ethics*.
15. F.D. Miller, Jr., *Nature, Justice and Rights in Aristotle's Politics*, Oxford: Clarendon Press, 1995, p. 7.
16. A. MacIntyre, *Ethics and Politics: Selected Essays*, Vol. 2, Cambridge: Cambridge University Press, 2006, p. 3.

17. R. Kraut, *Aristotle: Political Philosophy*, Oxford: Oxford University Press, 2003, pp. 181–91.
18. Aristotle, *Politics*, edited and translated by E. Barker, London: Oxford University Press, 1958, p. 1.
19. *Ibid.*, pp. 104–105.
20. *Ibid.*, p. 181.
21. *Ibid.*, pp. 119–20.
22. M.C. Nussbaum, 'Shame, Separateness, and Political Unity: Aristotle's Criticism of Plato', in A.O. Rorty (ed.), *Essays on Aristotle's Ethics*, Berkeley: University of California Press, 1980.
23. M.C. Nussbaum, *The Fragility of Goodness*, Cambridge: Cambridge University Press, 1986, p. 352.
24. Except, perhaps, for a few philosopher kings and queens.
25. Aristotle, *Politics*, p. 123.
26. J. Waldron, 'The Wisdom of the Multitude: Some Reflections on Book III, Chapter 11 of Aristotle's *Politics* in R. Kraut and S. Skultety (eds), *Aristotle's Politics: Critical Essays*, Lanham: Rowman & Littlefield Publishers, 2005, p. 146.
27. *Ibid.*, p. 151.
28. J. Ober, 'Aristotle's Natural Democracy', in R. Kraut and S. Skultety (eds), *Aristotle's Politics: Critical Essays*, Lanham: Rowman & Littlefield Publishers, 2005, p. 226.
29. J. Waldron, 'The Wisdom of the Multitude: Some Reflections on Book III, Chapter 11 of Aristotle's *Politics*', p. 158.
30. Aristotle, *Politics*, p. 182
31. J.L. Ackrill, 'Explanation in Natural Science', in *Aristotle the Philosopher*, New York: Oxford University Press, 1981.
32. J.L. Ackrill, *Aristotle the Philosopher*, p. 41.
33. *Ibid.*, pp. 51–52.
34. F.D. Miller, Jr., *Nature, Justice and Rights in Aristotle's Politics*, Oxford: Clarendon Press, 1995, pp. 27–45.
35. R. Kraut, *Aristotle: Political Philosophy*, Oxford: Oxford University Press, 2003, p. 251.
36. *Ibid.*, p. 249.
37. Aristotle, *Politics*, pp. 244–46.
38. *Ibid.*, p. 298.
39. *Ibid.*, p. 302.

## READING LIST

Ackrill, J.L., *Aristotle the Philosopher*, New York: Oxford University Press, 1981.

Kraut, R., *Aristotle: Political Philosophy*, Oxford: Oxford University Press, 2003.

Kraut, R. and S. Skultety (eds), *Aristotle's Politics: Critical Essays*, Lanham: Rowman & Littlefield Publishers, 2005.

MacIntyre, Alasdair, *After Virtue: A Study in Moral Theory,* Notre Dame: University of Notre Dame Press, 2007.

McKeon, Richard (ed.), *The Basic Works of Aristotle,* New York: Random House, 1941.

Miller, F.D. Jr., *Nature, Justice and Rights in Aristotle's Politics,* Oxford: Clarendon Press, 1995.

Nussbaum, M.C., *The Fragility of Goodness,* Cambridge: Cambridge University Press, 1986.

Rorty, A.O. (ed.), *Essays on Aristotle's Ethics,* Berkeley: University of California Press, 1980.

## CENTRAL THEMES

1. **The goal of moral action:** Aristotle, like many other ancient Greek thinkers, gives a lot of importance to human beings acting morally. What is his conception of moral action? How does he define a moral act? How do the different components of moral action—choice, deliberation, good character and practical wisdom—come together in his theory?
2. **The state and the moral development of its members:** For Aristotle, the state is the agency which brings about the moral development of individuals. How do the other functions of the state fit in with its main purpose of developing its members morally? What is Aristotle's conception of the state and what is meant by his claim that the state is natural to human beings?
3. **The polity and the other constitutions:** In the *Nichomachean Ethics,* Aristotle contrasts the realms of nature and morality, yet in *Politics,* he presents the state, the primary moral agency, as natural to human beings. In this conception, how does he explain the variety of states or constitutions that existed in his time, including the 'perverted' constitutions? What are his views regarding the polity as one of the three good constitutions?
4. **Aristotelian teleology:** In Aristotle's theory of causation, explanatory primacy is given to the 'final cause' or the telos. How would one elaborate Aristotle's 'four-fold' theory of causation, with first place being given to teleological principles, in the realm of nature or in the realm of social and political institutions?

# FOUR

# Augustine and Thomas Aquinas: Christian Political Thought in the Middle Ages

The advent of Christianity gave rise to scepticism about the link between individual virtue and the design of political institutions, established in Greek thought. Typically, in classical Greek thought, the political community was considered to be of immense importance to an individual's well-being. Not only was the *polis* essential to fulfil the material needs of individuals, it was also required to fulfil a person's moral and spiritual needs. Even when the form of the political community changed from that of a *polis* to that of an empire, thinkers still debated the merits of a life spent in service to the political community. With the emergence and eventual dominance of Christianity, however, we see the pre-eminence of the political community being displaced by the religious community, in this case, the Christian community. The goal of human beings, even now, was to live a life of virtue, but individual virtue now began to be linked to one's religious life instead of one's political life. Between the time of the Stoics and that of Machiavelli, Europe was dominated by the intellectual and philosophical system of Christianity, and we will, in this chapter, by discussing the work of Aurelius Augustine and Thomas Aquinas, look at the place of politics and of the political community in such a religious world view.

The early history of Christianity is a history of struggle and oppression. Christian groups and communities faced persecution at the hands of the officials of the Roman Empire for 300 odd years. Things began to change in the 4th century, after the conversion of Constantine, the Roman Emperor, to Christianity in 312 CE. In the 390s, after the official enforcement of Christianity by another Roman Emperor, Theodosius I, with legislation being passed to ban non-Christian pagan religions, the Empire seemed to have become the 'vehicle of the Christian religion'. Many Christians now began to see the Roman Empire as 'God's providentially intended instrument for the establishment of Christianity in the world... The rule of Rome was now the reign of Christ in the world'.[1] Other Christian thinkers, however, remained deeply suspicious of, and questioned this alignment between the political and religious authorities. Given this transition of the political power from an agency of persecution to an enabling agency, how did Christian thinkers conceptualize the role of the political regime in the salvation of individuals?

The spread of Christianity was accompanied by the establishment of the Roman Catholic Church which eventually developed into an extremely powerful institution of the middle ages. The Church, with its hierarchy of the pope, cardinals, bishops and priests over the mass of lay believers, generated its own model of how authority should be organized, in order to hold together members belonging to the same community. This hierarchical organization was the subject of much debate between Christian thinkers. It was, for instance, sharply contested by the conciliar movement of the 14th century. The organization of the Church could be seen as providing a complementary or competing model of how political power should be organized. Were the members of the political community to be administered in the same manner as those of the religious community? If the functions of the state and the Church differed fundamentally, did it follow that their principles of organization had to be different too? What was the relation between the religious and political communities? These were some of the new political questions that were thrown up by the middle ages, and in this chapter we will also look at some of the answers to these questions.

## SAINT AUGUSTINE (354–430 CE)

Aurelius Augustine was born in 354 CE in Thagaste, a Roman town in North Africa, in an area which is now part of Algeria. Being an outstanding student, he was sent to Carthage for his higher education, in 371 CE, after completing which he found employment as a teacher of rhetoric. In spite of his academic duties, he led a rather dissolute life as a young man. In Carthage, Augustine came under the influence of Manichaenism, which was a form of Gnostic doctrine. Emphasizing the duality between form and matter, Manichaenism saw the material world, including all human political and social arrangements, as intrinsically evil. Augustine finally became disappointed with Manichaen teachings after about a decade, and left for Italy. By 385 CE he had become a renowned professor of rhetoric in Milan. In 386 CE, as is written in his *Confessions*, he went through a 'spiritual awakening' and converted to Catholicism. Within a few years, he had returned to North Africa where he was first ordained a priest and later, in 396 CE, made the Bishop of Hippo, a port city in modern day Algeria. He remained the Bishop of Hippo till his death in 430 CE. He was canonized by the Roman Catholic Church in 1303 CE. Augustine was a prolific writer, having penned about a hundred books, and numerous letters and sermons. Among his famous works are *Confessions*, written around 400 CE, which is considered to be the first autobiography in the Western tradition, and *City of God*, which took over 10 years to complete (413–427 CE).

The tradition of ancient philosophy was alive in Augustine's time, with several of the Hellenistic schools, like the New Academy and Stoicism, still thriving. Augustine himself was greatly influenced by neo-Platonists like Plotinus and Porphyry, and some scholars have interpreted his philosophy to be a form of ancient philosophy with a Christian gloss. If one were to go only by Augustine's earliest writings, which show a belief in the possibility of human society becoming part of the divinely ordained cosmic order, through the agency of a wise ruler, then one could hold this position. 'This was Augustine's youthful vision of a "rational myth of the state", founded on a conception of a cosmic order akin to and accessible to reason and a human destiny which could be achieved by human intellectual and moral resources.'[2] By the time Augustine wrote *Confessions*, however, he had given up this classical Greek hope in a universal order. Many scholars have highlighted Augustine's differences from the ancient Greek way of thinking and presented him as the first important Christian thinker. Augustine expended much effort in putting down three significant Christian heresies of the time—Donatism, Manichaenism and Pelagianism—and thus, ended up defining Christian orthodoxy.[3]

One of these heresies—Pelagianism—claimed that if we have an obligation to be without sin, then it is within our power to be without sin. Disagreeing strongly, Augustine put forward his 'Doctrine of Original Sin, according to which, apart from the grace of God, none of us is capable of being without sin.'[4] Augustine's doctrine of original sin was part of his attempt to explain the problem of evil in the world. Anguished by the presence of evil in the world, Augustine writes, in *Confession*, 'Here is God and see what God has created. God is good and…being God, he created good creatures. See how God surrounds and fills them. Then where and whence is evil? How did it creep in? What is its root and what is its seed? ... Where then does it come from, since the good God made everything good? Certainly the greatest and supreme Good made lesser goods; yet the Creator and all he created are good. What then is the origin of evil?'[5] In order to create human beings as moral beings, Augustine argues, God had to make them creatures with free will. (We are already familiar with the conceptual link between morality and choice, having studied Aristotle) The existence of free will allows evil an entry into the world. In Book 3 of *On Free Choice of the Will*, Augustine states, 'Just as a stray horse is better than a stone which is not astray, since the stone does not have its own motion or perception, so the creature who sins of his own free will is more excellent than the creature who does not sin because he has no free will'.[6] However, Augustine seems to undermine his position about free will and goodness by claiming, that ultimately, it is only through God's grace that human beings can find salvation. It has been said that Augustine, 'more than any other prominent Christian, rejects the idea that we can merit salvation'.[7] Why then, is it important for human beings to be able to acquire merit by doing good acts out of their own choice if their salvation does not depend on that but on God's grace?

Further, if salvation, that is, 'communion with God and with similar others', is the ultimate end that Christians strive for, and if this salvation is dependent basically on God's grace, then one's political context is of no relevance to this salvation. As Augustine put it, 'as for this mortal life, which ends after a few days' course, what does it matter under whose rule a man lives, being so soon to die'.[8] Augustine did not spend much time thinking about political institutions because he believed that the political community, of whichever kind, was not capable of fulfilling the real end of all human beings.

What was of grave concern to Augustine was not the mere possibility of evil, but its preponderance in the world. Ever since the original sin of Adam and Eve, men seemed to have used their free will not to do good things, but primarily to be wicked. Augustine believed that even though the human race was created by God in his own image, human beings were weak and sinful creatures. They were always tempted to do wrong, and could be kept on the right path only by force. 'For early Christianity and the Fathers of the Church, typified in the writings of St. Augustine, political life was corrupted by man's hereditary inclination to evil, and the state was a coercive institution designed to maintain a minimum of order in a sinful world. The ruler, even if he was a Christian, could only strive to moderate human power drives and impose a minimal justice on the earthly city that would make it possible for the members of the heavenly city to reach their eternal reward.'[9] Augustine took Plato's condemnation of the realm of becoming as the realm of falsehood further, and condemned the whole of human life on earth as tainted by sin. Earthly life was of such little worth, that to engage in a discussion of politics was not of much point. Yet, as human beings had to live on earth, some modicum of order was necessary. For Augustine, political order could only be maintained by an absolute monarch with enough power to keep the disorderly subjects under control. 'All the institutions of political and judicial authority and their administrative and coercive agencies serve this object: that the wicked be held in check and the good given a space to live in innocence.'[10]

In *City of God,* Augustine sets up a contrast between the earthly city and the heavenly city: 'The earthly city is not to be identified with any secular state nor the heavenly city with the Catholic Church.' All human groups are mixed, in that they contain individuals belonging to both these cities. The two cities are 'inextricably interwoven in the Roman Empire as in the Christian Church or indeed in any social group'.[11] The heavenly city is 'constituted of those who love God correctly, who find their enjoyment only in him'.[12] The earthly city, on the other hand, is made up of individuals who make the error of 'pursuing the human functions or goods, like health, family or social life, or knowledge, as *ends in themselves* or as *ultimate ends*'.[13] For Augustine, the 'radical opposition' between the two cities as to their 'ultimate loves' or the 'fundamental orientation of their wills', went hand in hand with the fact that 'the satisfaction of material needs, security from attack and orderly intercourse are valued by citizens of both the cities. This is what Aristotle calls the earthly peace. It is everybody's concern to maintain it, though people are bound to wish to maintain it for the sake of different ultimate objectives.'[14] Individuals belonging to the two cities might share some goals, but we must not forget how different they are from each other. Those belonging to the heavenly city only aspire to an 'earthly peace' as a means to reach their goal of communion with God. Unlike the denizens of the earthly city, they never seek earthly goods for their own sake.

Augustine's belief in the worthlessness of the earthly city as compared to the heavenly city becomes clear in an exchange of letters between him and Nectarius. Nectarius of Calama (a town near Hippo) intercedes with Bishop Augustine on behalf of his fellow citizens, who, having burnt the church in their city, now have to face punishment. Nectarius pleads with Augustine not to bring pain and retribution to his city. The earthly city is to be protected because it is 'the city in which we were born and brought into life, which first granted us the enjoyment of the light we see, which nourished us and brought us up'.[15] Furthermore, passage to the heavenly city is only guaranteed to those who have served the earthly city. 'The people who have served the town of their birth well are promoted to the city above; the people who are shown to have secured safety for their own homeland, by their advice or their efforts, are the ones who will live closer to God.'[16] In response, Augustine exalts the heavenly city. He replies that Nectarius should not be concerned about the trials and tribulations of the earthly city, since what is of real value is the city beyond. He exhorts Nectarius to worry about 'discharging [his] duties to a much finer city'.[17] Nectarius can do this by thinking about the real interests of his fellow citizens and make them realize their sins through punishment, instead of pandering to their wishes.

In another Letter, Augustine defends Christianity against the charge that it is contrary to the ethics of citizenship, since it subordinates the earthly city to the heavenly city. The charge states that 'under the Christian emperors the empire is in a very bad way, even though they have on the whole observed the Christian religion'.[18] This implies that there is something in Christianity which leads its followers to neglect their political community. To this Augustine replies, that the earthly city can no longer serve the moral needs of its people. In earlier conceptions, the political community not only served the material but also the moral and spiritual needs of individuals. For Augustine, it can no longer do so. Hence, for Augustine, the earthly community loses its importance. Nevertheless, Augustine always preached complete obedience to the political rulers. His affirmation of the heavenly city did not lead him to encourage any kind of dissent to the rulers of the earthly cities, however venal they might be. If citizenship can be defined as loyal obedience to one's ruler, then one can say that for Augustine, Christianity did not undermine the virtues of citizenship.

## THOMAS AQUINAS (1224–1274)

Thomas Aquinas was born near Naples into 'a wealthy and influential' family of Sicily. His father was the Count of Aquino and his mother, the Countess of Teano. His family was related to a number of European royal families including that of Emperor Frederick II of the kingdom of Sicily. St. Thomas began his studies at the age of five at the Benedictine monastery of Monte Cassino, and at thirteen, he began attending the University of Naples to study the liberal arts. In 1245, Aquinas joined the Dominican Order, and went to Paris and Cologne to study theology. In 1256, he received his licence to teach, and from 1256 to 1259, he served as a master of theology at the University of Paris. For the next decade, he taught in the Italian cities of Orvieto, Rome, Naples and Viterbo, returning to Paris as a professor in 1269. He stayed and taught theology in Paris till his death in 1274.[19]

Although Aquinas was a member of the Faculty of Theology and not of the Faculty of Arts, he was a strong advocate of the role of philosophy in religious knowledge. Religion was not a system of revelation alone. A large part of religious knowledge was based on rational deliberation and many of the claims of religion could be approached through rational argument. Taking seriously Aristotle's dictum that, 'all human beings by nature desire to know', Aquinas took a position against Augustine's denunciation of man's curiosity, and instead celebrated the human desire for knowledge as a sign, not of human hubris, but of human perfectibility.

Aquinas lived at the time when the works of Aristotle (apart from the already available books on logic) became available for the first time in Europe in Latin translations. Aristotle's works had fallen into disarray, because the Catholic Church, allied with neo-Platonism had followed a conscious policy of sidelining them. Fortunately, Aristotle's works were safeguarded by Muslim and Jewish scholars in Andalusia, in Spain. In 1270, the Church condemned 13 propositions of Aristotle and repeated the condemnation in 1277. Aquinas, however, persevered in his attempt to marry Aristotelianism with Christianity. Aquinas himself wrote as many as 12 commentaries on Aristotle's work between 1269 and 1272 and tried to assimilate many of Aristotle's arguments into the teachings of Christianity. Aquinas developed his arguments in his famous works, *Summa contra gentiles, Summa Theologiae* (1259–1269) and *On the Government of Princes* (1265–1267). Aquinas was canonized in 1323. Much later, after the edict of 1879, his works were used to counter the influence of liberalism in Christianity. He is owed a place in the history of political thought for turning our gaze back to politics, through his recovery of Aristotle. In the secular academia as well, pace the Thomistic Aristotelianism of scholars like A. MacIntyre, we can see the use of Aquinas to counter the dominance of liberalism in political theory.

## The Place of Politics in Christian Thought

In the Christian *weltanschauung*, as we have already seen, politics and government were signifiers of man's fallen nature. Men were essentially wicked, and therefore, they were required to be disciplined into submission, by the force of the king's sword. Aquinas interpreted the existence of political communities in a different manner. For him, political rule was not a sign of sinfulness because political rule existed even before sin, when man was in a state of innocence. Aquinas explains, 'man is by nature a social animal, and so in the state of innocence would have lived a social life. But there cannot be social life among a multitude of people save under the direction of someone who is to look to the common good; for many, as such, seek many things, whereas one attends only to one'.[20] Political rule is conducive to human welfare and not an aspect of human sinfulness. A more detailed explanation can be found in the first chapter of *On the Government of Princes*, where Aquinas makes the argument, that since man, unlike other animals, is not provided, with a coat of fur as protection and sharp claws, horns and teeth as armour, he is compensated by nature with the gift of reason. 'Now each man is imbued by nature with the light of reason, and he is directed towards his end by its action within him.'[21] Man is not only a rational animal; 'man is by nature a social and political animal, who lives in a community'.[22] Only in a community, with the help of others, is man able to provide for all his needs. Reason alone cannot fulfil all of man's needs. 'It is therefore necessary for man to live in a community, so that each man may devote his reason to some particular branch of learning: one to medicine, another to something else, another to something else again. And this is shown especially by the fact that only man has the capacity to use speech, by means of which one man can reveal the whole content of his mind to another.'[23] Through speech, men can benefit from each other's reason. Men need political rule to be able to effectively carry out this process of useful exchange. 'If, therefore, it is natural for man to live in fellowship with many others, it is necessary for there to be some means whereby such a community of men may be ruled.'[24]

Aquinas, unlike Augustine, does not think that political rule has to be tolerated as a necessary evil. His primary concern is to discern which kind of political rule is the most beneficial to man. He spends some time considering which is better: a kingship or rule by the many. He argues, that given that the common good aimed at in a political community is unity or peace, this end is better realized in a monarchy. To explain his stance, Aquinas asks us to look at the model of nature. 'Those things are best which are most natural, for in every case nature operates for the best; and in nature government is always by one… If those things which come about through art do so by imitation of those which exist in nature, and if a work of art is better to the degree that it achieves a likeness to what is in nature, it is necessarily true in the case of human affairs that that community is best which is ruled by one.'[25] Aquinas uses several arguments in support of monarchy as the best form of government, but he also concedes that sometimes government by the many might be better. In doing this, Aquinas was introducing a new idea, because 'until the 13th century, it was assumed that monarchy was not only the best form of government but also the only one that was in accordance with divine intention'.[26] Aquinas wrote, 'Experience therefore seems to show that a single city governed by rulers who hold office for one year only can sometimes accomplish more than a king can even if he has three or four cities, and that small services exacted by kings bear more heavily than great burdens imposed [on itself] by a community of citizens.'[27] Aquinas argues that a monarch might not be able to encourage his subjects to make their best efforts for the common good because in a monarchy, the common good is seen to be just the king's interest. In a republic, however, the citizens might feel that the common good is really being considered, and therefore, give of their best.

Aquinas might have used Aristotle's classification of constitutions, but many of the arguments he used to support different kinds of government vary from those of Aristotle. For instance, he never advocated monarchy for the Aristotelian reason that when one man outshines all others so much in virtue, it would be unjust to not make him king. Here we can see Aquinas as a Christian thinker for whom all individuals are God's creation, and so all individuals have reason in them. His support for monarchy is on the grounds of the principle of unity being better. That is his reason for finally choosing the monarchical form of government over the republican one. Where the many rule, dissension easily breaks out, and this leads to tyranny which is the worst form of government. 'Again, the rule of many turns into tyranny more rather than less frequently than that of one.'[28] The problem with the government of the many is that the dissensions which break out under it are 'contrary to the good of peace, which is the foremost goal of any social community.'[29]

Although the jury may still be out on whether just rule by one or by the many is better, it is incontrovertible that tyranny is the worst form of government, Aquinas believes that though monarchy and tyranny seem closely related, experience shows that it is actually the rule of the many that more frequently descends into tyranny. The rule of the many leads to civil war, which, in turn, leads to tyranny. Moreover, the tyranny that results from one corrupt monarch is less harmful than the tyranny that is a result of an entire body of authority that is corrupt. The monarch as tyrant can only take away individual goods, but when the regime of the many turns corrupt, peace itself is disrupted.

In the seventh chapter of *On the Government of Princes,* Aquinas discusses the possible courses of action, when the ruler becomes a tyrant. Should the people rebel against the tyrant and attempt to depose him? 'In cases where it belongs by right to a community to provide a ruler for itself, that community can without injustice depose or restrain a king whom it has appointed, if he should abuse royal power tyrannically. Nor should such a community be thought disloyal if it acts to depose a tyrant even if the community has already pledged itself to him in perpetuity; for the tyrant who has failed to govern the community faithfully, as the office of king requires, has deserved to be treated in this way.'[30] This support of rebellion by the people overturns the Augustinian picture of constant obedience, and actually sits quite uneasily with how Aquinas himself ends the chapter. Aquinas concludes by stating that God lets tyrants rule as punishment to sinners, 'because of the sins of the people'. 'Guilt, therefore, must first be taken away, so that the scourge of tyranny may cease.'[31]

The Christian elements in Aquinas's political thought can also be seen in his exhortation to monarchs to always rule in the common interest. Monarchs are to rule justly, for the common good, and must not aim for personal wealth or power. Personal riches and power should not be an incentive, but neither should a desire for honour or glory motivate the king. Honour or glory is gained when a man's virtue is publicly attested by his fellows. Aquinas writes that men are fickle and if the ruler is constantly seeking their approval, he may be led to do things which are harmful to the general welfare of the people. The reward that kings should aim at, instead, should be the reward of heavenly blessedness. To achieve this state, they should always be just. Not only does justice get the reward of heaven, but it also gets riches, honour, glory and friendship.

## A CONCEPTION OF LAW

An important aspect of Aquinas's political theory is his theory of law. For him, as we already saw, a good monarch maintains justice in his kingdom by ruling through laws. 'Law is a kind of rule and measure of acts, by which someone is induced to act or restrained from acting.'[32] Aquinas defines law as 'an ordinance of reason for the common good, made and promulgated by him who has care of the community'.[33] The justice of laws derives from three things: 'Laws are said to be just from their end, from their author, and from their form—when burdens are imposed upon subjects according to equality of proportion and with a view to the common good.'[34] Aquinas subscribes to an intellectualist conception of law rather than a voluntarist one, because, according to him it is more important for a law to be in accord with reason, than it is to be the authoritative command of a lawgiver.

Aquinas talks about four kinds of law in his writings: the eternal law, which is the rational order of the universe (the whole community of the universe is governed by Divine reason); the natural law, which is the eternal law as it applies to us human beings; human law (if the human law is at variance with the law of nature, then it is no longer law, but a corruption of law); and finally, divine law, which governs our conscience.

Human law, in the form of the law of nations, and civil law must conform to natural law in order to be considered law. Aquinas, however, accepts that in some cases (like in the case of private property, slavery and usury), such institutions which may be against natural law, may be required for human ends. Who, however, was to be the interpreter of the law? Who was to judge whether the law was in accord with reason? For Aquinas, unlike for Aristotle, reason is an attribute of every human being and not just a quality of the privileged few. God gives reason to everybody. Custom has the force of law and is the interpreter of law.

We see in Aquinas, that 'political organization, chiefly through the instrumentality of human law, has the capacity of furthering the human condition'.[35] Even though Aquinas agrees with Augustine that perfect happiness lies only in union with God through God's grace and the Christian virtues of faith, hope and charity or love, unlike Augustine, he does not see our enjoyment of our natural human functions of gaining knowledge, or living with family and friends as a form of evil but as a form of happiness, albeit an imperfect happiness.[36]

Initially, because of his association with Aristotle's writings, Aquinas had to bear the brunt of the Church's condemnation of Aristotle. However, things soon changed. In 1323, Aquinas was declared a saint, and his writings were widely taught by the Dominican brothers. In 1879, his teachings were declared to be the official philosophy of the Roman Catholic Church by Pope Leo XIII.

## THE CONCILIAR MOVEMENT

In Christian thought, there was a gradual emergence of the idea, that it is important to deliberate over how the political community should be organized. What brought about this change in thinking was the realization that the rightly organized political community could aid in achieving Christian goals. This was also a result of the trend, in the Christian community, of questioning the way authority was organized within the community itself. This takes us to a discussion of the conciliar movement. The conciliar movement was a 14th–15th century reform movement within the Catholic Church. The main tenet of conciliarism was that the final authority in spiritual matters lay with the Church as a corporation of Christians, as represented by a general Council, and not with the pope. The Catholic Church had become, by the middle ages, the 'principal carrier of Roman-imperial absolutism', and by attacking the pope's authority, conciliarism became an inspiration for Western constitutionalism as well.

Much before Luther, the Catholic Church had begun to come in for a lot of criticism from a variety of sources. Some of these critiques were fundamental, for instance, those questioning the very idea of the Church as a mediator between the individual believer and God. The critique that we are interested in, however, was directed at the way authority was organized in the Church, with the pope having immense power as its head. During the 12th century, power in the hands of the Pope increased greatly and this raised concerns over that power being misused. As early as the 1190s, Huguccio, the Bishop of Pisa, had maintained that a General Council of the Church 'must have the authority to sit in judgement on the pope';[37] this attack on papal supremacy or papal absolutism laid the 'foundations for the entire conciliar movement'.

Conceptually, a Church is a collective body. The Catholic Church claims to be a universal Church open to people of all races, nationalities and to either sex. Christ refuses no one from God's grace and he sent his apostles to preach to all mankind. This was in fact, one of the primary factors aiding the spread of Christianity, in its early years. For instance, Christianity did not deprive women—who were practically given no rights in the Roman community—of God's grace. As part of this community, then, members of the Church are united by a common interest. Members of the Church have a common faith and they are a united fraternity.

The conciliarists claimed that the ultimate religious authority lay with the Church as a collective body: 'The Church as the mystical union of the faithful in Christ is the immediate recipient of divine authority.'[38] However, it was not possible for this authority to be exercised by the Church as a whole. In actual practice, this authority could only be exercised by a smaller body. According to the conciliarists, the only way the Church could exercise its authority, was through a general council consisting of its leading members. Conciliarists pointed to the early history of the Church to argue that decisions should be taken in a council and not by one person, namely, the pope. Initially, the conciliar movement advocated that power be shared between the pope and bishops-in-council. Later, however, it demanded unlimited sovereignty for the internally democratic council of bishops. The Church Council of Constance (1414–1418), for instance, issued two decrees: The first held that a general council was superior to a pope in matters of doctrine, schism and reform, the second stated that henceforward councils must meet at regular intervals.

Within the conciliar movement, the issue of how a large collective body was to act was problematized. Since this collectivity was assumed to have a common interest, a smaller group or even one person could act in its name. According to Juan de Segovia, a 15th century theologian, collective bodies with a common interest can be represented by one person who 'somehow loses his individual unity and dons the united community, so as to be said to wear or represent the person not of one but of many'.[39] With a ruler or a Pope acting in its name, this does not mean that the larger collective body ceases to exist, and if it becomes possible for this larger collective body to gather in its plurality, its pronouncements carry more weight than those of its representative: 'But if it happens that this whole community assembles together, and its assertions and wishes contradict those of the president, since truth is preferred to fiction, the community will deservedly prevail. For the truth is that this community is many persons, and the fiction is that this president, who is really one person, is said to be many by representation.'[40]

Arguments like these were used by the conciliarists to place limits on the claim to absolute authority by different popes. The political rulers of Europe, who wanted their own authority to be unhindered by the pope, enthusiastically supported the conciliarists and they regularly interfered in the election of several popes in an attempt to keep the power of the popes in check. From 1305 to 1450, there were several episodes of rival claimants to the papacy jockeying with each other with the support of different political powers. With one line of popes established at Rome, there was another papacy in exile at Avignon (1305–1377), which had the support of French kings. By the 1418 Council of Constance, unity was achieved, and a pope acceptable to all was established at Rome.

This interference in Church elections was to boomerang on the budding absolute monarchies of Europe. It fostered the slow emergence of the idea that just as the authority of the Christian church was to be seen as devolving to the community of the Christian church as a whole, and not just to the person of the pope, similarly, the political community was not to be led by the person of the monarch, but was to be in the hands of a larger, perhaps elective body. A heated discussion began over the issue of how a monarch could justify himself as a representative of all his subjects, especially since all his subjects did not seem to be united by any one or common interest. Alternatively, could kingship be justified on the grounds that, while the Church was a strongly united body, enabling it to act as one, the looser unity of secular polities required the unifying force of kingship? We will see the resonance of these debates in the writings of political thinkers of the coming centuries.

## NOTES

1. J.H. Burns (ed.), *The Cambridge History of Medieval Political Thought c.350–c.1450*, Cambridge: Cambridge University Press, 2005, p. 103.
2. *Ibid.*, p. 109.
3. Gareth B. Matthews, *Augustine*, Malden: Blackwell Publishing, 2005.
4. *Ibid.*, p. 14.
5. *Ibid.*, p. 107.
6. *Ibid.*, p. 110.
7. *Ibid.*, p. 113.
8. M.J. White, *Political Philosophy: A Historical Introduction*, Oxford: Oneworld Publications, 2003, p. 79.
9. Paul E. Sigmund, 'Law and Politics', in Norman Kretzmann and Eleonore Stump (eds), *The Cambridge Companion to Aquinas*, Cambridge: Cambridge University Press, 1993, p. 218.
10. J.H. Burns (ed.), *The Cambridge History of Medieval Political Thought*, p. 110.
11. *Ibid.*, p. 106.
12. M.J. White, *Political Philosophy*, p. 81.
13. *Ibid.*, p. 84.
14. J.H. Burns (ed.), *The Cambridge History of Medieval Political Thought*, p. 107.
15. Augustine, 'Letter 103', in E.M. Atkins and R.J. Dodaro (eds), *Augustine: Political Writings*, Cambridge: Cambridge University Press, 2001, p. 9.
16. *Ibid.*

17. Augustine, 'Letter 91', in E.M. Atkins and R.J. Dodaro (eds), *Augustine: Political Writings*, p. 2.
18. Augustine, 'Letter 136', in E.M. Atkins and R.J. Dodaro (eds), *Augustine: Political Writings*, p. 29.
19. Introduction to, Norman Kretzmann and Eleonore Stump (eds), *The Cambridge Companion to Aquinas,* Cambridge: Cambridge University Press, 1993.
20. R.W. Dyson (ed.), *Aquinas: Political Writings*, Cambridge: Cambridge University Press, 2002, p. 4.
21. *Ibid.*, p. 5.
22. *Ibid.*, p. 6.
23. *Ibid.*
24. *Ibid.*, p. 7.
25. *Ibid.*, p. 11.
26. Paul E. Sigmund, 'Law and Politics', in Norman Kretzmann and Eleonore Stump (eds), *The Cambridge Companion to Aquinas*, pp. 219–220.
27. R.W. Dyson (ed.), *Aquinas: Political Writings*, p. 15.
28. *Ibid.*, p. 17.
29. *Ibid.*, p. 16.
30. *Ibid.*, p. 20.
31. *Ibid.*, p. 21.
32. *Ibid.*, p. 77.
33. *Ibid.*, pp. 82–83.
34. *Ibid.*, p. 143.
35. M.J. White, *Political Philosophy*, p. 78.
36. *Ibid.*, p. 100.
37. Quentin Skinner, *The Foundations of Modern Political Thought,* Vol. 2, Cambridge: Cambridge University Press, 1978, p. 37.
38. J.H. Burns (ed.), *The Cambridge History of Medieval Political Thought.*
39. *Ibid.*, p. 581.
40. *Ibid.*

## READING LIST

Burns, J.H. (ed.), *The Cambridge History of Medieval Political Thought c.350–c.1450*, Cambridge: Cambridge University Press, 2005.

Dyson, R.W. (ed.), *Aquinas: Political Writings*, Cambridge: Cambridge University Press, 2002.

Kretzmann, Norman, and Eleonore Stump (eds), *The Cambridge Companion to Aquinas*, Cambridge: Cambridge University Press, 1993.

Matthews, Gareth. B., *Augustine*, Malden: Blackwell Publishing, 2005.

Skinner, Quentin, *The Foundations of Modern Political Thought,* Vol. 2, Cambridge: Cambridge University Press, 1978.

White, M.J., *Political Philosophy: A Historical Introduction*, Oxford: Oneworld Publications, 2003.

## CENTRAL THEMES

1. **Virtue and Salvation:** For Augustine, since human beings have free will, their lives have a valuable moral dimension. If this freedom of will allows evil an entry into the world, so also can it lead to the doing of good acts. Having highlighted the importance of free will and moral action, why then does Augustine place human salvation on the mantle of God's grace alone?
2. **The secular ruler and religious goals:** When some of the Roman emperors took it upon themselves to spread Christianity, then was established the Holy Roman Empire. Why does Augustine remain wary of seeing political power as a handmaiden to the Church? How does he conceive of the role of political institutions in human life?
3. **The best political regime:** Aquinas taking the trouble of comparing different forms of government to discover that which is the best, implies a view of government as furthering human ends. What is Aquinas's conception of the role of government in human affairs?
4. **Aquinas and Aristotelian philosophy:** In his acceptance of the human functions of acquiring knowledge and living with friends and family, as well in his conception of law as not only eternal and divine, but also natural and human, Thomas Aquinas shows the influence of Aristotle's philosophy. How did Aquinas bring together Aristotelian and Christian elements in his moral and political philosophy, and did this generate any conceptual problems?
5. **Conciliarism:** What kinds of arguments did the conciliar movement throw up about how, and by whom, the interests of members of a religious community could best be represented? Can some of these arguments be applied to construct principles of representation for a political community?

# FIVE

# Machiavelli (1469–1527): Humanism and Republicanism

## THE REPUBLICAN CITY-STATES OF ITALY

In our popular imagination of the European middle ages, alongside the large landed estates of the countryside, are also placed the many vibrant city-states of late medieval Italy. The city-states of the Lombardy and Tuscany regions of northern Italy—Milan, Venice, Verona, Padua, Ravenna, Modena, Genoa, Florence, Arezzo, Bologna and Pisa—to name only a few, had all emerged by the end of the first millennium. Ever vigilant of their independence not only from the Holy Roman Emperor, but also from the Roman Catholic Church, these city-states defined their liberty in terms of rule by the people of the city, rather than by a few selected notables.[1] By the end of the 12th century, in most of the Italian city-states, the government was in the hands of a *podesta,* who was an official, usually from another city, selected or elected by the people to run the city's affairs for a mere six months before he was replaced by another. The *podesta* ruled with the help of the People's Council. He also had to submit himself to an audit at the end of his term, before being allowed to return to his original city. According to Skinner, this distinctive system of republican government was well established in several Italian city-states. 'The cities were generally controlled by chief magistrates known as *podesta,* so called because they were vested with supreme power or *potestas* over the citizens under their charge. A *podesta* normally held office for a period of six months or at most a year, and conducted his administration by means of a series of executive councils. All the members of such councils, including the *podesta* himself, enjoyed a status no higher than that of public servants of the commune that elected them. The system thus represented a complete repudiation of the familiar medieval principles of lordship and hereditary rule.'[2] Fiercely independent of any external control, whether from the papacy or the Holy Roman Emperor, these city-republics questioned the use of this independence if internally their people had to submit to the control of an absolute prince.

These city-republics of northern Italy were surrounded, in Italy itself, by the kingdoms of Naples and of the pope, and just across the borders of Italy, by the powerful monarchies of France, Spain and England. Even in the city-republics, in the spate of the next two hundred years, by the mid-14th century, the *podestas* had been replaced by the *signori,* or executive boards, whose governing powers were much more authoritarian. The transition from the *podesta* to the *signori* was repeated in city-state after city-state in Italy, and Florence, the city-state to which Machiavelli belonged, was one such city-state. In Florence, there was a slow weakening of republican institutions. In 1393, the office of the *podesta* was replaced by that of the *signori.* Although the *signori* were more powerful than the *podesta,* there still remained checks on their executive authority. When the Medici family established their regime in 1434, these checks were done away with, and the Medici princes ruled more like kings until the republic was re-established in 1494, when the Consiglio Grande (Great Council) was set up. The Great Council, which was set up by the famous law of December 1494, had the power to approve all new laws and taxes. Members of the middle class could have their say through the Great Council.[3] The Great Council or the Consiglio Grande gave the regime the character of a 'governo largo' because more than 3,000 citizens could participate in it. Not only were many non-aristocratic elements included in the Consiglio Grande, they also had the right to election to the Signoria, the chief executive board as well as to several other administrative boards. A *gonfaloniere* was the third element of this constitution.[4] From 1494 to 1498, the leadership of the Florentine republic was in the hands of a Dominican priest called Savonarola who was severely critical not only of the corruption of the Catholic Church, but also of the art and humanist culture of the wealthy Florentines. The latter plotted to get rid of him, and in 1498, he was replaced by a secular leader, Piero Soderini, who later became *gonfaloniere* for life, in 1502.

Born in 1469, Machiavelli had already come of age when the Medicis were overthrown and his first job, at the age of 29, was to work as a bureaucrat for the newly established republic. Machiavelli came from an ordinary Florentine family, 'neither rich, nor highly aristocratic'. His father was a lawyer, who took great care of his son's education and sent him off to the University of Florence to complete his studies in the humanities. Machiavelli's teacher at the University was Marcello Adriani, who became the head of the first chancery of the republic. Perhaps, it was at his insistence that Machiavelli was appointed as secretary to the second chancery. The first chancery was supposed to be responsible for foreign affairs and matters of war, while the second chancery looked after internal affairs and the domestic bureaucracy. By the time of Machiavelli's appointment in June 1498, however, the functions of the two chanceries had begun to overlap.[5] In fact, it was Machiavelli who was sent on many diplomatic missions for the republic to several places, like France, Spain and the Vatican. When the republic fell, in 1512, and the Medicis came back, Machiavelli was imprisoned and nearly executed. Fortunately, an amnesty was granted to him, and he was exiled to the outskirts of Florence, to his farm. It is there that he wrote the many books for which he is so famous—*The Prince, Discourses, Art of War, History of Florence,* and *Discourse on the Reform of the Government of Florence*. Machiavelli became the most famous of the philosophical historians of Florence, including Guicciardini and Francesco Vettori. Unlike Guicciardini, who was allied to the Medicis, Machiavelli and Vettori were republicans.

## THE INTELLECTUAL CONTEXT

The history of republican institutions in the Italian city-states has generated a heated debate among Machiavelli scholars. According to Hans Baron, these republican institutions existed in some kind of theoretical vacuum. Although the city-states enjoyed republican political practices, a political theory of republicanism had not yet developed. That had to wait till the Renaissance civic humanists as well as the publication of Machiavelli's *Discourses*. For Baron, Machiavelli's originality and contribution lies in developing a political theory of republicanism.

Skinner's position, on the other hand, is that, right from the middle of the 12th century, many tracts celebrating the fine points of 'free government' existed in the Italian city-states. Skinner cites the work of Brunetto Latini (1266) as an example of tracts on city government, using references to the Roman thinkers Sallust and Cicero, to make the point that only a free government could ensure justice, which was necessary for the common good, which, in turn, brought about concord in the city, which, then, allowed the city to achieve greatness. It is such 12th and 13th century arguments about the advantages of elected government versus a monarchy that form the backdrop for Machiavelli's *Discourses*. The *Discourses,* then, according to Skinner, shows a continuity between these pre-humanist writers of city government, Renaissance humanism and Machiavelli.

It was also in the 13th century that several advice books, 'intended for the guidance of the *podesta* and city magistrates' were written. Skinner refers to *The Pastoral Eye* (1222) and to *The Government of Cities* (1240), and states that these 'early advice-books' helped to set a pattern for the later mirror-for-princes literature by emphasizing the virtues a good ruler should possess'.[6] The trend of writing of advice books for princes reached its peak in the latter part of the 15th century, by which time almost all republican institutions had been overtaken by princely governments. During these years, many writers, including Patrizi, Bartolomeo Saachi and Giovanni Pontano wrote advice books for rulers. *The Prince*, by Machiavelli, belongs to this mirror-for-princes genre.

The 15th century advice books belonged to writers of the Italian Renaissance. Therefore, apart from the influence of the pre-humanist Republican writings, Machiavelli's work also shows the stamp of the Renaissance. The Italian Renaissance celebrated the values of human power and human creativity, the ability of human beings to shape their own destiny, or to make things better for themselves by their own effort. That is why the dominant idea of the Renaissance is said to be humanism. The humanists rejected the 'entire Augustinian picture of human nature' by insisting on man's creative powers. The so-called 'Manifesto of the Renaissance', *An Oration on the Dignity of Man*, written by Giovanni Pico della Mirandola, and published in 1486, expresses this beautifully. In his oration, Pico writes:

> He [God] therefore took man as a creature of indeterminate nature and, assigning him a place in the middle of the world, addressed him thus: 'a fixed abode nor a form that is thine alone nor any function peculiar to thyself have we given thee, Adam, to the end that according to thy longing and according to thy judgement thou mayest have and possess what abode, what form and what functions thou thyself shalt desire. The nature of all other beings is limited and constrained within the bounds of laws prescribed by Us. Thou, constrained by no limits, in accordance with thine own free will, in whose hand We have placed thee, shall ordain for thyself the limits of thy nature.'[7]

If Pico was saying that it is in this indeterminacy that man's greatness lies, then we can already glimpse the road that Machiavelli will take in his writings. Which nature was man to choose, according to the humanists? These creative powers were to be spent in activities useful to the community. There was a growing belief in Renaissance humanism that 'a life devoted to pure leisure and contemplation (*otium*) is far less likely to be of value—or even to foster wisdom—than a life in which the pursuit of useful activity (*negotium*) is most highly prized'.[8] It is at the intersection of these different strains—Republican political practice mediated by Republican tracts, Renaissance humanism and its mirror-for-princes genre—that Machiavelli's contribution to Western political thought lies.

## PRINCELY *VIRTU* AND FORTUNA

Why do we read *The Prince* today, rather than the countless other advice books available in the mirror-for-princes literature? What has made *The Prince* a classic, whereas the rest of the genre is today, read only by specialist historians? It is because, as Skinner writes, *The Prince* 'succeeded in making a contribution to the genre of advice-books for princes which at the same time revolutionized the genre itself'.[9] All the different tracts in this genre in late 15th century Italy agreed that the goal of the prince should be honour, glory and fame, which he could gain by developing his *virtu*. They also agreed that the main obstacles in achieving this goal were the vagaries of fortune since fortune was governed by the whimsical and capricious goddess, Fortuna. The means the prince could use to overcome this obstacle of Fortuna to reach his goal of glory was to develop his *virtu*. By *virtu*, the writers meant both the classical Greek cardinal virtues, as well as the Christian virtues of piety and clemency. *The Prince* discusses the same goal of glory for the prince and his struggle with Fortuna, and *virtu* is also the central concept of *The Prince*. But it is the startling new meaning that Machiavelli gives to this term that has made his work stand out, among all the rest.

**Box 5.1**

**ON THE ROLE OF FORTUNE IN HUMAN AFFAIRS:**

It is not unknown to me how many men have had, and still have, the opinion that the affairs of the world are in such wise governed by fortune and by God that men with their wisdom cannot direct them and that no one can even help them; and because of this they would have us believe that it is not necessary to labour much in affairs, but to let chance govern them. This opinion has been more credited in our times because of the great changes in affairs which have been seen, and may still be seen, every day, beyond all human conjecture. Sometimes pondering over this, I am in some degree inclined to their opinion. Nevertheless, not to extinguish our free will, I hold it to be true that Fortune is the arbiter of one-half of our actions, but that she still leaves us to direct the other half, or perhaps a little less. I compare her to one of those raging rivers, which when in flood overflows the plains, sweeping away trees and buildings, bearing away the soil from place to place; everything flies before it, all yield to its violence, without being able in any way to withstand it; and yet, though its nature be such, it does not follow therefore that men, when the weather becomes fair, shall not make provision, both with defences and barriers, in such a manner that, rising again, the waters may pass away by canal, and their force be neither so unrestrained nor so dangerous. So it happens with fortune, who shows her power where valour has not prepared to resist her, and thither she turns her forces where she knows that barriers and defences have not been raised to constrain her.

*The Prince*, Chapter 25

To be successful, to achieve greatness for his city, a Prince must have 'virtu'. The world of human affairs is governed by Fortuna who is capricious and whimsical. But human beings cannot simply ignore her, because Fortuna also holds the goods that come with fortune and which human beings desire—glory and wealth—and therefore, Machiaveli says that they must develop the qualities which will persuade the goddess to be on their side. Here, we see an important difference between Machiavelli and his classical sources. The Stoics and Skeptics had scoffed at the goods of fortune and considered them irrelevant for the health of the human soul. For Machiavelli, riches and glory, the two finest gifts that fortune can bring, are certainly important for human happiness. *Virtu*, for Machiavelli, is the ability to deal with any contingency that Fortuna places before one. If we are well prepared for the contingencies of Fortuna, then she will smile at us and will let us have our way (see Box 5.1).

Machiavelli explains, that in order to be well prepared for any contingency, the prince must be a changeling. He must be able to change himself to act differently according to circumstances (see Box 5.2). How far have we travelled from Aristotle, and even from Cicero! For Aristotle, through

**Box 5.2**

**ON THE IMPORTANCE OF CHANGING WITH THE TIMES:**

And hence it comes that a commonwealth endures longer, and has a more sustained good fortune than a princedom, because from the diversity in the characters of its citizens, it can adapt itself better than a prince can to the diversity of times. For, as I have said before, a man accustomed to follow one method, will never alter it; whence it must needs happen that when times change so as no longer to accord with his method, he will be ruined. Piero Soderini, of whom I have already spoken, was guided in all his actions by patience and gentleness, and he and his country prospered while the times were in harmony with these methods. But, afterwards, when a time came when it behoved him to have done with patience and gentleness, he knew not how to drop them, and was ruined together with his country. Pope Julius II, throughout the whole of his pontificate, was governed by impulse and passion, and because the times were in perfect accord, all his undertakings prospered. But had other times come requiring other qualities, he could not have escaped destruction, since he could not have changed his methods nor his habitual line of conduct.

As to why such changes are impossible, two reasons may be given. One is that we cannot act in opposition to the bent of our nature. The other, that when a man has been very successful while following a particular method, he can never be convinced that it is for his advantage to try some other. And hence it results that a man's fortunes vary, because times change and he does not change with them. So, too, with commonwealths, which, as we have already shown at length, are ruined from not altering their institutions to suit the times.

*The Discourses Book III*, Chapter 9

habit, human beings acquired a second nature which ensured for them a virtuous disposition and the ability to act morally. Machiavelli, on the contrary, is arguing that being virtuous is not, say, to be able to tell the truth if the circumstances require it, but also to be able to be devious if that is necessary. To have *virtu* is not to be virtuous in the Christian or classical sense—it is to be a changeling.

A prince needs to have this kind of flexibility in successfully governing a city, because he has not only to deal with Fortuna, but also with corruption. Faced with a corrupt population, and wanting to set his city on the road to greatness, a prince cannot let his goals be defeated by moral qualms. Machiavelli did not have any idealistic notions about human nature. He believed that human beings were prone to wickedness, and that they only acted righteously under compulsion.

According to Machiavelli, since human beings were essentially wicked, their cities and communities invariably fell into corruption. Here, we can see the hold of the Christian doctrine of original sin on Machiavelli, despite his antipathy to the Catholic Church. In order to overcome Fortuna and corruption, a prince needs *virtu* of the Machiavellian sort. Fortuna and corruption make it necessary for the prince to use certain means for the preservation of the state. A prince of *virtu* would study the necessity involved between means and ends and then act for reasons of state.

Machiavelli's opinion is that political efficacy requires the cruelty and violence of the lion and the cunning of the fox. 'There are two methods of fighting, the one by law, the other by force: the first method is that of men, the second of beasts; but as the first method is often insufficient, one must have recourse to the second. It is therefore necessary for a prince to know well how to use both the beast and the man…a prince being thus obliged to know well how to act as a beast must imitate the fox and the lion.'[10] Machiavelli is different from the other mirror-for-princes writers, especially because of the amount of emphasis he places on the requirement of force, in all its manifestations, in running a state. Not only must the prince be well versed in the art of warfare, not only must there be a citizen militia, but the prince must also be a master at using violence economically and effectively. Unlike the earlier 13th century writers giving advice to the *podestas*, Machiavelli is quite clear that apart from the rhetorical skills of persuasion, the prince must learn the more important skill of using force (see Box 5.3).

This position has led to the accusation that Machiavelli wanted to separate politics from morality. Isaiah Berlin, in 'The Originality of Machiavelli', defends Machiavelli against this charge by arguing that Machiavelli was not contrasting an immoral political realm with a moral personal realm; rather, he was showing us the conflict between two moralities: public and private. The desire to achieve public goals sometimes

Box 5.3

**ON SUCCESS IN POLITICS:**

You must know there are two ways of contesting, the one by the law, the other by force; the first method is proper to men, the second to beasts; but because the first is frequently not sufficient, it is necessary to have recourse to the second. Therefore it is necessary for a prince to understand how to avail himself of the beast and the man. .. A prince, therefore, being compelled knowingly to adopt the beast, ought to choose the fox and the lion; because the lion cannot defend himself against snares and the fox cannot defend himself against wolves. Therefore, it is necessary to be a fox to discover the snares and a lion to terrify the wolves. Those who rely simply on the lion do not understand what they are about. Therefore a wise lord cannot, nor ought he to, keep faith when such observance may be turned against him, and when the reasons that caused him to pledge it exist no longer. If men were entirely good this precept would not hold, but because they are bad, and will not keep faith with you, you too are not bound to observe it with them.

Therefore it is unnecessary for a prince to have all the good qualities I have enumerated, but it is very necessary to appear to have them. And I shall dare to say this also, that to have them and always to observe them is injurious, and that to appear to have them is useful; to appear merciful, faithful, humane, religious, upright, and to be so, but with a mind so framed that should you require not to be so, you may be able and know how to change to the opposite.

And you have to understand this, that a prince, especially a new one, cannot observe all those things for which men are esteemed, being often forced, in order to maintain the state, to act contrary to fidelity, friendship, humanity, and religion. Therefore it is necessary for him to have a mind ready to turn itself accordingly as the winds and variations of fortune force it, yet, as I have said above, not to diverge from the good if he can avoid doing so, but, if compelled, then to know how to set about it.

*The Prince*, Chapter 18

clashes with personal moral concerns. According to Machiavelli, even if one decides not to act in such a situation, one is still accountable for the consequences that result because of one's inaction. Moreover, Machiavelli clearly shows, that unless the public sphere is well looked after, the private sphere cannot be protected. A well functioning private sphere requires a healthy public sphere. Thus, according to Berlin, Machiavelli shows us that we cannot excuse ourselves from public action on the grounds of being concerned with our moral selves.

> There are two worlds, that of personal morality and that of public organization. There are two ethical codes, both ultimate; not two 'autonomous' regions, one of 'ethics', another of 'politics', but two (for him) exhaustive alternatives between two conflicting systems of value. If a man chooses the 'first good way', he must, presumably, give up all hope of Athens and Rome, of a noble and glorious society in which human beings can thrive and grow strong,

> proud, wise and productive; indeed, they must abandon all hope of a tolerable life on earth: for men cannot live outside society; they will not survive collectively if they are led by men who (like Soderini) are influenced by the first, 'private' morality; they will not be able to realize their minimal goals as men; they will end in a state of moral, not merely political, degradation.[11]

Soderini was not able to defend the republic, which fell into the hands of the Medicis, again, in 1512. From the Machiavellian point of view, it was Soderini's ineffectiveness caused by his moral dilemmas, which was ultimately responsible for this road to perdition for Florence.

According to Berlin, Machiavelli retains the classical link between public good and private interests. *Virtu* is required for a vibrant and stable political community, which, in turn, is essential for individuals to lead a happy life. Machiavellian *virtu*, however, has entirely altered the classical meaning of the term. Machiavelli, moreover, defines individual happiness as the enjoyment of property and family life, rather than as something that can be obtained solely in the practice of *virtu*.

It would also be interesting to examine the significance of Fortuna. What does Fortuna actually represent? If Fortuna, the goddess of luck, represents contingency, then does she not stand for the efficacy of the acts of different individuals? Is Machiavelli trying to grope at the democratic idea, that it is not just the actions of kings and emperors that govern human history, but equally, one has to be attentive to the unforeseen consequences of the acts of myriad individuals? Further, even though Machiavelli is influenced by humanism in emphasizing the ability of human beings to shape their own futures, his use of the concept of Fortuna shows that he was contesting the position which, in the words of another philosopher, 'makes us think of the core of ourselves as self-sufficient, not in need of the gifts of fortune'. This also fits in with Machiavelli's emphasis on the public sphere—a point that we just saw being underlined by Berlin. Unless we focus on the social and political conditions which structure the actions of other individuals, there will be no guarantee for happiness in our own personal lives.

## CIVIC *VIRTU* AND LIBERTY

If *Prince* is about princely *virtu*, *Discourses* is about civic *virtu*, that is, about the qualities that the citizens of a republican city must have. We know that Machiavelli was in favour of a republican form of government. He believed that liberty was best [reserved in such a government, in which power was shared between the nobles and the people (see Box 5.4).

As we have mentioned earlier, the advocates of republicanism in the Italian city-states had laid out, much earlier, the benefits of this form of

**Box 5.4**

**ON HOW LIBERTY IS PRESERVED IN A REPUBLICAN FORM OF GOVERNMENT:**

And looking to the other circumstances of this city, I affirm that those who condemn these dissensions between the nobles and the commons, condemn what was the prime cause of Rome becoming free; and give more heed to the tumult and uproar wherewith these dissensions were attended, than to the good results which followed from them; not reflecting that while in every republic there are two conflicting factions, that of the people and that of the nobles, it is in this conflict that all laws favourable to freedom have their origin, as may readily be seen to have been the case in Rome.

As touching reasons, it may be pleaded for the Roman method, that they are most fit to have charge of a thing, who least desire to pervert it to their own ends. And, doubtless, if we examine the aims which the nobles and the commons respectively set before then, we shall find in the former a great desire to dominate, in the latter merely a desire not to be dominated over, and hence a greater attachment to freedom, since they have less to gain than the others by destroying it. Wherefore, when the commons are put forward as the defenders of liberty, they may be expected to take better care of it, and, as they have no desire to tamper with it themselves, to be less apt to suffer others to do so.

*Discourses, Book I,*
Chapters 4 and 5

government. In *Discourses,* Machiavelli further builds up his argument that it is in a republican form of government that individual liberty can best be preserved and the city can achieve greatness. In a republic all the citizens would contribute their talents for the glory of their city. With no fear of the arbitrary actions of a prince, and neither the fear that a jealous king might suddenly strike an outstanding citizen down, citizens would not hesitate to make themselves and their city better. In Machiavelli's own words, 'And it is easy to understand whence that affection for liberty arose in the people, for they had seen that cities never increased in dominion or wealth unless they were free.' 'Only those cities and countries that are free can achieve greatness. Population is greater there because marriages are more free and offer more advantages to the citizen; for people will gladly have children when they know that they can support them, and that they will not be deprived of their patrimony, and where they know that their children not only are born free and not slaves, but, if they possess talents and virtue, can arrive at the highest dignities of the state. In free countries we also see wealth increase more rapidly, both that which results from the culture of the soil and that which is produced by industry and art; for everybody gladly multiplies those things, and seeks to acquire those goods the possession of which he can tranquilly enjoy.'[12]

For Machiavelli, individual liberty can best be preserved in a republic, and not in a principality. Machiavelli defines individual liberty as the liberty of one's possessions and of one's family life. There is less threat to liberty in a republic, but a republic can only be maintained if its citizens display civic *virtu*. According to Machiavelli, the mark of *virtu* is not nobility or wealth, but a contribution to the common good. A republic can only be sustained if the common good is furthered. Let us consider Machiavelli's take on the defence of the city-state and the citizen army. Instead of relying on auxiliaries or mercenaries, cities should always depend on a civic militia. The citizens should not shirk their military duty, and should always put their country before their life. Machiavelli also advises these citizens not to let their moral qualms hinder them from acting in ways necessary for the benefit of their city. 'For where the very safety of the country depends upon the resolution to be taken, no considerations of justice or injustice, humanity or cruelty, nor of glory or of shame, should be allowed to prevail. But putting all other considerations aside the only question should be, what course will save the life and liberty of the country?'[13]

Skinner has argued that by relating civic *virtu* to individual liberty, Machiavelli provided political theory with a third conception of liberty. The meaning of individual liberty was given by each individual citizen–liberty meant being able to do whatever it was that one wanted to do. For such a liberty to be achievable, however, it was necessary that the law constrain the citizens towards civic *virtu*. Without a display of such *virtu* by the citizens, they would be threatened internally by a despot or externally by a conqueror, which would result in a suppression of individual liberties. Thus, civic *virtu* was essential for individual liberty. Machiavelli also pointed out that this civic *virtu* could only flourish in city-states in which there was some equality between the citizens. He categorically denounced the idle-rich of the large landed estates as detrimental to a republic (see Box 5.5). Here is Machiavelli's own advice on this issue: 'If anyone should wish to establish a republic in a country where there are many gentlemen, he will not succeed until he has destroyed them all; and whoever desires to establish a kingdom or principality where liberty and equality prevail, will equally fail.'

What is puzzling about Skinner's position on the relationship between liberty and *virtu* in Machiavelli, is the dynamic between individual liberty and corruption. Liberty is defined as being able to do what one wants to, and Machiavelli says that what the majority of citizens want, is to lead their private lives peacefully. But corruption is also defined as being focused too strongly on one's private affairs. If corruption is antithetical to civic *virtu*, which is a requirement of individual liberty, then surely Skinner can see that the conceptual space between corruption and individual liberty needs to be wider? It is not hard to find, in *Discourses*, passages in which Machiavelli writes about the 'private' in unfavourable terms.

**Box 5.5**

**ON THE REPUBLICAN FORM OF GOVERNMENT AND ECONOMIC EQUALITY:**

These republics in which a free and pure government is maintained will not suffer any of their citizens either to be, or to live as gentlemen; but on the contrary, while preserving a strict equality among themselves, are bitterly hostile to all those gentlemen and lords who dwell in their neighbourhood; so that if by chance any of these fall into their hands, they put them to death, as the chief promoters of corruption and the origin of all disorders.

But to make plain what I mean when I speak of gentlemen, I say that those are so to be styled who live in opulence and idleness on the revenues of their estates, without concerning themselves with the cultivation of these estates, or incurring any other fatigue for their support. Such persons are very mischievous in every republic or country. But even more mischievous are they who, besides the estates I have spoken of, are lords of strongholds and castles, and have vassals and retainers who render them obedience. Of these two classes of men the kingdom of Naples, the country round Rome, Romagna, and Lombardy are full; and hence it happens that in these provinces no commonwealth or free form of government has ever existed; because men of this sort are the sworn foes to all free institutions.

*Discourses, Book I,* Chapter 55

In Box 5.6, for example, we see Machiavelli warning us against addressing any form of injustice privately. If instead of through the law, any wrong committed is punished privately, this will elicit resentment, leading to factionalism and the eventual ruin of the state. If the same wrongs are addressed through the law, which as a public institution, is less infected by arbitrariness, the sanctions imposed are found more tolerable. We need, therefore, to keep Machiavelli's contrasting of the 'private' and the 'public' in mind as we consider Skinner's interpretation of Machiavelli's conception of individual liberty.

A less difficult puzzle that needs to be solved with respect to *Discourses,* is how to read it consistently with *The Prince.* While *Discourses* sings the praise of a republic, the *Prince* is full of praise for a completely opposed form of government, the monarchy. What unites the two books is Machiavelli's humanism. Whether it is with reference to one man, the prince, or the entire community in a republic, Machiavelli is convinced of the human ability and power to create conditions which are conducive to their well being. Both the books express faith in human ingenuity and prowess. It seems quite clear that Machiavelli is a republican. The princely form of government seems to be, for him, a transitional form. It is necessary when the people of a city have become very corrupt, but once the prince has established new laws, Machiavelli advises him to relinquish his power and transfer it to republican institutions. Only a republic can best maintain the liberty of its citizens; only a republic is a stable form of government; only as a republic can a city achieve greatness; and only as a republic can one solve easily the problem of succession.

### Box 5.6

To those set forward in a commonwealth as guardians of public freedom, no more useful or necessary authority can be given than the power to accuse, either before the people, or before some council or tribunal, those citizens who in any way have offended against the liberty of their country.

A law of this kind has two effects most beneficial to a State: first, that the citizens from fear of being accused, do not engage in attempts hurtful to the State, or doing so, are put down at once and without respect of persons: and next, that a vent is given for the escape of all those evil humours which, from whatever cause, gather in cities against particular citizens; for unless an outlet be duly provided for these by the laws, they flow into irregular channels and overwhelm the State. There is nothing, therefore, which contributes so much to the stability and permanence of a State, as to take care that the fermentation of these disturbing humours be supplied by operation of law with a recognized outlet. This might be shown by many examples, but by none so clearly as by that of Coriolanus related by Livius, where he tells us, that at a time when the Roman nobles were angry with the plebeians (thinking that the appointment of tribunes for their protection had made them too powerful), it happened that Rome was visited by a grievous famine, to meet which the senate sent to Sicily for corn. But Coriolanus, hating the commons, sought to persuade the senate that now was the time to punish them, and to deprive them of the authority which they had usurped to the prejudice of the nobles, by withholding the distribution of corn, and so suffering them to perish of hunger. Which advice of his coming to the ears of the people, kindled them to such fury against him, that they would have slain him as he left the Senate House, had not the tribunes cited him to appear and answer before them to a formal charge.

In respect of this incident I repeat what I have just now said, how useful and necessary it is for republics to provide by their laws a channel by which the displeasure of the multitude against a single citizen may find a vent. For when none such is regularly provided, recourse will be had to irregular channels, and these will assuredly lead to much worse results. For when a citizen is borne down by the operation or the ordinary laws, even though he be wronged, little or no disturbance is occasioned to the state: the injury he suffers not being wrought by private violence, nor by foreign force, which are the causes of the overthrow of free institutions, but by public authority and in accordance with public ordinances, which, having definite limits set them, are not likely to pass beyond these so as to endanger the commonwealth. For proof of which I am content to rest on this old example of Coriolanus, since all may see what a disaster it would have been for Rome had he been violently put to death by the people. For, as between citizen and citizen, a wrong would have been done affording ground for fear, fear would have sought defence, defence have led to faction, faction to divisions in the State, and these to its ruin. But the matter being taken up by those whose office it was to deal with it, all the evils which must have followed had it been left in private hands were escaped.

*Discourses, Book I,* Chapter 7

## CIVIC *VIRTU* AND RELIGION

Machiavelli writes, 'Religion is the most necessary and assured support of any civil society.'[14] How does one explain these words of Machiavelli, given his virulent criticism of Christianity and the Roman Catholic Church? Machiavelli's scathing criticism, that the nearer we get to the Vatican city, the more corruption we find among the population, since the people just follow the example set by the church, seems at odds with this statement. The Roman Catholic Church was notorious in the 16th century for the lavish and decadent lifestyle of its higher officers. But Machiavelli also makes the argument that even if the church could return to its pristine days—of the time of Jesus Christ—Christianity would still remain a force antithetical to the prosperity of a city. Christianity teaches its followers otherworldliness, humility and docility in the face of troubles, all of which are against Machiavelli's concept of *virtu*. So why, then, does Machiavelli present religion as important to a city? This is because, religion, according to Machiavelli, can be used by the state to serve its purposes. Religion should be subordinated to the state and made to serve political ends. For instance, religious sanctions always kept the Romans in check. A fear of the wrath of God if they did not do their patriotic duty, kept the Romans loyal to their city. Thus, religion could serve as an effective tool in statecraft. Once we realize that this is Machiavelli's message, then there is no contradiction between this subordination of religion and his idea that the prince must not let his moral and religious qualms prevent him from doing what is necessary for the good of the city.

Machiavelli explicitly writes that religious sentiments will better fulfil political goals in places where the population of a city is illiterate, because

**Box 5.7**

**ON THE ROLE OF RELIGION:**

Though Rome had Romulus for her first founder, and as a daughter owed him her being and nurture, nevertheless, when the institutions of Romulus were seen by Heaven to be insufficient for so great a State, the Roman senate were moved to choose Numa Pompilius as his successor, that he might look to all matters which Romulus had neglected. He finding the people fierce and turbulent, and desiring with the help of the peaceful arts to bring them to order and obedience, called in the aid of religion as essential to the maintenance of civil society, and gave it such a form, that for many ages God was nowhere so much feared as in that republic. The effect of this was to render easy any enterprise in which the senate or great men of Rome thought fit to engage. And whosoever pays heed to an infinity of actions performed, sometimes by the Roman people collectively, often by single citizens, will see, that esteeming the power of God beyond that of man, they dreaded far more to violate their oath than to transgress the laws.

*Discourses, Book I,* Chapter 11

then, the political leaders will be able to easily instil in them the fear of the wrath of God and manipulate this fear to make them obey laws. He cites the example of a Roman general who lied about the result of a religious ritual (the examination of the entrails of a slaughtered goat) to convince his soldiers about an impending victory. Machiavelli shows no concern for religion as a system of truth; he is only interested in its function for the state.

What makes religion valuable for Machiavelli is that it compels people to obey civil laws. If the laws of the state are followed, the state will be strong and stable. This is the purpose of Machiavelli's political theory: how to establish a stable, prosperous state which is able, not only to defend itself against external aggression, but also to conquer other states, if necessary. This is what the science of politics, which is a historical science, teaches us. That is the goal of politics: how to ensure a collective, stable, prosperous and glorious life for the state.

## PROBLEMS WITH MACHIAVELLI'S POLITICAL THEORY

Machiavelli was severely criticized after the publication of *The Prince*. Shakespeare used the name 'Machiavel' to signify devious characters, which was just one among several negative contemporary reactions. Machiavelli was roundly denounced for propagating a doctrine of evil. There was some attempt to defend Machiavelli by the argument that he deliberately advised rulers in *The Prince* to act immorally, in the hope that the current Medici prince would be gullible enough to follow his advice, leading to the rebellion of the people and the reestablishment of the republic. This argument, however, did not have many takers. Critics point out that Machiavelli's political theory leads to the concentration of political power in the hands of evil individuals who are cruel and devoid of moral qualms and demand to know how, this can be a strategy for the welfare of the community. Even though Machiavelli states that his 'Prince' is not like the tyrant Agathocles of Syracuse who used his political power for personal aggrandizement, critics continue to believe that his advice of being willing to use violence and deception for higher ends will only produce corrupt rulers and is certainly not a recipe for pulling a state out of its corrupt condition. Given Machiavelli's jaundiced view of human nature, it was difficult to understand how he could argue that a prince would use his access to concentrations of political power only for the public good, and not for his personal munificence.

To make being forceful so integral a component of *virtu*, has also put Machiavelli in trouble with feminists. Machiavelli's depiction of the contest between the female Fortuna and the man of *virtu*, and his suggestion that Fortuna only smiles at those young men who use force against her, sounds like a typically chauvinistic, anti-woman stance. Details from Machiavelli's personal life have hardly helped in this case. Among his contemporaries, Machiavelli was known as a libertine in his dealings with women. It has been suggested in one of his biographies, that one of the reasons for his inability to get some political office after the Medici came back, had to do with his reputation for his licentious behaviour. For Machiavelli then, as with many other thinkers in the history of political thought, women's good or women's freedom was not seen as part of the public good or the human freedom that was being argued for.

Nevertheless, Machiavelli remains a thinker for whom the public good is an important concept. If individuals completely ignore the public good for the sake of their private interests, the state will become corrupt, and that will endanger the fulfilment of private interests as well. This attempt at striking a balance between private and public interests will become a significant part of subsequent political thought. A change in the meaning of public and private, as well as in their relative significance, will also be a feature of this thought.

## NOTES

1. Quentin Skinner, Chapter 1 in *The Foundations of Modern Political Thought*, Vol. 1, Cambridge: Cambridge University Press, 1978.
2. Quentin Skinner, 'Machiavelli's *Discorsi* and the Pre-Humanist Origins of Republican Ideas', in Gisela Bock, Quentin Skinner and Maurizio Viroli (eds), *Machiavelli and Republicanism*, Cambridge: Cambridge University Press, 1993, p. 121.
3. See F. Gilbert, Chapter 1 in *Machiavelli and Guicciardini: Politics and History in Sixteenth Century Florence*, New Jersey: Princeton University Press, 1965.
4. For some of these details, see John G.A. Pocock, Chapter 4 in *The Machiavellian Moment: Florentine Political Thought and the Atlantic Republican Tradition*, New Jersey: Princeton University Press, 1975.
5. M.J. White, *Political Philosophy: A Historical Introduction*, Oxford: Oneworld Publications, 2003, pp. 44–45.
6. Quentin Skinner, *The Foundations of Modern Political Thought*, p. 34.
7. Giovani Pice della Mirandola, *An Oration on the Dignity of Man.*
8. Quentin Skinner, *The Foundations of Modern Political Thought*, p. 109.
9. *Ibid.*, p. 118.
10. Niccolo Machiavelli, *The Prince* in Max Lerner (ed.), *The Prince and the Discourses*, (*The Prince* translated by Luigi Ricci and *The Discourses* translated by Christian E. Detmold), New York: Random House, 1950, p. 64.
11. Isaiah Berlin, 'The Originality of Machiavelli', in H. Hardy (ed.), *Against the Current: Essays in the History of Ideas*, Oxford: Oxford University Press, 1981, p. 50.

12. Niccolo Machiavelli, *The Discourses* in *The Prince and the Discourses* edited by Max Lerner, translated by Luigi Ricci, p. 287.
13. *Ibid.*, p. 528.
14. *Ibid.*, p. 146.

## READING LIST

Bock, Gisela, Quentin Skinner and Maurizio Viroli (eds), *Machiavelli and Republicanism*, Cambridge: Cambridge University Press, 1993.

Hardy, H. (ed.), *Against the Current: Essays in the History of Ideas*, Oxford: Oxford University Press, 1981.

Lerner, Max (ed.), *The Prince and the Discourses*, New York: Random House, 1950.

Pocock, John G.A., *The Machiavellian Moment: Florentine Political Thought and the Atlantic Republican Tradition*, New Jersey: Princeton University Press, 1975.

Skinner, Quentin, *Machiavelli: A Very Short Introduction*, Oxford: Oxford University Press, 2000.

Skinner, Quentin, *The Foundations of Modern Political Thought*, Vol. 1, Cambridge: Cambridge University Press, 1978.

## CENTRAL THEMES

1. **Renaissance humanism:** Machiavelli's political thought shows the influence of the tradition of Renaissance humanism which rejected the Augustinian denigration of man and of other things human. What is meant by Renaissance humanism and how does Machiavelli exemplify some of its tenets it his writings?
2. ***Virtu* and *Fortuna*:** For Machiavelli, the context of political action is provided by Fortuna and in this context, to successfully act in politics, one must have *virtu*. How does Machiavelli develop his concept of *virtu*? How does his concept of *virtu* differ from the detailing of a leader's qualities that was part of the mirror-of-princes literature of the 15th century?
3. **Republicanism:** Machiavelli's political theory lies at the cusp of Renaissance humanism and the earlier republicanism of the Italian city states. What is Machiavelli's theory of the benefits of republican government, as developed in the *Discourses*? How can one reconcile the advocacy of princely government in the *Prince* with the advocacy of the republican form of government in the *Discourses*?
4. **The ill of corruption:** *Virtu* is a bulwark not only against *Fortuna*, it is also a safeguard against corruption. The bane of corruption was a significant motif in the thought of this period—take for instance, the growing critique of the corruption of the Roman Catholic Church. How does Machiavelli define corruption? How is corruption related to his ideas of the private and public?

SIX

# Thomas Hobbes (1588–1679): Contract as the Basis of Political Obligation

## THE HISTORICAL CONTEXT

The English Civil War of the 17th century formed the backdrop to the writings of Thomas Hobbes and John Locke. This conflict between the Stuart kings and the supporters of the Parliament had many strands, with the economic, religious and political dimensions of the struggle all being equally significant. The economic dispute was over Charles I's attempts to stop the enclosure movement. The enclosure movement was backed by the English Parliament, which, in the 18th century, had come to be known as 'the committee of landlords'[1] because it never gave up on its project of helping English landlords in their attempt to drive the small farmers off their land.

Most members of this Parliament were also against the principle of religious liberty. As the supporter or rather, the overlord of the established Anglican Church, Parliament was against granting religious liberty to other non-conforming denominations such as the Independents and the Puritans, as well as the Catholics. It was the Stuart kings, several of whom professed Catholicism, who tried to use their qualified advocacy of the idea of religious freedom to gain more supporters.

Anti-poor, and against the idea of religious dissent by the people, the Parliament, nevertheless presented itself as the champion of the people and of democracy, fighting for the people against absolute monarchy. The monarch could not, by definition, be pro-people, because he saw his authority as deriving not from the people, but from God. Parliament's claim, on the other hand, to be the supreme authority, was based on it being the representative of the people. Let us look at this economic, religious and political upheaval in more detail.

## THE ECONOMIC CONFLICT

In the 16th and 17th centuries, although the so-called 'commercial revolution' was in full swing, agriculture still provided the majority of the population with their livelihood. The nature of agriculture, however, was changing. Due to the the stimulus gained from the wool trade (England had already become the largest and most important source of fine wool), commercialized agriculture became the trend. With an emerging profitable trade in wool, and later in grain, many of England's landlords were themselves responsible for the commercialization of agriculture. The raising of sheep required large tracts for pasture, and the capitalist farming of grain also required large tracts of land. This led, already in the 16th century, to the enclosure, of ever larger pieces of land, including village commons by manor lords as well as their tenant farmers, as a result of which ordinary peasants lost their customary rights to the village commons, as well as to their small strips of land on the landlord's estate. Prior to the Civil War, these enclosures took the form of 'encroachments made by lords of manors or their farmers upon the land over which the manorial population had common rights or which lay in the open arable fields'.[2] During the 16th and 17th centuries, approximately half-a-million acres were enclosed.[3] With this commercialization of landholding, land began to be seen more as an income yielding investment than as a source of status.

The peasants, on being thrown off their land, went either into poor relief or gathered in the disease-ridden towns to try to earn a living by selling their labour. Thus was born the class of wage labourers and the idea of labour as a commodity. Just as land had been transformed from a locus of status and obligation to a commodity, the value of which lay in its price, similarly, labour was also now a commodity to be bought and sold in the market. Charles I tried to stop the destruction of the peasantry by attempting to prevent Parliament from bringing about these enclosures. When the members of Parliament opposed him, he tried to rule without Parliament. This led to the English Civil War of 1642.

## THE RELIGIOUS CONFLICT

Many significant developments in the relationship between religious belief and political authority took place in this period. This was the time when the explosion of conflict over religion moved from Central to Western Europe. We have already seen, in Machiavelli's writings of the early 16th century, the corruption of the Catholic Church come under attack. Luther's denunciation in 1517, of the sale of Indulgences by the Catholic Church resonated widely across Middle Europe. Protestantism spread like wildfire among many communities, leading to enormous armed conflict between Catholic rulers and Protestant princes. This conflict was sought to be resolved in 1555, by the Peace of Augsburg, which laid down the principle of *cuius region, eius religio* ('Whose reign, that religion' or, 'In the Prince's land, the Prince's religion'). As long as the ruler was Roman Catholic or Lutheran, the religion of the ruler determined the religion of his subjects. No longer could the Roman Catholic Church claim universal jurisdiction.

Although the Peace of Augsburg seemed to be about the independence of monarchs, it was also the harbinger of the religious liberty of subjects, because one of the clauses of the treaty laid down, that religious dissenters were to be allowed to emigrate peacefully to the lands of another prince whose religion was the same as theirs. Article 24 stated, 'In case our subjects, whether belonging to the old religion or the Augsburg confession should intend leaving their homes with their wives and children in order to settle in another, they shall be hindered neither in the sale of their estates after due payment of the local taxes nor injured in their honour'.

All of these issues now came to the boil in the western European countries of Spain, France and England. In England, the break with the Roman Catholic church had come much earlier with the establishment of the Church of England or, the Anglican church, in the reign of Henry VIII. In 1534, Henry had also passed an Act of Supremacy according to which the English monarch was supreme over the English church. We can see here an example of a European state not only establishing its independence against overarching institutions like the Roman Catholic church, but also asserting its sovereignty over its own church.

By the 17th century however, England contained many different religious groups: apart from the Anglicans, there were the Presbyterians, the Independents and many other radical Puritan (an English form of Calvinism) groups. As an established Church, the Anglicans firmly believed that 'in every state there should be one church and one uniform method of worshipping God'.[4] The Presbyterians basically concurred with this idea, but they wanted the Church of England to move away from its closeness to Catholic ritual. They wanted 'the Church of England transformed into a tightly organized national Calvinist church'.[5] The Independents and the Puritans 'rejected any sort of compulsory state church, whether Anglican or Presbyterian, and advocated religious toleration for a variety of voluntary, autonomous, Puritan churches'.[6] To this mix was added, the attempt by some of the Stuart royalists to restore Catholicism in England, so that the Pope would continue to be the religious head of the English people. The Catholics, Independents and Puritans, all granted the Church ecclesiastical jurisdiction that was independent of the state, although they diverged on just what they meant by the church. Catholics regarded the church as an international institution under the Pope, while the Independents viewed it as an individual congregation. What is interesting is that, if not Charles I, certainly his successors were open to this idea of religious difference, and being secret Catholics, did not want to impose the Anglican code on their subjects. Parliament, on the other hand, was divided between the Presbyterians, with their project of some kind of national Church, and the Independents and the Puritans, who wanted more freedom for different religious congregations. When the Royalists lost the Civil War in 1648, to Cromwell's Parliamentary Army, the Independents gained an upper hand, since Cromwell was an Independent. However, with Cromwell's death, in 1658, and the Restoration, in 1660, the Anglican establishment was back in the control of Parliament, which passed the Clarendon Code with the purpose of harassing all nonconforming sects. Parliament was now divided between the Whigs (the liberals) and the Tories (the conservatives). But when James II came to the throne and as a practising Catholic, suspended Parliament's penal laws against Catholics and nonconformists, with the boast that he wanted to 'make all people of our dominions members of the Catholic Church', the Tories and the Whigs united in order to lead a movement to depose him, and succeeded in 1688. Thus, religious strife continued in England till the Toleration Act of 1689 permitted nonconformists (but not Catholics) to worship publicly (although, in comparison with the Anglicans, they remained second class citizens).

## THE POLITICAL CONFLICT

As the 17th century unfolds, then, we have a Parliament insisting on curtailing the powers of the monarch. The English Civil War that breaks out in 1642 hangs on the rejection of absolute monarchy, on the notion, that the king cannot rule without Parliament, which is the representative of the people. The king, on the other hand, who takes umbrage at Parliament trying to limit his power, is willing to let his secular power be limited by religious authorities. Parliament, interestingly, insisting on limiting the absolute power on the king, will brook no challenge from any religious body to its own absolute power as the people's representative. We clearly see, here, the emergence of the theory of Parliamentary sovereignty.

The army that fought the war on behalf of Parliament was led by Oliver Cromwell, an Independent. Cromwell had the difficult task of not only trying to gain a military victory against the king's forces, but also of keeping both the conservative and the radical lobbies among the supporters of Parliament, at bay. The conservatives wanted to establish the Anglican code, whereas the radicals not only wanted total religious freedom, but they also wanted to extend the suffrage as widely as possible. After all, their support for Parliament as a representative body meant that this representation was to be as wide as possible. These conflicting positions on how representative a body like Parliament was to be, can be seen in the famous Putney debates which took place in October and November 1647, between factions of Cromwell's New Model Army and members of the radical group, the Levellers. The radical position was that all soldiers and others, as long as they were not servants or beggars, ought to have a voice in electing those who would represent them in Parliament, even if they had less than forty shillings per annum in free hold land. As Colonel Rainsborough put it, 'that the poorest he that is in England hath a life to live, as the greatest he; and therefore its clear, that every man that is to live under a government ought first by his own consent to put himself under that government; and I think that the poorest man in England is not bound in strict sense to that government that he hath not had a voice to put himself under.'[7] Cromwell and his allies wanted a much more restricted franchise, restricted to only freeholders. The more radical elements in their army followed the Levellers in proclaiming that the franchise must not be restricted on the basis of property; it should be denied only to those who were dependent on others for their livelihood.

It is in this context of overlapping conflicts that we have to see Hobbes writing the various versions of his political theory, beginning with *The Elements of Law* in the 1630s, *De Cive* in 1642 and *Leviathan* in 1651. Hobbes was born in 1588, the year in which the Spanish Armada, sent by Philip II of Spain, who saw himself as the main defender of the Catholic faith in Europe, was defeated by the Protestant monarch of England. Hobbes was born in the small town of Malmesbury. His father was a small town religious preacher. Hobbes was brought up by his paternal uncle who paid for his education. Hobbes did well at school and won himself a place at the University of Oxford, where he studied from 1603 to 1608.[8] As we have already shown, the beginning of the 17th century was a time of great political, religious and economic ferment in England. Politically, there was the long-standing conflict between the king and Parliament. Since the 13th century, when Parliament emerged as a countervailing force to the king's power, the monarchs of England had tried to suppress it, but at the beginning of the 17th century, this struggle took the form of a full fledged civil war. In 1629, the English king, Charles I, began to rule without consulting Parliament. After 11 years of struggle, in 1640, Parliament tried to abolish the king's discretionary powers. When Charles I attempted to suspend the Parliament in 1642, the Civil War began. After some reversals, the Parliamentary faction won and Charles I was executed in 1649. For the next 11 years there was no monarchy in England and it was restored only in 1660, on a constitutional basis. However, things did not really settle down till about 30 years later, with the so-called Glorious Revolution. It was in trying to think about how to resolve this conflict that Hobbes came up with his new concepts in political theory.

Living in England in these turbulent times, Hobbes's first published work, in 1628, was an English translation of Thucydides's *History of the Peloponnesian War*. Apparently, Hobbes wanted to use Thucydides's attack on Athenian democracy to turn his fellow Englishmen away from any inclination they might have for this form of government. By the late 1630s, Hobbes had written two tracts: *Human Nature, or, the Fundamental Elements of Policie* and *De corpore politico, or, The elements of law, moral and politick,* although he published them, together, only in 1650. In these writings, Hobbes stressed the need for absolute sovereignty. When these manuscripts were circulated, around 1640, among the members of the English parliament who had been struggling to limit the powers of the sovereign, they created an uproar and Hobbes had to flee for his life to Europe. He spent the next 11 years in exile, returning to England only in 1651. During these years of exile, he wrote *De Cive,* in Latin, in 1642, which he published in 1651 in English as *Philosophical Rudiments concerning Government and Society.* He became part of the Royalist circle and began teaching mathematics to the future Charles II, who was also in exile in Paris. It was during these years that Hobbes produced the third and final version of his political theory, his masterpiece, *Leviathan,* which he published in 1651. In spite of reiterating the argument for absolute sovereignty, *Leviathan* (for reasons we will go into later) so offended the Royalist lobby that they might have killed Hobbes had he not returned to England in 1651 and sought the protection of the revolutionary government. Having offended the Parliamentarians, the Royalists and the religious establishment, Hobbes led a precarious existence in England. The political work that he wrote next, *Behemoth,* his version of the English Civil War, was refused permission for publication, and only came out posthumously.

Hobbes's writings include not only the many works on political philosophy mentioned above, but several pieces on scientific method as well. As a young man, when employed as a tutor by the Cavendish family, Hobbes had made a few trips to Europe and become part of the philosophical circles there. His meetings with the mathematicians Mersenne and Gassendi, and with Descartes and Galileo in Europe, as well as his discussions with Francis Bacon in England, had convinced him of the rightness of his turn away from scholasticism. Hobbes wanted to construct a theory of politics based on scientific method. The science that attracted him most was geometry, and he saw himself as proving theorems about politics in *Leviathan*.

Before beginning our discussion of *Leviathan*, let us remember that it is Hobbes's philosophy, which marks a clear transition from classical and medieval political thought. If virtue was the dominant idea of classical and medieval Western political philosophy, then liberty can be said to be the clarion call of modern political philosophy. Machiavelli has to be seen as a Janus-faced figure, because by insisting, as we saw in the previous chapter, that civic virtue was a requirement of individual liberty, instead of replacing the earlier value with that of liberty, he tried to establish a strong link between the two. Hobbes, in my opinion, marks a sharper break from earlier political thought, because he not only foregrounds liberty, but makes the idea of moral goodness dependent on liberty, instead of the other way around. Liberty, henceforth, becomes the touchstone of everything. Hobbes originates the tradition of contractarian political theory, according to which, all relations in which human beings enter, are binding only if they are entered into freely or voluntarily. This foregrounding of liberty is evident in each one of Hobbes's central concepts. Is this conceptual break in the history of political thought to be explained by changing economic and social relations? We will leave for later the interesting question of why is it that it is from Hobbes's time that the idea of individual virtue was replaced by the idea of individual liberty as the goal of political design. It is interesting to see liberty being foregrounded at a time when there was so much conflict in society. Hobbes had to deal with the question of how to retain liberty without ending up in conflict.

As we saw earlier, Hobbes came out with his first attempt at political philosophy in 1640, in the form of *Human Nature* and *De corpore politico*. In 1642, he wrote *De Cive*. In this exposition, however, we will focus mainly on the third version, published in 1651, of his political principles. The 1651 work is titled, *Leviathan, or, The Matter, Form, and Power of a Commonwealth, Ecclesiastical and Civil*. It is divided into four parts, and we will be mainly concerned here with the first two parts: 'Of Man' and 'Of Commonwealth'. In a brief introduction to his work, Hobbes reminds us that when we praise God for his wonderful creation, man, we must realize that God's creation, men, have created something even more wonderful, 'of greater stature and strength'. They have made an 'Artificial Man'—the Commonwealth or State—for the protection and defence of these natural men. The coming together of a large number of men into a political community is the creation of this new entity, 'Artificial Man', or what Hobbes calls the state. This state is called *Leviathan* because it is so much more powerful and effective than individual men, and being so powerful, the state merits our attempt to understand it. It is not virtue that allows men to lead happy lives, but a strong state which is necessary to fulfil our requirements. That is why we need to study the state. In his book, Hobbes writes that some of the things that he will consider with respect to this state or Artificial Man will be: a) its matter and artificer, both of which is man, b) how and by what covenants it is made, and c) what preserves and dissolves it.

## HOBBES ON HUMAN NATURE

Since Hobbes says that to understand the state, the first thing we must do is to understand 'its matter and artificer', both of which is man, let us begin with his view of human nature. A human being, for Hobbes, is matter in motion, there being two kinds of motion: vital motions, like the circulation of blood or, the beating of one's pulse, and voluntary motions. Voluntary motions or 'endeavour', as Hobbes calls them, are basically of two kinds: either towards an object or away from an object. 'This Endeavour, when it is toward something which causes it, is called Appetite or Desire… and when the Endeavour is fromward something, it is generally called Aversion.'[9] Human beings are nothing but bundles of appetites and aversions, and life consists in satiating one desire after another. For Hobbes, the cessation of desire is what we call death, and felicity or happiness is the movement from one fulfilled desire to another. 'Continual success in obtaining those things which a man from time to time desires, that is to say, continual prospering, is that men call Felicity; I mean the Felicity of this life. For there is no such thing as perpetual Tranquillity of mind, while we live here; because Life itself is but Motion, and can never be without Desire.'[10] Life itself is about the continuous fulfilment of one's desires, and human beings take the help of their reason in order to satisfy their desires. Human beings do not just have passions, they have reason too, but their reason is a mere slave of their passions, and its role is to devise the most efficient means of achieving these passions. How far have we come here from the Greek view of reason as the master of our desires (see Box 6.1)!

As for the Greeks, for Hobbes, too, happiness remains the goal of life, but that is where the similarity ends. Defining happiness or felicity as the

**Box 6.1**

**HOBBES ON APPETITES AND AVERSIONS:**

These small beginnings of motion within the body of man, before they appear in walking, speaking, striking, and other visible actions, are commonly called endeavour.

This endeavour, when it is toward something which causes it, is called appetite, or desire, the latter being the general name, and the other oftentimes restrained to signify the desire of food, namely hunger and thirst. And when the endeavour is fromward something, it is generally called aversion.

*Leviathan*

continuous satisfaction of our desires, Hobbes makes desire the engine of all human action. Human beings are no longer conceived of as struggling to find out what virtue is through their reason; reason has now merely to follow desire. For Hobbes, as we see clearly in Box 6.2, what we call virtuous is simply that which we desire. Individuals desire different things, so there is no one action which can be termed virtuous.

Box 6.2

**HOBBES ON THE SUBJECTIVE NATURE OF GOOD AND EVIL:**

But whatsoever is the object of any man's appetite or desire, that is it which he for his part calleth good; and the object of his hate and aversion, evil; and of his contempt, vile and inconsiderable. For these words of good, evil, and contemptible are ever used with relation to the person that useth them: there being nothing simply and absolutely so; nor any common rule of good and evil to be taken from the nature of the objects themselves; but from the person of the man, where there is no Commonwealth; or, in a Commonwealth, from the person that representeth it; or from an arbitrator or judge, whom men disagreeing shall by consent set up and make his sentence the rule thereof.

*Leviathan*

## THE STATE OF NATURE

With this conception of human nature, Hobbes presents us with the concept of the state of nature. The state of nature represents the interaction of human beings with each other in the absence of any kind of relations of political authority. Given his human beings, Hobbes's state of nature represents a state of war. Ceaselessly pursuing their desires, with no agreement on good and bad, human beings come in conflict with each other. Since the state of nature is a state of freedom and equality, with everyone having the right to do as he will, and no one being naturally inferior to anyone else, it adds to the level of hostility, because no one draws back from pursuing that which they desire. In fact, the attempt to acquire 'power after power' never ceases, because everyone is trying to ensure that no one can stop them from fulfilling their desires. Not only is it part of human nature to continuously want to fulfil new desires, one desire that is 'part of the nature of man' is the desire for glory. Human beings cannot stand for any sign of others undervaluing them. This creates a situation of ever present hostility in which there is no point in undertaking long-term projects, like cultivating a farm, for instance, since there is no security that one will get to enjoy the fruits of this agricultural labour. 'In such condition, there is not place for Industry; because the fruit thereof is uncertain; and consequently no Culture of the Earth; no Navigation,…no commodious Building; no Knowledge of the face of the Earth; no account of Time; no Arts; no Letters; no Society; and which is worst of all, continual fear, and danger of violent death; And the life of man, solitary, poor, nasty, brutish, and short.'[11]

Many contemporary political scientists have popularized Hobbes's concept of the state of nature by asking the question of whether it can be modelled as a prisoner's dilemma. The classic prisoner's dilemma is an important tool of rational choice theory and it represents a situation the dynamic of which is such that the two actors have no choice but to act in ways which make both of them worse off. The structure of the situation itself prevents the actors from choosing options to their mutual benefit. Several recent commentators on Hobbes have wondered whether it is fair to present him as the original rational choice theorist. After all, in the state of nature, given freedom and equality, it is only rational to seek power after power, with the end result being a suboptimal one of constant insecurity (see Box 6.3).[12]

Box 6.3

**THE STATE OF NATURE AS THE STATE OF WAR:**

Hereby it is manifest that during the time men live without a common power to keep them all in awe, they are in that condition which is called war; and such a war as is of every man against every man. For war consisteth not in battle only, or the act of fighting, but in a tract of time, wherein the will to contend by battle is sufficiently known: and therefore the notion of time is to be considered in the nature of war, as it is in the nature of weather. For as the nature of foul weather lieth not in a shower or two of rain, but in an inclination thereto of many days together: so the nature of war consisteth not in actual fighting, but in the known disposition thereto during all the time there is no assurance to the contrary. All other time is peace.

Whatsoever therefore is consequent to a time of war, where every man is enemy to every man, the same consequent to the time wherein men live without other security than what their own strength and their own invention shall furnish them withal. In such condition there is no place for industry, because the fruit thereof is uncertain: and consequently no culture of the earth; no navigation, nor use of the commodities that may be imported by sea; no commodious building; no instruments of moving and removing such things as require much force; no knowledge of the face of the earth; no account of time; no arts; no letters; no society; and which is worst of all, continual fear, and danger of violent death; and the life of man, solitary, poor, nasty, brutish, and short.

*Leviathan*

## THE LAWS OF NATURE

Since human beings have reason, Hobbes argues, they can see in the state of nature that there must be a more efficient way of fulfilling these desires.

Here Hobbes also introduces his third major idea: the idea of the laws of nature. There are passages in *Leviathan*, which present the laws of nature as the precepts of reason, as rational rules which show the way as to how to achieve one's desires. Hobbes lists as many as 19 laws of nature, with some of the important ones being the following: The first law of nature commands men 'to seek Peace, and to follow it'. The second law of nature states, 'That a man be willing, when others are so too, as far-forth, as for Peace, and defence of himself he shall think it necessary, to lay down his

Box 6.4

**HOBBES ON NATURAL RIGHTS AND THE LAWS OF NATURE:**

The right of nature, which writers commonly call jus naturale, is the liberty each man hath to use his own power as he will himself for the preservation of his own nature; that is to say, of his own life; and consequently, of doing anything which, in his own judgement and reason, he shall conceive to be the aptest means thereunto.

By liberty is understood, according to the proper signification of the word, the absence of external impediments; which impediments may oft take away part of a man's power to do what he would, but cannot hinder him from using the power left him according as his judgement and reason shall dictate to him.

A law of nature, lex naturalis, is a precept, or general rule, found out by reason, by which a man is forbidden to do that which is destructive of his life, or taketh away the means of preserving the same, and to omit that by which he thinketh it may be best preserved. For though they that speak of this subject use to confound jus and lex, right and law, yet they ought to be distinguished, because right consisteth in liberty to do, or to forbear; whereas law determineth and bindeth to one of them: so that law and right differ as much as obligation and liberty, which in one and the same matter are inconsistent.

And because the condition of man (as hath been declared in the precedent chapter) is a condition of war of every one against every one, in which case every one is governed by his own reason, and there is nothing he can make use of that may not be a help unto him in preserving his life against his enemies; it followeth that in such a condition every man has a right to every thing, even to one another's body. And therefore, as long as this natural right of every man to every thing endureth, there can be no security to any man, how strong or wise soever he be, of living out the time which nature ordinarily alloweth men to live. And consequently it is a precept, or general rule of reason: that every man ought to endeavour peace, as far as he has hope of obtaining it; and when he cannot obtain it, that he may seek and use all helps and advantages of war. The first branch of which rule containeth the first and fundamental law of nature, which is: to seek peace and follow it. The second, the sum of the right of nature, which is: by all means we can to defend ourselves.

From this fundamental law of nature, by which men are commanded to endeavour peace, is derived this second law: that a man be willing, when others are so too, as far forth as for peace and defence of himself he shall think it necessary, to lay down this right to all things; and be contented with so much liberty against other men as he would allow other men against himself.

*Leviathan*

right to all things; and be contented with so much liberty against other men, as he would allow other men against himself.' The third law of nature commands men to 'perform their covenants made', the ninth commands that 'every man acknowledge the other for his equal by Nature', and the seventeenth that 'no man be allowed to be judge in his own case'.[13] If we look at the content of these laws of nature, we can see how Hobbes would argue that human reason, in the form of the laws of nature, would persuade human beings that they would have a better chance of fulfilling their desires, if they got out of the state of nature. Although the laws of nature exist in the state of nature, they are not followed because no one is able to enforce them. What needs to be done is to set up somebody as an enforcer of these very same laws (see Box 6.4).

## THE SOCIAL CONTRACT AND THE CREATION OF THE STATE

Thus enters the idea of the social contract. All the individuals in the state of nature make a promise to each other that henceforth they will each give up their natural right in favour of the sovereign and will obey his laws. They promise each other that in choosing their sovereign, they are to be understood to be authorizing all his future actions. The contract is of the form: 'I Authorise and give up my Right of Governing myself, to this Man, or to this Assembly of men, on this condition, that you give up your Right to him, and Authorise all his Actions in like manner. This done, the Multitude so united in one Person, is called a Commonwealth, in Latin Civitas.'[14]

Here is another version of how the state is created through the Hobbesian social contract: 'A *Commonwealth* is said to be *Instituted,* when a *Multitude* of men do Agree, and *Covenant, every one, with every one,* that to whatsoever *Man,* or *Assembly of Men,* shall be given by the major part, the *Right to Present* the Person of them all, (that is to say, to be their *Representative*); every one, as well he that *Voted for it,* as he that *Voted against it,* shall *Authorise* all the Actions and Judgements, of that Man, or Assembly of men, in the same manner, as if they were his own, to the end, to live peaceably amongst themselves, and be protected against other men.'[15]

The social contract creates a sovereign, and at the same time, another new entity called the state. The fact that it is by choosing a sovereign that the people also create the state, should not make us miss the separateness of the state from the sovereign. When we undertake the covenant, we make ourselves, a multitude, into one person, the person of the state. The state is an artificial person, and therefore needs a natural person/s to bear its persona. Without this persona, it cannot act. We choose an individual or a body of men to bear this persona and authorize his/their actions. When he/they act, it is the state that is acting. It is state that is the repository of power, with the sovereign as its representative, and the subjects owe allegiance to the sovereign as the representative of the state (see Box 6.5).

Box 6.5

**THE SOCIAL CONTRACT AND THE CREATION OF THE COMMONWEALTH:**

The only way to erect such a common power, as may be able to defend them from the invasion of foreigners, and the injuries of one another, and thereby to secure them in such sort as that by their own industry and by the fruits of the earth they may nourish themselves and live contentedly, is to confer all their power and strength upon one man, or upon one assembly of men, that may reduce all their wills, by plurality of voices, unto one will: which is as much as to say, to appoint one man, or assembly of men, to bear their person; and every one to own and acknowledge himself to be author of whatsoever he that so beareth their person shall act, or cause to be acted, in those things which concern the common peace and safety; and therein to submit their wills, every one to his will, and their judgements to his judgement. This is more than consent, or concord; it is a real unity of them all in one and the same person, made by covenant of every man with every man, in such manner as if every man should say to every man: I authorize and give up my right of governing myself to this man, or to this assembly of men, on this condition; that thou give up, thy right to him, and authorize all his actions in like manner. This done, the multitude so united in one person is called a COMMONWEALTH; in Latin, CIVITAS. This is the generation of that great LEVIATHAN, or rather, to speak more reverently, of that mortal god to which we owe, under the immortal God, our peace and defence. For by this authority, given him by every particular man in the Commonwealth, he hath the use of so much power and strength conferred on him that, by terror thereof, he is enabled to form the wills of them all, to peace at home, and mutual aid against their enemies abroad. And in him consisteth the essence of the Commonwealth; which, to define it, is: one person, of whose acts a great multitude, by mutual covenants one with another, have made themselves every one the author, to the end he may use the strength and means of them all as he shall think expedient for their peace and common defence.

And he that carryeth this person is called sovereign, and said to have sovereign power; and every one besides, his subject.

*Leviathan*

Earlier, the monarch did not just represent the state; he or she *was* the state. Hobbes posits the state as something independent of the king, who is just someone who acts for the state. Just as Hobbes displeased the king's lobby by insisting that even an absolute monarch is chosen by the people and not appointed by God, similarly, by explaining that the sovereign assumes the persona of the state, or that the sovereign plays the role of the state, Hobbes introduced a distinction between the sovereign and the state, with far-reaching consequences. Skinner argues that this distinction between the monarch and the state was made earlier as well, by the republican and constitutionalist traditions. What Hobbes did was not just to separate the king from the state, but also to distinguish between the people and the state. For Hobbes, whether the state was represented by a democratic government or a monarchical one, the seat of sovereignty was the state, not the king or the people. For Skinner, it is with Hobbes that a new discourse of the state enters political thought.[16]

## SOVEREIGNTY

For Hobbes, the people can choose to vest sovereignty in one person, or in an assembly of persons; what is more important, is that the sovereign, whoever it may be, is absolute. In *Leviathan,* both in the chapter on the rights of the sovereign, as well as in the chapter on the dissolution of the commonwealth, one can easily see the absolute nature of Hobbes's sovereign. Consider the long list of the rights of the sovereign in Chapter 18: The people cannot, without the sovereign's permission, make a new contract to change the form of government; they cannot ever accuse the sovereign of any act of injustice, or punish him/them for such acts; the sovereign has the right to be the sole judge of which policy is best for the peace and defence of the people; the sovereign has the right of censorship; and so on. In Chapter 29, Hobbes reinforces his point about absolute sovereignty by stating, right at the beginning of the chapter, that it is the want of absolute power that leads to the dissolution of a commonwealth. If the people are allowed to judge for themselves what is good and evil, if their property is considered to be out of bounds of the sovereign's fiat, and if the sovereign is considered to be subject to his/their own laws, then one can be sure that the state will not be able to maintain itself. Any questioning of the absolute power of the sovereign is a step towards the dissolution of the commonwealth and a return to the state of nature, which, as we saw earlier, is akin to a terrible state of war. We must remember, that what Hobbes is doing here, is highlighting the absolute power of the state. Suppose the form of government that the people choose is a democracy with the sovereign being an 'Assembly of men'. The same rights of sovereignty will inhere in this 'Assembly of men', who will exercise these rights in the name of the state. It is the state which is now, for example, the overlord of the people's property.

The right to life, in fact, is the only right that Hobbes allows individuals to retain from the state of nature, as they make their transition into becoming members of a commonwealth. Hobbes clearly states that this retention does not mean that the state or sovereign has a duty to respect his subjects' right to life. Since the sovereign is not a party to the social contract, he has no obligations towards the subjects. The sovereign retains his natural right to do as he will. However, if the sovereign wills the death of any one subject, that subject has the right to defend his life. It is only the subject as an individual who retains this right of self-defence. No one has the right to help another—be it one's friend, or one's blood brother—in escaping the sword of the sovereign.

You may wonder how this seems like a rational plan. This does not look like a rational plan to get out of the state of war. As Locke wrote in the 1670s, this was like advising somebody to jump from the mouth of a fox into the jaws of a lion. Or, as Sabine said much later, the individualism of Hobbes' egoistic, desire driven humans sits ill with the absolute sovereign. The power of the absolute sovereign can crush all individual desire. The point of arguing that we have authorized this individual or this body of men to bear the person of the state was to signal that this act of authorization by the subjects was also one of marking boundaries. Those bearing the person of the state had to stay within the bounds of their authorization. But Hobbes turned the idea of authorization upside-down. For Hobbes, 'The concept of the political covenant is not a means of limiting the powers of the crown; properly understood, it shows that the powers of the crown have no limit at all.' 'Not only do the members of the multitude have no remaining right to question the actions of their sovereign; they have a positive duty to "own" whatever actions their sovereign may undertake in seeking their safety and contentment. But this is to say, according to Hobbes's theory of attributed action, that the public acts of the sovereign, and hence of the state, are nothing other than the acts of the individual members of the multitude. So it will not merely be unjust for them to oppose their sovereign; it will actually be self-contradictory, for they will be opposing themselves.'[17]

In his defence, Hobbes states that his commonwealth is an absolute but minimal state. There might not be any unjust laws—since justice is defined by law, and law is the command of the sovereign—but Hobbes does distinguish between good and bad laws (see Box 6.6). In answering his own question, 'what is a good law?', Hobbes writes that 'the use of Laws is not to bind the People from all Voluntary actions; but to direct and keep them in such a motion, as not to hurt themselves by their own impetuous desires, rashness, or indiscretion, as Hedges are set, not to stop travellers, but to keep them in the way. And therefore a Law that is not Needful, having not the true End of a Law, is not Good... Unnecessary Laws are not good Laws; but traps for Money.'[18] The purpose of law is to maintain order, to prevent individuals from physically harming each other. Good laws are those which do not interfere too much with the life of the citizens, for instance, in their economic dealings with one another, in how they educate their children, the institution of the family, etc. The distinction between the private and the public is crucial here. The private realm, which is the space of individual desire, is left alone. A good monarch is one who, by not interfering in this private space, allows his subjects the maximum amount of liberty to pursue their desires.

Box 6.6

**HOBBES ON THE LAWS OF THE SOVEREIGN:**

The office of the sovereign, be it a monarch or an assembly, consisteth in the end for which he was trusted with the sovereign power, namely the procuration of the safety of the people, to which he is obliged by the law of nature, and to render an account thereof to God, the Author of that law, and to none but Him. But by safety here is not meant a bare preservation, but also all other contentments of life, which every man by lawful industry, without danger or hurt to the Commonwealth, shall acquire to himself... For the use of laws (which are but rules authorized) is not to bind the people from all voluntary actions, but to direct and keep them in such a motion as not to hurt themselves by their own impetuous desires, rashness, or indiscretion; as hedges are set, not to stop travellers, but to keep them in the way. And therefore a law that is not needful, having not the true end of a law, is not good. A law may be conceived to be good when it is for the benefit of the sovereign, though it be not necessary for the people, but it is not so. For the good of the sovereign and people cannot be separated. It is a weak sovereign that has weak subjects; and a weak people whose sovereign wanteth power to rule them at his will. Unnecessary laws are not good laws, but traps for money which, where the right of sovereign power is acknowledged, are superfluous; and where it is not acknowledged, insufficient to defend the people.

*Leviathan*

In the state of nature individuals had the freedom to do anything at all, for there were no laws there forbidding them from performing any action. The laws of nature existed, but in the absence of enforcement, as Hobbes said, a law is not really a law. What constrained an individual's liberty in the state of nature was not law, but rather, other individuals, who often, by use of brute force, prevented each other from obtaining that which they desired. When these individuals sign the social contract and establish a commonwealth, they have to live under the enforceable laws of the monarch. They no longer have the liberty to do anything at all, but since the state prevents other persons from physically constraining them, and as a minimal state, frames as few laws as possible, these individuals are able to enjoy more liberty in the commonwealth. This is how Hobbes understands the relationship between individual liberty and the state.

For Hobbes, the public good merely means individuals being able to satisfy their own desires. There is no longer any harmony assumed between one person's felicity and another person's. In his effort to make himself happy, an individual will probably make another person unhappy.

This assumption is, in fact, one of conflict and it becomes the function of the state to prevent individuals from interfering in each other's happiness or liberty. The state is to maintain the liberty of each person to do as he pleases without infringing on another's liberty.

## HOBBES ON LIBERTY

If liberty, and not virtue, is the leitmotif of modern political theory, it is Hobbes who provides us with a specifically modern understanding of liberty. By defining liberty as the 'absence of external impediments to motion', Hobbes became the progenitor of what Berlin later called the negative theory of freedom. 'A Free Man, is he, that in those things, which by his strength and wit he is able to do, is not hindered to do what he has a will to.'[19] In this definition, it is clear that Hobbes is distinguishing between liberty and power. If a person is ill and is therefore unable to get out of bed, we can describe his position as exactly that: an inability to get up. We do not say that he is not free to get up, which we could say if he was chained to the bed. Similarly, a lack of financial resources to do something should be characterized as a lack of power, and not as a lack of freedom. For Hobbes, the only things one is not free to do, are those things which the sovereign has expressly forbidden by its laws. Liberty, then, is the silence of the laws. 'The Liberty of a Subject lies therefore only in those things, which in regulating their actions, the Sovereign has permitted: such as is the Liberty to buy, and sell, and otherwise contract with one another, to chose their own abode, their own diet, their own trade of life, and institute their children as they themselves think fit; and the like.'[20]

Just as the absence of power does not necessarily mean absence of freedom, similarly, for Hobbes, the presence of fear does not make one devoid of freedom, either. In *Leviathan*, Hobbes gives us the example of a highway robber threatening a traveller with a weapon and demanding all his money. If the traveller parts with his money, we cannot say that he did not do so freely. Hobbes is making this same point when he argues that in both ways of establishing a commonwealth—by institution or by acquisition—the subjects must be said to have consented to the rule of the sovereign of their own free will. A commonwealth is instituted when individuals voluntarily come together in a social contract. A commonwealth is established by acquisition, however, when it is conquered by a new sovereign. Even in this case, if the subjects choose to stay in the commonwealth, and obey the new laws out of fear, they are to be taken as having consented to the new sovereign. To understand Hobbes's conception of liberty, then, we must remember its relationship with power, fear and necessity.

## HOBBES'S THEORY OF POLITICAL OBLIGATION

The absolute sovereign must be obeyed—that seems to be Hobbes's message. If the absolute sovereign is the pre-condition for the enjoyment of individual liberty, it is important for Hobbes to instil in the subjects a sense of loyalty to the sovereign, so that they do not do anything to destabilize him. This is the issue of political obligation. According to many theorists, the basis of the long term stability of any government is the obligation its people feel to obey its laws. Now, obligation is a moral concept, being obliged to do something, for instance, often means to be duty-bound to do something. Why is it our duty to obey our government's laws? The medieval answer was that our obligation is derived from the will of God since the monarch was God's representative on earth. The modern answer is that this obligation is derived from our will since it is we who choose the government. What kind of theory of political obligation did Hobbes espouse, is an extremely controversial question. There are several positions on this.[21] There is what is called the traditional interpretation of Hobbes, associated with Watkins and Nagel, according to which *Leviathan* has no notion of moral obligation at all. When Hobbes writes that contracts have no standing in the state of nature because there is no one to enforce their being followed, he is accepting that contracts are obeyed only when there is fear of punishment, that is, for prudential reasons and not because one feels obliged because one has entered into a contract. From this, it would follow, that subjects will only obey the laws of a sovereign till the time they think him as capable of punishing their transgression. It would also follow from this, that if the sovereign is unable to withstand the attack of a powerful aggressor, the subjects will immediately transfer their allegiance to the new power. For these theorists, *Leviathan* contains only a prudential theory of obedience and not a theory of political obligation.

The position opposed to this is known as the Taylor–Warrender thesis. Warrender argued in his 1957 book that Hobbes did have a theory of moral obligation, but he did not derive obligation only from individual acts of covenanting.[22] For Warrender, Hobbes saw the laws of nature not merely as precepts of reason, but as the commands of God. Even as the commands of God, in the state of nature, 'the laws of nature oblige in *foro interno*, that is to say, they bind to a desire they should take place, but in *foro externo*, that is, to the putting them in act, not always.'[23] What obliges us to obey the laws of the state is not the promise to each other to obey the sovereign, but rather, the law of nature which commands us to keep our covenants. All the laws of nature have an obligatory force. But this is a suspended obligatory force, since there is no one in the state of nature to enforce these laws. When the sovereign is installed, he becomes the enforcer of these laws. But Warrender wants us to remember that the sovereign does not create the grounds of the obligation; he merely creates the conditions where the grounds work. Individuals do not just obey the laws of the state out of fear; they consider it their duty to obey them, deriving this duty, according to Warrender, from the commands of God. According to these scholars, Hobbes is able to sustain the position of the sovereign on the basis of a theory of political obligation, after all.

## SOME PROBLEMS IN HOBBES'S THEORY

Does Hobbes fulfil his promise of designing a political institution which gives individuals the highest degree of liberty to satisfy their desires? The Hobbesian claim is that an absolute sovereign is the lynchpin of such a political design. As we saw before, however, there were immediate objections to this claim. The absolute sovereign would, critics said, endanger the liberty of individuals instead of protecting it. Hobbes was being sanguine when he claimed that the absolute sovereign would run a minimal state. There was nothing in his theory to provide this guarantee.

Another point of criticism is that while Hobbes keeps emphasizing the importance of the absolute sovereign, he does not see that without a theory of political obligation, his absolute sovereign will be unstable. If the only way we can give Hobbes a theory of political obligation is by assuming that he understands the laws of nature as the commands of God, this creates other problems. Hobbes expressly said that he wanted to present a theory which would be built up, step by step, from a small number of self-evident propositions about human nature, passions and reason. To postulate a belief in God would be to introduce an extraneous factor not allowed by the theory. What if we go back to the idea of the laws of nature as rational precepts? After all, Hobbes did write that the laws of nature 'are not properly laws, but qualities that dispose men to peace, and to obedience. When a Commonwealth is once settled, then are they actually Laws, and not before.'[24] For something to be a law, it must be known or written down clearly. None of this applies in the case of the laws of nature. It is not clear, in *Leviathan,* how the laws of nature are to be interpreted. Both interpretations—the laws of nature as God's commands or, the laws as rational precepts—create problems for Hobbes' political theory.

Even if the political route to individual liberty that Hobbes outlines is problematic, at least one could say that the ideal of individual liberty upheld by him is attractive. But what many find unacceptable is his argument that liberty is consistent with fear. It is because of the value of individual liberty that the idea of consent as the basis of all relationships comes to the forefront. But the consent that Hobbes talks about is a hypothetical consent; or a consent that is given actually in a situation of fearing for one's life. Such ideas of liberty or consent, then, lose much of their appeal.

Hobbes's political ideas were a response to the changing conditions of 17th century England. From Robert Filmer to James Harrington to John Locke, many others also addressed the political conflicts of the day. It is to some of these other responses to emerging demands for religious liberty, political rights and economic restructuring that we now turn to, in the next few pages.

## NOTES

1. Barrington Moore, Jr., *Social Origins of Dictatorship and Democracy*, New York: Penguin Books, 1966, p. 19.
2. *Ibid.*, p. 9.
3. Richard S. Dunn, *The Age of Religious Wars: 1559–1715*, 2nd edition, New York: W.W. Norton & Company, 1979, p. 111.
4. Johann Sommerville, 'Leviathan and its Anglican Context', in Patricia Springborg (ed.), *The Cambridge Companion to Hobbes's* Leviathan, Cambridge: Cambridge University Press, 2007, p. 359.
5. Richard S. Dunn, *The Age of Religious Wars*, p. 174.
6. *Ibid.*
7. Crawford B. Macpherson, *The Political Theory of Possessive Individualism: Hobbes to Locke*, Oxford: Oxford University Press, 1962.
8. Quentin Skinner, Chapter 1 in *Visions of Politics: Hobbes and Civil Science*, Vol. 3, Cambridge: Cambridge University Press, 2002.
9. Thomas Hobbes, *Leviathan*, edited by Crawford B. Macpherson, Harmondsworth: Penguin Books, 1968, p. 119.
10. Thomas Hobbes, *Leviathan*, pp. 129–130. Remember the Greek idea of *eudaimonia*? One should think about how the Hobbesian concept of felicity captures the idea of happiness differently from Socratic *eudaimonia*.
11. Thomas Hobbes, *Leviathan*, p. 186.
12. See for instance, David Gauthier, *The Logic of Leviathan*, Oxford: Oxford University Press, 1969; Gregory Kavka, *Hobbesian Moral and Political Theory*, Princeton, Princeton University Press, 1986 and Jean Hampton, *Hobbes and the Social Contract Tradition*, Cambridge: Cambridge University Press, 1986.
13. Thomas Hobbes, Chapters 14 and 15 in *Leviathan*.
14. Thomas Hobbes, *Leviathan*, p. 227.
15. *Ibid.*
16. See Quentin Skinner, 'From the State of Princes to the Person of the State', *Visions of Politics: Renaissance Virtues*, Vol. 2, Cambridge: Cambridge University Press, 2002.
17. *Ibid.*, pp. 207–208.
18. Thomas Hobbes, *Leviathan*, p. 388.

19. *Ibid.*, p. 262.
20. *Ibid.*, p. 264.
21. See Edwin Curley, 'Reflections on Hobbes: Recent Work in his Moral and Political Philosophy', in R. Shaver, *Hobbes*, Dartmouth: Ashgate, 1999, pp. 187–189.
22. Howard Warrender, *The Political Philosophy of Hobbes: His Theory of Obligation*, New York: Oxford University Press, 2000, p. 1957.
23. Thomas Hobbes, *Leviathan*, p. 215.
24. *Ibid.*

## READING LIST

Gauthier, David, *The Logic of Leviathan*, Oxford: Oxford University Press, 1969.

Hampton, Jean, *Hobbes and the Social Contract Tradition*, Cambridge: Cambridge University Press, 1986.

Hobbes, Thomas, *Leviathan*, edited by Crawford B. Macpherson, Harmondsworth: Penguin Books, 1968.

Kavka, Gregory, *Hobbesian Moral and Political Theory*, Princeton, Princeton University Press, 1986.

Macpherson, Crawford B., *The Political Theory of Possessive Individualism: Hobbes to Locke*, Oxford: Oxford University Press, 1962.

Shaver, R., *Hobbes*, Dartmouth: Ashgate, 1999.

Skinner, Quentin, *Visions of Politics: Hobbes and Civil Science*, Vol. 3, Cambridge: Cambridge University Press, 2002.

Springborg, Patricia (ed.), *The Cambridge Companion to Hobbes's* Leviathan, Cambridge: Cambridge University Press, 2007.

Warrender, Howard, *The Political Philosophy of Hobbes: His Theory of Obligation*, New York: Oxford University Press, 2000.

## CENTRAL THEMES

1. **Individualism:** Hobbes spends many chapters of the *Leviathan* developing his conception of what a human being is, trying to unpack how a human being thinks and feels. It is this conception of human nature that is said to be the backbone of Hobbes's individualism. What problems do you perceive in Hobbes's conception of how individuals think and feel?
2. **The sovereign state:** Hobbes makes the monarch an absolute sovereign because the monarch represents the state, and for Hobbes, the state is defined in terms of its absolute sovereignty. The state is an entity separate from the monarch and from the people, although it can be represented either by the king or the people. What are the different aspects of the state's sovereignty that Hobbes fleshes out?
3. **Negative liberty:** Hobbes's theory of negative liberty seems to follow from his conception of human nature and his individualism. He sets up an absolute state

in order that individuals may enjoy their negative liberties. What is Hobbes's conception of negative liberty? How is the negative liberty of individuals safeguarded in the absolutist state?

4. **Law:** Although Hobbes writes in detail about the laws of nature, he is said to have overturned the natural law tradition through his nominalism. One can see that clearly in his conception of the laws of the state. Does Hobbes draw any analogies between the laws of nature and the positive laws of the state? Do you find any contradiction between what law means for Hobbes, in the state of nature, and in the political community?

SEVEN

# John Locke (1632–1704): Theological Premises and Liberal Limits on Government

John Locke was born in England in 1632. Although the English Civil War (in which Locke's father had fought on the side of Parliament) was over by the time Locke was a young man, the struggle between the king and Parliament for supremacy was very much alive. After the monarchy was restored in 1660, for some time under the rule of Charles II, things were quiet, but after his death in 1685, when his brother James II, who was a Catholic, came to the throne, the tension became palpable. Even the reign of Charles II, towards its end, was marked by the Exclusion Crisis (1679–1681), with Parliament attempting to exclude James II, a practising Catholic, from the throne. England, at that time, was rife with a fear of Catholicism. 'Locke's contemporaries believed that Catholics subjected their consciences to a spiritual tyranny exercised by the Pope, and that Catholic monarchs subscribed to a political theory of absolutism.'[1] When James II did become the king and attempted to rule England as an absolute monarch, it was as if these fears had come true, and the king's opponents responded by unsuccessfully trying to invade England, from Holland, under the leadership of the Duke of Monmouth. The struggle between the king and Parliament was also complicated by becoming intertwined with the problem of the religious freedom of the dissenters, including the Catholics. Before the Restoration, the Anglican Church and the king had taken a stance against religious freedom. Now, however, this position was taken by Parliament and by the Church, with the king advocating 'liberty of conscience' for his subjects. In December 1662, Charles II even issued a Declaration of Indulgence suspending penal laws against religious dissent. He was subsequently forced to rescind this declaration by Parliament.[2] As for John Locke, for whom the question of religious belief remained important throughout his life, not only did he take up the issue of the liberties of individuals subject to a church and a government, it is believed that he was also deeply involved in all the events—the Exclusion Crisis, the Rye House Plot to kill Charles II and his brother James (1681–1683), and the Monmouth Rebellion—in which this conflict was played out. More than once, in fact, for participating in these conspiracies, Locke had to flee England for exile in Europe.[3]

After finishing school, in 1652, Locke joined Christ Church College at the University of Oxford, where he also began to teach after getting his degree. The young Locke, surprisingly, was rather conservative. His early *Two Tracts on Government* (1660) shows him to be a supporter of absolute monarchy, and of religious uniformity. While fulfilling his teaching responsibilities, Locke developed an interest in medicine, became part of the burgeoning focus on 'natural philosophy' at Oxford, took up botany, and actually enrolled for the bachelor's degree in medicine. It was as a medical man that, in 1666, he first met and cured the 1st Earl of Shaftesbury, the leader of the parliamentary faction in English politics, and subsequently became part of his household. The two men developed a close relationship and it was as part of the Shaftesbury entourage that Locke was directly involved in the instability of English politics of that time. It is a matter of serious discussion among Locke scholars, as to whether it was because of Shaftesbury's influence that Locke's political positions changed so radically.[4] It has been stated by Locke's biographer, Maurice Cranston, that Locke 'learned his liberalism' from Shaftesbury, since, Locke's earlier writings allowed no space for the concept of right to property, or for dissent against the 'civil magistrate'.[5] Shaftesbury's influence seemed to have caused a dramatic change in Locke's views on the limits of government.

Locke did not publish anything 'of note' till he was middle aged. *Two Tracts on Government* and *Essays on the Law of Nature* were both written around 1660–1661. In these writings, we find Locke postulating the human condition as one of conflict and hostility, mitigated only by 'a benevolent God providing a set of rules for the direction of human beings'[6]. Some of these rules are covered by divine positive law, which is a 'revealed religious truth', but others, especially, the laws of nature, are not clearly expressed anywhere. However, if we always obey the laws and commands of our civil magistrate, our political ruler, then we can be certain that we are following the laws of nature, that is, the laws of God. 'One barely needs to know for practical purposes what the law of nature prescribes, all one needs to know is whom to obey.'[7] For the young Locke, the extensive powers of the civil magistrate are derived from 'God's purposes' for men. This wide ranging civil authority is also exercised over all 'indifferent things', that is, all matters of religious ceremonial not expressly revealed by God.

Subjects cannot cite their faith to justify any disobedience of the ruler's commands. Neither religious grounds nor any other grounds can be used to prevent the sovereign from exacting obedience from his subjects.

Surprisingly, this extreme position on political absolutism changed in *Essay on Toleration* (1667), written one year after Locke's association with Shaftesbury. In this essay, Locke argued that since the purpose of political rule was to maintain peace and security, the sovereign should not interfere with those of his subjects' actions which did not adversely impact on this peace. Religious beliefs were to be left alone, unless they led to actions subversive of general security. Moreover, since coerced religious beliefs had no value at all, the sovereign should not try to change them by force. If he did, the people had the right to disobey. 'Every man is obliged to worship his God in the way which he believes to be right... This right empowers men to refuse to engage in religious practices which they believe to be wrong.'[8] According to Dunn, the roots of Locke's later concerns can be detected here. 'The necessary autonomy of individual religious judgement had been proclaimed to the world of politics. The transposition of this theme from theology and epistemology to sociology and politics made each individual man the final judge of how far the society in which he lived had succeeded in avoiding force,... the avoidance of which was its sole end.'[9]

Locke's major works were all written and published rather late in his life. He is well known for *Essay Concerning Human Understanding* (1690), *Two Treatises of Government* (1690) and *Four Letters Concerning Toleration*, of which *Second Letter on Toleration* (1689) is most famous.

## PATERNAL AUTHORITY AND POLITICAL POWER

As students of political science, perhaps we can begin by looking more closely at *Two Treatises of Government*. This work was published anonymously in 1690 with the subheading 'In the former the false principles and foundation of Sir Robert Filmer and his followers are detected and overthrown', for the first treatise and 'the latter is an essay concerning the true original, extent and end of civil government' for the second.[10] According to Peter Laslett, Locke had already written 'Second Treatise', or at least most of it, by 1679–1680, but he decided to write and add 'First Treatise' in 1680, because it was only early that year that Filmer's famous *Patriarcha* was (re) published. Robert Filmer's earlier writings had been available since 1648, but his influence reached its zenith in the 1680s, with the publication of *Patriarcha, or the Natural Power of Kings* in 1680. In his work, Filmer justified the absolute power of contemporary kings as a paternal inheritance from Adam, the father of all mankind, and Locke's less read 'First Treatise' is a rebuttal of Filmer's arguments about a king's 'father-right' over his people. Having shown how Filmer's theory of the justification of political authority was erroneous, Locke proceeds, in 'Second Treatise', to construct his own theory of legitimate political authority.[11]

Locke begins his argument by stating clearly that paternal authority is not of the same kind, nor can it be justified on the same grounds, as political authority. A father's right of command over his children is based on the immaturity of the children, on their not being able to decide, when they are young, as to what is in their best interest. This 'non-age' is what allows a father's command to ignore issues of the children's consent. For Locke, 'the Freedom then of Man and Liberty of acting according to his own Will, is grounded on his having Reason.'[12] Since freedom is grounded in reason, and the human child becomes rational only at a certain age, until that time, the father can demand his children's obedience, for the sake of their own preservation. For Locke, like for Aristotle, since political authority, unlike paternal authority, is exercised over equals, it has to be based on consent. The people's consent, then, is the basis of all political power, which Locke defines thus at the end of the first chapter of *Second Treatise*. 'Political power then I take to be a Right of making Laws with penalties of Death, and consequently all less Penalties, for the Regulating and Preserving of Property, and of employing the force of the Community, in the Execution of such Laws, and in the defence of the Commonwealth from Foreign Injury, and all this only for the Public Good.'[13] Locke is defining political power as being made up of three types of power (see also Box 7.1). The power 'to make laws both to preserve and to regulate the lives, activities and possessions of subjects (legislative power)'; the power 'to use the force of the community to execute these laws with penalties of death and lesser penalties (executive power)'; and the power to wage wars to preserve the community, including colonies and subjects abroad, against other states (federative power)'.[14] If this is the definition of political power—the power to make laws, to execute them and to wage war—then for Locke, individuals already have political power, in the sense that political power originally lies in the hands of individuals. By making this claim, Locke distinguished himself not only from the 'natural subjection' theorists like Filmer, for whom 'political power resides naturally and originally in the monarch to whom lesser political bodies and all citizens are naturally subject',[15] but also from the 'natural freedom' position. Theorists in the tradition of natural freedom, like Hobbes and Grotius, believing that 'people are naturally free in the sense of not being subject to the will of another' gave these naturally free individuals the right to self-defence, but not to political power (the right to execute laws, for instance). For Grotius, political power 'immediately arises at the moment of constitution of government',[16] and it is not transferred to the government by the people. For Locke, on the other hand, 'political power is a natural property of individuals, who are capable of exercising it, and who, in fact, have the duty and right to exercise political power'. Tully calls this Lockean claim 'one of the major conceptual innovations in early modern political thought'[17]. So not only does Locke make political power different from paternal power, he also situates it originally in the hands of individuals, who can then consent to its transfer to a governmental institution.

Box 7.1

**ON THE DEFINITION OF POLITICAL POWER:**

Sect. 2. To this purpose, I think it may not be amiss, to set down what I take to be political power; that the power of a *magistrate* over a subject may be distinguished from that of a *father* over his children, a *master* over his servant, a *husband* over his wife, and a *lord* over his slave. All which distinct powers happening sometimes together in the same man, if he be considered under these different relations, it may help us to distinguish these powers one an--other and shew the difference betwixt a ruler of a commonwealth, a father of a family, and a captain of a galley.

Sect. 3. *Political power,* then, I take to be a *right* of making laws with penalties of death, and consequently all less penalties, for the regulating and preserving of property, and of employing the force of the community, in the execution of such laws, and in the defence of the common wealth from foreign injury; and all this only for the public good.

*Two Treatises of Government*, Chapter 1

## FREEDOM AND EQUALITY IN THE STATE OF NATURE

In order to explain his concept of political power, Locke uses the same devices as those used by the other social contract thinkers. Like Hobbes, for example, Locke too presents us with his concept of the state of nature and the social contract. The Lockean state of nature is a state of freedom and equality (see Box 7.2). The state of nature is 'a State of perfect Freedom to order their Actions, and dispose of their Possessions, and Persons as they think fit, within the bounds of the law of Nature. [It is] a State also of Equality, wherein all the Power and Jurisdiction is reciprocal, no one having more than another'.[18] The equality Locke finds in nature, denotes that in nature, everyone is equally free. Everyone is equally free to 'order their actions' and to exercise '(political) power and jurisdiction'. Since these equally free individuals already follow the law of nature in the state of nature, as well as have the power to execute the law of nature, the state of nature is peaceful with an orderly social interaction among its inhabitants. The state of nature is certainly not, as in the case of Hobbes, a state of war. Locke makes a sharp distinction between license and liberty, and defines liberty as doing what one wants as long as that is permitted by the law of nature. Locke writes that although the state of nature is 'a State of Liberty, yet it is not a State of License,... The State of Nature has a Law of Nature to govern it, which obliges every one: And Reason, which is that Law, teaches all Mankind, who will but consult it, that being all equal and independent, no one ought to harm another in his Life, Health, Liberty or Possessions'.[19] The equal freedom of individuals in the state of nature results in the existence, in the state of nature itself, of institutions like the family and society. Most men following the law of nature in the state of nature, 'here we have', Locke writes, 'the plain difference between the State of Nature, and the State of War', because the state of nature is 'a State of Peace, Good Will, Mutual Assistance, and Preservation'.[20] Several commentators have pointed out, that Locke's formulations here follow from his Christian theology. For Locke, all human beings are created by

**Box 7.2**

**ON LIBERTY AND EQUALITY IN THE STATE OF NATURE:**

Sect. 4. To understand political power right, and derive it from its original, we must consider, what state all men are naturally in, and that is, a *state of perfect freedom* to order their actions, and dispose of their possessions and persons, as they think fit, within the bounds of the law of nature, without asking leave, or depending upon the will of any other man.

A *state* also of wherein all the power and jurisdiction is reciprocal, no one having more than another; there being nothing more evident, than that the creatures of the same species and rank, promiscuously born to all the same advantages of nature, and the use of the same faculties, should also be equal one amongst another without subordination or subjection,...Sect. 6. But though this be a *state of liberty,* yet it is *not a state of licence:* though man in that state have an uncontrollable liberty to dispose of his person or possessions, yet he has not liberty to destroy himself, or so much as any creature in his possession, but where some nobler use than its bare preservation calls for it. The *state of nature* has a law of nature to govern it, which obliges every one: and reason, which is that law, teaches all mankind, who will but consult it, that being all *equal and independent,* no one ought to harm another in his life, health, liberty, or possessions: for men being all the workmanship of one omnipotent, and infinitely wise maker; all the servants of one sovereign master, sent into the world by his order, and about his business; they are his property, whose workmanship they are, made to last during his, not one another's pleasure: and being furnished with like faculties, sharing all in one community of nature, there cannot be supposed any such *subordination* among us, that may authorize us to destroy one another, as if we were made for one another's uses, as the inferior ranks of creatures are for our's. Every one, as he is *bound to preserve himself,* and not to quit his station wilfully, so by the like reason, when his own preservation comes not in competition, ought he, as much as he can, *to preserve the rest of mankind,* and may not, unless it be to do justice on an offender, take away, or impair the life, or what tends to the preservation of the life, the liberty, health, limb, or goods of another.

*Two Treatises of Government*, Chapter 2

God; they are his creatures made to serve his purposes. As his creatures, all humans have a duty to preserve themselves and others as well, if that does not conflict with their own preservation. We have no right to destroy ourselves, through, say, an act of suicide, because we belong to God. Moreover, Locke insists that we cannot consent to our own slavery because being a slave is inimical to our self preservation, and self preservation, while not so much a right, is a duty that we owe to God. As Waldron explains, 'Lockean self preservation is as much a duty as a right', and that 'what validates an individual's appetitive behaviour and his seeking for the satisfaction of any of his desires is not the bare fact that he has preferences which move him, but that his obtaining satisfaction of at least some of his desires is in accordance with God's purpose in creating him'.[21] We can preserve ourselves by making some of the common resources of nature into our own, and that leads Locke into a discussion of property, devoting all of Chapter 5 of *Second Treatise* to proving that a natural right to private property exists in the state of nature.

## PRIVATE PROPERTY IN THE STATE OF NATURE

Locke has to explain how has it come to pass, that given that nature and all its resources were given by God to mankind in common, there is private property in the world. Locke points out that although God gave nature to men in common, he also made each man the sole owner of all property in his own person (see Box 7.3). An individual's own body and the capabilities that flowed from that physical and mental being, for instance, the capability to labour, belonged to each individual alone. Since this was the case, therefore, when an individual mixed his labour with a common natural resource, for instance, when he plucked an apple from a

Box 7.3

**ON PROPERTY IN ONE'S OWN PERSON:**

Sect. 27. Though the earth, and all inferior creatures, be common to all men, yet every man has a *property* in his own *person:* this no body has any right to but himself. The *labour* of his body, and the *work* of his hands, we may say, are properly his. Whatsoever then he removes out of the state that nature hath provided, and left it in, he hath mixed his *labour* with, and joined to it something that is his own, and thereby makes it his *property.* It being by him removed from the common state nature hath placed it in, it hath by this *labour* something annexed to it, that excludes the common right of other men: for this *labour* being the unquestionable property of the labourer, no man but he can have a right to what that is once joined to, at least where there is enough, and as good, left in common for others.

*Two Treatises of Government,* Chapter 5

tree, that natural resource became his, that is, it became a form of private property.

So long as private property is a result of one's own labour, there does not seem to be much danger of there being much inequality in property ownership. Locke states clearly, that in the state of nature there are certain limitations on the right to private property. Apart from the limitation that only that property can be acquired which results from one's own labour, there is also the condition that one must acquire only that much property that one can use, and thereby does not spoil. For instance, one cannot pluck 100 apples if one needs 10. The third limitation, Locke states, is that one must 'leave as much and as good' for others. When it comes to acquiring land, for instance, Locke seems to say that one is not allowed to acquire all the fertile land while leaving only fallow land for others.

In the same chapter, however, Locke also shows us how all these limitations on the acquisition of property fall away. The labour limitation falls, because Locke says that the labour of a servant belongs to the employer of that servant. One can buy labour power, and by using this labour power, legitimately acquire large amounts of property. The spoilage limitation is done away with, with the invention of money, since property converted into the form of money does not spoil. Locke uses a productivity of labour argument to get rid of the third limitation. His claim is that if land and labour are the two factors needed for agricultural production, the contribution of land to that production is merely 10 per cent, while that of the labour is 90 per cent. So when one labours to acquire property, one is only increasing the stock of mankind.

Thus, Locke's explanation of the emergence of private property in the state of nature becomes a justification of severe inequalities of wealth in it. Obviously, Locke is not speaking of economic equality when he defines the state of nature as a state of equality. He says, quite clearly, that his reference to equality is not to equality in all its senses but only to political equality. 'Though I have said above, Chapter II, That all Men by Nature are equal, I cannot be supposed to understand all sorts of Equality...the Equality I there spoke of—being that equal Right that every Man hath, to his Natural Freedom, without being subjected to the Will or Authority of any other Man.'[22] Whether sharp inequalities in the ownership of private property in the state of nature will permit it to be a state of 'perfect freedom', or of political equality for those individuals who do not possess any or much property, is another matter.

## CIVIL/POLITICAL SOCIETY

Even though Locke distinguishes the state of nature from the state of war, he says that certain inconveniences in the state of nature persuade human beings to leave it. 'Thus Mankind, notwithstanding all the Privileges of the state of Nature, being but in an ill condition, while they remain in it, are quickly driven into Society.'[23] Locke lists three inconveniences in the state of nature (see Box 7.4): that 'there wants an established known law', 'there wants a known and impartial Judge' and that 'there wants the power to back and support the sentence when right and to give it due execution'. Perhaps it is also the disparities of wealth that make life in the state of nature inconvenient, although, Locke does not say so.

**Box 7.4**

**ON THE INCONVENIENCES OF THE STATE OF NATURE:**

Sect. 124. The great and *chief end,* therefore, of men's uniting into commonwealths, and putting themselves under government, *is the preservation of their property*. To which in the state of nature there are many things wanting.

—*First,* There wants an *established,* settled, known *law,* received and allowed by common consent to be the standard of right and wrong, and the common measure to decide all controversies between them: for though the law of nature be plain and intelligible to all rational creatures; yet men being biased by their interest, as well as ignorant for want of study of it, are not apt to allow of it as a law binding to them in the application of it to their particular cases.

Sect. 125. *Secondly,* In the state of nature there wants *a known and indifferent judge,* with authority to determine all differences according to the established law: for every one in that state being both judge and executioner of the law of nature, men being partial to themselves, passion and revenge is very apt to carry them too far, and with too much heat, in their own cases; as well as negligence, and unconcernedness, to make them too remiss in other men's.

Sect. 126. *Thirdly,* In the state of nature there often wants power to back and support the sentence when right, and to give it due *execution*. They who by any injustice offended, will seldom fail, where they are able, by force to make good their injustice; such resistance many times makes the punishment dangerous, and frequently destructive, to those who attempt it.

Sect. 127. Thus mankind, notwithstanding all the privileges of the state of nature, being but in an ill condition, while they remain in it, are quickly driven into society. Hence it comes to pass, that we seldom find any number of men live any time together in this state. The inconveniencies that they are therein exposed to, by the irregular and uncertain exercise of the power every man has of punishing the transgressions of others, make them take sanctuary under the established laws of government, and therein seek *the preservation of their property*.

*Two Treatises of Government*, Chapter 9

Individuals, therefore, decide to sign a social contract and set up a civil or political society. Locke uses the two terms 'civil society' and 'political society' interchangeably. Although society existed in the state of nature, the social contract creates a new civil/political society with a government, and the purpose of this creation is the preservation of the life, liberty and property of the members of this new civil/political society.

For Locke, liberty is a fence to one's life, because if one is not free then one's life is always in danger. Similarly, property is a fence to one's liberty, because if one is impecunious, then one has to depend on others, and is not able to take decisions independently. The relationship works the other way too. One's life is a fence to one's liberty and liberty is a fence to property. It is these connections which he draws between life, liberty and private property, which makes Locke announce the preservation of property as one of the main limits on the powers of the government.

## THE LIMITS ON GOVERNMENT

For Locke, the right to private property becomes one of the limitations on government. Any government, which encroaches on the individual's natural right to property, is an illegitimate government. The purpose of setting up a government, through the social contract and transiting from the state of nature, was to find a better way of protecting the rights to life, liberty and property. If the government goes against this foundational purpose, it can be overthrown and replaced by another.

For this reason, Locke has been accused of being a 'bourgeois' thinker by commentators such as Crawford B. Macpherson, who accuse Locke of setting up a government, the main purpose of which is the protection of private property.[24] Macpherson's claim has been contested by scholars like James Tully who point out that Locke clearly states—as we saw at the beginning of our discussion—that the purpose of government is to serve the public good. In order to fulfil this goal, the government will need to tax its citizens, and as long as this taxation is with the people's consent, it is legitimate. Here, Tully is making the point that taxation is an infringement of one's private property and Locke quite clearly allows taxation for the general good as long as the taxes are approved by a majority vote. Apart from that, Tully also points out that for Locke, the term 'property' had a much wider meaning than material possessions. 'Property' included a person's rights and liberties, civil as well as religious. The government had to protect the property of individuals in the sense of these rights.[25]

For some commentators, then, the valuable part in Locke's political theory is not his opinion on the defence of private property, but rather, his insistence on limited government. Primarily, the government is limited by the public good, and it is the people who decide whether governmental policy is beneficial for the public or not. The public good is composed of the life, liberty as well as property of the people. This is why Locke prohibits the government from imposing taxes on property without the consent of the people.

For Locke, when individuals sign the social contract and thus replace the state of nature with civil or political society, they make the legislature the supreme power in that civil/political society. It may be the supreme power, but the 'legislative' cannot go against 'the Law of Nature, the fundamental Law of Nature being the preservation of Mankind'. The preservation of the members of this newly created civil/political society requires the following four limits on the 'legislative':

> First, they are to govern by promulgated, established Laws, not to be varied in particular cases, but to have one rule for Rich and Poor, for the Favourite at Court, and the Country Man at Plough. Secondly, These Laws also ought to be designed for no other end ultimately but the good of the People. Thirdly, they must not raise Taxes on the Property of the People, without the Consent of the People, given by themselves, or their Deputies. Fourthly, the Legislative neither must nor can transfer the Power of making Laws to any body else, or place it anywhere but where the People have.[26]

The legislative being the highest power, it is still necessary, in all forms of government, for the executive to retain some discretionary powers. In Locke's time, these discretionary powers were known as the Prerogative of the monarch. 'This Power to act according to discretion, for the public good, without the prescription of the Law, and sometimes even against it, is that which is called Prerogative.'[27] Locke is quite clear that the preservation of the public good acts as a limit to the executive prerogative, just as it does on the powers of the legislative (see Box 7.5).

**Box 7.5**

**ON THE EXTENT OF THE POWER OF THE LEGISLATURE:**

Sect. 142. These are the *bounds* which the trust, that is put in them by the society, and the law of God and nature, have *set to the legislative power* of every commonwealth, in all forms of government.

- First, They are to govern by *promulgated established* laws, not to be varied in particular cases, but to have one rule for rich and poor, for the favourite at court, and the countryman at plough.
- Secondly, These laws also ought to be designed *for* no other end ultimately, but *the good of the people.*
- Thirdly, They must *not raise taxes* on the *property of the people, without the consent of the people,* given by themselves, or their deputies. And this properly concerns only such governments where the *legislative* is alw ays in being, or at least where the people have not reserved any part of the legislative to deputies, to be from time to time chosen by themselves.
- Fourthly, The *legislative* neither must *nor can transfer the power of making laws* to any body else, or place it any where, but where the people have.

*Two Treatises of Government*, Chapter 11.

## THE PHILOSOPHICAL AND RELIGIOUS BASIS OF LIMITED GOVERNMENT

Locke's advocacy of the idea of limited government can also be derived from his philosophical and religious presuppositions. According to Locke's epistemological theory, 'given the probable status of most knowledge claims…differences of opinion, even on the most important subjects, must be looked upon as an inherent feature of human action and the pursuit of knowledge.'[28] This would invalidate any defence of absolute government on grounds of its access to certain knowledge. Similarly, discussing the question of religious belief, Locke said that since 'the care of every man's soul is wholly his own responsibility, [and] he has an indispensable obligation to exercise his judgement with respect to matters of religion, his association with others in a particular church depends entirely upon his own personal consent.'[29] From the dictum that every man was responsible for the care of his own soul it followed, for Locke, that to compel individuals to follow a faith they did not believe in would be to damn them. 'God judges people on the sincerity, not the truth of their beliefs…to profess or act contrary to one's religious beliefs, even if the magistrate so orders, is now the paramount sin of hypocrisy and it would lead to eternal damnation.'[30] A policy of religious uniformity was therefore unacceptable because it was ungodly. Just as the idea, that all our beliefs are probable rather than certain, leads to the position that no absolute government had the authority to impose its beliefs, similarly, the idea that religious belief was a matter of personal judgement and integrity, led to the principle of toleration as a limit to the power of government.

It might be interesting to examine in greater detail, the religious dimensions of Locke's principle of limited government. We have already mentioned the conflict between the Catholic inclined Stuart monarchy, and the majority of the English people, who were Anglicans. This conflict had significant ramifications. In 1661–1662, the English Parliament passed the Clarendon Code which compelled uniformity to Anglican forms of worship and punished Presbyterians, Baptists, Quakers, Independents and Catholics as dissenters. The monarch, Charles II, tried to use his powers of prerogative to proclaim the Declaration of Indulgence to protect the dissenters. We see here an interesting connection between the institution of absolute monarchy and religious liberty. This means that the conflict to which Locke was responding in his writings, should not be constructed simply as a struggle between king and Parliament as the representative of the people; it was also a conflict between the majority of the people being represented by Parliament, and a minority of religious dissenters whom the king sought to protect. These religious dissenters, including not just Catholics but many Protestant Christian sects, had their property expropriated, and were often carted off and transported to the colonies. It has been said that it is Locke's writings on religious liberty that 'illuminate the property that the *Two Treatises* is written to defend. It is not the private property of the bourgeoisie, but the properties—the possessions and legal, political and religious rights—of an oppressed [religious] minority'.[31] This struggle over religious liberty also illuminates Locke's idea of limited government, for Locke saw that it was not the king, but Parliament which was encroaching upon the religious freedom of many. This made him conclude that all government, whether monarchical or parliamentary in form, needs to be limited.

Locke had written *Essay on Toleration* in 1667. He followed this up in 1685 with *A Letter Concerning Toleration*. In these writings, he argued against the uniformist position, that unless all the inhabitants of a kingdom believed in the same faith, there would be no civil peace. A policy imposing religious uniformity, he pointed out, would, in fact, lead to a sense of oppression among the dissenters. According to Locke, when people feel oppressed, they have a right to rebel. So it is not a policy of religious uniformity, but that of religious toleration that leads to civil peace. Of course, for Locke, this toleration extended only to all Protestant Christian sects. Locke did not stretch the principle of toleration to include atheists or Catholics, whose beliefs cannot limit the government's power to persecute them.

## THE RIGHT TO RESISTANCE

In the last two chapters of *Second Treatise*, namely, the chapter titled 'Tyranny' as well as the one titled 'Of the Dissolution of Government', Locke argues repeatedly for the right of the people to rebel against a government which fails in preserving their life, liberty and property. Noting the objection, that a political theory which gives so much importance to the right of resistance 'will unhinge and overturn all Polities, and instead of Government and Order, leave nothing but Anarchy and Confusion',[32] Locke constructs a detailed argument in his own defence. He begins by stating that a government or prince, acting against the interest of the people, puts 'himself into a State of War with his People',[33] and so the government/prince, is responsible for the disorder or anarchy, and not the resisting people.

Locke also points out, that if the people have grievances they will first try to get redress through legal means, and it is only when the government itself is breaking the law and acting illegally, and these arbitrary actions of the government affect a large mass of the people, do the people begin to resist. 'For till the mischief be grown general, and the ill designs of the

Rulers become visible, or their attempts sensible to the greater part, the People, who are more disposed to suffer, than right themselves by Resistance, are not apt to stir.'[34]

Finally, making a distinction between the dissolution of government and the dissolution of society, Locke states that when a government betrays the trust of the people, it stands dissolved. The dissolution of the government does not entail the dissolution of society and it is the society which chooses a new government (see Box 7.6). In Locke's own words, 'Whensoever the Legislative shall endeavour to grasp themselves, or put into the hands of any other an Absolute Power over the Lives, Liberties, and Estates of the People, by this breach of Trust, they forfeit the power, the People had put into their hands, and it devolves to the People, who have a Right to resume their original Liberty, and by the Establishment of a new Legislative, provide, for their own Safety and Security, which is the end for which they are in Society'.[35]

**Box 7.6**

**ON THE RIGHT OF THE PEOPLE TO CHANGE THEIR GOVERNMENT:**

The reason why men enter into society is the preservation of their property; and the end why they choose and authorize a legislative is that there may be laws made and rules set as guards and fences to the properties of all the members of the society to limit the power and moderate the dominion of every part and member of the society; for since it can never be supposed to be the will of the society that the legislative should have a power to destroy that which every one designs to secure by entering into society, and for which the people submitted themselves to legislators of their own making. Whenever the legislators endeavour to take away and destroy the property of the people, or to reduce them to slavery under arbitrary power, they put themselves into a state of war with the people who are thereupon absolved from any further obedience, and are left to the common refuge which God has provided for all men against force and violence. Whensoever, therefore, the legislative shall transgress this fundamental rule of society, and either by ambition, fear, folly, or corruption, endeavour to grasp themselves, or put into the hands of any other, an absolute power over the lives, liberties, and estates of the people, by this breach of trust, they forfeit the power the people had put into their hands for quite contrary ends, and it develops to the people, who have a right to resume their original liberty and, by the establishment of a new legislative, such as they shall think fit, provide for their own safety and security, which is the end for which they are in society.

*Two Treatises of Government*, Chapter 19

## THE LIMITS OF LOCKE'S LIBERALISM

Early critics of Locke like Crawford B. Macpherson, tended to focus on the issue of private property. For them, Locke's insistence on property as a natural right and his claim that the purpose of government was the preservation of property, pigeonholed him as a bourgeois thinker. Macpherson emphasized Locke's bourgeois refusal to allow the state to regulate inequalities of property ownership, and used this to cast doubt on Locke's democratic credentials. As a typically liberal thinker, Locke's political thought was seen as embodying all the weaknesses of liberal democracy.

The grounds of criticism of Locke have shifted somewhat from the days of Macpherson. The trope of 'possessive individualism' is no longer considered to be adequate for capturing the thought of any 17th century English thinker, including Locke, since the emergence of incipient capitalism, which this trope sought to capture, is now seen to be an 18th century phenomenon. As a 17th century writer, Locke's concerns were different. Criticism is focused now, not so much on Locke's concept of property, but on his concept of consent. For Locke, the legitimacy of the political power of the government was based on the people's consent. However, he is said to have built his theory only on ideas of hypothetical and tacit consent with no scope for real consent. Locke clearly states, that to use any of the facilities provided by the government, even to accept one's inheritance, is to imply one's consent to all the laws of the government one is living under. In this criticism, Locke's democratic credentials are questioned not through his concept of property, but through his concept of consent.[36]

Like the other social contractualists, Locke has also come under attack by feminists for supporting the subordination of women to men. In Locke too, the story of the social contract is said to hide the story of the sexual contract. Women are not seen as party to the social contract, yet they are seen as consenting to the prevailing sexual arrangements in order to justify their subordination. Ostensibly, Locke denounced patriarchalism, and the concept of the king as a paternal ruler. According to critics, however, under the cover of this denouement, he developed a theory of modern patriarchy by advocating rule of men over women.[37]

Whatever the shortcomings of his theory, Locke's writings served to draw up a picture of the central elements of a liberal polity. Whereas Locke's response to the political struggles of his day was to suggest the setting up of a liberal political system, this liberal solution was rejected by many subsequent political thinkers.

## NOTES

1. Richard Ashcraft, *Locke's* Two Treatises of Government, London: Allen and Unwin, 1987, p. 25.
2. See John Marshall, Chapter 2 in *John Locke: Resistance, Religion and Responsibility*, Cambridge: Cambridge University Press, 1994.
3. For a background on English politics of the time, and Locke's role in these political events, see Richard Ashcraft, *Revolutionary Politics and Locke's Two Treatises of Government*, Princeton: Princeton University Press, 1986.

4. John Locke, Chapter 2 in *Two Treatises of Government*, edited by Peter Laslett, Cambridge: Cambridge University Press, 1970.
5. Richard Ashcraft, *Locke's Two Treatises of Government*, p. 21.
6. John Dunn, Chapters 2–3 in *The Political Thought of John Locke: An Historical Account of the Argument of the 'Two Treatises of Government'*, Cambridge: Cambridge University Press, 1969.
7. *Ibid.*, p. 22.
8. *Ibid.*, p. 38.
9. *Ibid.*, p. 39.
10. John Locke, *Two Treatises of Government*, p. 134.
11. Although 'Second Treatise' was written before 'First Treatise', when the work was published, in 1690, it seemed as if *Second Treatise* was a logical continuation of *First Treatise*. See John Locke, *Two Treatises of Government*.
12. John Locke, *Two Treatises of Government*, p. 309.
13. *Ibid.*, p. 268.
14. James Tully, *An Approach to Political Philosophy: Locke in Contexts*, Cambridge: Cambridge University Press, 1993, p. 14.
15. *Ibid.*, p. 16.
16. *Ibid.*, p. 18.
17. *Ibid.*, p. 15.
18. John Locke, *Two Treatises of Government*, p. 269.
19. *Ibid.*, p. 271.
20. *Ibid.*, p. 280.
21. Jeremy Waldron, *God, Locke, and Equality: Christian Foundations in Locke's Political Thought*, Cambridge: Cambridge University Press, 2002, pp. 156–157.
22. John Locke, *Two Treatises of Government*, p. 304.
23. *Ibid.*, p. 352.
24. Crawford B. Macpherson, *The Political Theory of Possessive Individualism*, Oxford: Oxford University Press, 1962.
25. For Locke on property see James Tully, *A Discourse on Property: Locke in the Natural Law Tradition*, Cambridge: Cambridge University Press, 1979 and James Tully, *A Discourse on Property: John Locke and his Adversaries*, Cambridge: Cambridge University Press, 1980.
26. John Locke, *Two Treatises of Government*, p. 363.
27. *Ibid.*, p. 375.
28. Richard Ashcraft, *Locke's Two Treatises of Government*, p. 24.
29. *Ibid.*, p. 250.
30. James Tully, *An Approach to Political Philosophy: Locke in Contexts*, p. 53.
31. *Ibid.*, p. 59.
32. John Locke, *Two Treatises of Government*, p. 401.
33. *Ibid.*
34. John Locke, *Two Treatises of Government*, pp. 417–418.
35. *Ibid.*, pp. 412–413.
36. See C. Pateman, *The Sexual Contract*, Stanford: Stanford University Press, 1988.
37. See Chapter 4 in D. Coole, *Women in Political Theory*, Wheatsheaf, 1988.

## READING LIST

Ashcraft, Richard, *Locke's Two Treatises of Government*, London: Allen and Unwin, 1987.

Ashcraft, Richard, *Revolutionary Politics and Locke's Two Treatises of Government*, Princeton: Princeton University Press, 1986.

Dunn, John, *The Political Thought of John Locke: An Historical Account of the Argument of the 'Two Treatises of Government'*, Cambridge: Cambridge University Press, 1969.

Locke, John, *Two Treatises of Government*, edited by Peter Laslett, Cambridge: Cambridge University Press, 1970.

Macpherson, Crawford B., *The Political Theory of Possessive Individualism*, Oxford: Oxford University Press, 1962.

Marshall, John, *John Locke: Resistance, Religion and Responsibility*, Cambridge: Cambridge University Press, 1994.

Pateman, C., *The Sexual Contract*, Stanford: Stanford University Press, 1988.

Tully, James, *An Approach to Political Philosophy: Locke in Contexts*, Cambridge: Cambridge University Press, 1993.

Waldron, Jeremy, *God, Locke, and Equality: Christian Foundations in Locke's Political Thought*, Cambridge: Cambridge University Press, 2002.

## CENTRAL THEMES

1. **Natural rights and limited government:** For Locke, all human beings are born with certain rights. Since it is nature which gives us these rights and not society, it is the purpose of social and political institutions to safeguard these rights. Every government is limited by these rights in the sense that any government that encroaches on these rights is illegitimate. What do you think of this conception of natural rights as a limit to governmental power?
2. **The rights to life, liberty and property:** For Locke, the three rights to life, liberty and property are pre-conditions of each other; in his words, one's liberty is a 'fence' to one's property, and one's property is a 'fence' to one's liberty. But what happens when your right to property conflicts with someone else's right to life? Is Locke's idea of majority rule a way of resolving the question of the conflict between the rights of different individuals?
3. **Property:** How is Locke able to prove that every individual has a natural right to private property? Does Locke's conception of property substantiate the claim that he was a 'bourgeois' thinker? Is his conception of property defensible?
4. **A theory of resistance:** When the government betrays the trust of the people, the people have the right to rebel against such a government. To justify the people's right to overthrow the government is not to encourage political instability. How does Locke defend himself against the charge that his theory of resistance is not the same as a theory of political disorder?
5. **A theory of consent:** For Locke, as for all contractarian political philosophy, legitimate government is created by the consent of the people. How does Locke define consent? What are the different forms that this consent takes, for Locke? Why has Locke been accused of providing us merely with a theory of hypothetical consent?

EIGHT

# Rousseau (1712–1778): The General Will and Moral and Political Liberty

Rousseau may be the third thinker in the social contractarian triumvirate of Hobbes, Locke and himself, but he remains one of the first thinkers to offer us a strong critique of modern social and political institutions in the name of the modern values of equality, liberty and democracy. Rousseau's pulling down of modern institutions is not done in the name of, for example, their having overturned the natural order of hierarchy; instead, he shows us again and again their failure to match their promise of embodying equal and free rights for all. In a very important sense, Rousseau begins the counter tradition of questioning the progressiveness of modernity.

Jean Jacques Rousseau was born in Geneva, a republican city-state surrounded by large monarchical kingdoms. As a republic, Geneva had a general council which theoretically could be attended by all its eligible male heads of households. However, it has been estimated that in the middle of the 18th century, in a population of 25,000, no more than 1,500 citizens could vote in the general council. Real political power lay in the hands of the small council, a much smaller body of 20 members, all drawn from patrician families. The general council may not have enjoyed any real powers (it could not convene its own meetings, nor introduce any new legislation) but its existence crystallized the claim of the ordinary 'citizens' and the 'bourgeois' (that is, the urban citizens) to a greater share in political decision making. From 1707 to 1738, the conflict between the patrician faction and the citizens' lobby in Geneva often erupted into overt struggles. Rousseau was born in 1712, and growing up in a neighbourhood of Geneva 'largely populated by artisans and notorious as a centre of popular agitation',[1] he was familiar with the arguments for popular sovereignty. When Rousseau left Geneva, he took with him a dream of the possibility of democracy, which remained with him throughout his wanderings.

Rousseau's mother came from an upper-class family, while his father was a watchmaker. As his mother died within a week of Rousseau's birth, Rousseau was brought up by his father, who however, abandoned Geneva and his son when Rousseau turned 10. Rousseau was taken in by his mother's brother, and for the next few years he attended a reputed school with his cousin. The cousin, having completed his schooling, was sent off to begin his training as an army officer, whereas Rousseau was reminded that he had to earn his living and was apprenticed to an engraver, when he was 13. At 16, Rousseau had had enough and he ran away from his apprenticeship, converted to Catholicism, (thus forfeiting his Genevan citizenship) and began moving from one European city to another. He was like a vagabond, with no formal education or university training. Patronized by much older and richer women like Madame de Warens, whom he called *maman*, and Madame d'Epinay who provided him later with his pastoral retreat, Rousseau was self-taught and used his musical talents to establish himself in Paris. He also became friends with French *philosophes* like Diderot and d'Alembert and was soon contributing articles to their *Encyclopaedia*, as well as writing popular musical operas. In 1756, however, when he was at the height of his musical career, he left Paris, as if rejecting city life, and settled down in a cottage in the countryside, where he wrote such masterpieces as *Social Contract* and *Emile*. Both of these books were published in 1762, both were condemned by the French parliament, causing Rousseau to flee to Switzerland. He also spent a year in England under the protection of David Hume, but returned to France in 1767.[2]

Rousseau began writing his masterpieces in 1750, and in a spate of 12 years or so, he had written 'Discourse on the Arts and Sciences' (1750), 'Discourse on Inequality' (1755), the *Encyclopaedia* article titled 'Political Economy' (1755), *Emile* (1762), and *The Social Contract* (1762). His other political works include the *Constitution for Corsica* (1765) and an essay titled 'Government of Poland' (1771). Rousseau also wrote a number of autobiographical works, the most famous of which is *Confessions*, published posthumously, in two parts, in 1782–1789. In 1776, he wrote *Rousseau: Judge of Jean Jacques*, in which Rousseau analyses and 'judges' the work of a thinker called Rousseau, that is, himself. In 1776, he began *Reveries of the Solitary Walker*, a work which is divided into 10 'walks' during which the walker talks to himself. Disturbed by the banning of his books, much of Rousseau's autobiographical writings are actually a defence of his philosophical and political ideas.

## ROUSSEAU AND ROMANTICISM

Let us begin our discussion of Rousseau with an analysis of his first major piece, the 1750 'Discourse on the Arts and Sciences', which won the first prize of the Academy of Dijon. The Academy had decided on 'Whether the progress of the arts and sciences has contributed to the purifying of morals?' as the question posed for their annual essay competition and Rousseau's first discourse was an answer to this question. Rousseau begins 'Discourse on the Arts and Sciences' by seemingly setting up 'natural man' and 'rational man' as adversaries that is, by contrasting nature with man. 'It is a noble and beautiful spectacle to see man raising himself, so to speak, from nothing by his own exertions; dissipating by the light of reason, all the thick clouds in which he was, by nature enveloped; encompassing... with giant strides the vast extent of the universe; and, what is still grander and more wonderful, going back into himself, there to study man and get to know his own nature, his duties and his end.'[3] Philosophy, the sciences, the arts, literature—these seem to be the means by which man has raised himself, but Rousseau soon lets us know that his judgement on these is resoundingly negative: 'Our minds have been corrupted in proportion as the arts and sciences have improved', or, as he puts it later, 'the progress of the arts and sciences has added nothing to our real happiness; it has corrupted our morals.'[4]

Both the arts and sciences have contributed to the moral corruption of human beings. The arts and sciences were not to be praised as the fruits of civilization. If civilization was to be equated with the development of the arts and sciences, then it was civilization which was responsible for the fall of man. Rousseau states that it is not so much that he is against the arts and sciences, but that he is on the side of virtue. According to him, the cultivation of the arts and sciences has always been prejudicial to military and moral qualities. For Rousseau, this truth is a historical constant. Wherever the arts and sciences had reached a pinnacle, there morality had degenerated, and Rousseau cites the examples of Egypt, Athens, Rome and China to substantiate his claim. Rousseau goes so far as to show how each of the specific arts and sciences originated from a particular vice. Astronomy was born, he writes, of the vice of superstition, eloquence of flattery and ambition, geometry of avarice, physics of idle curiosity and moral philosophy of human pride.[5]

Not only are the arts and sciences antithetical to our morality, they are also opposed to our freedom. The arts and sciences are like flowers bedecking our chains; they are the illusion that makes us unaware of the unhappy position we are in. 'The arts, literature and the sciences, less despotic though perhaps more powerful, fling garlands of flowers over the chains which weigh them down. They stifle in men's breasts that sense of original liberty, [and] cause them to love their own slavery.'[6]

Rousseau's essay made him infamous. 'Discourse on the Arts and Sciences' elicited a large number of critical responses in which it was argued that he was completely mistaken about the simplicity of the early barbarians who were far crueller than us moderns. In his replies to these critics, the argument that Rousseau was to make in 'Discourse on Inequality' and *The Social Contract,* is prefigured. Rousseau's reply was that the culprit behind the corruption of human beings was wealth, private property and inequality. These were the causes of our moral turpitude, not so much the arts and the sciences.

## NATURAL DIFFERENCES AND SOCIAL INEQUALITIES

In his next well known essay, 'Discourse on Inequality', Rousseau develops this argument in much greater detail by sketching a picture of the history of mankind. Early man, Rousseau writes, lived an animal-like existence. He was a solitary creature, and his interactions with other human beings were episodic and casual, conducted for the purposes of a hunt, or to satisfy a sexual instinct. Early man had no fixed abode, and no continuous social interaction. 'Let us conclude then, that man in a state of nature, wandering up and down the forests, without industry, without speech, and without home, an equal stranger to all ties, neither standing in need of his fellow creatures, nor having any desire to hurt them, and perhaps not even distinguishing them one from another.'[7]

Here, Rousseau also presents us with his concept of human nature. At this stage in the life of the species, like other animals, man is also characterized by the two natural sentiments of self-love and pity. Every sentient being, Rousseau claims, shares these two emotions. Self-love is the interest every sentient being has in preserving itself, and pity, or compassion is the repugnance every such being feels at the suffering of another living being. Rousseau often gives the example of horses being unwilling to trample live bodies. Self-love, or *amour de soi* is not the same as *amour propre* which is an emotion akin to self-aggrandizement. *Amour propre* develops only in society. Rousseau mentions two characteristics which distinguish human beings from animals: free will and the capacity for self-improvement, which he calls 'perfectibility' (see Box 8.1). Not only did human beings have the capacity to determine their choices, they were also able to improve themselves. Rousseau believed that whereas 'Nature exercised an internal constraint upon animal behaviour', humans were 'capable of choice', 'because they could always satisfy natural impulses in a variety of ways, [for example] their flexible diet could comprise either fruit or meat, [they could not be said to be] bound by the instincts which impelled and controlled all other creatures.'[8] Because human nature is indeterminate, human beings could either improve themselves or become worse than before. This, for Rousseau, was the human faculty of self-improvement, which allowed human beings to have, unlike other animals, a history.

**Box 8.1**

**ON HUMAN AGENCY AND HUMAN PERFECTIBILITY:**

It is not, therefore, so much the understanding that constitutes the specific difference between the man and the brute, as the human quality of free-agency. Nature lays her commands on every animal, and the brute obeys her voice. Man receives the same impulsion, but at the same time knows himself at liberty to acquiesce or resist: and it is particularly in his consciousness of this liberty that the spirituality of his soul is displayed. For physics may explain, in some measure, the mechanism of the senses and the formation of ideas; but in the power of willing or rather of choosing, and in the feeling of this power, nothing is to be found but acts which are purely spiritual and wholly inexplicable by the laws of mechanism.

However, even if the difficulties attending all these questions should still leave room for difference in this respect between men and brutes, there is another very specific quality which distinguishes them, and which will admit of no dispute. This is the faculty of self-improvement, which, by the help of circumstances, gradually develops all the rest of our faculties, and is inherent in the species as in the individual: whereas a brute is, at the end of a few months, all he will ever be during his whole life, and his species, at the end of a thousand years, exactly what it was the first year of that thousand. Why is man alone liable to grow into a dotard? Is it not because he returns, in this, to his primitive state; and that, while the brute, which has acquired nothing and has therefore nothing to lose, still retains the force of instinct, man, who loses, by age or accident, all that his *perfectibility* had enabled him to gain, falls by this means lower than the brutes themselves? It would be melancholy, were we forced to admit that this distinctive and almost unlimited faculty is the source of all human misfortunes; that it is this which, in time, draws man out of his original state, in which he would have spent his days insensibly in peace and innocence; that it is this faculty, which, successively producing in different ages his discoveries and his errors, his vices and his virtues, makes him at length a tyrant both over himself and over nature.

*A Discourse upon the Origin and the Foundation of the Inequality Among Mankind*

Coming back to the process of human development, Rousseau points out, that gradually, these isolated and solitary human beings began some kind of settled and collective existence. Families formed and began to live together, and language developed. Rousseau terms this simple, rustic, communal life, the first revolution in the history of man, calling it the golden age of mankind. The invention of metallurgy and agriculture constituted, for Rousseau, the second revolution in the life of the human species. Rousseau states categorically that 'it was iron and corn, which first civilized men, and ruined humanity'.[9] Once human beings learned the skill of agriculture and especially, to make the same piece of land grow crops regularly, it became profitable to try to have sole possession of that land. This is how the concept of private property emerged.

Once private property was accepted, the distinction between the rich and poor emerged. Over time economic inequalities became extreme, the few rich families became afraid of the poor, who were more in number. In order to safeguard their property, the rich came up with the idea of government and law, and apparently impartial administrators who would, ostensibly, look after everybody's interests. This, according to Rousseau, was the original social contract, a trick played by the rich on the poor, because, as Rousseau points out, this government was not impartial. It pretended to be, but it actually looked after the interests of the rich against the poor.

The distinction between the rich and poor is the first term of inequality, the distinction between the government and governed is the second term of inequality and the distinction between the master and slave is the last and final term of inequality (see Box 8.2). Once government comes to be established, Rousseau argues, those in government use their political power to usurp everybody's rights, including those of the rich. Very few individuals become, as it were, the masters of the whole community. Once economic inequality is introduced, it will inexorably lead to this extreme political inequality of master and slave, in which situation, there will be a loss not only of natural equality, but also of natural liberty.

Ostensibly, Rousseau's purpose in writing the second discourse was to refute the suggestion that moral or political inequalities, like the inequalities of wealth and power, are related to natural differences, like the

**Box 8.2**

**ON THE FOUR KINDS OF SOCIAL INEQUALITY:**

If we follow the progress of inequality in these various revolutions, we shall find that the establishment of laws and of the right of property was its first term, the institution of magistracy the second, and the conversion of legitimate into arbitrary power the third and last; so that the condition of rich and poor was authorized by the first period; that of powerful and weak by the second; and only by the third that of master and slave, which is the last degree of inequality, and the term at which all the rest remain, when they have got so far, till the government is either entirely dissolved by new revolutions, or brought back again to legitimacy.

*A Discourse upon the Origin and the Foundation of the Inequality Among Mankind*

differences in age, bodily strength and wit (see Box 8.3). Whatever differences in bodily strength or wit there may be, and these are slight, they are of no significance in man's natural state. Whereas for Hobbes and Locke there is a natural equality among men, which is of great significance to what happens in the state of nature, for Rousseau, in the state of nature, men are naturally different from each other. This fact, however, has no significant bearing on their behaviour. These natural differences cannot be held responsible for the social and economic inequalities of society. It is only in society that these inequalities of wealth and power arise and Rousseau holds these social inequalities responsible for man's corruption. Again, while for the other contractarians, Hobbes and Locke, the transition from the state of nature is to a civil society, for Rousseau, the society created after the emergence of private property is not 'civil' at all; it is characterized, above all, by exploitative and antagonistic relations. No wonder, then, that Colletti calls Rousseau, Marx's precursor.[10]

**Box 8.3**

**ON NATURAL AND MORAL INEQUALITY:**

I conceive that there are two kinds of inequality among the human species; one, which I call natural or physical, because it is established by nature, and consists in a difference of age, health, bodily strength, and the qualities of the mind or of the soul: and another, which may be called moral or political inequality, because it depends on a kind of convention, and is established, or at least authorized by the consent of men. This latter consists of the different privileges, which some men enjoy to the prejudice of others; such as that of being more rich, more honoured, more powerful or even in a position to exact obedience.

It is useless to ask what is the source of natural inequality, because that question is answered by the simple definition of the word. Again, it is still more useless to inquire whether there is any essential connection between the two inequalities; for this would be only asking, in other words, whether those who command are necessarily better than those who obey, and if strength of body or of mind, wisdom or virtue are always found in particular individuals, in proportion to their power or wealth: a question fit perhaps to be discussed by slaves in the hearing of their masters, but highly unbecoming to reasonable and free men in search of the truth.

*A Discourse upon the Origin and the Foundations of the Inequality Among Mankind*

## SOCIAL INSTITUTIONS AND MORAL MAN

As we already pointed out earlier, prior to reason, man was characterized by the two sentiments of self-love and pity for other sentient beings. These pure emotions are corrupted in society. Society, characterized by inequality, becomes responsible not only for the corruption of human beings, but also for the lack of liberty in their lives. It is due to these views of Rousseau, that he is often associated with the slogan 'Back to Nature'. The early Rousseau, of the two discourses, seems to give us an extremely negative judgement on society and civilization. Is this judgement reiterated in *Emile*? In *Emile* in 1762, Rousseau, writes that, 'Everything is good as it comes from the hands of the Author of Nature; but everything degenerates in the hands of man.'[11] A little later, he laments that, 'All our wisdom consists in servile prejudices, all our customs are but servitude, worry and constraint. Civilized man is born, lives and dies in a state of slavery...and as long as he preserves the human form, he is fettered by our institutions.'[12]

*Emile,* interestingly enough, is a treatise on education. However, if Rousseau really had this contempt for human learning, then why would he write a work on education? By this time, Rousseau had come to the conclusion that education, organized along the right lines, would build on the strengths of our human nature instead of perverting it. Therefore, he advocates the education of Emile, in the countryside; close to nature, and away from the city. Emile is a child who is removed from his parents and sent away, with a tutor, to the countryside. The tutor ensures that the child has the freedom to move about freely in this natural and solitary environment, and keeps him away from any books till the age of 12. Rousseau thinks that the child should learn to reason for himself, on the basis of his experience and not because of what he learns from books. Between 12 and 15, the only book Emile is to be allowed access to, is *Robinson Crusoe*. During this time Emile is also to learn some basic manual skill or a useful art, like carpentry. As an adolescent, Emile naturally experiences a sexual urge which the tutor is to sublimate into 'friendship and the general sense of human community', by using the natural sentiment or pre-rational natural instinct of compassion. It is only when the boy has turned 15, that the tutor introduces him to the study of philosophy and religion. From playing in the lap of nature, when the student turns to metaphysics and religion, he acquires a sense of being part of the natural order. As a created natural order, nature has purposes or ends imbued in it, and with this realization, Emile comes to know himself as a moral being. Rousseau seems to be implying here 'a natural and painless transition from the study of Nature to the search for its author; and when the idea of God is acquired, as the most reasonable explanation of the cosmos, it follows that with the natural love of self, there will be associated a natural love of the Creator of the self and the universal order, of which the self feels itself to be an integral part...[then is born] an active conscience which, although it operates through feeling, does not supplant reason, but supplements it.'[13] As a moral being, Emile now has a conscience, which, for Rousseau, is based both on the sentiments and on reason.

It is at the end of this stage, by about the early twenties, that Emile learns that the order of which he is part, is also a social order, and that he has grown up not merely to be a man, but also a citizen. The individualism of Emile does not imply that men in general can find personal fulfilment outside society. 'Emile is not a primitive, but an artificially-produced natural man for an artificially-produced natural society.'[14]

Just as *Emile* is for a certain kind of education completing or perfecting our nature, similarly, is not *The Social Contract* about the rightly organized political society building on what nature already provides us with? In the state of nature, not only do we have free will, we also enjoy natural liberty, since 'no man has a natural authority over his fellow in the state of nature'. However, we have no moral liberty in the state of nature, because we have not yet developed a moral sense. This moral sense can only be born in society, and we need to establish a society in which, not only do we preserve the liberty of the state of nature, but also provide the conditions for us to achieve moral freedom. In place of a society in which a few rule over the many, human beings need to set up a society guaranteeing civil and moral freedom for all. Rousseau defined freedom thus: 'Obedience to a law which we prescribe to ourselves is liberty.'[15] Which kind of society, however, will establish such freedom?

Rousseau seems to suggest that human beings need to come together in society to achieve a better life, but he is also makes it clear that this society has to be organized on certain lines. As he puts it, 'The problem is to find a form of association which will defend and protect with the whole common force the person and goods of each associate, and in which each, while uniting himself with all, may still obey himself alone, and remain as free as before.'[16] Rousseau's solution to this problem is a social contract (see Box 8.4), which states that 'each of us puts his person and all his power in common under the supreme direction of the general will, and, in our corporate capacity, we receive each member as an indivisible part of the whole'.[17]

'At once, in place of the individual personality of each contracting party, this act of association creates a corporate and collective body....This public person, so formed by the union of all other persons,...now takes [the name] of Republic or body politic; it is called by its members "State" when passive, "Sovereign" when active, and "Power" when compared with others like itself. Those who are associated in it take collectively the name of people, and severally are called citizens, as sharing in the sovereign authority, and subjects, as being under the laws of the State.'[18]

In simpler terms, Rousseau's idea is to vest sovereignty with all the people signing the hypothetical contract, so that the same people are both the sovereign as well as the subjects. It is the people who collectively make the laws, and it is the same people who then obey these laws. Since,

**Box 8.4**

**ON THE SOCIAL CONTRACT AND THE CREATION OF THE BODY POLITIC:**

"The problem is to find a form of association which will defend and protect with the whole common force the person and goods of each associate, and in which each, while uniting himself with all, may still obey himself alone, and remain as free as before." This is the fundamental problem of which the *Social Contract* provides the solution.

The clauses of this contract are so determined by the nature of the act that the slightest modification would make them vain and ineffective; so that, although they have perhaps never been formally set forth, they are everywhere the same and everywhere tacitly admitted and recognized, until, on the violation of the social compact, each regains his original rights and resumes his natural liberty, while losing the conventional liberty in favour of which he renounced it.

These clauses, properly understood, may be reduced to one—the total alienation of each associate, together with all his rights, to the whole community; for, in the first place, as each gives himself absolutely, the conditions are the same for all; and, this being so, no one has any interest in making them burdensome to others.

Moreover, the alienation being without reserve, the union is as perfect as it can be, and no associate has anything more to demand: for, if the individuals retained certain rights, as there would be no common superior to decide between them and the public, each, being on one point his own judge, would ask to be so on all; the state of nature would thus continue, and the association would necessarily become inoperative or tyrannical.

Finally, each man, in giving himself to all, gives himself to nobody; and as there is no associate over whom he does not acquire the same right as he yields others over himself, he gains an equivalent for everything he loses, and an increase of force for the preservation of what he has.

If then we discard from the social compact what is not of its essence, we shall find that it reduces itself to the following terms:

*Each of us puts his person and all his power in common under the supreme direction of the general will, and, in our corporate capacity, we receive each member as an indivisible part of the whole.*

At once, in place of the individual personality of each contracting party, this act of association creates a moral and collective body, composed of as many members as the assembly contains votes, and receiving from this act its unity, its common identity, its life and its will. This public person, so formed by the union of all other persons, formerly took the name of *city*, and now takes that of *Republic* or *body politic*; it is called by its members *State* when passive, *Sovereign* when active, and *Power* when compared with others like itself. Those who are associated in it take collectively the name of *people*, and severally are called citizens, as sharing in the sovereign power, and *subjects*, as being under the laws of the State.

*The Social Contract*

according to Rousseau liberty is living according to self-prescribed rules, in civil society all the people are free, because they live as subjects under laws which they have framed themselves.

If we establish a society following these steps, we replace the natural liberty of the state of nature, with civil and moral liberty. These two kinds of liberty can only exist if sovereignty in civil society is vested, not simply in the people, but more specifically, in the general will of the people. Therefore, we now have to examine what one means by the term 'general will'.

## THE GENERAL WILL

Rousseau states that for the general will to be truly general, it must be general in its origin, in its object, in its form, and lastly, it can only exist if there is economic equality. The sovereign is only that general will which is general in its origin. This means that everyone must have a voice in the decision taken by the general will. Everyone, for instance, must have a vote by which he expresses his decision. This shows that Rousseau was critical of a representative democracy, where representatives vote in the place of the people. In such a case, it is not the general will which is sovereign, because representative democracy denies the principle that the general will must be general in its origin. Rousseau contemptuously claimed that the English people are free only for one day in five years: the day they vote, that is, the only day the general will is really general in its origin.

Next, Rousseau points out that the general will must be general in its object, that is, the people must be thinking about the common good when taking a decision (see Box 8.5). Even when the general will is general in its origin, that is, every adult member of the community has voted and expressed his decision, if these voters have voted in their own individual or private interest, or in the interest of some association less than the political community, then the collective decision cannot be said to be an expression of the general will. Such decisions can only be called the will of all, which, for Rousseau, is not the same as the general will. 'There is often a great deal of difference between the will of all and the general will—the latter considers only the common interest, while the former takes private interest into account, and is no more than a sum of particular wills.'[19]

This idea, that the general will requires more than the consent of everybody, is already prefigured in the second discourse, in Rousseau's rejection, of the original contract that the rich persuaded the poor to enter into. Mere consent or agreement is not enough to create the general will. In *The Social Contract*, Rousseau states that once a new political entity has been created in which the general will is sovereign, the question arises of the framing of laws, which will determine how individuals are to act. Rousseau presents this problem in the form of two contradictory propositions. He first states that 'the people, being subject to the laws, ought to be their author: the conditions of the society ought to be regulated solely by those who come together to form it',[20] but then goes on to ask, 'How can a blind multitude, which often does not know what it wills, because it rarely knows what is good for it, carry out for itself so great and difficult an enterprise as a system of legislation?'[21] Rousseau's solution to bringing together 'the idea of the will, and the idea that what is willed will be good and just',[22] is to introduce the person of the legislator as necessary for 'public enlightenment' leading to 'the union of understanding and will in the social body'. However, despite this, Rousseau insists that 'sovereignty cannot be attributed to the legislator and remains with the whole body of citizens'.[23] The source of the obligation to obey the law remains the will of the citizens. Political obligation is not derived from the goodness of the law. If the general will is to exist, it must then, be general both in its origin and in its object.

Box 8.5

**ON THE GENERAL WILL:**

There is often a great deal of difference between the will of all and the general will; the latter considers only the common interest, while the former takes private interest into account, and is no more than a sum of particular wills: but take away from these same wills the pluses and minuses that cancel one another, and the general will remains as the sum of the differences.

If, when the people, being furnished with adequate information, held its deliberations, the citizens had no communication one with another, the grand total of the small differences would always give the general will, and the decision would always be good. But when factions arise, and partial associations are formed at the expense of the great association, the will of each of these associations becomes general in relation to its members, while it remains particular in relation to the State: it may then be said that there are no longer as many votes as there are men, but only as many as there are associations. The differences become less numerous and give a less general result. Lastly, when one of these associations is so great as to prevail over all the rest, the result is no longer a sum of small differences, but a single difference; in this case there is no longer a general will, and the opinion which prevails is purely particular.

It is therefore essential, if the general will is to be able to express itself, that there should be no partial society within the State, and that each citizen should think only his own thoughts: which was indeed the sublime and unique system established by the great Lycurgus. But if there are partial societies, it is best to have as many as possible and to prevent them from being unequal, as was done by Solon, Numa and Servius.

*The Social Contract*

Another aspect of the general will is that it must also be general in its form. This means that the laws formulated by the general will must be in the form of general propositions without mentioning particular individuals. 'But when the whole people decrees for the whole people, it is considering only itself; and if a relation is then formed, it is between two aspects of the entire object, without there being any division of the whole. In that case the matter about which the decree is made is, like the decreeing will, general. This act is what I call a law.'[24]

Finally, the last condition is that of equality. It is important to remember that by equality Rousseau is referring to economic equality, without which, he states, social and political equality cannot exist. Remember also that for Rousseau the purpose of making the general will sovereign was to protect individual liberty and Rousseau writes explicitly that liberty cannot exist without equality. By equality, Rousseau says he does not mean that 'riches are to be absolutely identical for everybody [but] that, in respect of riches, no citizen shall ever be wealthy enough to buy another, and none poor enough to be forced to sell himself'.[25] Where there are such economic disparities, people naturally feel that there is no common interest and when taking their decision, begin to focus only on their particular interests. The general will cannot be arrived at, in such a situation. Rousseau, in *The Social Contract*, accepts the existence of private property, even though he had berated the emergence of private property as the source of inequality and other ensuing evils in the second discourse. But allowing for private property, Rousseau is nevertheless careful to specify a kind of agrarian economy made up of independent farmers owning small plots of land more or less equal in size.

Only, given such a general will, general in its object, origin and form, and existing in conditions of equality, can be given the attributes of sovereignty–its indivisibility, its inalienability, its infallibility and its absolute nature. It is to such a general will that the people alienate their rights, including their rights to life, liberty and property. Unlike Hobbes, Rousseau does not even allow the individuals entering civil society to retain their right to life against the sovereign; when the general will commands one of its members to put his life at risk, he has to do so. In Rousseau's words, when it is 'expedient for the State that you should die, he ought to die, because it is only on that condition that he has been living in security up to the present, and because his life is no longer a mere bounty of nature, but a gift made conditionally by the State'.[26] Unlike in Locke, Rousseau's sovereign is not limited, it is absolute and omnipotent. Rousseau seems to think that because it is the people in whom sovereignty is located, this absolute power vested in the sovereign, will not be detrimental to individual liberty. In fact, he is also famous for saying, that if an individual refuses to abide by the general will, he must be compelled to obey the general will, and in thus being forced, he is actually being forced to be free, because in following the general will, he is only following his own real will.

Like equality, another precondition for the existence of the general will, which Rousseau discusses elsewhere, is that the political community must overlap with a small culturally homogeneous society. In *Considerations on the Government of Poland*, written in 1772, Rousseau said that, a nation is 'unified by customs and character, not by regulations and laws but by the same kind of life and food and the common influence of climate'.[27] We know that Rousseau was a staunch democrat. The only kind of democracy that was acceptable to him, as a defender of individual liberty, was a form of direct democracy. Here, he was pointing to the link between democracy and another phenomenon: the phenomenon of nationalism. We can see in Rousseau, how nationalism rides piggyback on a concept of strong democracy. The assumption is that it will be easier for the general will to exist if the people are already united in terms of cultural factors like religion and language. As we see in Box 8.6, taking up the case of religion, Rousseau emphasizes the necessity of a civil religion where one's faith is more a matter of inculcating the sentiments that make one sociable and a good citizen.

Box 8.6

**ON CIVIL RELIGION:**

There is therefore a purely civil profession of faith of which the Sovereign should fix the articles, not exactly as religious dogmas, but as social sentiments without which a man cannot be a good citizen or a faithful subject. While it can compel no one to believe them, it can banish from the State whoever does not believe them—it can banish him, not for impiety, but as an anti-social being, incapable of truly loving the laws and justice, and of sacrificing, at need, his life to his duty. If any one, after publicly recognizing these dogmas, behaves as if he does not believe them, let him be punished by death: he has committed the worst of all crimes, that of lying before the law.

The dogmas of civil religion ought to be few, simple, and exactly worded, without explanation or commentary. The existence of a mighty, intelligent and beneficent Divinity, possessed of foresight and providence, the life to come, the happiness of the just, the punishment of the wicked, the sanctity of the social contract and the laws: these are its positive dogmas.

*The Social Contract*

## ROUSSEAU'S PARADOXES

As we said at the beginning of this chapter, it was Rousseau's purpose to show us how modern institutions had failed to live up to their own promise of democracy, liberty and equality. Rousseau has long been a favourite of democratic theorists who have argued, that while Hobbes and Locke were more interested in propagating liberal principles, it was only Rousseau who was a true believer in democracy. Rousseau showed up liberal democracy for the sham it was, and argued for its replacement by his model of democracy. Do the political institutions designed by Rousseau capture better our ideals of democracy, liberty and equality?

If you were reading Rousseau from a woman's perspective, your answer would surely be negative. Rousseau argues against liberal democracy, saying that a person's will cannot be represented by others, but in the case of women, he is all too willing to allow their interests to be represented by men. He argues for keeping women away from politics, because he is afraid that women will always put the interests of their families before that of the public's. Actually, Rousseau's ambivalence about nature also applies to his views about women, since he considered them to be closer to nature. We saw that Rousseau's early condemnation of reason in comparison to nature, slowly gave way to an advocacy of reason that was based on rather than divorced from the sentiments. By analogy, we find Rousseau arguing that women's role in the family is essential to the upbringing of young male citizens, because it is their mothers who teach them the sentiments of sympathy and love. For the same reason, however, Rousseau denies women entry into the public sphere. He believes that a woman's love is always directed toward a particular (for example, a member of her family); it cannot transcend particulars for the general. For this reason, he is able to ignore the fact that none of his strictures for guaranteeing equality and liberty for all citizens apply to the position of women, and for this he has been castigated by many women, beginning with Mary Wollstonecraft, who had this to say about him: 'The rights of humanity have thus been confined to the male line from Adam downwards. Rousseau would carry his male aristocracy still further [as he] proceeds to prove that woman ought to be weak and passive, because she has less bodily strength than man; and hence infers, that she was formed to please and to be subject to him; and that it is her duty to render herself agreeable to her master.'[28]

Another problem, which is more general, arises from Rousseau's insistence on the absolute sovereignty of the people. When the people act collectively as the sovereign, no individual member of this collectivity has any rights against them. Even if we keep all of Rousseau's safeguards in mind—for instance, only that general will is absolute which is general both in its origin and its object—we are left with a sense of uneasiness. It is probably possible to ensure the first safeguard, although as we just pointed out, Rousseau himself forgot his principle of the generality of origin in the case of women. How do we ensure, however, that every member of the general will keeps the general interest in mind when taking a decision on any particular issue? Even if we could visualize societies which were much more egalitarian than the ones we are familiar with today, our experience of deep divisions within most societies makes it difficult to accept Rousseau's faith in an identifiable common interest. In that case, we might need to come up with some other democratic mechanism rather than vesting absolute sovereignty in the people. It is because of this, that in spite of his reputation as a democrat, there are critics of Rousseau who accuse his theory of the general will of having totalitarian consequences. Actually, this notion, that in a democracy, while the government may be limited, the people's sovereignty cannot be bound, is still very much alive today, and is widely debated by the constitutionalists and the democrats.

For Rousseau, freedom was an inalienable right, but we could be forced to be free; reason was unnatural and artificial but without reason we could not be moral; cosmopolitanism was a virtue but democracy required nationalism. Rousseau's writings seemingly contain a plethora of paradoxes. Do these paradoxes result from Rousseau's rejection of many features of modernity while at the same time holding on to the modern ideas of equality and liberty? Is it these paradoxes that are responsible for the fascination of Rousseau's writings, while at the same time opening up these writings to wildly divergent interpretations?

## THE SOCIAL CONTRACT TRADITION

'The 17th and 18th centuries are commonly and accurately represented as the great age of social contract theory: the still popular doctrine that political legitimacy, political authority, and political obligation are derived from the consent of those who create a government.'[29] For all the differences between them, Hobbes, Locke and Rousseau belong to the same contractarian tradition, because each of them saw the origin of political authority as lying in a contract. For each of them, the basis of political authority was the consent of those over whom this political authority was exercised. This was the only way that political authority could be made compatible with the natural equality and freedom of individuals. Through these propositions, the contractarians strengthened a new way of thinking about the ends and basis of political authority.

Of course, each social contract thinker had, as we have already seen, his own theory of the interaction between naturally free and equal individuals. For Hobbes, this interaction between human beings as bundles of appetites and aversions represented a 'state of war'. Hobbes believed that there could never emerge a voluntary consensus on good and bad or right and wrong in the state of nature. For Locke, equal and free individuals lived peacefully in a state of nature where the laws of nature were not only followed for the most part, but their infringement could also be punished.

Locke's state of nature is 'a divinely created order expressing the purposes of its Creator; the laws of nature articulate these purposes to human beings as rationally intelligible authoritative commands'.[30] Rousseau, on the other hand, traced the evolution of isolated, almost animal-like human beings, characterized by self-love, pity and perfectibility, into first societies. Beginning from different conceptions of how equal and free individuals originally lived with each other, the social contract thinkers have presented us with three different forms of the social contract and of the consequences of that social contract.

For Hobbes, the social contract transforms a multitude into one person, which he calls the State. At the same time, the contract also establishes the individual or the body of men who represent the persona of the State. For Locke, the contract creates a new political community which then entrusts the legislature and the government with the representation of its interests. Rousseau also differentiates between the establishment of the political community and the setting up of the government. Hobbes and Rousseau, however, present a picture of an absolute and indivisible sovereignty while Locke limits the power of the sovereign legislative in many different ways.

Political authority, having originated in the consent of naturally free and equal individuals, is meant to safeguard this freedom and equality of individuals. Why would these individuals consent to the establishment of a government, with the attendant loss of equality and freedom (government, by definition, has more power than any individual, and can curtail individual liberty through its laws and officials), unless they expect that in spite of this loss, government will somehow be beneficial for individuals. Defining freedom as the absence of external impediments, Hobbes expects the sovereign established by the social contract to set up a minimal state with just a few essential laws, thereby not interfering with the freedom of individuals in the economic, educational and other private spheres. For Locke, liberty is not license and therefore, liberty does not exist only in the absence of the law. There are, according to Locke, some things which individuals are not free to do, and therefore, liberty has to exist within the bounds of the law. For Rousseau, the idea of freedom has a strong moral component and he contrasts the moral and civil liberty of civil society to natural liberty which is devoid of morality. This moral and civil liberty exists when one follows the laws formed by the general will.

The purpose of the state being to safeguard the life and liberty of its members, that state which goes against this purpose becomes illegitimate, and can, according to Locke, be resisted. Locke not only places limits on the supreme legislative power of the state, but gives the people a collective right to resistance if these limits are crossed. Hobbes, on the other hand, while allowing each individual to protect his life, even against the commands of the sovereign, expressly forbids anyone to help protect an individual from the sovereign. In effect, then, he leaves each individual helpless against the might of the sovereign. For Rousseau, the sovereign being the general will of the people, the people as separate individuals have no right to resist this general will.

The social contract tradition of political thought was a way of understanding and supporting the new political practices of the 17th and 18th centuries. The modern state would continue to be the main object of analysis, with the relationship between individual freedom and the modern state being analysed in still different ways.

## NOTES

1. James Miller, *Rousseau: Dreamer of Democracy,* New Haven: Yale University Press, 1984, p. 18.
2. For biographical details about Rousseau, see Robert Wokler, *Rousseau: A Very Short Introduction* Oxford, Oxford University Press, First Indian edition, 2006.
3. Jean-Jacques Rousseau, *The Social Contract and Discourses,* translated by G. D. H. Cole, London: J. M. Dent and Sons, 1973, p. 4.
4. *Ibid.*, p. 7, 24.
5. *Ibid.*, p. 14.
6. *Ibid.*, pp. 4–5.
7. *Ibid.*, p. 72.
8. Robert Wokler, *Rousseau: A Very Short Introduction*, pp. 55–56.
9. Jean-Jacques Rousseau, *The Social Contract and Discourses*, p. 83.
10. See Part III in Lucio Colletti, *From Rousseau to Lenin: Studies in Ideology and Society,* New Delhi: Oxford University Press, 1978.
11. Jean-Jacques Rousseau, *Emile: General Principles of Education*, p. 158.
12. *Ibid.*, p. 162.
13. Jack H. Broome, *Rousseau: A Study of His Thought*, London: E. Arnold, 1963, p. 95.
14. *Ibid.*, p. 104.
15. Jean-Jacques Rousseau, *The Social Contract and Discourses*, p. 178.
16. *Ibid.*, p. 174.
17. *Ibid.*, p. 175.
18. *Ibid.*
19. Jean-Jacques Rousseau, *The Social Contract and Discourses*, p. 185.
20. *Ibid.*, p. 193.
21. *Ibid.*
22. See Patrick Riley, Chapter 4 in *Will and Political Legitimacy*, Cambridge: Harvard University Press, 1982.
23. Roger D. Masters, *The Political Philosophy of Rousseau,* Princeton: Princeton University Press, 1968, p. 355.
24. Jean-Jacques Rousseau, *The Social Contract and Discourses*, p. 192.
25. *Ibid.*, p. 204.

26. *Ibid.*, p. 189.
27. Jean-Jacques Rousseau, *Considerations on the Government of Poland and on Its Proposed Reformation*, April 1772.
28. Mary Wollstonecraft, *A Vindication for the Rights of Woman*, New York: Dover Publications, 1996, pp. 89, 79.
29. Patrick Riley, *Will and Political Legitimacy*, p. 1.
30. John Dunn, *Rethinking Modern Political Theory*, Cambridge: Cambridge University Press, 1985, p. 49.

## READING LIST

Broome, Jack H., *Rousseau: A Study of His Thought*, London: E. Arnold, 1963.

Colletti, Lucio, *From Rousseau to Lenin: Studies in Ideology and Society*, New Delhi: Oxford University Press, 1978.

Masters, Roger D., *The Political Philosophy of Rousseau*, Princeton: Princeton University Press, 1968.

Miller, James, *Rousseau: Dreamer of Democracy*, New Haven: Yale University Press, 1984.

Riley, Patrick, *Will and Political Legitimacy*, Cambridge: Harvard University Press, 1982.

Rousseau, Jean-Jacques, *The Social Contract and Discourses*, translated by G. D. H. Cole, London: J. M. Dent and Sons, 1973.

Wollstonecraft, Mary, *A Vindication for the Rights of Woman*, New York: Dover Publications, 1996.

## CENTRAL THEMES

1. **Nature as 'pure' and society as 'corrupt':** Rousseau's early writings put the blame for man's corrupt nature—his selfishness, his self-aggrandizement, his pleasure at the suffering of others—on society's door. In the state of nature, man's nature did not have the above attributes. Anything that needs society for its development—the arts and sciences, for example, even reason, is criticized by Rousseau in his early work as antithetical to human well being. What do you think of this conception of the downfall of the 'noble savage' in Rousseau's early work?
2. **Equality and liberty:** Rousseau justifies the transition to the democratic political community in the name of freedom, with natural freedom being replaced by moral and political freedom. This liberty cannot exist in the absence of social, economic and political equality. What is Rousseau's conception of equality and how does he relate it to liberty?
3. **The general will and the will of all:** Rousseau makes much of the difference between the general will and the will of all, and sets down stringent conditions for the existence of the general will. What do you think of the role played by the concept of the general will in Rousseau's theory of direct democracy?

4. **Women and nature:** We could say that a novel feature of modern thought is its emphasis on the break between the natural world and the human world. The human world is constructed through a withdrawal, in some sense, from nature. Rousseau is one thinker who stresses this break from nature as well as harps on taking nature as our guide. How does Rousseau use the relationship he constructs between women and nature to define women's relationship to politics?

# NINE

# Jeremy Bentham (1748–1832): Representative Government as the Maximizer of Utility

Jeremy Bentham was born in 1748, in London, in the family of a wealthy and successful English attorney. He was a precocious child, reading Latin when he was three years old, and Locke's difficult philosophical works before he hit his teens. At 12, he was already enrolled at Oxford University. After an Oxford education at Queen's College where he did both his B.A. and M.A. (1760–1766), Bentham began attending the London law courts. He was called to the bar in 1769, although he never practised as a lawyer. In those days, the only way for would-be lawyers to learn about law was by attending court proceedings. It was Bentham's good fortune that for the last few years, the University of Oxford had been organizing a series of lectures by William Blackstone, the English jurist and professor of law. Bentham attended these lectures in 1763, and when Blackstone began publishing his lectures as *Commentaries on the Laws of England* in 1765, Bentham created quite a stir by writing an extremely critical commentary on a few introductory paragraphs of this work, poking fun at Blackstone's 'antipathy to reformation'. Once he began, Bentham never seemed to stop writing, although most of his writings were fragmentary. It was his friend, Etienne Dumont, a Genevan, who translated them into French and published his writings in a book form as *A Theory of Legislation* in 1802. This work became available to Bentham's countrymen only when it was translated back into English in the 1820s. Among the writings of Bentham published originally in English, are *A Fragment on Government* (1776), *Introduction to the Principles of Morals and Legislation* (1789), *Plan of Parliamentary Reform* (1817), *Bentham's Radical Reform Bill* (1819) and the *Constitutional Code* (1830). The *Constitutional Code* was supposed to be his magnum opus, and he had planned it as a three-volume work. However, he was able to publish only the first volume in his lifetime.

Bentham was never a practising lawyer, and he saw himself as more of a legal reformer. Most of his works were written with the purpose of bringing about legal and political change in Britain. He even went to Russia, in 1785, as an adviser to Catherine the Great and spent three years there. Back home, in the 1790s, he entered into a contract with the British government to undertake prison reform and as a part of this reform, to design and build a structure called the Panopticon. The Panopticon, according to Bentham, would be an ideal prison. Extremely disappointed when this project fell through, he turned to the reform of political institutions. In the 1820s, when he was in his 70s, his motivation to write such an ambitious work like *Constitutional Code,* came from the hope that its proposals would be adopted by the new liberal governments of Spain and Portugal. When that hope dimmed, Bentham planned to write some legal codes for Greece and he even went so far as to send an early draft of *Constitutional Code* to Greece in 1823–1824. When that project also fell through, he 'was still hopeful that one of the new states of Latin America would adopt it'.[1] Much of Bentham's work was done in association with James Mill, whom he first met in 1808 and who was to become his lifelong associate. With him, Bentham set up *The Westminster Review* in 1824, a journal devoted to the philosophy of utilitarianism. Bentham died in 1832 when the struggle for Parliamentary reform in England was on.

Bentham was the inspiration behind a group of intellectuals in England known as the Philosophical Radicals. This group believed, with Bentham, that societies could be reformed and improved with the help of philosophical knowledge; that the way forward was not to rely on inherited experience or on customary law, but to use one's reason to judge existing social and legal institutions. We live in an age in which 'knowledge is rapidly advancing towards perfection… Correspondent to discovery and improvement in the natural world, is reformation in the moral'.[2] Here, we find a classic formulation of the concept of a knowledge-based society. Unlike Burke, Bentham was a supporter of the French revolution, and his frame of mind has been called typically French. 'Like the revolutionists across the Channel, he is a rationalist in thought and radical in conduct [for whom] the present is not continuous, but only contiguous, with the past. At any moment we can break with what has gone before and reorganize the world *ab initio* in accordance with our enlightened, carefully thought-out plan'.[3] In Bentham's case, this plan was based on the principle of utility. We need to, therefore, examine his philosophy of utilitarianism and show the links between his political philosophy and his utilitarianism. Bentham acknowledged his debt to Hume, Helvetius and Priestley in developing his own philosophy of utilitarianism. From Hume and Helvetius he said he got the idea of utility, and from Priestley the idea of the good and happiness of the majority of the members of any society.[4]

## UTILITARIAN PRINCIPLES

Bentham began the first chapter of *The Principles of Morals and Legislation* thus:

> Nature has placed mankind under the governance of two sovereign masters, pain and pleasure. It is for them alone to point out what we ought to do, as well to determine what we shall do. On the one hand the standard of right and wrong, on the other the chain of causes and effects, are fastened to their throne. They govern us in all we do, in all we say, in all we think…a man may pretend to abjure their empire: but in reality he will remain subject to it all the while. The principle of utility recognizes this subjection, and assumes it for the foundation of that system, the object of which is to rear the fabric of felicity by the hands of reason and of law.[5]

For Bentham, utilitarianism was both a descriptive and normative theory. It not only described how human beings act so as to maximize pleasure and minimize pain, but it also prescribed or advocated such action. According to the principle of utility (or, the 'greatest happiness' principle, or, the 'felicity' principle), the cause of all human action, that which motivates human beings to act, is a desire for pleasure. Utility or happiness is defined in terms of pleasure. A thing or action is useful if it brings about happiness, that is, pleasure. 'By utility is meant that property in any object, whereby it tends to produce benefit, advantage, pleasure, good or happiness.'[6] A person's interest also has the same content: pleasure. 'A thing is said to promote the interest, or to be for the interest, of an individual, when it tends to add to the sum total of his pleasures: or, what comes to the same thing, to diminish the sum total of his pains.'[7]

For Bentham, pleasure and pain are the primary sensations experienced by human beings. 'Pleasures and pains are basic to our phenomenal experience and are commonly experienced by everyone.'[8] Bentham believed that sensations being the 'original mental entities', ideas are simply 'the subsequent mental copies of sensations, fainter than the originals but available to experience even when the originals are no longer present'.[9] With sensations being basically of three kinds—pleasant, painful and indifferent—pleasant and painful sensations have stronger associations and leave a more lasting impression on us, and the ideas that they engender also stay with us longer.

In *The Principles of Morals and Legislation*, Bentham listed 14 kinds of simple pleasures that move human beings, including the pleasures of sense, wealth, skill, a good name, power, benevolence, malevolence, memory, imagination and of relief. Diminishing pain also means more pleasure. There are twelve kinds of pain which individuals seek to avoid like, the pain of privation, of the senses, of enmity or of an ill name, of benevolence and of malevolence. These simple pleasures and pains can combine to form compound ones.[10]

It is these pleasures and pains that determine all our actions. 'Directly or indirectly, well-being, in some shape or other, is the subject of every thought, and object of every action, on the part of every known Being, who is, at the same time a sensitive and thinking Being... This being admitted, Eudaemonics,...may be said to be the object of every branch of art, and the subject of every branch of science. Eudaemonics, [is] the art, which has for the object of its endeavours, to contribute in some way or other to the attainment of well-being.'[11]

The science of utility maximization, Eudaemonics, is a kind of master science. For Bentham, all our efforts to gain knowledge are to be directed to the knowledge of how to increase our well-being. The claim to attention of any knowledge, however consummate it may be, lies in its use for the augmentation of happiness. All branches of knowledge are part of Eudaemonics and knowledge is of no value if it cannot be used to promote happiness. 'But except in so far as in some shape or other it leads to and is productive of well-being—a balance on the side of happiness—what is the value of all the knowledge in the world? Just nothing.'[12]

Just as Bentham links knowledge with well-being, similarly, he couples morality with the idea of happiness. Not only do individuals seek to maximize their pleasure and minimize their pain, but they also use the evaluative terms of good and bad to name those activities which bring them pleasure or pain. Now this is a position as old as Hobbes, with the crucial difference being that every individual's goal is no longer to maximize his own pleasure and minimize his own pain, but rather, to maximize the total amount of pleasure and minimize the total amount of pain generated by his action. In order to calculate this, he has to take into consideration the effect of his action on the pleasure and pain of relevant others. We can, here, see the difference in the Hobbesian and the utilitarian position on happiness. The Hobbesian individual does not bother about the pleasant and painful sensations of others, and we have seen many commentators claim the lack of a sense of moral obligation in Hobbes. For Hobbes, what is moral or good for an individual is what makes him happy. In the utilitarian position, when it is said that 'the sole evidence it is possible to produce that anything is desirable, is that people actually do desire it', what is meant is that which is moral, or good, or desirable, is that which increases the happiness of the maximum number of individuals, not just of one individual. One has to be oriented not merely towards one's own happiness, but the happiness of others as well, when deciding what one should do. In fact, it is essential that one not give more weight to one's own pleasure than to the pleasure of others.[13] What is new with Bentham and his claim of utilitarianism being a moral theory, is the advocacy of such action. As early as 1776, in the preface to *A Fragment on Government*, Bentham writes, 'it is the greatest happiness of the greatest number that is the measure of right and wrong'.[14]

This is how Bentham answers the question of what is so moral about an individual seeking his pleasure. His defence against the charge of utilitarianism being, instead of a theory of morality, a theory actually of selfish psychological hedonism, is that utilitarianism does not propose that one seek only one's own pleasure. In deciding in what manner to act, one has to be impartial between one's own pleasure and that of all those affected by that act. If all happiness is either that happiness of the agent himself or the happiness of others, then we can clearly show that utilitarianism is also concerned with the happiness of others. Let us take the example of punishment. If punishment is to have some utility, and to have utility is to generate happiness then punishment is obviously not going to make the person who is being punished, happy. It will instead, make others happy by making it less probable that the crime is committed again. It is true, that for Bentham, the community is a fictitious entity; nothing more than the individual members constituting it. 'The community is a fictitious body, composed of the individual persons who are considered as constituting as it were its members. The interest of the community then is…the sum of the interests of the several members who compose it.'[15] It remains true, however, that the interests (happiness) of others are to count as much as the interest of oneself.

The context of one's action determines the circle of individuals affected by it. For government officials, all the members of their political community are affected by their action, so the government has to calculate the balance of pleasure and pain on a countrywide scale. A private individual has only to consider the pleasures and pains of those few directly affected by his action. The government is concerned about the happiness or welfare of all its citizens, and the individual is to think of the happiness of others as well, apart from himself. This is how utilitarianism is a moral theory.

Bentham also provided a calculus for determining the balance between pleasure and pain gained from any action. According to this felicific calculus (see Box 9.1), one must give a numerical value to the intensity, duration, certainty or uncertainty, and propinquity or remoteness of the pleasures and pains of the persons affected by one's actions, and one must undertake the action only if the value of the pleasure is higher than the value of the pain. One should also factor in the fecundity (the chance it has of being followed by sensations of the same kind) of the pleasure producing act, as well as the purity (the chance it has of not being followed by sensations of the opposite kind) and extent (the number of persons to whom it extends) of the pleasure being produced. By thus suggesting a procedure for the empirical measurement of the sum total of pleasure, Bentham felt that he had provided an objective basis for moral claims.

Box 9.1

**THE MEASUREMENT OF PLEASURE AND PAIN:**

Pleasures then, and the avoidance of pains, are the *ends* that the legislator has in view; it behoves him therefore to understand their *value*. Pleasures and pains are the instruments he has to work with: it behoves him therefore to understand their force, which is again, in other words, their value.

To a person considered by *himself*, the value of a pleasure or pain considered by *itself*, will be greater or less, according to the four following *circumstances*:

1. Its *intensity*.
2. Its *duration*.
3. Its *certainty or uncertainty*.
4. Its *propinquity* or *remoteness*.
   These are the circumstances which are to be considered in estimating a pleasure or a pain considered each of them by itself. But when the value of any pleasure or pain is considered for the purpose of estimating the tendency of any act by which it is produced, there are two other circumstances to be taken into the account; these are,
5. Its *fecundity*, or the chance it has of being followed by sensations of the same kind: that is, pleasures, if it be a pleasure: pains, if it be a pain.
6. Its *purity*, or the chance it has of not being followed by sensations of the *opposite* kind: that is, pains, if it be a pleasure: pleasures, if it be a pain.

These two last, however, are in strictness scarcely to be deemed properties of the pleasure or the pain itself; they are not, therefore, in strictness to be taken into the account of the value of that pleasure or that pain. They are in strictness to be deemed properties only of the act, or other event, by which such pleasure or pain has been produced; and accordingly are only to be taken into the account of the tendency of such act or such event.

To a *number* of persons, with reference to each of whom to the value of a pleasure or a pain is considered, it will be greater or less, according to seven circumstances: to wit, the six preceding ones; viz.,

1. Its *intensity*.
2. Its *duration*.
3. Its *certainty* or *uncertainty*.
4. Its *propinquity* or *remoteness*.
5. Its *fecundity*.
6. Its *purity*.
   And one other; to wit:
7. Its *extent*; that is, the number of persons to whom it *extends*; or (in other words) who are affected by it.

*An Introduction to the Principles of Morals and Legislation*, Chapter IV

In calculating pleasure and pain, one must be careful to abstract from the object which is the source of the pleasure or pain, as well as from the person whose pleasure or pain is being calculated. This means that the pleasures of a philosopher are not to count for more than the pleasures of an illiterate person. Every one is to count as one, and the pleasure from a worthwhile activity like writing a history of Egypt is not by definition of higher value than that from gambling with a deck of cards. We find it difficult to accept this principle, because the thing or activity that gives us pleasure becomes associated in our mind with that pleasure, and we begin to believe that it is the thing or activity that is valuable to us, and not the pleasure. But for Bentham, when 'a pleasure or pain becomes attached to other sensations or ideas, it remains a distinct mental entity… Relational properties such as "being a pleasure of listening to Beethoven" or "being a pleasure of watching a soap opera", are irrelevant to the measurement of value of the pleasure. For Bentham the only good-making characteristics of pleasure are intensity and duration, and thus only these properties are considered in the measurement of value.'[16]

Human beings generally seek their own happiness, and to harmonize the happiness of a large group of individuals becomes a matter of political design. Here we need to quickly glance at Bentham's theory of human motivation. Bentham identified four general motives for human action (see Box 9.2). The purely social motive of benevolence motivates a few individuals. Such benevolent individuals pursue the happiness of others

**Box 9.2**

**THE CLASSIFICATION OF HUMAN MOTIVES:**

A more commodious method, therefore, it should seem, would be to distribute them according to the influence which they appear to have on the interests of the other members of the community, laying those of the party himself out of the question: to wit, according to the tendency which they appear to have to unite, or disunite, his interests and theirs. On this plan they may be distinguished into *social, dissocial,* and *self-regarding*. In the social class may be reckoned,

1. Good-will.
2. Love of reputation.
3. Desire of amity.
4. Religion. In the dissocial may be placed,
5. Displeasure. In the self-regarding class,
6. Physical desire.
7. Pecuniary interest.
8. Love of power.
9. Self-preservation; as including the fear of the pains of the senses, the love of ease, and the love of life.

With respect to the motives that have been termed social, if any farther distinction should be of use, to that of good-will alone may be applied the epithet of *purely-social;* while the love of reputation, the desire of amity, and the motive of religion, may together be comprised under the division of *semi-social:* the social tendency being much more constant and unequivocal in the former than in any of the three latter. Indeed these last, social as they may be termed, are self-regarding at the same time.

*An Introduction to the Principles of Morals and Legislation,* Chapter X.

even at the cost of their own happiness. An individual, who acts out of the semi-social motive of love of praise, pursues others' happiness only when it promotes his own as well. The majority of human kind act out of the asocial motive of self-interest, and pursue their own happiness taking care not to cause others pain, but do not go the extent of pursuing others' happiness. Finally, there are some individuals moved by dissocial motives, who actually experience pleasure by harming others.

Human beings are then, generally always seeking their own pleasure. It is a truism to say that every man, on every occasion, pursues his own interest. When the interests of some group of men are opposed to the general interest, there is not much point, therefore, in exhorting these men not to act in such a way that gives them pleasure but gives many more pain. For Bentham, it was the proper end or object of every political arrangement (not of every private individual's action) that the greatest happiness of the greatest number be realized (see Box 9.3). It was up to the legislator to ensure, by attaching sanctions to the 'sinister' interests opposed to the general interest that nobody would be motivated to act on those sinister interests because their realization would now, instead of resulting in pleasure, produce instead the pain of punishment.

**Box 9.3**

**THE DIFFERENCE BETWEEN PRIVATE ETHICS AND THE ART OF LEGISLATION:**

Let us recapitulate and bring to a point the difference between private ethics, considered as an art or science, on the one hand, and that branch of jurisprudence which contains the art or science of legislation, on the other. Private ethics teaches how each man may dispose himself to pursue the course most conducive to his own happiness, by means of such motives as offer of themselves: the art of legislation (which may be considered as one branch of the science of jurisprudence) teaches how a multitude of men, composing a community, may be disposed to pursue that course which upon the whole is the most conducive to the happiness of the whole community, by means of motives to be applied by the legislator.

*An Introduction to the Principles of Morals and Legislation*, Chapter XVII.

What is required, in general, for human beings to reach the happiness they are searching for? Human happiness, for Bentham, depended on individuals not being motivated to follow their sinister interests, rendering, instead, services to each other. The government can ensure these services by creating a system of rights and obligations. Political society exists because government is necessary to compel individuals to render services to each other, in order to increase their happiness. This, then, is how Bentham made the transition from his utilitarianism to his political philosophy.

## BENTHAM'S POLITICAL PHILOSOPHY

'Government can not be exercised without coercion; nor coercion without producing unhappiness.'[17] Now unhappiness is to be avoided, thus one may justify a government by claiming, that without it more unhappiness would be produced in society. The *raison d'etre* of government is that it attaches sanctions to certain unhappiness producing actions (for the majority of citizens), so that individual citizens will not be motivated to perform them. Or, as we said at the end of the previous section, this coercion, which is, by definition, part of the nature of government, is essential to create a system of rights and obligations to further the welfare of society.

Governmental coercion underpins the legal obligations of citizens by holding out the threat of punishment for reneging on these obligations. Bentham claimed that theorists like Blackstone were wrong in justifying this punishment on the grounds that governments had come into existence from an 'original contract' in which the people had promised to obey the government's laws, and so if any person went back on his promise and broke the law, he could be justifiably punished. Bentham scoffed at the use of fictions like the 'original contract' to explain the nature of government. 'For what reason is it, that men ought to keep their promises? The moment any intelligible reason is given, it is this: that it is for the advantage of society they should keep them; it is for the advantage of the whole number that the promises of each individual should be kept... Such is the benefit (pleasure) to gain, and mischief (pain) to avoid, by keeping them, as much more than compensates the mischief (pain) of so much punishment as is requisite to oblige men to it.'[18] Bentham pointed out, that since any promises to obey the ruler at all events, even if he governs his subjects 'to their destruction', are void, the obligation to obey the laws, as well as the punishments in lieu thereof, are to be justified by considerations of utility alone and not by some specious 'original contract'.

It is here that Bentham also criticizes the idea of a state of nature. First, he defines a political society as follows: 'When a number of persons (whom we may style *subjects*) are supposed to be in the *habit* of paying *obedience* to a person, or an assemblage of persons, of a known and certain description (whom we may call *governor* or *governors*) such persons altogether (*subjects* and *governors*) are said to be in a state of *political* SOCIETY.'[19] He then goes on to define a natural society: 'When a number of persons are supposed to be in the habit of *conversing* with each other, at the same time that they are not in any such habit as mentioned above, they are said to be in a state of *natural* SOCIETY.'[20] For Bentham, there was no pure natural society or political society, but there was a continuum between the two. 'Between these two states, there is not that explicit separation which these names, and these definitions might teach one, at first sight, to expect... Governments accordingly, in proportion as the habit of obedience is more perfect, recede from, in proportion as it is less perfect, approach to, a state of nature.'[21]

The general function of government is to ensure the greatest happiness of the greatest number. In specific terms, the ends of government are 'subsistence, abundance, security, and equality; each maximized, in so far as it is compatible with the maximization of the rest'.[22] Bentham defined subsistence as the absence of everything, leading to positive physical deprivation, and he advised the government to encourage industrialization to generate employment, so that each individual could look after his own subsistence. The government was also to set up a common fund from contributions from the rich, for the well-being of the poor.

If subsistence prevents the citizens from being unhappy, abundance is necessary to maximize their happiness. By ensuring prosperity, that is, surplus wealth in the hands of individuals after their basic needs are met, the government encourages the citizens to fulfil all their desires. Bentham thought that affluence could best be increased by guaranteeing each man the due reward of his work, and security of his possessions. He felt that the state should also encourage the invention of new tools and gadgets, offer rewards for socially useful inventions, develop technical manpower, and encourage thrift and hard work. 'Above all it should highlight those aspects of religious thought that encourage men to despise comforts and luxury.'[23]

For Bentham, security was an important factor that the government had to look into. The government had to consider each individual's security of person, property, power, reputation and condition of life. Each person's security, in each of these aspects, was to be provided for by the government. Security of property, for instance, was to be provided by seeing to it that valid contracts are kept by everyone.

Bentham was concerned about four kinds of inequality: moral, intellectual, economic and political. He did not propose any measures to reduce moral and intellectual inequalities, but inequalities of wealth and power, he felt, were to be mitigated. 'The more remote from equality are the shares possessed by the individuals in question, in the mass of instruments of felicity, the less is the sum of felicity produced by the sum of those same shares'.[24] However, although differences between the rich and poor were to be evened out, it was not to happen at the expense of the security of property. Inequalities of power could be 'minimized by reducing the amount of power attached to public offices to the barest minimum, by declaring every sane adult eligible for them, and by making their incumbents accountable to those subject to their power'.[25]

The last service to be provided by the government was that of encouraging benevolence in the citizen body, so that every member of the body politic voluntarily, and with enjoyment, performed the 'countless small services' of which the fabric of the felicity of society was built. The government could, for example, 'fight the religious and sectarian prejudices which warp men's sympathies and incline them to treat outsiders as less than fully human'.[26]

So far, we looked at how the government fulfils its goals in specific ways. What is of greater importance, is Bentham's theory of how the government reaches its goals in general. Bentham believed that a man was a creature so dependent on others for his well-being, that human life would be unlivable and impossible if men did not render various types of services to one another. Society, according to Bentham, is ultimately only a system of services that men render one another. Government can ensure some of these services by creating a system of obligations and rights. It does so by putting in place a system of offences with their corresponding punishments (see Box 9.4). Not paying taxes, for example, is deemed an offence as is taking away someone else's money. These punishable offences ground the services men render to each: the positive service, or obligation of contributing to the fund of common resources, and the negative service, or obligation of not interfering with someone's right to property. These services, or obligations, in turn, ground everybody's rights: right to subsistence, and right to property. Each right only exists because of a corresponding obligation, and the government is to be very careful in specifying these

**Box 9.4**

**THE PRINCIPLE OF UTILITY AND PUNISHMENT:**

The general object which all laws have, or ought to have, in common, is to augment the total happiness of the community; and therefore, in the first place, to exclude, as far as may be, every thing that tends to subtract from that happiness: in other words, to exclude mischief.

But all punishment is mischief: all punishment in itself is evil. Upon the principle of utility, if it ought at all to be admitted, it ought only to be admitted in as far as it promises to exclude some greater evil.

It is plain, therefore, that in the following cases punishment ought not to be inflicted. Where it is *groundless:* where there is no mischief for it to prevent; the act not being mischievous upon the whole.

Where it must be *inefficacious:* where it cannot act so as to prevent the mischief.

Where it is *unprofitable,* or too *expensive:* where the mischief it would produce would be greater than what it prevented.

Where it is *needless:* where the mischief may be prevented, or cease of itself, without it: that is, at a cheaper rate.

*An Introduction to the Principles of Morals and Legislation,* Chapter XIII.

obligations. 'My rights may or may not be a source of pleasure to me, but the corresponding obligations they impose on others are certain sources of pain to them. The government therefore should never create rights, "instruments of felicity" though they are, unless it can be absolutely certain that their probable advantages would more than compensate for their certain disadvantages.'[27]

In a political society the sovereign can get the citizens to act as he wants in two ways: by influencing their will, which Bentham calls 'imperation', and by the threat of corporeal punishment, which Bentham calls 'contrectation'. Although the former power is based on the latter, which is the basis of the ruler's sovereignty, Bentham points out that a political society based on imperation is more stable and longer lasting than a society based on contrectation.

How is one to ensure that the government will create that system of rights and obligations which will fulfil the greatest happiness of the greatest number? Bentham's utilitarianism led him to believe that the government that would best serve the people's interests would be the democratic form of government. It is a democratic government which best fulfils the functions of any government. Instead of getting into the controversy over whether Bentham had been inclined towards democracy right from the time of the French revolution, or whether this democratic bent appeared much later, in 1808, after he met James Mill, let us, for now, just note how some of Bentham's utilitarian principles fit the ideals of a democratic government. If it is held, that 'the happiness of any one individual has no more value than the equal happiness of another, that all individuals have both an equal capacity for and an equal desire for happiness, then, assuming that all individuals have an equal capacity of judging the tendency of an action to increase happiness, the best form of government would be that in which everyone had a vote.'[28] In fact, in a tract that Bentham wrote in 1789, he advocated universal adult suffrage for all French citizens who could read, including women. Later, however, he grew cautious about universal suffrage on the grounds that it would allow the 'misjudgement of the ill informed classes' a role in political decision making, given that everyone did not have an equal capacity for judging the effectiveness of an action in promoting happiness. A decade or so later, however, Bentham was back to arguing for democratic ascendancy, except that now he had a new justification for democracy. We have already discussed how Bentham thought that the function of any government was to guard against the sinister interests of any group, by attaching appropriate sanctions to certain actions. But what if the most sinister interest which was to be guarded against, was the sinister interest of the political establishment? Bentham gradually came to the conclusion that social and legal reform was not being undertaken in Britain because, since the political class benefited from the old ways of doing things, the British government had a sinister interest in not bringing about any such reform. 'Rulers were like other individuals, in that their self-regarding interest predominated over their regard for the interests of the community. Their self-regarding interest led them to maintain every abuse which they found established, whether or not they derived any profit from it, since to expose the mischievousness of an unprofitable abuse would at the same time expose that of the profitable.'[29] The only way of preventing the government officials from giving into their sinister interests was to make them accountable to their constituents in regular, frequent elections, which is what he advocated in his writings of 1817 and 1819, on parliamentary reform in Britain.

Only in such a democratic government, could a harmony between the interests of the governed and those in government be engineered. In a democracy, what maximizes the happiness of the rulers is to be returned to office, and they know that the only way they can ensure that this happens is if they maximize the happiness, or in other words, look after the welfare and interests of the ruled. They know that if they go against the interests of the ruled, they will be voted out of office. From this argument, Bentham logically derived that the right of every adult to vote, frequent national elections, as frequent as every year, transparency of government business, which meant a free press, unlimited access to government offices, and the right to attend legislative sessions, could help establish democratic government which would ensure the happiness of the public. 'Once annual election, universal franchise, and fullest publicity are established, no government, Bentham thinks, would ever "dream" of pursuing its interest at the cost of the community.'[30]

## THE PANOPTICON: SURVEILLANCE AND CHOICE

Rosen's claim for Bentham as having a theory of representative democracy 'far superior in scope, depth and subtlety' than that of J.S. Mill, can be contrasted with a view of Bentham, the creator of the Panopticon, as the advocate of modern forms of subjugation. The Panopticon is the name that Bentham gave to a model prison that he designed for the British government in the 1790s. A piece of land was bought by the government, on which Bentham was to supervise the construction of the new prison. However, much to Bentham's disappointment, around 1802, the project fell through.

The design of the Panopticon was to serve as a model for any disciplinary institution. Not just a jail house, but any school, hospital, factory and military barracks could have the same structure as well. The idea of the

Panopticon has become important again today, with Foucault crediting Bentham with creating a new technology of power. The Panopticon 'represents one component in the history of repression—the transition from the inflicting of punishment to the imposition of surveillance'.[31] This is how Foucault describes the architecture of the prison building:

> A perimeter building in the form of a ring. At the centre of this, a tower pierced by large windows opening on to the perimeter face of the ring. The outer building is divided into cells each of which traverses the whole thickness of the building. These cells have two windows, one opening on to the inside, facing the windows of the central tower, the other, outer one allowing daylight to pass through the whole cell. All that is then needed is to put an overseer in the tower, and place in each of the cells a lunatic, a patient, a convict, a worker or a school boy. The lighting enables one to pick out from the central tower the little captive silhouette in each of the cells. In short, the principle of the dungeon is reversed; daylight and the overseer's gaze capture the inmate more effectively.[32]

The prisoners, who have no contact with each other, feel as if they are under the constant watch of the guards. 'There is no need for arms, physical violence or material constraints. Just a gaze. An inspecting gaze, which each individual, under its weight will end by interiorizing to the point that he is his own overseer, each individual thus exercising this surveillance over, and against, himself.'[33]

## PROBLEMS WITH BENTHAM'S THEORY

Bentham has become infamous for introducing this new model of power in which the subject is made to, almost voluntarily, exercise control over himself. The Panopticon is also said to mirror the relationship between government and citizens in liberal democracies, where all horizontal links between citizens are devalued, and what unites them into one community is their separate political obligation to obey the sovereign. This, then, becomes a travesty of the ideals of liberal democracy.

Bentham has also been faulted for believing that human beings only search for the experience of pleasure, a mental state. To prove that 'value does not reside in simple mental states'[34] we can use the example of Nozick's 'experience machine'. Nozick doubts whether we would plug ourselves into such a machine which could give us any experience we desired because what we want is 'to do certain things, and not just have the experiences of doing them'.[35] If one could hook oneself to a machine which constantly generated sensations of pleasure, without having to do anything else, that would not satisfy one at all. Human beings undertake certain activities for the sake of those activities, not only for the pleasurable sensations they get from doing them. A related criticism is that, what we value are 'states of the world' not just states of our mind. 'If a father wants his children to be happy, what he wants, what is valuable to him, is a state of the world, not a state of his mind; merely to delude him into thinking that his children flourish, therefore, does not give him what he values.'[36] Value, or utility, is tied into 'an external reality, to certain states of the world'. A quantitative hedonism like that of Bentham's is problematic because it 'does not have a means to distinguish experiences on any basis other than quantity of satisfaction and thus is more pressed to explain why hallucinatory experiences are less valuable than the real thing'.[37]

Another oft-made criticism of utilitarianism is that the project of maximizing happiness in a society, means trampling the rights of minority groups. If there is a large majority whose members get intense pleasure from an action that creates pain for a minority, then Bentham's utilitarianism does not have the theoretical resources to forbid such action.

## NOTES

1. Frederick S. Rosen, *Jeremy Bentham and Representative Democracy: A Study of the Constitutional Code*, Oxford: Clarendon Press, 1983, p. 7.
2. Jeremy Bentham, *A Fragment on Government*, edited by J.H. Burns and H.L.A. Hart, Cambridge: Cambridge University Press, 1988, p. 3.
3. W.T. Jones, *Masters of Political Thought, Volume Two: Machiavelli to Bentham*, Boston, MA Houghton Mifflin, 1963, p. 366.
4. Philip Schofield, *Utility and Democracy: The Political Thought of Jeremy Bentham*, Boston, MA: Oxford: Oxford University Press, 2006, pp. 2–5.
5. Jeremy Bentham, *The Principles of Morals and Legislation*, New York: Prometheus Books, 1988, pp. 1–2.
6. *Ibid.*
7. *Ibid.*
8. Wendy Donner, *The Liberal Self: John Stuart Mill's Moral and Political Philosophy*, Ithaca: Cornell University Press, 1991, p. 13.
9. *Ibid.*
10. See Jeremy Bentham, Chapter 5 in *The Principles of Morals and Legislation*.
11. Philip Schofield, *Utility and Democracy*, pp. 9–10.
12. As quoted in Philip Schofield, *Utility and Democracy*, p. 26.
13. See Bhikhu Bhikhu Parekh (ed.), *Bentham's Political Thought*, London: Croom Helm, 1973, pp. 15–16.
14. Jeremy Bentham, *A Fragment on Government*, p. 3.
15. Jeremy Bentham, *The Principles of Morals and Legislation*, p. 3.
16. Wendy Donner, *The Liberal Self*, p. 14.
17. Jeremy Bentham, *Constitutional Code*, as quoted in Bhikhu Parekh (ed.), *Bentham's Political Thought*, London: Croom Helm, 1973, p. 195.

18. Jeremy Bentham, *A Fragment on Government*, p. 55.
19. *Ibid.*, p. 40.
20. *Ibid.*
21. *Ibid.*
22. Jeremy Bentham, *Constitutional Code*, p. 196.
23. Bhikhu Parekh (ed.), *Bentham's Political Thought*, p. 41.
24. Jeremy Bentham, *Constitutional Code*, p. 200.
25. Bhikhu Parekh, *Bentham's Political Thought*, p. 41.
26. *Ibid.*, p. 42.
27. *Ibid.*, p. 35.
28. Philip Schofield, *Utility and Democracy*, p. 79.
29. Philip Schofield, *Utility and Democracy*, pp. 159–160.
30. Bhikhu Parekh, *Bentham's Political Thought*, p. 31.
31. Michel Foucault, *Power/Knowledge: Selected Interviews and Other Writings 1972–1979* (ed.), Colin Gordon, New York: Pantheon Books, 1980, p. 38.
32. *Ibid.*, p.147
33. *Ibid.*, p.155
34. Wendy Donner, *The Liberal Self*, p. 69.
35. *Ibid.*, p. 70.
36. *Ibid.*
37. Wendy Donner, *The Liberal Self*, p. 73.

## READING LIST

Bentham, Jeremy, *A Fragment on Government*, edited by J.H. Burns and H.L.A. Hart, Cambridge: Cambridge University Press, 1988.

Bentham, Jeremy, *Constitutional Code*, as quoted in Bhikhu Parekh (ed.), *Bentham's Political Thought*, London: Croom Helm, 1973.

Bentham, Jeremy, *The Principles of Morals and Legislation*, New York: Prometheus Books, 1988.

Rosen, Frederick S., *Jeremy Bentham and Representative Democracy: A Study of the Constitutional Code*, Oxford: Clarendon Press, 1983.

Schofield, Philip, *Utility and Democracy: The Political Thought of Jeremy Bentham*, Oxford: Oxford University Press, 2006.

## CENTRAL THEMES

1. **The principle of utility:** According to Bentham, the principle of utility can help us reorganize our societies to our benefit. What is meant by Bentham's claim that it is the principle of utility which recognizes that both 'the standard of right and wrong' as well as 'the chain of causes and effects' are fastened to the 'throne of pain and pleasure'? How can utilitarianism be said to be a theory of moral action?
2. **The felicific calculus:** Bentham develops a detailed procedure for calculating the utility of any action. What are the different elements of his felicific calculus?

Do you agree with the position that the felicific calculus provides us with an objective basis for comparing conflicting moral claims?

3. **The idea of sinister interests:** How does Bentham's idea of sinister interests lead him to develop a theory of representative government? Which sinister interests are thwarted, in which way, by the institutions of representative government?
4. **Government as a system of rights and obligations:** What does Bentham mean by specifying the ends of government as 'subsistence, abundance, security and equality: each maximized in so far as it is compatible with the maximization of the rest.' How does Bentham conceive of government as fulfilling these ends by creating a system of rights and obligations?

TEN

# John Stuart Mill (1806–1873): The Benefits of the Liberty of Men and Women for Society

John Stuart Mill was born in 1806, in London, as the oldest son of the Scottish historian and philosopher, James Mill. His father almost immediately put Mill on a pedagogic diet well beyond his years, teaching him Greek when he was only three years old, and Latin when he was eight, by which time Mill had also read several of Plato's dialogues. Before he entered his teens, Mill began studying logic and mathematics, and soon after, also mastered the political economy of Smith and Ricardo. During all this time, Mill also read a lot of history.

All of Mill's education was supervised by his father and his father's philosopher friend, Jeremy Bentham. Mill neither went to a regular school and nor to a university like Oxford or Cambridge, but he read so much at home that, while still in his teens, he began contributing articles to the *Westminster Review*, the journal of the Philosophic Radicals.[1] Later, as one of the Philosophic Radicals himself, well versed in their utilitarian principles, he became the editor of their new journal, the *London and Westminster Review*.

Perhaps, under the pressure of so much intellectual work, Mill had a nervous breakdown just as he crossed 20, and in 1826, he fell into a deep depression, which lasted almost two years. Later in life, Mill would fault the pedagogic principles derived from his father's and Bentham's utilitarianism for this emotional paralysis of his youth. Mill pulled himself out of his depression by reading the poetry of the English Romantics. In 1827, he began working for the British East India Company and continued to work for the company for three decades. It was during these years that he wrote many of his famous works.

From 1865 to 1868, Mill was a member of the British Parliament, trying to push through legislation granting women's suffrage and worker's rights. He was also the Lord Rector of the University of Saint Andrews in Scotland, during these years. In 1851, Mill married Harriet Taylor, who was not only a good friend, but also someone he had been in love with, for nearly 20 years. Unfortunately, she died not long after their marriage, in 1858. Mill acknowledged her influence on his writings in several places.

Mill was a prolific writer, producing work in several disciplines. His *A System of Logic*, which he wrote in 1843, was followed by *Principles of Political Economy* in 1848. In 1859, he wrote *On Liberty*. In 1861, he wrote *Considerations on Representative Government* followed by *Utilitarianism* in 1863. *The Subjection of Women* was published in 1869, while *Autobiography* and *Three Essays on Religion*, were published posthumously in 1873 and in 1874, respectively. As we can see, Mill's oeuvre was wide ranging, covering methodological issues in the sciences, questions of moral and political philosophy, as well as the discipline of political economy. Mill's ideas not only greatly influenced intellectuals in England in the 19th century, but some of his theories—his methodological individualism, his version of utilitarianism and his emphasis on liberty and democracy—fuel philosophical debates even today, and resonate in some of our contemporary political struggles for liberty and equal rights.

## AN EQUAL FREEDOM FOR WOMEN

Twenty years ago, undergraduate students of political science studying John Stuart Mill read mainly *On Liberty*, and his *Considerations on Representative Government*. Students today are fortunate in that they make their acquaintance with Mill through *The Subjection of Women*, a work which was far ahead of its time in its application of the principle of liberty to the position of women. If the paramount value espoused by Mill in his writings is liberty, then certainly *The Subjection of Women* should be read as a companion text to *On Liberty*. After all, it was in the former work that Mill wrote, 'After the primary necessities of food and raiment, freedom is the first and strongest want of human nature'.[2]

I begin this discussion of Mill with *The Subjection of Women*. Mill zealously advocated the liberty of women as well the liberty of the working class. Mill rued the fact that a great majority of the working class were still forced by poverty to be 'chained to a place, to an occupation, and to conformity with the will of an employer'.[3] In *The Subjection of Women* we can see what happens to an idea of liberty when it is developed as a weapon to fight the subordination of women. We can also track whether Mill's defence of women's equality and liberty is based on the principle of utility or whether this defence takes him beyond utilitarianism.

*The Subjection of Women* begins with the revolutionary statement that 'the principle which regulates the existing social relations between the two sexes—the legal subordination of one sex to the other—is wrong in itself, and now one of the chief hindrances to human improvement; and...it ought to be replaced by a principle of perfect equality, admitting no power or privilege on the one side, not disability on the other'.[4] Mill's referent for the legal subordination of women was the mid-19th century English law about the marriage contract. Mill was so opposed to this law that when he married Harriet Taylor in 1851, he wrote out a formal protest against the laws that would govern their marriage.[5] By these laws, married Englishwomen could hold no property in their own name, and even if their parents gifted them any property, that too, belonged to their husbands. Unless a woman was legally separated from her husband (divorce, in those days, was an expensive and difficult process), even if she lived away from him, her earnings belonged to him. By law, only the father and not the mother was the guardian of a couple's children. Mill also cited the absence of laws on marital rape to prove the inequality suffered by the Englishwomen of that time.

What Mill found paradoxical was that in the modern age, when the principles of liberty and equality were being espoused, these very rights were being denied to women. No one believed in slavery anymore, yet women were sometimes treated worse than slaves. Mill wanted to explain this resistance to women's equality in the context of the general acceptance of the principles of equality and liberty. Perhaps, women's inequality was seen as 'a fact of nature', since women had been treated unequally over the ages and across the continents. Other oppressive practices, however, such as slavery, had been eschewed with the rise of modernity, whereas women were still entrenched in oppressive, patriarchal practices. The reason why women's subjection, unlike slavery or political absolutism, found such few opposers, Mill argued, was not because it was 'natural', but because, whereas only slave-holders and despots had an interest in holding on to slavery and despotism, all men had an interest in women's subordination.

This is what made women's subordination so difficult to resist. Men wanted to hold on to it because they benefited from it. Their self-esteem got a boost from the mere sense of being male, as they could control the labour and resources of another human being. Women, on the other hand, had no choice but to live with their husbands, were afraid that their complaints about their position would only lead to worse treatment from them, and suffered in silence. This did not mean that they accepted their subordinate position voluntarily. Many women had actually written tracts against women's inequality and hundreds of women were already demonstrating in the streets of London, for women's suffrage. Mill also claimed that since all women were brought up from childhood to believe 'that their ideal of character is the very opposite to that of men; not self-will, and government by self-control, but submission, and yielding to the control of others',[6] what was remarkable was not that some women accepted their subordination willingly, but that so many women resisted it.

Attacking every defence of women's inequality, Mill went on, in *The Subjection of Women*, to marshal further arguments for why the oppression of women should be resisted. Saying, that 'there are many persons for whom it is not enough that the inequality has no just or legitimate defence; they require to be told what express advantage would be obtained by abolishing it',[7] Mill detailed how society would benefit, in four different ways, if women were to be granted equal rights.

The first advantage would be that the family would no longer be 'a school of despotism'.[8] According to Mill, the patriarchal family compels all its members to live in hierarchical relationships, since all power is concentrated in the hands of the husband/father/master and the wife, children and servants have to obey him. For Mill, such families were an anachronism in modern democratic polities, which were based on the principles of equality and liberty (see Box 10.1). Individuals who live in such families cannot be good democratic citizens because they do not know how to treat another citizen as an equal. 'Any sentiment of freedom which can exist in a man whose nearest and dearest intimacies are with those of whom he is absolute master, is not the genuine love of freedom, but, what the love of freedom generally was in the ancients and in the middle ages—an intense feeling of the dignity and importance of his own personality; making him disdain a yoke for himself,...but which he is abundantly ready to impose on others for his own interest or glorification.'[9] If democracy is a form of self-government, it assumes its members to be free citizens who participate in this self-government. Looking at the concept of free citizens through the lens of the condition of women, makes Mill define liberty in a particular manner. Freedom is to be defined such that the liberty of one is consistent with the liberty of others, and if women are to be as free as men, they must first enjoy equality with them. For women to be free, they must enjoy an equal legal status with men, and have an equal access to education and employment. In the interests of democratic citizenship then, it was necessary to obtain equality for women in the family.

Another advantage of women's equality, Mill pointed out, would be the 'doubling of the mass of mental faculties'[10] available to society. Society would benefit not only because there would be more doctors, engineers, teachers and scientists, but men in the professions would also perform

Box 10.1

**THE SOCIAL ILL EFFECTS OF THE SUBORDINATION OF WOMEN:**

But the true virtue of human beings is fitness to live together as equals; claiming nothing for themselves but what they as freely concede to every one else; regarding command of any kind as an exceptional necessity, and in all cases a temporary one; and preferring, whenever possible, the society of those with whom leading and following can be alternate and reciprocal. To these virtues, nothing in life as at present constituted gives cultivation by exercise. The family is a school of despotism, in which the virtues of despotism, but also its vices, are largely nourished. Citizenship, in free countries, is partly a school of society in equality; but citizenship fills only a small place in modern life, and does not come near the daily habits or inmost sentiments. The family, justly constituted, would be the real school of the virtues of freedom. It is sure to be a sufficient one of everything else. It will always be a school of obedience for the children, of command for the parents. What is needed is, that it should be a school of sympathy in equality, of living together in love, without power on one side or obedience on the other. This it ought to be between the parents. It would then be an exercise of those virtues which each requires to fit them for all other association, and a model to the children of the feelings and conduct which their temporary training by means of obedience is designed to render habitual, and therefore natural, to them. The moral training of mankind will never be adapted to the conditions of the life for which all other human progress is a preparation, until they practise in the family the same moral rule which is adapted to the normal constitution of human society. Any sentiment of freedom which can exist in a man whose nearest and dearest intimacies are with those of whom he is absolute master, is not the genuine or Christian love of freedom, but, what the love of freedom generally was in the ancients and in the middle ages—an intense feeling of the dignity and importance of his own personality; making him disdain a yoke for himself, of which he has no abhorrence whatever in the abstract, but which he is abundantly ready to impose on others for his own interest or glorification.

*The Subjection of Women*, Chapter 2

better, because of competition from their female counterparts. Mill describes this benefit as 'the benefit of the stimulus that would be given to the intellect of men by the competition; or (to use a more true expression) by the necessity that would be imposed on them of deserving precedency before they could expect to obtain it'.[11]

Thirdly, women enjoying equality would have a better influence on mankind. Under relations of subordination, women have to resort to perverse means to assert their will. If they are treated equally, they will no longer need to do this.

Finally, by giving women equal rights, their happiness would be increased manifold and this would satisfy, Mill argued, the utilitarian principle of the greatest happiness of the greatest number:

> Thus far, the benefits which it has appeared that the world would gain by ceasing to make sex a disqualification for privileges and a badge of subjection, are social rather than individual; consisting in an increase of the general fund of thinking and acting power, and an improvement in the general conditions of the association of men with women. But it would be a grievous understatement of the case to omit the most direct benefit of all, the unspeakable gain in private happiness to the liberated half of the species; the difference to them between a life of subjection to the will of others, and a life of rational freedom.[12]

In arguing for women to enjoy the same freedoms as men—the freedom to vote, to attend university, to go to work, to do what they willed with their earnings—Mill linked up the idea of freedom to other ideas important to him, that is, the ideas of equality, democracy and utility. Only when women accessed the same privileges as men, would democracy be strengthened. Mill was not saying that the democratic project was incomplete because half the population was not being allowed to participate in the project of self-government. Rather, his claim was that without the reform of the patriarchal family, even the men would not know how to be truly democratic. Democracy in the political/public sphere would remain faulty unless democratic citizens were brought up and created in egalitarian families.

In *The Subjection of Women*, Mill declares that equality, liberty and democracy are bound up together. Can this constellation of values be justified on the grounds of utility? Having looked at Mill's ideas about equality and liberty for women, let us look at what he says more generally about the principle of liberty and its usefulness.

## THE IMPORTANCE OF INDIVIDUAL LIBERTY

Why does Mill hold the value of liberty so dear? Why is it so important to him that the liberty of individuals, including that of women, be protected? Mill believed that when individuals are free to make their own choices, they use many of their faculties. 'The human faculties of perception, judgement, discriminative feeling, mental activity, and even moral preference, are exercised in only making a choice… The mental and moral, like the muscular powers, are improved only by being used… He who chooses his plan for himself, employs all his faculties. He must use observation to see, reasoning and judgement to foresee, activity to gather materials for decision, discrimination to decide, and when he has decided, firmness and self-control to hold to his deliberate decision.'[13] Individuals, who act in a certain fashion only because they have been told to do so, do not develop any of these faculties. Emphasizing that what is important is 'not only what men do, but also what manner of men they are that do it',[14] Mill said that what while we might be able to 'guide' individuals in 'some good path' without allowing them to make any choices, the 'worth' of such human beings would be doubtful. The point of liberty then seems to be the 'improvement' of the 'moral and mental powers' of human beings (see Box 10.2).

This improvement of the mental and moral faculties of individuals, for both men and women, will take place, Mill argued, when they exercise three specific liberties: the liberty of thought and expression, including the

**Box 10.2**

**THE VALUE OF LIBERTY IN AN INDIVIDUAL'S LIFE:**

The human faculties of perception, judgement, discriminative feeling, mental activity, and even moral preference, are exercised only in making a choice. He who does anything because it is the custom, makes no choice. He gains no practice either in discerning or in desiring what is best. The mental and moral, like the muscular powers, are improved only by being used. The faculties are called into no exercise by doing a thing merely because others do it, no more than by believing a thing only because others believe it. If the grounds of an opinion are not conclusive to the person's own reason, his reason cannot be strengthened, but is likely to be weakened by his adopting it: and if the inducements to an act are not such as are consentaneous to his own feelings and character (where affection, or the rights of others are not concerned), it is so much done towards rendering his feelings and character inert and torpid, instead of active and energetic.

He who lets the world, or his own portion of it, choose his plan of life for him, has no need of any other faculty than the ape-like one of imitation. He who chooses his plan for himself, employs all his faculties. He must use observation to see, reasoning and judgement to foresee, activity to gather materials for decision, discrimination to decide, and when he has decided, firmness and self-control to hold to his deliberate decision. And these qualities he requires and exercises exactly in proportion as the part of his conduct which he determines according to his own judgement and feelings is a large one. It is possible that he might be guided in some good path, and kept out of harm's way, without any of these things. But what will be his comparative worth as a human being? It really is of importance, not only what men do, but also what manner of men they are that do it. Among the works of man, which human life is rightly employed in perfecting and beautifying, the first in importance surely is man himself. Supposing it were possible to get houses built, corn grown, battles fought, causes tried, and even churches erected and prayers said, by machinery—by automatons in human form—it would be a considerable loss to exchange for these automatons even the men and women who at present inhabit the more civilized parts of the world, and who assuredly are but starved specimens of what nature can and will produce. Human nature is not a machine to be built after a model, and set to do exactly the work prescribed for it, but a tree, which requires to grow and develop itself on all sides, according to the tendency of the inward forces which make it a living thing.

*On Liberty*, Chapter 3

liberty of speaking and publishing; the liberty of action and the liberty of association. We will follow Mill's argument for each of these cases (see Box 10.3).

**Box 10.3**

**LIBERTY IN ITS DIFFERENT FORMS:**

This, then, is the appropriate region of human liberty. It comprises, first, the inward domain of consciousness; demanding liberty of conscience, in the most comprehensive sense; liberty of thought and feeling; absolute freedom of opinion and sentiment on all subjects, practical or speculative, scientific, moral, or theological. The liberty of expressing and publishing opinions may seem to fall under a different principle, since it belongs to that part of the conduct of an individual which concerns other people; but, being almost of as much importance as the liberty of thought itself, and resting in great part on the same reasons, is practically inseparable from it. Secondly, the principle requires liberty of tastes and pursuits; of framing the plan of our life to suit our own character; of doing as we like, subject to such consequences as may follow; without impediment from our fellow-creatures, so long as what we do does not harm them even though they should think our conduct foolish, perverse, or wrong. Thirdly, from this liberty of each individual, follows the liberty, within the same limits, of combination among individuals; freedom to unite, for any purpose not involving harm to others: the persons combining being supposed to be of full age, and not forced or deceived.

*On Liberty*, Chapter 1

We begin with the liberty of thought and expression. 'If all mankind minus one, were of one opinion, and only one person were of the contrary opinion, mankind would be no more justified in silencing that one person, than he, if he had the power, would be justified in silencing mankind.'[15] Mill's reasons for espousing freedom of expression were the following: For Mill, since the dominant ideas of a society usually emanate from the class interests of that society's ascendant class, the majority opinion may not reflect the truth and may not benefit the society as a whole. It is more than likely that the suppressed minority opinion is true and those suppressing it will only prevent or deter mankind from knowing the truth. Human beings are fallible creatures and their certainty that the opinion they hold is true is justified only when their opinion is constantly opposed to contrary opinions. Mill wanted us to give up the assumption of infallibility—when our certainty about our beliefs makes us crush all contrary points of view so that our opinion is not subject to criticism.

But what if the minority opinion is false? Mill gave three reasons for why the minority should be allowed freedom of expression, nevertheless.

It's only by constantly being able to refute wrong opinions, that we hold our correct opinions as living truths. If we accept an opinion, even if correct, simply because it belongs to an authority figure or institution or majority group, that opinion becomes a dead dogma. Neither do we understand its grounds, and nor does it mould our character or move us to action. Finally, Mill argued that truth is a multifaceted thing and usually every argument and opinion contains a part of the truth. Suppressing one opinion then, leads to the suppression of one part of the truth. 'Conflicting doctrines, instead of being one true and the other false, share the truth between them; and the nonconforming opinion is needed to supply the remainder of the truth, of which the received doctrine embodies only a part. Popular opinions…are often true, but seldom or never the whole truth. They are a part of the truth; sometimes a greater, sometimes a smaller part, but exaggerated, distorted, and disjoined from the truths by which they ought to be accompanied and limited. Heretical opinions, on the other hand, are generally some of these suppressed and neglected truths.'[16]

When it comes to liberty of action, Mill asserted that 'the sole end for which mankind are warranted, individually or collectively, in interfering with the liberty of action of any of their number, is self-protection…the only purpose for which power can be rightfully exercised over any member of a civilized community, against his will, is to prevent harm to others. His own good, either physical or moral, is not a sufficient warrant'.[17] We have already seen that for Mill, the purpose of liberty is improvement. In an earlier section, we also saw Mill rejecting the meaning of liberty as the domination of others. Yet, none of this prevents Mill from insisting that this improvement or, the choice of non-domination, cannot be forced on anyone (see Box 10.4). Mill did acknowledge that it was difficult to draw a line between action that affects self, and action that affects the other, and he provided some hypothetical examples as proof of this difficulty. If a man destroys his own property, this is an action affecting the other, because others dependent on that man will be affected. Even if this person has no dependants, his action can be said to affect others, who, influenced by his example, might behave in a similar manner.

Against this, Mill said that only when one has specific obligations to another person, can one be said to affect his or her interests; therefore, the case of an individual affecting others by setting an example, will not stand. Mill cited all kinds of restrictions like not eating pork or beef, or priests being required to be celibate, as examples of unnecessary restrictions on action that affect the self. Other examples are Sabbatarian legislation which prevents individuals from working, or even singing and dancing on Sundays.

Mill wrote that sometimes even in the case of actions that affect others, no restrictions can be placed on one. For instance, if one wins a job through a competition, this action can be said to affect others' interests since by winning that job, that person is depriving his other competitors of that job. Similarly, trade has social consequences, but as a believer in the principle of free trade, Mill argued that lack of restrictions on trade actually leads to better pricing and better quality of products.

**Box 10.4**

**THE REGULATION OF INDIVIDUAL LIBERTY BY THE HARM PRINCIPLE:**

The object of this Essay is to assert one very simple principle, as entitled to govern absolutely the dealings of society with the individual in the way of compulsion and control, whether the means used be physical force in the form of legal penalties, or the moral coercion of public opinion. That principle is, that the sole end for which mankind are warranted, individually or collectively in interfering with the liberty of action of any of their number, is self-protection. That the only purpose for which power can be rightfully exercised over any member of a civilized community, against his will, is to prevent harm to others. His own good, either physical or moral, is not a sufficient warrant. He cannot rightfully be compelled to do or forbear because it will be better for him to do so, because it will make him happier, because, in the opinions of others, to do so would be wise, or even right. These are good reasons for remonstrating with him, or reasoning with him, or persuading him, or entreating him, but not for compelling him, or visiting him with any evil, in case he do otherwise. To justify that, the conduct from which it is desired to deter him must be calculated to produce evil to someone else. The only part of the conduct of any one, for which he is amenable to society, is that which concerns others. In the part which merely concerns himself, his independence is, of right, absolute. Over himself, over his own body and mind, the individual is sovereign.

*On Liberty*, Chapter 1

Mill defended liberty of association on three grounds: first, 'when the thing to be done is likely to be done better by individuals than by government, speaking generally, there is no one [as] fit to conduct any business, or to determine how or by whom it shall be conducted, as those who are personally interested in it'.[18] Secondly, allowing individuals to get together to do something, even if they do not do it as well as the government might have done it, is better for the mental education of these individuals. The right of association becomes, for Mill, a 'practical part of the political education of a free people, taking them out of the narrow circle of personal and family selfishness, and accustoming them to the comprehension of joint concerns: habituating them to act from public or semi-public motives, and guide their conduct by aims which unite instead of isolating them from one another'.[19] Further, government operations tend to be everywhere alike. With individuals and voluntary associations, on the contrary, there are varied experiments, and endless diversity of experience. Thirdly, if we let the government do everything, then there we facilitate in aggrandizing its power. 'If the roads, the railways, the banks, the insurance offices, the great joint-stock companies, the universities, and the public charities, were all of them branches of the government; if, in addition, the municipal corporations and local boards, with all that now devolves on them, became departments of the central administration; if the employees of all these different enterprises were appointed and paid by the government, and looked to the government for every rise in life; not all the freedom of the press and popular constitution of the legislature would make this or any other country free otherwise than in name.'[20]

Mill's ideal was improvement. He wanted individuals to constantly better themselves morally, mentally and materially. It was individual liberty, which was instrumental in achieving this ideal. 'The only unfailing and permanent source of improvement is liberty, since by it there as many possible independent centres of improvement as there are individuals.'[21] Individuals improving themselves would naturally lead to a better and improved society.

## REPRESENTATIVE GOVERNMENT

Freedom of association is one of the central tenets of modern democracies, and it seems obvious that the liberties of individuals would find most protection in a democratic form of government. Surprisingly, here, Mill sounds a warning about democracies by arguing that civil liberties are under greater threat in democratic than in despotic regimes. In the absolutist states of earlier times, the ruler's interest was seen as opposed to that of the subjects, who were especially vigilant against any encroachment on their existing freedoms. In modern democracies based on the principle of self-government, the people usually do not feel threatened by their own government. Mill berated this laxity and said that individuals needed to be more vigilant about the threat to their liberty, not only from the government, but also from social morality and custom.[22]

However, as long as the citizens are vigilant, democracy, or in Mill's words, 'representative government', is the best form of government. Still, if indeed in a democracy, there is is always the danger of the self-governed people encroaching on individual liberties, then how is this form of government the most beneficial? Mill began *Considerations on Representative Government* by stating that we can decide the best form of government only by examining which form of government fulfils most adequately the purposes of government. For Mill, the point of having a government was its performing two main functions: it must use the existing qualities and skills of the citizens to best serve their interests, and it must improve the moral, intellectual and active qualities of these citizens (see Box 10.5). A despotic government, let us say, an enlightened despotism, may be able to fulfil the first purpose, but will fail in the second. Only a representative government is able to fulfil both these functions. It is a representative government that by judiciously combining the two principles of competence and participation is able to fulfil the two functions of protecting and educating the citizens.[23]

**Box 10.5**

**ON THE TWO ELEMENTS OF GOOD GOVERNMENT:**

The first element of good government, therefore, being the virtue and intelligence of the human beings composing the community, the most important point of excellence which any form of government can possess is to promote the virtue and intelligence of the people themselves. The first question in respect to any political institutions is how far they tend to foster in the members of the community the various desirable qualities, moral and intellectual, or rather (following Bentham's more complete classification) moral, intellectual, and active. The government which does this the best has every likelihood of being the best in all other respects, since it is on these qualities, so far as they exist in the people, that all possibility of goodness in the practical operations of the government depends.

We may consider, then, as one criterion of the goodness of a government, the degree in which it tends to increase the sum of good qualities in the governed, collectively and individually, since, besides that their well-being is the sole object of government, their good qualities supply the moving force which works the machinery. This leaves, as the other constituent element of the merit of a government, the quality of the machinery itself; that is, the degree in which it is adapted to take advantage of the amount of good qualities which may at any time exist, and make them instrumental to the right purposes.

*Considerations on Representative Government*, Chapter 2

Let us look at what Mill had to say about the first function of government. Mill began his discussion of this subject by introducing Bentham's concept of sinister interests. How does a representative government ensure that the common interest of society is being furthered instead of the partial and sinister interest of some group or class? Even though Mill distinguished between short term and long term interests, he was certain that every individual and every class is the best judge of its own interests. He scoffed at the idea that some human beings may not be aware of their 'real' interests, retorting that given these persons' current habits and dispositions, what they choose reflects their real interests. It follows, then, that every individual must be allowed a say in controlling the government and thus given an opportunity to protect his or her interests. It is on this basis that Mill demanded that women be given the right to vote. He advocated that barring those who were illiterate, did not pay taxes or were on parish relief, everyone be allowed to vote.

Mill, as an advocate of the extension of suffrage, supported Hare's system of proportional representation for electing deputies to Parliament. Under the erstwhile system, Mill pointed out, minorities went unrepresented, and since they too needed to protect their interests, a different electoral mechanism was required to ensure their representation.

While his belief in participation led him to advocate a widening of the franchise, his belief in competence led him to recommend plural voting. In fact, he said that the franchise should not be widened without plural voting being introduced. Plural voting meant that with everyone having at least one vote, some individuals would have more than one vote because they were presumably more qualified. It assumed 'a graduated scale of educational attainments, awarding at the bottom, one additional vote to a skilled labourer and two to a foreman, and at the top, as many as five to professional men, writers and artists, public functionaries, university graduates and members of learned societies'[24]. Plural voting would ensure that the votes of the better calibre of, or more competent, deputies would carry more weight, and so the general interest would not be hampered by the poor qualities of members of Parliament.

Mill sought to combine the two principles of competence and participation in every institution of representative democracy. Take the representative assembly again, for instance. Mill said that this body must be 'a committee of grievances' and 'a congress of opinions'. Every opinion existing in the nation should find a voice here; that is how every group's interests have a better chance of being protected. At the same time, Mill argued that this body was suited neither for the business of legislation nor for administration. Legislation was to be framed by a Codification Commission made up of a few competent legal experts. Administration should be in the hand of the bureaucracy, an institution characterized by instrumental competence, that is, the ability to find the most efficient means to fulfil given goals. Mill's argument employed two kinds of competence: instrumental and moral. Instrumental competence is the ability to discover the best means to certain ends and the ability to identify ends that satisfy individuals' interests as they perceive them. Moral competence is the ability to discern ends that are intrinsically superior for individuals and society. Morally competent leaders are able to recognize the general interest and resist the sinister interests that dwell not only in the government but also in the democratic majority. Just as it is important to ensure that morally competent leaders get elected to the legislature, similarly, it has to be ensured that the Codification Commission include morally competent legal experts.

What about the other goal of government, that of making its citizens intellectually and morally better? Again, it is a representative government that is based on a combination of participation and competence, which is able to improve the quality of its citizens in the mental, moral and practical aspects. Let us look at some of the specific institutional changes recommended by Mill. He wanted to replace the secret ballot with open voting, that is, everyone must know how one has voted. For Mill, the franchise was not a right. Unlike, say, the right to property, which allows one to dispose of one's property in any arbitrary manner, the franchise is a trust, or a public duty. One must cast one's vote for the candidate whose policies seem to best further the common interest. It is the need to justify one's vote to others, which makes the vote an instrument of one's intellectual and moral growth. A vote cannot be cast arbitrarily, based on insignificant grounds, like, say, the colour of someone's eyes. Everyone must have the franchise, but it must be open. This is how Mill combined the principle of participation and competence in the suffrage to ensure the moral and intellectual growth of the voting citizens.

We find here, again, the motif of improvement. Representative government scores over despotism not because it better protects the given interests of the citizens, but because it is able to improve these citizens (see

**Box 10.6**

**ON REPRESENTATIVE GOVERNMENT BEING THE BEST FORM OF GOVERNMENT:**

There is no difficulty in showing that the ideally best form of government is that in which the sovereignty, or supreme controlling power in the last resort, is vested in the entire aggregate of the community, every citizen not only having a voice in the exercise of that ultimate sovereignty, but being, at least occasionally, called on to take an actual part in the government by the personal discharge of some public function, local or general.

...it is evident that the only government which can fully satisfy all the exigencies of the social state is one in which the whole people participate; that any participation, even in the smallest public function, is useful; that the participation should everywhere be as great as the general degree of improvement of the community will allow; and that nothing less can be ultimately desirable than the admission of all to a share in the sovereign power of the state. But since all cannot, in a community exceeding a single small town, participate personally in any but some very minor portions of the public business, it follows that the ideal type of a perfect government must be representative.

*Considerations on Representative Government*, Chapter 3

Box 10.6). The citizens develop their capabilities by being able to participate in the affairs of their state, by casting their vote, and by actually taking decisions in local government.

In Mill's time the franchise was restricted not just by gender but by property qualifications as well. Mill was wary of giving the vote to the uneducated members of the working class, because he believed that they would end up choosing incompetent policies for the nation. At the same time, he believed that the only way individuals could improve themselves, was by participation. It is this tension between his two principles, participation and competence, that we see in his suggested institutional reforms. It must be mentioned here that Mill highlighted participation as a feature not only of political democracy, but of economic democracy as well. He advocated partnerships between owners and workers to run businesses, as well as worker co-operatives running industrial concerns so that workers could develop their intellectual powers by taking decisions themselves. According to some scholars, Mill seemed to be actually more sanguine about the effect of participation on efficiency and competence in economic concerns than in politics.[25]

## BEYOND UTILITARIANISM

In looking at Mill's writings on liberty and democracy, we asked the question of the link between these concepts and the idea of utility. When answering this query, we must remember that Mill never gave up his self-characterization as a utilitarian, no matter how far his principles seemed to have moved away from that creed. When he spoke about rights, for instance, he subsumed rights under the concept of utility, defining rights as nothing else but some extremely important utilities. As we all know, Mill's father, James Mill, was the closest associate of Jeremy Bentham, the founder of utilitarianism. Mill grew up in the shadow of utilitarianism, and even after the emotional crises of his early twenties, he managed to write a defence of utilitarianism. Throughout his work, we have seen him applying the standard of utility. One consideration for giving equality to women was that it would increase their happiness, and the principle of liberty was defended on the grounds of its social utility. Social progress depended on individual freedom. A modified liberal democracy was characterized as the best form of government because of its usefulness in improving the quality of its citizens.

*Utilitarianism* is the slim tract which Mill put together not only to answer all the objections that had been raised against this philosophy, but also to make certain modifications to the existing theory of utilitarianism, so that it would become consistent with his ideas of liberty and democracy.

The work begins by Mill pointing out that there has been, over the centuries, little agreement on the criteria of differentiating right from wrong. Rejecting the idea of human beings having a moral sense like our sense of sight or smell, which can sense what is right in concrete cases, Mill put forward the criteria of 'utility' or, the 'greatest happiness' principle as the basis of morality. That action is moral which increases pleasure and diminishes pain. In defending utilitarianism here, Mill made a significant change from Bentham's position. Pleasure is to be counted not only in terms of quantity but also in terms of quality. A qualitatively higher pleasure is to count for more than lower pleasures. 'It is quite compatible with the principle of utility to recognise the fact, that some kinds of pleasure are more desirable and more valuable than others... It is better to be Socrates dissatisfied than a pig satisfied.'[26]

Mill's utilitarianism differed from Bentham's by being a qualitative hedonism. According to Mill, in order to calculate the value of a pleasure one has to factor in the nature of the activity from which that pleasure is being derived. Since the activity enters into the evaluation of the pleasure, utilitarianism is no longer about brain states or mental states, but about what we actually do. 'The superiority of qualitative hedonism over the quantitative alternative lies partly in its ability to discriminate among numerous experiences and rank them on the basis of their differences, even as it is recognized that it is only experiences that can be candidates for value. Although Mill was concerned centrally to answer the objection that hedonism is "a doctrine worthy only of swine" and thus to rule out degrading satisfactions, the theory equally can downgrade or rule out entirely inauthentic, hallucinatory, or self-deceptive experiences.'[27]

Having responded to the criticism that utilitarianism assumes an animal-like human nature, Mill moved to the next serious problem. Why would individuals be interested in the happiness of others? Mill answered in terms of the 'social feelings of mankind; the desire to be in unity with our fellow creatures, a powerful principle of human nature.'[28] Claiming that 'the social state is at once so natural, so necessary and so habitual to man, that...he never conceives himself otherwise than as a member of a body',[29] Mill found our tendency of taking an interest in others' happiness not surprising at all.

Finally, the only objection that Mill took seriously was that justice, instead of utility is the foundation of morality. Mill's response was first to link justice with rights—an injustice is done when someone's rights are violated—and then to assert that rights are to be defended because of their utility. 'To have a right, then, is to have something which society ought to defend me in the possession of. If the objector goes on to ask, why it ought? I can give him no other reason than general utility.'[30] A society in which individuals are certain of enjoying their rights is the one, which according to Mill, is able to progress. Thus, rights do not replace the concept of utility. For Mill, utility was the justification for rights.

## FAULT LINES

If Mill's vision was one of men and women improving themselves, and thereby making their society better by speaking out freely, acting freely and forming associations freely, then some problems remain in his writings. In *The Subjection of Women*, for instance, he claims that women choosing to marry are in effect choosing a career of taking care of their husband and children, and there seems to be no place for these women in the public sphere of associational life. How will these women improve themselves when they have no opportunity of lifting themselves out of the 'narrow circle of personal and family selfishness'?[31] Similarly, we find in Mill, a concern for the liberty of the working classes, together with an advocacy of free market and free trade policies. Without governmental intervention in the sphere of economic policy, it is difficult to establish some kind of equality for the poor, and we have seen Mill accepting the link between equality and liberty. In Mill's defence, however, one can say that in his later years he did turn towards a more socialist economic policy.

For all his concern about the liberty of women and the working classes in England, Mill did not think it right that another subjugated group—the colonized in India—should enjoy liberty. Both Mill and his father had worked for the British East India Company for nearly a score years, and both had retired as Chief Examiners in charge of the memoranda guiding the company's policies in India. James Mill had also written *History of British India*, in 1818. John Stuart Mill was convinced that the Indian natives were not rational enough to be given freedom. The harm principle did not apply to children or to persons with not enough reason, and Indians, according to him, were a race without reason.

Many critics of Mill have also pointed out that his attempt to modify Benthamite utilitarianism to accommodate his own emphasis on liberty ultimately failed. Trying to link liberty with self-improvement, Mill had to introduce the distinction between the quantity and quality of pleasures. Given this distinction, who was to judge that a certain pleasure was qualitatively superior to another? 'The test of quality, and the rule for measuring it against quantity, being the preference felt by those who, in their opportunities of experience, to which must be added their habits of self-consciousness and self-observation, are best furnished with the means of comparison.'[32] Some individuals, then, are more competent than others in the valuation of pleasure. It is this same idea of differential competence that became the basis of Mill's advocacy of plural voting in politics. This meant, however, giving up one of the valuable insights of utilitarianism: that each person had to be counted as of equal value. Mill's apparent defence of utilitarianism actually led him to reject some of its essential tenets.

## NOTES

1. The Philosophic Radicals were a group of British thinkers, led by James Mill and Bentham, who distinguished themselves both from the Tories and the Whigs. The Tories were agrarian conservatives, but even the liberal Whigs were wary of the extreme proposals of the Radicals, especially when it came to religious reforms. Later, in the 1840s, the Whigs and the Radicals joined to form the Liberal Party.
2. John Stuart Mill, 'On Liberty' in Stefan Collini (ed.), *On Liberty and Other Writings*, Cambridge: Cambridge University Press, 1989, p. 212.
3. As quoted in C.L. Ten, 'Democracy, socialism and the working classes', in John Skorupski (ed.), *The Cambridge Companion to Mill*, Cambridge University Press, 1998.
4. John Stuart Mill, 'The Subjection of Women', in Stefan Collini (ed.), *On Liberty and Other Writings*, p. 119.
5. See M.L. Shanley, 'The Subjection of Women' in John Skorupski (ed.), *The Cambridge Companion to Mill*.
6. John Stuart Mill, 'The Subjection of Women' in Stefan Collini (ed.), *On Liberty and Other Writings*, p. 132.
7. *Ibid*., p. 196.
8. *Ibid*., p. 160.
9. *Ibid*.
10. *Ibid*., p. 199.
11. *Ibid*.
12. *Ibid*., pp. 211–212. An interesting collection of essays on this work of Mill is Maria H. Morales (ed.), *Mill's* The Subjection of Women: *Critical Essays*, Lanham, MD: Rowman and Littlefield, 2004.
13. John Stuart Mill, 'On Liberty' in Stefan Collini (ed.), *On Liberty and Other Writings*, p. 59.
14. *Ibid*.
15. *Ibid*., p. 20.
16. *Ibid*., p. 47.
17. *Ibid*., p. 13.
18. *Ibid*., p. 109.
19. *Ibid*., pp. 109–110.
20. *Ibid*., p. 110.
21. *Ibid*., p. 70.
22. This argument reminds us of Berlin's position that democracy and liberty are concepts which do not refer to the same things.
23. See Dennis F. Thompson, *John Stuart Mill and Representative Government*, New Jersey: Princeton University Press, 1976.

24. *Ibid.*, p. 285.
25. See Wendy Donner, *The Liberal Self: John Stuart Mill's Moral and Political Philosophy*, Ithaca: Cornell University Press, 1991, pp. 208–217.
26. John Stuart Mill, *Utilitarianism, Liberty, Representative Government*, London: J.M. Dent and Sons Ltd, 1960, pp. 7–9.
27. Wendy Donner, *The Liberal Self*, p. 76.
28. *Ibid.*, p. 29.
29. *Ibid.*
30. John Stuart Mill, *Utilitarianism, Liberty, Representative Government*, p. 60.
31. John Stuart Mill, 'On Liberty', in Stefan Collini (ed.), *On Liberty and Other Writings*, pp. 109–110.
32. Wendy Donner, *The Liberal Self*, p. 40.

## READING LIST

Collini, Stefan (ed.), *On Liberty and Other Writings*, Cambridge: Cambridge University Press, 1989.

Donner, Wendy, *The Liberal Self: John Stuart Mill's Moral and Political Philosophy*, Ithaca: Cornell University Press, 1991.

Mill, John Stuart, *Utilitarianism, Liberty, Representative Government*, London: J.M. Dent and Sons Ltd, 1960.

Skorupski, John (ed.), *The Cambridge Companion to Mill*, Cambridge: Cambridge University Press, 1998.

Thompson, Dennis F., *John Stuart Mill and Representative Government*, New Jersey: Princeton University Press, 1976.

## CENTRAL THEMES

1. **The value of individual liberty:** Mill mounts a defence of individual liberty in the name of the development of human intellectual and moral capacities. What, for Mill, is liberty good for? Does the 'harm' principle sit well with the claim that what liberty is good for is for creating 'better' individuals?
2. **Mill as a feminist:** Mill's emphasis on individual liberty is consistent with his insistence, almost unique in the canon of Western political thought, that women must also enjoy the right to individual liberty. How does Mill develop his critique of women's subordination and what reasons does he give for demanding equality for women?
3. **The reformulation of utilitarianism:** Dissatisfied with some aspects of Bentham's theory, Mill introduced some new ideas into utilitarianism. What are some of the ways in which Mill reformulates the utilitarian position and does this reformulation generate its own problems?
4. **Mill on representative government:** For Mill, given his conception of what government is for, representative government is the best form of government. How does representative government realize the two principles of competence and participation, and is there any conflict between the fulfilment of these two principles?

# ELEVEN

# G.W.F. Hegel (1770–1831): The Social Conditions for a Non-Contractual Theory of Freedom

Georg Wilhelm Friedrich Hegel was a central figure in the philosophical tradition known as German Idealism. The emergence of German Idealism has long been associated with Immanuel Kant whose classic work, *The Critique of Pure Reason*, was published in 1781. Fichte and Schelling developed this tradition further and Hegel, who was a contemporary and a friend of Schelling, is often seen to be the culmination of this philosophical tradition. In contrast to British empiricist writers like Locke and Hume, and later on Mill, who considered all our knowledge to be derived from sense-impressions, the German Idealists gave a primary role to our thoughts and our ideas as the building blocks of human knowledge. German Idealism inherited the epistemological question—How do human beings get to know their world?—from the empiricists. Beginning with this question, and analysing different forms of knowledge, like science (pure reason) and moral knowledge (practical reason), Kant moved from the realm of epistemology to that of moral and political philosophy. In Hegel we find epistemological questions linked even more strongly to moral and political concerns.

Hegel was born in 1770, in Stuttgart, in what is now south-western Germany. He went to school there, after which he studied philosophy and theology at Tubingen. On completing his studies in 1793, he worked for some time as a tutor for wealthy families in Switzerland and in Frankfurt. During these years, Hegel wrote a few essays on religion, which he never published in his lifetime, but which were published posthumously as *Early Theological Writings*. In these essays, he grappled both with Kantian philosophy (which states that the most important attribute of human nature is reason) and the teachings of Jesus (which states that the most important attribute of human nature is love). In these early essays, Hegel seemed to favour Jesus's position over that of Kant's,[1] but he would later go on to affirm freedom as the most important attribute of human nature and to analyse the relationship of human freedom to human reason and love.

When Hegel was about 30 years old, he began teaching at the University of Jena, and it is here that he wrote his greatest work, *Phenomenology of Spirit*. In a famous letter to his friend, Hegel wrote that he was penning down the last page of *Phenomenology of Spirit* as Napoleon was riding into the city of Jena, with his troops. Hegel came of age during the turbulent years of the French Revolution, and the Napoleonic conquests of different parts of Europe, and these events certainly affected Hegel's thinking.

It is not only contemporary political events that a thinker responds to, but the intellectual currents of the day also influence his or her thoughts. The revolution in ideas of the 18th century named the Enlightenment had its own local flavour in Scotland, England, France, and in the area that we now know as Germany. The German Enlightenment was mediated very strongly by the Romantic movement and its advocacy of individual self-expression. Goethe, who was the towering figure of German Romanticism, and several other important German Romantics, like Holderlin and the Schlegel brothers, were Hegel's close friends. Thus, Hegel was a figure whose thought straddles both the German Enlightenment as well as German Romanticism.[2]

After Napoleon captured Jena, its university closed down and Hegel had to work for about a year as a newspaper editor in Bamberg. Then he became the headmaster of a high school at Nuremberg, where he remained for nine years. In 1816, he finally moved to the University of Heidelberg, and after a short stint there, took up the chair of philosophy at the University of Berlin, in 1818. He worked and taught there till his death, in November 1831. By the time he died, philosophy departments all over Europe were dominated by Hegelian philosophy.[3]

Since Hegel taught philosophy for so long, many of his works have survived in the form of lecture notes, like, *Lectures on the Philosophy of History*, *Lectures on Aesthetics*, and *Lectures on the History of Philosophy*. Hegel was also a prodigous writer. After publishing *Phenomenology of Spirit*, in 1807, he brought out *Science of Logic* in three volumes, followed by *Encyclopaedia of the Philosophical Sciences*, and finally, in 1821, *Philosophy of Right*.

Hegel's work has been subject to many interpretations. As soon as he died, his work generated the two schools of the right Hegelians and the left Hegelians. The former interpreted Hegel as a conservative thinker who was attempting to defend the *status quo*, whereas the left Hegelians, in whose ranks were included Feuerbach and Marx, saw Hegel's work as having radical implications. More recently, there has been a tendency to interpret Hegel as a liberal thinker,[4] but this interpretation is sharply contested by those who want to use Hegel's work to develop a non-communist, yet radical alternative to liberalism.[5] Let us now begin a discussion of some Hegelian ideas to see how these alternative interpretations can find a foothold in his concepts.

## THE CONSCIOUSNESS OF FREEDOM

In my opinion, for Hegel, as for the social contractualists, the central modern value was that of individual freedom. Hegel repeatedly interpreted different historical events as struggles which had the realization of freedom as their aim. He also stated that the criterion for the legitimacy of political institutions was whether they hampered or facilitated individual freedom. In this emphasis on freedom, Hegel was as one with modern political philosophy. At the same time, he developed his own distinctive concept of freedom, very different from that of Hobbes or of Kant. Hegel did not see freedom as the Hobbesian fulfilment of unobstructed desire, and neither did he see it in Kantian terms as something that is opposed to sensuous desires. Central to the meaning of freedom for Hegel was the idea of embodiment in an 'other'. Embodiment in otherness in general becomes a requirement of individual freedom. We have to now examine what Hegel meant by defining freedom as self-determination in otherness, and see how he constructed his political theory on this foundational principle.

Before we begin our explanation, we must deal with an objection. Many scholars have insisted that individual freedom could not be a central value for Hegel, because, according to these scholars, Hegel defined freedom in such a way as to make it look very much like non-freedom. Let us look at this argument briefly. Hegel claimed that whereas animals could not be called free, because they were governed by drives and instincts, it was part of human nature to be free, because human beings, unlike animals, had the faculty of willing. See Box 11.1 for Hegel's own description of a human will that is free. What is the will, for Hegel? The will, unlike theoretical reason, is thought which results in action. 'For Hegel, the will is not a faculty separate from thinking but rather, "a particular way of thinking—thinking translating itself into existence, thinking as the drive to give itself existence".'[6] Since human beings have the faculty of consciousness, when a human being performs an action in order to fulfil his desires, this action differs from when an animal does the same, because a human being represents to himself the object of his desire.

Box 11.1

**THE THREE ELEMENTS OF THE WILL:**

The will contains (a) the element of pure indeterminateness, i.e., the pure doubling of the I back in thought upon itself. In this process every limit or content, present though it be directly by way of nature, as in want, appetite or impulse, or given in any specific way, is dissolved. Thus we have the limitless infinitude of absolute abstraction, or universality, the pure thought of itself.

*Note.*—Those who treat thinking and willing as two special, peculiar, and separate faculties, and, further, look upon thought as detrimental to the will, especially the good will, show from the very start that they know nothing of the nature of willing—a remark which we shall be called upon to make a number of times upon the same attitude of mind.

—The will on one side is the possibility of abstraction from every aspect in which the I finds itself or has set itself up. It reckons any content as a limit, and flees from it. This is one of the forms of the self-direction of the will, and is by imaginative thinking insisted upon as of itself freedom. It is the negative side of the will, or freedom as apprehended by the understanding. This freedom is that of the void, which has taken actual shape, and is stirred to passion. It, while remaining purely theoretical, appears in Hindu religion as the fanaticism of pure contemplation; but becoming actual it assumes both in politics and religion the form of a fanaticism, which would destroy the established social order, remove all individuals suspected of desiring any kind of order, and demolish any organization which then sought to rise out of the ruins. Only in devastation does the negative will feel that it has reality. It intends, indeed, to bring to pass some positive social condition, such as universal equality or universal religious life. But in fact it does not will the positive reality of any such condition, since that would carry in its train a system, and introduce a separation by way of institutions and between individuals.

But classification and objective system attain self-consciousness only by destroying negative freedom. Negative freedom is actuated by a mere solitary abstract idea, whose realization is nothing but the fury of desolation.

*Addition.*—This phase of will implies that I break loose from everything, give up all ends, and bury myself in abstraction. It is man alone who can let go everything, even life. He can commit suicide, an act impossible for the animal, which always remains only negative, abiding in a state foreign to itself, to which it must merely get accustomed. Man is pure thought of himself, and only in thinking has he the power to give himself universality and to extinguish in himself all that is particular and definite. Negative freedom, or freedom of the understanding, is one-sided, yet as this one-sidedness contains an essential feature, it is not to be discarded. But the defect of the understanding is that it exalts its one-sidedness to the sole and highest place. This form of freedom frequently occurs in history. By the Hindus, e.g., the highest freedom is declared to be persistence in the consciousness of one's simple identity with himself, to abide in the empty space of one's own inner being, like the colourless light of pure intuition, and to renounce every activity of life, every purpose and every idea. In this way man becomes Brahma; there is no longer any distinction between finite man and Brahma, every difference having been swallowed up in this universality. A more concrete manifestation of this freedom is the fanaticism of political and religious life. Of this nature was the terrible epoch of the French Revolution, by which all distinctions in talent and authority were to have been superseded. In this time of upheaval and commotion any specific thing was intolerable. Fanaticism wills an abstraction and not an articulate association.

It finds all distinctions antagonistic to its indefiniteness, and supersedes them. Hence in the French Revolution the people abolished the institutions which they themselves had set up, since every institution is inimical to the abstract self-consciousness of equality. (b) The I is also the transition from blank indefiniteness to the distinct and definite establishment of a definite content and object, whether this content be given by nature or produced out of the conception of spirit. Through this establishment of itself as a definite thing the I becomes a reality. This is the absolute element of the finitude or specialization of the I.

*Note.* This second element in the characterization of the I is just as negative as the first, since it annuls and replaces the first abstract negativity. As the particular is contained in the universal, so this second phase is contained already in the first, and is only an establishing of what the first is implicitly. The first phase, if taken independently, is not the true infinitude, i.e., the concrete universal, or the conception, but limited and one-sided. In that it is the abstraction from all definite character, it has a definite character. Its abstract and one-sided nature constitutes its definite character, its defect and finitude.

The distinct characterization of these two phases of the I is found in the philosophy of Fichte as also in that of Kant. Only, in the exposition of Fichte the I, when taken as unlimited, as it is in the first proposition of his "Wissenschaftslehre," is merely positive. It is the universally and identity made by the understanding. Hence this abstract I is in its independence to be taken as the truth, to which by way of mere addition comes in the second proposition, the limitation, or the negative in general, whether it be in the form of a given external limit or of an activity of the I.

To apprehend the negative as immanent in the universal or self-identical, and also as in the I, was the next step, which speculative philosophy had to make. Of this want they have no presentiment, who like Fichte never apprehend that the infinite and finite are, if separated, abstract, and must be seen as immanent one in the other.

*Addition.*—This second element makes its appearance as the opposite of the first; it is to be understood in its general form: it belongs to freedom but does not constitute the whole of it. Here the I passes over from blank in determinateness to the distinct establishment of a specific character as a content or object. I do not will merely, but I will something. Such a will, as is analysed in the preceding paragraph, wills only the abstract universal, and therefore wills nothing. Hence it is not a will.

The particular thing, which the will wills is a limitation, since the will, in order to be a will, must in general limit itself. Limit or negation consists in the will willing something. Particularizing is thus as a rule named finitude. Ordinary reflection holds the first element, that of the indefinite, for the absolute and higher, and the limited for a mere negation of this indefiniteness. But this indefiniteness is itself only a negation, in contrast with the definite and finite. The I is solitude and absolute negation. The indefinite will is thus quite as much one-sided as the will, which continues merely in the definite

(c) The will is the unity of these two elements. It is particularity turned back within itself and thus led back to universality; it is individuality; it is the self-direction of the I. Thus at one and the same time it establishes itself as its own negation, that is to say, as definite and limited, and it also abides by itself, in its self-identity and universality, and in this position remains purely self-enclosed.— The I determines itself in so far as it is the reference of negativity to itself; and yet in this self-reference it is indifferent to its own definite character. This it knows as its own, that is, as an ideal or a mere possibility, by which it is not bound, but rather exists in it merely because it establishes itself there.

—This is the freedom of the will, constituting its conception or substantive reality. It is its gravity, as it were, just as gravity is the substantive reality of a body.

*Philosophy of Right*

If it is the nature of animals to follow their drives, it is the nature of human beings to be determined by their will. To be self-determined is to be determined by one's will, or in other words, to let the will determine itself. For example, if I am hungry, and I eat, this is an example of free action because I could choose not to eat. But even though the choice would be mine, the content of that choice—to eat or not to eat—would not be given by the will. Does that mean that for Hegel, for the will to be free, it must also determine when I feel hungry? Only when we determine all aspects of ourselves, can the will be said to determine itself, and only then can we be said to be self-determined.

This understanding of freedom seems rather different from the common understanding of the concept. Generally, to follow our desires unhindered, and not to fret about the source of those desires, is considered to be freedom. It also seems rather different from Hegel's definition of freedom, because this is not how Hegel defined freedom. Hegel often defined freedom as, 'being at home with oneself in one's other'.[7] This could mean, for instance, that we become conscious of our body, let us say, as an 'other' with its own needs. We accept the needs of the body, like the need for food and the need for exercise as necessary for the body's and thereby our own health. Once we accept these needs of our body as a part of us, the body no longer seems like an 'other', as something which is a constraint or an obstacle to our will. The needs of the body are no longer an infringement on our freedom. 'The freedom of man, as regards natural impulses, consists not in his being rid of such impulses altogether and thus striving to escape from his nature but in his recognition of them as a necessity and as something rational.'[8] Human beings can recognize the rational order among their natural impulses, and they are engaged in precisely this attempt when they try to make themselves happy. 'In happiness, thought already has some power over the natural force of the drives, for it is not content with the instantaneous, but requires a whole of happiness.'[9]

We can see, here, why many scholars argue that Hegel overturned the usual meaning of freedom, although, as we just discussed, the sense of freedom as the absence of constraints seems to be included in Hegel's understanding of freedom. The problem is that one's acceptance of the 'rational order of the impulses' or of the 'rational order of specific political institutions and social relations' would mean that one does not see those impulses or those institutions as a constraint to one's freedom. Freedom, then, becomes just another name for reconciliation. Individual freedom is, as theorists point out, about how external elements constrain one's desires, but Hegel seems to make it out primarily to be about what one does to oneself. For these theorists, Hegel diminishes the idea of individual freedom by equating it with self-control or with self-acceptance. It remains true, however, that in Hegel's writings, we frequently find an attempt to define individual freedom as a relationship between the 'self' and the 'other'. Let us look at this relationship as set out by Hegel, to see whether his conception of freedom can hold true against the objections we have been referring to.

By using the term 'self-determination' for freedom, Hegel focused our attention on the 'self' which is attempting to determine itself. Self-consciousness, which is the minimal condition to be fulfilled for there to be a sense of self, only arises, Hegel said, through an interaction with another self, that is, an 'other'. By insisting on this, Hegel opened up the whole idea of the social requirements of freedom, requirements which are much more stringent than the liberal absence of restraint. For liberals, individual freedom is only possible under certain social and political conditions, which can be encapsulated in the idea of the absence of the 'other'. In liberalism, until the state prevents others from interfering with one's life, as well as does not itself encroach upon one's space, there can be no individual freedom. Liberals often think of freedom as existing when no one stops one from doing as one desires. One must be free to follow one's desires and aims. Taking an almost opposite position, Hegel pointed out, that even if this were the definition of freedom, what the freedom of the individual requires is not the absence, but the presence of the other.

'Self-consciousness exists in and for itself when, and by the fact that, it so exists for another, that is, it exists only in being acknowledged.'[10] If we take this statement of Hegel to mean that our sense of ourselves is mediated through the acknowledgement of others, then we see how others can be perceived as threatening to us. The 'other' can make us feel estranged from ourselves; we look down on ourselves because the 'other' looks down on us. To get rid of this self-alienation, for which the 'other' is responsible, we feel an urge to get rid of, destroy or subjugate the 'other', who has cast our self-certainty about ourselves in doubt. This is the famous struggle between the 'master' and the 'slave' to which we will also be referring to later. It is here that Hegel points out that dominating the 'other' is no solution to the problem of self-consciousness. If the self subjugates the 'other', then that other's consciousness cannot be a source of the certainty of the 'self'. The 'other' must be recognized as an equal and only through this 'mutual recognition' between two equals, do these two separate 'selves' become conscious of themselves as having the capacity of and the right to freedom.

It is not only for a sense of being a 'self' with the capacity of freedom[11] that the presence of the 'other' is required. If we consider the next step, which is the 'self' having certain goals, for the achievement of which this 'self' wants to be free in the first place, the other enters the picture in yet another way. Hegel believed that all 'selves' are constituted in society. It is by growing up as members of particular societies that human beings acquire their aims, desires and purposes, and are thereby constituted as individual selves. The 'other', thus, is always present in the 'self'. Hegel was distinguishing one kind of presence of the 'other', which we can call 'situatedness', from another kind of the presence of the 'other', which we have called 'mutual recognition'. In all historical societies, we are situated beings, in the sense that our aims and desires develop in and through our belonging to such societies. It is in modern societies alone, though, that there is a mutual recognition between individuals, of being free, of consciously choosing to pursue the aims and purposes given to us in society. When our self-consciousness is a consciousness of ourselves as free beings, for Hegel, this means that such 'selves' follow some goals and purposes not merely because these are the purposes that are followed in their society, but because these 'selves' consider these purposes to be rational. Hegel rejected the idea that following one's desires was to be free or self-determined, on the ground that these desires came to one from external social forces. However, if these desires are made one's own through a process of rational deliberation, then one can be said to be free.

For Hegel, this consciousness of freedom develops progressively in human history. In *Philosophy of History*, Hegel claimed that all of human history was to be understood as a progressive realization of the idea of freedom. In earlier societies, for example, in the 'oriental despotisms' of China, India and Persia, the belief system sustaining these societies was that only one individual, the monarch, was entitled to be free. In other ancient societies that were slave-owning democracies, for instance, several Greek city-states, the dominant ideology was that not one, but some men—the free born Greek males—were meant to be free. The development of Christianity in the Roman empire, and more significantly, the Reformation, brought about the modern idea that individual freedom is an entitlement of all human beings.[12] It should be clear by now that the human consciousness of freedom is not, according to Hegel, inborn. The modern idea that all human beings, male or female, of whatever rank, caste, class or educational status, are entitled to be free, emerges only after a long historical process.

**Box 11.2**

**HEGEL ON WORLD HISTORY:**

As states are particular, there is manifested in their relation to one another a shifting play of internal particularity of passions, interests, aims, talents, virtues, force, wrong, vice, and external contingency on the very largest scale. In this play even the ethical whole, national independence, is exposed to chance. The spirit of a nation is an existing individual having in particularity its objective actuality and self-consciousness.

Because of this particularity it is limited. The destinies and deeds of states in their connection with one another are the visible dialectic of the finite nature of these spirits. Out of this dialectic the universal spirit, the spirit of the world, the unlimited spirit, produces itself. It has the highest right of all, and exercises its right upon the lower spirits in world-history. The history of the world is the world's court of judgement.

*Lectures on the Philosophy of History*

If this long historical process tells us the one story of the human consciousness of freedom, this would imply that for Hegel, all of human history is a seamless web (see Box 11.2). Not only does the history of different societies mark, as we just saw, different moments in our consciousness of freedom, each stage in the historical development of, say, philosophy in Germany, becomes part of the same story of the development of human consciousness. In *Phenomenology of Spirit*, Hegel sought to trace the growth of this human consciousness by looking at the evolution of the intellectual culture of the West through its art, religion and philosophy. When Hegel's *Phenomenology of Spirit* traces the unfolding of consciousness to itself, it constantly takes particular schools of Western philosophy to embody different and progressive moments of this unfolding. Seventeenth century empiricism, for instance, is consciousness understanding itself to be merely the reflection of external objects, whereas Kantian philosophy is consciousness realizing that its consciousness of external objects is also a self-consciousness. This whole story, with its different moments being the various understandings of what it means for a human being to be free, is told in *Phenomenology*, through an interpretation of different moments in Western art, religion and philosophy, with philosophy being, for Hegel, a clearer expression of human consciousness than art or religion.

## THE EMBODIMENT OF FREEDOM

The story of human freedom cannot, obviously, be told as the story of art, religion and philosophy alone. For Hegel, it is equally the story of social practices and social institutions. This brings us to the other aspect of the

Hegelian philosophy of freedom, that is, the relationship he posited between ideas and their material embodiment. For Hegel, the principle of embodiment was crucial, since it is through its embodiment that the reality of anything is expressed. For instance, according to Hegel, for a human being to know himself, he has to embody himself in a reality outside of his 'self', in something that is not his 'self'. Only when he expresses his 'self', does his 'self' gain a reality and he gains knowledge of his 'self'. Thus, an idea must be embodied in something material, for example, in some practice, for us to know what that idea is an idea of. To explain it in religious terms, for Hegel, it is not so much that the world cannot exist without the Absolute (a Hegelian term which some have taken to be a reference to God) but that the Absolute cannot exist without the world, because without embodying itself in the world, the Absolute cannot even know itself. Peter Singer describes well this Hegelian idea of embodiment. 'For Hegel sees God not as eternal and immutable, but as an essence that needs to manifest itself in the world, and having made itself manifest, to perfect the world in order to perfect itself.'[13]

Earlier, we had described the struggle of consciousness for recognition. The outcome of this struggle is the famous Hegelian master–slave dialectic which has to run its course for the realization of the need for 'mutual recognition' to dawn. Before this recognition takes place, only one consciousness wins recognition for its freedom and Hegel terms this consciousness that of the master. The consciousness who loses the battle for recognition is that of the slave. The master, freeing himself from labour, uses the slave to do all the work. It is the slave who 'transforms nature and himself through work… He works in terms of an abstract idea, a project to be realized. He forms the external world which acquires a consistency of its own and bears his mark, and he forms himself by separating himself from his instincts and by becoming an apprentice in abstract general notions, language and thought. Thus, through the slave's work, both the world of technique and society itself on the one hand, and the world of thought, art and religion on the other are constituted.'[14] Even though this relationship is not a consciousness of freedom for either the master or the slave, for Hegel, it is the position of the slave which captures one moment of freedom, that of embodiment.

The institutional embodiment of the idea of individual freedom in social practices becomes, then, an essential component of the reality of individual freedom. If the human consciousness of freedom is not inborn, if it is a historical consciousness, emerging or being engendered through interaction with others, then, the social is the location of individual freedom. Individual freedom, for Hegel, is situated in the social. The social (social practices and institutions) is the site of individual freedom. The modern consciousness of freedom, Hegel wrote, is expressed in the social institutions that make up modern life. In *Philosophy of Right*, Hegel gives us his analysis of how individual freedom is embodied in the modern institutions of the family, civil society and the state, since it is belonging to these institutions that makes up a person's life in modern societies. Hegel believed that it was the modern family, civil society and the modern state, that were the institutional embodiments of a 'mutual recognition' based freedom (see Box 11.3).

**Box 11.3**

**THE RELATIONSHIP OF PHILOSOPHY TO THE STATE AND ITS PRACTICES:**

Further, as to rights, ethical observances, and the state, the truth is as old as that in which it is openly displayed and recognized, namely, the law, morality, and religion. But as the thinking spirit is not satisfied with possessing the truth in this simple way, it must conceive it, and thus acquire a rational form for a content which is already rational implicitly. In this way the substance is justified before the bar of free thought.

Free thought cannot be satisfied with what is given to it, whether by the external positive authority of the state or human agreement, or by the authority of internal feelings, the heart, and the witness of the spirit, which coincides unquestioningly with the heart. It is the nature of free thought rather to proceed out of its own self, and hence to demand that it should know itself as thoroughly one with truth.

*Philosophy of Right*

For Hegel, the modern family is based on the principle of consent. Whether the marriage through which a new family comes into being results from an arrangement between the partners' parents, or whether it takes place because two individuals fall in love with each other, Hegel claimed that it must always be based on the consent of the marriage partners. The 'subjective will' of the two partners must be satisfied, and it is in this sense that the modern family expresses the idea of individual freedom. In one of his early essays, Hegel had stated that 'love is somewhat analogous to reason in that it finds itself in other people'.[15] Looking at the institution of the family in light of this statement, we find that for Hegel, the family is, first of all, a union of two individuals. A husband and a wife are supposed to find themselves in each other, and in that sense, the family is based on 'mutual recognition'. The union of the family is also voluntary; the recognition granted to each other must be freely given. In Hegel's words, 'The subjective origin of marriage may lie to a greater extent in the particular inclination of the two persons who enter this relationship, or in the foresight and initiative of parents etc. But its objective origin is the free consent of the persons concerned, and in particular their consent to constitute a single person and to give up their natural and individual personalities within this union. In this respect, their union is a self-limitation, but since they attain their substantial self-consciousness within it, it is in fact their liberation.'[16]

The family is only the first unit of social organization. Next, Hegel took up an analysis of the social and economic interactions of individuals belonging to different families. These interactions take place in the sphere of civil society. Civil society is a much wider realm than the economy for Hegel. It is made up of at least four different systems or institutions: the system of needs, the administration of justice, the police and the corporations.[17] By the system of needs, Hegel was referring to the production and exchange of commodities by individuals, in the attempt to satisfy their material needs. This exchange makes individuals conscious of their dependence on each other to satisfy their needs (see Box 11.4). The exchange of commodities also presupposes a certain system of rights. Individuals in modern society have the right to own and alienate property and the justice system protects these rights and punishes their encroachment. Next, Hegel moves to a discussion of the 'police', justifying the transition thus: 'In the system of needs, the livelihood and welfare of each individual are a possibility whose actualization is conditioned by the individual's own arbitrary will and particular nature, as well as by the objective system of needs. Through the administration of justice, infringements of property or personality are annulled. But the right which is actually present in particularity means not only that... the undisturbed security of persons and property should be guaranteed, but also that the livelihood and welfare of individuals should be secured—that is, that particular welfare should be treated as a right and duty actualized.'[18] As Wood explains, Hegel's term 'police' covers 'what we would call the "welfare" system'.[19] The 'police' or 'public authority' provides for the welfare of all individuals in civil society. The welfare institution of the 'police' ensures that all individuals in civil society have a source of livelihood, and access, for example, to educational and health facilities. The welfare state becomes essential for individual freedom given Hegel's belief that poverty stricken individuals must not be dependent on someone's charity in order to sustain themselves. It is their right that they be sustained by the welfare state. In his third lecture series, of 1819–1820, on 'right, ethics and the state', Hegel conceded that 'the emergence of poverty in general was a consequence of civil society'; yet he called poverty 'a corruption of civil society'. 'The poor man is conscious of himself as an infinite, free being and thus arises the demand that his external existence should correspond to this consciousness'. But in his condition of poverty, his self-consciousness 'appears driven to the point where it no longer has any rights, where freedom has no existence',[20] and so if the modern state is to be the realization of individual freedom, poverty must be dealt with by the 'public authority'.

The fourth element of civil society, for Hegel, is the corporations. The corporations are mainly associations of workers in trade and industry who share the same profession. Members who belong to the same corporation see their fellow members almost as family members and realize that the fulfilment of the needs of fellow members is beneficial to their own interests. As members of different corporations, individuals acquire an idea of a collective interest. Hegel called the corporations the second ethical root of the state after the family, because each corporation encourages its members to see the complementarity of their interests. Here, again, we see Hegel positing that individual freedom, as the fulfilment of one's interest, is mediated by the interests of others.

**Box 11.4**

HEGEL'S CONCEPT OF CIVIL SOCIETY:

The civic community is the realm of difference, intermediate between the family and the state, although its construction followed in point of time the construction of the state. It, as the difference, must presuppose the state. On the self-dependent state it must rely for its subsistence. Further, the creation of the civic community belongs to the modern world which alone has permitted every element of the idea to receive its due. When the state is represented as a union of different persons, that is, a unity which is merely a community, it is only the civic community which is meant. Many modern teachers of political science have not been able to develop any other view of the state. In this society every one is an end to himself; all others are for him nothing. And yet without coming into relation with others he cannot realize his ends. Hence to each particular person others are a means to the attainment of his end.

But the particular purpose gives itself through reference to others the form of universality, and in satisfying itself accomplishes at the same time the well-being of others. Since particularity is bound up with the conditioning universal, the joint whole is the ground of adjustment or mediation, upon which all individualities, all talents, all accidents of birth or fortune disport themselves. Here the fountains of all the passions are let loose, being merely governed by the sun of reason. Particularity limited by universality is the only standard to which the particular person conforms in promoting his well-being. 183. The self-seeking end is conditioned in its realization by the universal. Hence is formed a system of mutual dependence, a system which interweaves the subsistence, happiness, and rights of the individual with the subsistence, happiness, and right of all. The general right and well-being form the basis of the individual's right and well-being, which only by this connection receives actuality and security. This system we may in the first instance call the external state, the state which satisfies one's needs, and meets the requirements of the understanding.

*Philosophy of Right*

The preceding positive description of the different institutions of civil society cannot do away with the fact that for Hegel, 'concrete freedom' is only realized through the modern state. Hegel uses the term 'state' in different senses. Sometimes, the term includes the other institutions that make up modern society, since the state is the precondition of these social institutions; otherwise, Hegel used the term in the narrow sense of specifically governmental institutions consisting of a bicameral legislature, a meritocracy based executive and a constitutional monarchy.

For Hegel, the idea of the state was that of a political community, a collective effort by a group of people to define itself in managing its collective life together. The political community subsumes all other kinds of social life or communities because it is the decisions made at the level of the state that govern other kinds of social interaction. In that sense, Hegel is clear that social interaction is not given by nature, but comes about consciously and depends on rules that are made at a political level. The family, for instance, is not a natural institution but its form is decided by the political community.[21] It is in that sense that the state or political community is prior to other communities like the family or civil society. Given that the modern family and civil society are embodiments of freedom, the modern state, as their precondition, thus also becomes a realization of human freedom (see Box 11.5).

**Box 11.5**

**FREEDOM IN THE MODERN STATE:**

**260.** The state is the embodiment of concrete freedom. In this concrete freedom, personal individuality and its particular interests, as found in the family and civic community, have their complete development. In this concrete freedom, too, the rights of personal individuality receive adequate recognition. These interests and rights pass partly of their own accord into the interest of the universal. Partly, also, do the individuals recognize by their own knowledge and will the universal as their own substantive spirit, and work for it as their own end. Hence, neither is the universal completed without the assistance of the particular interest, knowledge, and will, nor, on the other hand, do individuals, as private persons, live merely for their own special concern. They regard the general end, and are in all their activities conscious of this end. The modern state has enormous strength and depth, in that it allows the principle of subjectivity to complete itself to an independent extreme of personal particularity, and yet at the same time brings it back into the substantive unity, and thus preserves particularity in the principle of the state.

*Lectures on the Philosophy of History*

In the narrowly political sense as well, the institutions of the state embody individual freedom. The modern state is based on the principle of political equality, and for Hegel, all members of the modern state participate in some measure in making the rules that determine their collective life. In so far as the legislature is concerned, Hegel believed that the debates in the legislative assembly must be made public, because it is by listening to these debates that the public can participate in the decision making. Endorsing the publicity with which the proceedings of the Estates (Hegel's term for the legislature) are conducted, Hegel said that 'Public opinion has been a major force in all ages, and this is particularly true in our own times, in which the principle of subjective freedom has such importance and significance. Whatever is to achieve recognition today no longer achieves it by force, and only to a small extent through habit and custom, but mainly through insight and reasoned argument.'[22] Hegel believed that the citizens, by being attentive to and attending the public proceedings of the legislative Estates, and using their freedom of expression and the freedom of the press to generate a vocal public opinion, could be said to be participating in governmental decision making. Hegel was not a supporter of our modern principle of universal adult franchise because he thought that the vote merely 'atomized' the individual citizen further.

The same principle of freedom requires that the executive power be in the hands of a bureaucracy chosen by an open competition, and based on merit. Hegel called the members of the bureaucracy the universal class because he believed that they would serve the common interest of the community. Hegel was also insistent that the monarch must be a constitutional monarch, whose role basically would be to sign on the dotted line.

Taken together, these social and political institutions complete the story of Hegelian freedom. They reflect, as well as reinforce the idea that each human being has the right to be free. Their structure also clarifies what it is that Hegel meant when he discussed freedom as self-determination in his different writings.

## CRITICAL RESPONSES TO HEGEL

Today, in many quarters, Hegel is not very popular as a thinker. Many people have taken to heart his dictum that history is the progressive realization of the idea of freedom. You must have seen reports about several world leaders who have claimed to be acting for the sake of spreading freedom in the world. For most of them, the spread of freedom means the establishment of liberal democracy. They believe that individual freedom is maximized under liberal democracy, and therefore, they are unhappy with Hegel's criticism of liberal democracy. His strictures against 'subjective freedom' and his rejection of the English Reform Bill of 1831 which sought to extend the suffrage, brand him, in the eyes of these critics, as a conservative for whom individual freedom was not really a central value. When freedom becomes identified with liberal democracy, any reservations about the latter are seen as an attack on freedom itself. Hegel, in such a world view, becomes an enemy of individual freedom.

Of course there are many theorists today, who agree with Hegel that freedom as self-determination requires much more than liberal democracy. For these thinkers, to view the idea of freedom as no one or nothing stopping one from doing as one desires, within a framework of minimal laws, is to make a travesty of the value of freedom. To understand the Hegelian idea of freedom, we need to ask ourselves why we consider freedom for individuals so valuable. What is freedom good for, and how does it enhance human flourishing? Or, is freedom human flourishing itself? Is it because Hegel had a certain view of human flourishing of which freedom was an important part, that he refused to define freedom as just doing what one wants? For these critics, Hegel's importance as a political philosopher lies in that he complicated the idea of freedom as self-determination. Even these theorists, however, have given up on Hegel's idea that history is the march of human freedom. So, by his supporters, too, Hegel is branded as a conservative thinker. Hegel is attacked for holding on to the Enlightenment ideas of 'progress', 'science', and 'reason', and for not seeing that these ideals actually mask the domination of large groups of people. Hegel's claim of having individual freedom as his central value again comes under attack when his philosophical system is faulted for not having the intellectual resources to unmask domination. For these critics, to see all of human history as progressing towards a goal of spreading freedom, is to be unacceptably teleological. The attempt to posit one end for the entire world and then turn the gaze backwards into history, obviously led Hegel to misinterpret different histories to fit the *telos* that he had already set.

## NOTES

1. See W.H. Walsh, 'The Origins of Hegelianism', in M. Inwood (ed.), *Hegel*, Oxford: Oxford University Press, 1985.
2. See Charles Taylor, *Hegel*, Cambridge: Cambridge University Press, 1975, pp. 3–50.
3. For biographical details about Hegel, see Peter Singer, Chapter 1 in *Hegel*, Oxford: Oxford University Press, 1983. This book is a short and excellent introduction to Hegel's main ideas.
4. See Steven B. Smith, *Hegel's Critique of Liberalism: Rights in Context*, Chicago: University of Chicago Press, 1989.
5. See John O'Neill (ed.), *Hegel's Dialectic of Desire and Recognition*, Albany: State University of New York Press, 1996, and Robert R. Williams, *Hegel's Ethics of Recognition*, Berkeley: University of California Press, 1998.
6. Paul Franco, *Hegel's Philosophy of Freedom*, New Haven: Yale University Press, 1999, p. 157.
7. *Ibid.*, p. 155.
8. *Ibid.*, p. 167.
9. *Ibid.*

10. Georg W.F. Hegel, *Phenomenology of Spirit* translated by A.V. Miller, Oxford: Oxford University Press, 1977, p. 111.
11. 'I am somebody with my own aims and purposes and I have a right to fulfil these aims.'—This idea does not come to one automatically. This consciousness arises in one, according to Hegel, as a result of interaction with others, under certain social conditions.
12. See George W.F. Hegel, *Philosophy of History* translated by J. Sibree, New York: Dover Publications, 1956. Hegel divided *Philosophy of History* into four parts, with the first part discussing the 'Oriental World' of China, India and Persia, the second part the 'Greek World', the third part the 'Roman World' in which a discussion of Christianity is included, and the fourth part the 'German World', containing a section on the 'modern time' and the Reformation, the Enlightenment and the French Revolution.
13. Peter Singer, *Hegel*, p. 83.
14. Pierre Hassner, 'George W.F. Hegel' in Leo Strauss and Joseph Cropsey (eds), *History of Political Philosophy*, 3rd edition, Chicago: University of Chicago Press, 1987, p. 735.
15. George W.F. Hegel, *Three Essays (1793–1795): The Tubingen Essay, Berne Fragments, The Life of Jesus*, translated by P. Fuss and J. Dobbins, Notre Dame: University of Notre Dame Press, 1984, p. 46
16. George W.F. Hegel, *Elements of the Philosophy of Right*, edited by A.W. Wood, translated by H.B. Nisbet, Cambridge: Cambridge University Press, 1991, p. 201.
17. *Ibid.*, p. 226.
18. *Ibid.*, p. 260.
19. *Ibid.*, p. 450.
20. Hegel lectured on the topics of 'right, ethics and the state' seven times. This quotation is from the third lecture series, transcribed probably by one of Hegel's students, and quoted in George W.F. Hegel, *Elements of the Philosophy of Right*, pp. 453–454.
21. The legal rules that govern the family will differ, for example, from one historical period to another.
22. George W.F. Hegel, *Elements of the Philosophy of Right*, p. 353.

## READING LIST

Franco, Paul, *Hegel's Philosophy of Freedom*, New Haven: Yale University Press, 1999.

Hegel, George W.F., *Elements of the Philosophy of Right*, edited by A.W. Wood, translated by H.B. Nisbet, Cambridge: Cambridge University Press, 1991.

Hegel, George W.F., *Philosophy of History* translated by J. Sibree, New York: Dover Publications, 1956.

Inwood, M., (ed.), *Hegel*, Oxford: Oxford University Press, 1985.

O'Neill, John (ed.), *Hegel's Dialectic of Desire and Recognition*, Albany: State University of New York Press, 1996.

Singer, Peter, *Hegel*, Oxford: Oxford University Press, 1983.
Smith, Steven B., *Hegel's Critique of Liberalism: Rights in Context*, Chicago: University of Chicago Press, 1989.
Taylor, Charles, *Hegel*, Cambridge: Cambridge University Press, 1975.
Williams, Robert R., *Hegel's Ethics of Recognition*, Berkeley: University of California Press, 1998.

## CENTRAL THEMES

1. **Hegel's conception of individual freedom:** Individual freedom is defined by Hegel as some kind of 'being with the self in the other'. What does Hegel mean by the 'other', and what are the different ways in which Hegel shows us that the 'other' becomes part of our freedom?
2. **History and the Idea of Freedom:** For Hegel, history is the story of the consciousness of human freedom. What are the different stages traced by Hegel in this story of human freedom? What role does Hegel's idea of the cunning of reason play in this conception of history?
3. **Hegel's conception of ethical life:** For Hegel, individuals are always to be seen as part of some community or other. In his conception, how do the principles which integrate individuals with each other in the modern family, civil society and the modern state differ? How does his concept of ethical life incorporate these three forms of community?
4. **Hegel's conception of civil society and the state:** Hegel's concept of civil society became one of sources of the idea of civil society which became important in the 1980s. What are the four different aspects of civil society that Hegel discusses in the *Philosophy of Right*? Why does he call civil society the 'external state'? On what basis does he distinguish between civil society and the state?

TWELVE

# Karl Marx (1818–1883): The State and Class Struggle

The most important idea that I associate with Karl Marx is his critique of capitalism as a system lacking freedom. Taking seriously the Hegelian idea that individual freedom was the result of specific social conditions, Marx concluded that the modern social conditions exemplified by the capitalist mode of production were antithetical to freedom. Marx took his project to be the demonstration of how, as a class society, capitalism not only leads to the subordination of the oppressed class of the proletariat, but that capitalism is a society of systemic 'unfreedom' for all its members.

Before we analyse Marx's theory of the lack of freedom in capitalist societies, let us take a brief biographical detour.[1] Marx was born in 1818 in Trier, on the banks of the river Moselle, in western Prussia, into a middle-class Jewish family. His father was a lawyer who became a Protestant in order to escape discrimination. Marx went to school at Trier, and then on to the University of Bonn to study law. Not finding his son paying much attention to his legal studies, Marx's father sent him from Bonn to the University of Berlin, where Marx switched from studying law to studying Hegelian philosophy. Finishing his doctorate, but not finding any work in the teaching profession, he began to write for the daily newspaper, *Rheinische Zeitung*, in Cologne, in 1842. Here, he also came into contact with Moses Hess who introduced him to socialist circles. When Marx wrote a number of pieces criticizing the Prussian government's policy towards the poverty-stricken Moselle winegrowers, the government responded by closing the paper down, and Marx left for Paris where he met Engels and other activists who were organizing regular meetings of the working classes in France. It was in Paris, in 1844, that he wrote *Economic and Philosophical Manuscripts*. At the behest of the Prussian government, he was hounded out of Paris in January 1845, and left with Engels for Brussels, where they stayed for the next three years. In 1847, the Communist League was established in London, and as one of its founder members, Marx wrote its manifesto which was publishing in February 1848 as the *Manifesto of the Communist Party*. Within a month, the Belgian government expelled Marx from Brussels and Marx and Engels returned to Cologne where they founded a new radical newspaper, the *Neue Rheinische Zeitung*. Within a year, Marx had to flee again and this time, in 1849, he left for England where he remained till his death in 1883. Marx spent many years in London, doing his painstaking research for *Capital*, at the British Museum and finally published the work in 1867. Marx was a prolific writer and his other well-known works include *The German Ideology, The Poverty of Philosophy, Manifesto of the Communist Party, A Contribution to the Critique of Political Economy, The Civil War in France*, as well as the three volumes of *Capital*.

## MARX ON THE HUMAN SPECIES

Lenin once said that Marx's theory was a mixture of German philosophy, British political economy and French socialism. As a university student in Germany, Marx was part of a group called the young Hegelians, who were trying to push Hegel's philosophy to its radical limits. Marx accepted Hegel's insistence on the active nature of human beings but rejected his idealism.

For Marx, human consciousness is always an embodied consciousness, which means that in order to be able to think and feel, human beings first have to be alive. In that sense, human beings are part of the order of nature and are dependent on nature in order to survive; human beings are natural beings. Unlike other natural creatures like animals, however, human beings are 'universal' creatures in that they can use all of nature for their survival instead of being limited, for example, instinctually to certain food sources. The consciousness of a human being, for Marx, goes much beyond his or her instincts.

Human beings are active natural beings, with their active nature being embodied not in thought alone, but in 'sensuous human activity'. As material beings, human beings live from nature. To live from nature, human beings must do certain things. Living from nature requires sensuous human activity. Marx pointed out that whereas 'the animal is immediately one with its life activity, man makes his life activity itself an object of his will and consciousness. He has conscious life activity'.[2] Human beings make the whole of nature not only their direct means of life, but the matter, the object and the tool of their life activity. This means that in reproducing themselves materially, because they are not one with their life-activity, human beings produce or create a whole new world. This is what it means to part of the human species, to be human. It is then, part of our nature, of our species-being, to produce this new world not only intellectually, in our consciousness, but materially and actually. Human activity is sensuous and conscious activity. It is this dialectic between consciousness and matter that becomes the stamp of our species-being.

In his *Theses on Feuerbach*, Marx pointed out that his materialism did not share the defects of a 'contemplative' materialism. 'The chief defect of all hitherto existing materialism is that the thing, reality, sensuousness, is conceived only in the form of the object, or of contemplation, but not as sensuous human activity, practice, not subjectively. Hence, in contradistinction to materialism, the active side was developed abstractly by idealism—which, of course, does not know real, sensuous activity as such.'[3] It is their material being which creates the possibility of consciousness in humans. Gradually, as human beings mediate their interaction with nature through their interaction with each other, they create a new world. It is this 'new world', the result of their own practice, their sensuous human activity, which becomes their object-world—the object of their thought and practice. When this 'object'—the objectified form of their own activity—begins to feel strange, when they find it difficult both to understand it and to mould it to their own purposes, that is when human beings experience alienation.

## MARX'S THEORY OF ALIENATION

Like Rousseau before him, and Nietzsche and Freud after, Marx stands in that line of thinkers for whom the social conditions that replaced feudalism had much that was problematic about them. For all these theorists, to tell the human story as the story of the march of progress, of the dispelling of the darkness of ignorance by the enlightenment of knowledge, of the abolishing of human dependence on nature by the application of knowledge in technology, was only to tell half the tale. The missing half was always the suppressed story of inequality, exploitation, alienation and repression.

To understand Marx's concept of alienation, we must remember, as Steven Lukes said, that the experience of alienation is an experience of a loss of freedom. If we look at the section on 'Estranged Labour' with which the first manuscript of Marx's *Economic and Philosophical Manuscripts* ends, we find that the term 'alienation' covers the twin processes of 'objectification' and 'estrangement'. 'The product of labour is labour embodied and made material in an object, it is the objectification of labour. The realization of labour is its objectification. In the sphere of political economy this realization of labour appears as a loss of reality for the worker, objectification as loss of and bondage to the object, and appropriation as estrangement, as alienation.'[4] When workers employed by a capitalist produce an object through their labour—when they realize or objectify their labour in a product—this object or product is not in their control, but under the control of their employer, the capitalist. Therefore, the workers are alienated from the products of their own labour, and feel dominated by these objects.

'The estrangement of the object of labour merely summarizes the estrangement, the alienation in the activity of labour itself.'[5] In capitalism, workers sell their labour power to a capitalist—for a certain number of hours in a day, their capacity to labour belongs to another. Their labour becomes external to them. The worker is related 'to his own (labouring) activity as something which is alien and does not belong to him… the worker's own physical and mental energy, his personal life,—for what is life but activity—becomes an activity directed against himself, which is independent of him and does not belong to him. This is self estrangement.'[6] Here we see Marx defining labour as a need. Human beings need to give vent to their creative energies, but when labour becomes a necessity in order to satisfy needs other than itself, that is a form of alienated labour. It is part of man's species-being to be productive and objective, that is, to objectify himself through his labour. Labour is 'the release and cultivation

**Box 12.1**

**MARX ON THE ALIENATION OF LABOUR:**

The *devaluation* of the human world grows in direct proportion to the *increase in value* of the world of things. Labour not only produces commodities; it also produces itself and the workers as a *commodity* and it does so in the same proportion in which it produces commodities in general.

This fact simply means that the object that labour produces, its product, stands opposed to it as *something alien*, as a power independent of the producer. The product of labour is labour embodied and made material in an object, it is the *objectification* of labour. The realization of labour is its objectification. In the sphere of political economy, this realization of labour appears as a *loss of reality* for the worker, objectification as loss of and bondage to the object, and appropriation as estrangement, as *alienation*.

Up to now, we have considered the estrangement, the alienation of the worker, only from one aspect – i.e., ***the worker's relationship to the products of his labour***. But estrangement manifests itself not only in the result, but also in the *act of production*, within the *activity of production* itself. How could the product of the worker's activity confront him as something alien if it were not for the fact that in the act of production he was estranging himself from himself? After all, the product is simply the resumé of the activity, of the production. So if the product of labour is alienation, production itself must be active alienation, the alienation of activity, the activity of alienation. The estrangement of the object of labour merely summarizes the estrangement, the alienation in the activity of labour itself.

*Economic and Philosophical Manuscripts*

of human energy', so to be alienated from one's labour means to be alienated from one's species-being.

'An immediate consequence of man's estrangement from the product of his labour, his life activity, his species being, is the estrangement of man from man.'[7] As workers, we are alienated from our products, from our labour, from ourselves, from nature and from other human beings (see Box 12.1). We relate to our own activity as 'unfree activity, as activity in the service, under the rule, coercion and yoke of another man'.[8]

For Marx, the capitalists also suffer a kind of alienation in that they are confronted by the laws of the market which they must follow if they are to survive. A capitalist is not free to give his workers wages that are not in conformity with the market rate, if he is to remain a capitalist. Marx also pointed out that freedom under capitalism really becomes reduced to a freedom of buying things. One feels that one has expressed one's freedom because one is free to choose which cereal to buy from among 20 different brands. Self-determination becomes the consumption of commodities. An individual's freedom also gets conceived of, as we see in Box 12.2, as

**Box 12.2**

**THE INDIVIDUAL AS A MEMBER OF CIVIL SOCIETY, AND AS A MEMBER OF THE POLITICAL COMMUNITY:**

None of the so-called rights of man, therefore, go beyond egoistic man, beyond man as a member of civil society – that is, an individual withdrawn into himself, into the confines of his private interests and private caprice, and separated from the community. In the rights of man, he is far from being conceived as a species-being; on the contrary, species-like itself, society, appears as a framework external to the individuals, as a restriction of their original independence. The sole bond holding them together is natural necessity, need and private interest, the preservation of their property and their egoistic selves.

It is puzzling enough that a people which is just beginning to liberate itself, to tear down all the barriers between its various sections, and to establish a political community, that such a people solemnly proclaims (*Declaration* of 1791) the rights of egoistic man separated from his fellow men and from the community, and that indeed it repeats this proclamation at a moment when only the most heroic devotion can save the nation, and is therefore imperatively called for, at a moment when the sacrifice of all the interest of civil society must be the order of the day, and egoism must be punished as a crime. (*Declaration of the Rights of Man*, etc., of 1793) This fact becomes still more puzzling when we see that the political emancipators go so far as to reduce citizenship, and the *political community*, to a mere means for maintaining these so-called rights of man, that, therefore, the *citoyen* is declared to be the servant of egotistic *homme*, that the sphere in which man acts as a communal being is degraded to a level below the sphere in which he acts as a partial being, and that, finally, it is not man as *citoyen*, but man as private individual [*bourgeois*] who is considered to be the *essential* and *true* man.

*On the Jewish Question*

something that has to be protected from the freedom of others from which it (that is, one's freedom to acquire as much as possible) is constantly under threat.

## FROM ALIENATED LABOUR TO COMMODITY FETISHISM

In his later writings, instead of alienation, Marx used the concept of commodity fetishism to characterize what was wrong with capitalism. To understand commodity fetishism, we must begin with the distinction between use value and exchange value. A bar of gold may not have much use value but it has enormous exchange value as it can be exchanged for a large number of things. For Marx, capitalism was an economic system in which exchange values completely overtake use values, in the sense, that even if a thing has a use value, it will not be produced in a capitalist society unless it has exchange value, that is, unless there is someone willing and able to pay a price for it. Under capitalism, it is as if the world of commodities—a commodity being defined as a thing which has exchange value—has come to dominate the world of human beings (see Box 12.3).

The exchange value of anything, according to Marx, is determined by the amount of human labour embodied in it, but as the world of commodities becomes dominant, we begin to see the commodity as having

**Box 12.3**

**MARX ON THE BOURGEOISIE ESTABLISHING A WORLD MARKET:**

The bourgeoisie cannot exist without constantly revolutionizing the instruments of production, and thereby the relations of production, and with them the whole relations of society. Conservation of the old modes of production in unaltered form, was, on the contrary, the first condition of existence for all earlier industrial classes. Constant revolutionizing of production, uninterrupted disturbance of all social conditions, everlasting uncertainty and agitation distinguish the bourgeois epoch from all earlier ones. All fixed, fast-frozen relations, with their train of ancient and venerable prejudices and opinions, are swept away, all new-formed ones become antiquated before they can ossify. All that is solid melts into air, all that is holy is profaned, and man is at last compelled to face with sober senses his, real conditions of life, and his relations with his kind.

The need of a constantly expanding market for its products chases the bourgeoisie over the entire surface of the globe. It must nestle everywhere, settle everywhere, establish connexions everywhere.

The bourgeoisie has through its exploitation of the world market given a cosmopolitan character to production and consumption in every country.

*Manifesto of the Communist Party*

value in itself, and we devalue the contribution of those who made the commodity. Ironically, labour power itself becomes a commodity. Labour power is a strange kind of commodity because it cannot be separated from the person to whom it belongs. If we are to distinguish capitalism from slavery, however, then we cannot be said to be buying and selling persons; we are instead, buying and selling labour power, which is a fictitious commodity. In this way, human beings and human relationships also become commodified in capitalism. Just as in religion, 'the products of the human brain appear as autonomous figures endowed with a life of their own, which enter into relations with each other and with the human race, so it is in the world of commodities with the products of men's hands. I call this the fetishism which attaches itself to the products of labour as soon as they are produced as commodities.'[9] In terms of our everyday experience, we can understand commodity fetishism as the sense of accomplishment we get when we buy new things, even though we have not much use for them.

In capitalism, the flooding of the market with an excess of commodities also leads to another problem. Commodities are not produced out of thin air; they are the result of human labour acting upon natural resources. The more commodities there are, the more natural resources are used. When there is a glut of unsold commodities, they may often be destroyed, or sold at throwaway prices, but the production of these unnecessary commodities has already reduced the planet's stock of precious energy resources.

## MARX'S THEORY OF EXPLOITATION

Under capitalism, workers are not only alienated, they are also exploited. The capitalists exploit the members of the proletariat by extracting 'surplus value' from them. In the capitalist mode of production, the worker is someone who owns no forces of production except his labour power. Since he does not, unlike the artisan in earlier economic systems, own any means of production, he is forced to sell his labour power to someone who does own or can buy raw materials, land and machines. In return for his labour power, the worker receives a wage. Now labour power is the only commodity, in using which, new value is produced. That is the only reason that it finds a market for itself. The capitalist outlays his capital in the form of constant and variable capital. Constant capital is the name given to the value laid out for the means of production and this value 'is simply transferred to the product during the production process'. When means of production are used up in the production process, their value simply 'reappears in the product in a new form'.[10] But when labour power is consumed in the production process, new value is also created.

For Marx, surplus value is the difference between the value a worker produces and the value of his labour power. The value of labour power is calculated on the same basis as the value of every other commodity, that is, according to the amount or duration of undifferentiated labour expended to produce it. Marx was here continuing the argument of classical political economy according to which 'labour is the source of value,... the amount of labour embodied in a good is thus related to the amount of value in the good, and... the relative values of two goods must be in proportion to the relative amounts of labour embodied in them'. The value of labour power is calculated on the basis of the socially necessary labour time needed to produce the goods that the workers need in order to reproduce themselves. The capitalist pays his workers a wage which is equivalent to the value of labour power, but he also makes the workers labour for much more than is necessary for the workers for their personal consumption items. The values that the workers produce through this extra labour of theirs, is appropriated by the capitalist. So the rate of surplus value or the rate of exploitation is determined by the following formula:

surplus value = surplus labour/necessary labour
= hours worker spends working for capitalist/hours worker spends working for personal consumption[11]

If the workers owned any means of production, they would not have to sell their labour power to some capitalist. Forced to sell their labour power, they are exploited because their wage only reflects the value of their labour power, not of the actual labour that they perform for their employer. So not only do the workers not have control over the objects they produce, they are not even recompensed for the values they produce.

## HISTORICAL MATERIALISM

Our analysis of different aspects of capitalism needs to now be set up against Marx's general theory of modes of production. The most succinct formulation of the theory of historical materialism (see Box 12.4) which describes the transitions of the modes of production was provided by Marx in *Contribution to a Critique of Political Economy*. He wrote, 'In the social production of their life, men enter into definite relations that are indispensable and independent of their will, relations of production which correspond to a definite stage of development of their material productive forces. The sum total of these relations of production constitutes the economic structure of society, the real basis, on which rises a legal and political superstructure, and to which correspond definite forms of social consciousness. The mode of production of material life conditions the social, political and intellectual life process in general.'[12]

Each society has an economic system with two main constituents: forces of production which include the means of production, such as raw materials, and the instruments of production such as land, machines and capital, and labour power; and the relations of production which describe the relationship of ownership or control between individuals and the forces of production. Historically, for example, slaves were individuals who owned absolutely no forces of production; even their labour power did not belong to them. The proletariat is made up of individuals who own no means of production but do own their own labour power. The serfs of feudal times, however, did own some means of production and also had partial control over their labour power. Together, these forces and relations of production form the economic basis of a society; a base which supports an entire superstructure of social and political institutions.

> At a certain stage of their development, the material productive forces of society come in conflict with the existing relations of production, or, what is but a legal expression for the same thing, with the property relations within which they have been at work hitherto. From forms of development of the productive forces, these relations turn into their fetters. Then begins an epoch of social revolution. With the change of the economic foundation, the entire immense superstructure is more or less rapidly transformed... In broad outlines, Asiatic, ancient, feudal, and modern bourgeois modes of production can be designated as progressive epochs in the economic formation of society.[13]

Marx mainly talked of three main modes of production, the slave, the feudal and the capitalist, although he did mention others, like the Oriental and the Germanic modes of production. Prior to the slave mode of production, Marx imagined a society in which no one owned any private property. Such a society was a classless society, since there was no distinction between property owners and the propertyless. It was also a society of scarcity, with everyone struggling hard, with inadequate tools, to sustain their livelihood. The slave mode of production is the first instance of a class society, where the owners of property, in the form of slave-owners, exploit the slaves. Under feudalism, land owning lords exploit the serfs and in capitalism the property-owning capitalists exploit the propertyless proletariat. With capitalism comes an enormous increase in productive forces. For many commentators, Marx was a technological determinist, that is, he understood historical change to be the result of the need for technical change.

Box 12.4

**MARX'S THEORY OF HISTORICAL MATERIALISM:**

In the social production of their existence, men inevitably enter into definite relations, which are independent of their will, namely relations of production appropriate to a given stage in the development of their material forces of production. The totality of these relations of production constitutes the economic structure of society, the real foundation, on which arises a legal and political superstructure and to which correspond definite forms of social consciousness. The mode of production of material life conditions the general process of social, political and intellectual life. It is not the consciousness of men that determines their existence, but their social existence that determines their consciousness.

At a certain stage of development, the material productive forces of society come into conflict with the existing relations of production or – this merely expresses the same thing in legal terms – with the property relations within the framework of which they have operated hitherto. From forms of development of the productive forces these relations turn into their fetters. Then begins an era of social revolution. The changes in the economic foundation lead sooner or later to the transformation of the whole immense superstructure.

In studying such transformations it is always necessary to distinguish between the material transformation of the economic conditions of production, which can be determined with the precision of natural science, and the legal, political, religious, artistic or philosophic – in short, ideological forms in which men become conscious of this conflict and fight it out. Just as one does not judge an individual by what he thinks about himself, so one cannot judge such a period of transformation by its consciousness, but, on the contrary, this consciousness must be explained from the contradictions of material life, from the conflict existing between the social forces of production and the relations of production. No social order is ever destroyed before all the productive forces for which it is sufficient have been developed, and new superior relations of production never replace older ones before the material conditions for their existence have matured within the framework of the old society.

Mankind thus inevitably sets itself only such tasks as it is able to solve, since closer examination will always show that the problem itself arises only when the material conditions for its solution are already present or at least in the course of formation. In broad outline, the Asiatic, ancient, feudal and modern bourgeois modes of production may be designated as epochs marking progress in the economic development of society. The bourgeois mode of production is the last antagonistic form of the social process of production—antagonistic not in the sense of individual antagonism but of an antagonism that emanates from the individuals' social conditions of existence—but the productive forces developing within bourgeois society create also the material conditions for a solution of this antagonism. The prehistory of human society accordingly closes with this social formation.

*Contribution to a Critique of Political Economy*

## MARX'S THEORY OF CLASS STRUGGLE

'The history of all hitherto existing society is the history of class struggles. Freeman and slave, patrician and plebian, lord and serf, guild master and journeyman, in a word, oppressor and oppressed, stood in constant opposition to one another, carried on an uninterrupted, now hidden, now open fight.'[14] These are the opening sentences of *Manifesto of the Communist Party*, and they show the centrality of the concept of class for Marx. For many Marxists, it is class struggle rather than the development of technology, which is the motor of historical change (see Box 12.5).

Marx did not define class membership in terms of income or education or status, but rather, in terms of an individual's relationships to the means of production. All those who are similarly placed with respect to the ownership or control of the forces of production, are members of the same class. In every society, there is always a class of individuals who owns or controls the means of production. This is the ruling class and it is opposed by those who do not own any means of production, or own very little of them, or merely own their labour power. This definition of class is termed as Marx's concept of a 'class in itself'. This means that members of such a class have identical interests, whether they are conscious of them or not. The real dividing line in society, in terms of interests, is not religion or

### Box 12.5

**MARX ON CLASSES IN SOCIETY:**

The history of all hitherto existing society is the history of class struggles.

Freeman and slave, patrician and plebeian, lord and serf, guild-master and journeyman, in a word, oppressor and oppressed, stood in constant opposition to one another, carried on an uninterrupted, now hidden, now open fight, a fight that each time ended, either in a revolutionary reconstitution of society at large, or in the common ruin of the contending classes.

In the earlier epochs of history, we find almost everywhere a complicated arrangement of society into various orders, a manifold gradation of social rank. In ancient Rome we have patricians, knights, plebeians, slaves; in the Middle Ages, feudal lords, vassals, guild-masters, journeymen, apprentices, serfs; in almost all of these classes, again, subordinate gradations.

The modern bourgeois society that has sprouted from the ruins of feudal society has not done away with class antagonisms. It has but established new classes, new conditions of oppression, new forms of struggle in place of the old ones.

Our epoch, the epoch of the bourgeoisie, possesses, however, this distinct feature: it has simplified class antagonisms. Society as a whole is more and more splitting up into two great hostile camps, into two great classes directly facing each other — Bourgeoisie and Proletariat.

From the serfs of the Middle Ages sprang the chartered burghers of the earliest towns. From these burgesses the first elements of the bourgeoisie were developed.

*Manifesto of the Communist Party*

language or community or gender, but class. In fact, Marx also said that the dividing line, not only in every society, but in the world as such was that of class; the working classes of all countries have a common interest against the capitalist class of these countries.

Another concept relating to class found in Marx's writings, is that of class for itself. A 'class for itself' is a large number of people who are conscious of the unity of their interests. Many commentators have claimed that for Marx, for a group to be a class, it has both to be a class in itself and a class for itself. This can be seen in Marx's dismissal of the peasantry, as not forming a class. The peasantry is a class in itself, because its members occupy identical positions with respect to the relations of production, but because peasants are disaggregated into separate villages, they do not become conscious of their identical interests, which leads Marx to liken them to a 'sack of potatoes', but definitely not a class.

> The small peasants form a vast mass, the members of which live in similar conditions, but without entering into manifold relations with one another. Their mode of production isolates them from one another, instead of bringing them into mutual intercourse... In so far as millions of families live under economic conditions of existence that divide their mode of life, their interests and their culture from those of other classes, and put them into hostile contrast to the latter, they form a class. In so far there is merely a local interconnection among these small peasants, and the identity of their interests begets no unity, no national union, and no political organization, they do not form a class.[15]

The working class, on the other hand, being concentrated in factories, is able to see its interests as common and thereby to become a class for itself. The members of the working class can see the contradictions of capitalism. They can see how production is organized as a social process requiring the collective effort of so many individuals. but the appropriation of the results of this socialized production process is done in the form of private property.

## MARX'S THEORY OF THE STATE AND REVOLUTION

For Marx, it is social classes, then, which are the agents of revolution. It was the newly emerging property owning class which brought about the new mode of production in the case of the slave, feudal and capitalist modes of production. Each new property-owning class bringing about the revolution in the name of all of society, after the transformation of the mode of production, establishes itself as the ruling class and exploits the property-less class. For Marx, it was only the proletariat which was the universal class since, after the worker's revolution, the proletariat would abolish all private property and therefore class society itself.

To bring about a revolution, it is imperative for a class to capture state power. The ruling class establishes itself as the ruling class by making the state serve its purposes. In *Manifesto of the Communist Party*, Marx calls the state the instrument of the ruling class. 'The executive of the modern State is but a committee for managing the common affairs of the whole bourgeoisie.'[16]

There has been much controversy over the Marxist theory of the state. For some Marxists, the control of the bourgeoisie over the functionaries of the state is direct, and is buttressed by the common social networks to which members of the bourgeoisie and the political class belong, and the by the financial dependence of the state on the bourgeoisie. For Marxists espousing the relative autonomy of the state thesis, the state is able to perform its task of managing the common affairs of the entire bourgeoisie only by maintaining a certain independence from different sections of it. These commentators also point out that in *The Eighteenth Brumaire of Louis Bonaparte*, Marx clearly showed how the state becomes powerful and maintains its own independent agenda when the social conditions are such that the emerging bourgeoisie is not able to establish itself fully. Besides, treating social, political, and cultural factors as mere epiphenomena of the economy has never found favour with important schools of Western Marxism, and the Althusserian concept of overdetermination is only one way in which the efficacy of the political or ideological forces has been asserted.

The importance of the state for Marx can also be seen in his belief that the proletariat must capture state power in order to bring about the workers' revolution. Marx was an advocate of the dictatorship of the proletariat, by which he meant that the proletariat would have to exclude the members of the bourgeoisie from the state till the time all private property was not expropriated. Once the basis of class society had been abolished, Marx said, the state would simply wither away, since the state was always an institution meant for maintaining class power.

## MARX IN THE NEW MILLENNIUM

Writing about Marx at the turn of the 21st century, when the last time the word 'revolution' was used widely, was to refer to the overthrow of communism in eastern Europe and in the Soviet Union at the end of the 1980s, is certainly fraught with difficulties. No matter how many times it is argued that Soviet and Chinese style communism was/is a travesty of Marxism, it remains true that Marx's prediction of a workers' revolution in advanced capitalist countries never came true. Capitalist countries have undergone periodic economic crises, but these have been temporary and have not resulted in any systemic breakdown. Whether through colonialism, or the welfare state or their complex class character, advanced capitalist societies have not experienced the radical transformation that Marx had talked about.

Marx had visualized a sharpening contradiction in these societies, between the capitalist class and the working class. The capitalist class was to become narrower and richer, confronted by a large mass of increasingly pauperized members of the working class. Capitalist societies, however, have increasingly disaggregated workers. There are blue collar and white collar workers, and then there are 'guest arbeiters'. These days, manufacturing is often outsourced to developing countries so the factory workers actually do not just belong to, but actually are in another country. Ownership of capital, even if it is ownership of a relatively small piece of it, is widely distributed in the form of stock options and public issue bonds. In this manner, there seem to be many more today with a stake in the capitalist system than just a few monopoly capitalists.

Another grouse that Marx had against capitalist economies was that they were anarchic, in the sense that they were not under the control of anybody, not even the few monopoly capitalists. Human beings had to follow the rules of the economic system, rather than the economic system serving their needs. Marx visualized the replacement of the capitalist mode of production not only by a system in which there would be no private property, but also by one which would be a planned economy. This idea has come in for a lot of criticism, with many pointing out that planned economies have proved to be inefficient and corrupt, and have been unable to coordinate the economic actions of numerous firms/individuals as capitalist economies have done.

Not only did Marx assume a heightening of the contradiction between capitalists and workers, he also thought of it as the only contradiction in capitalist society. This led him to characterize other movements, for example, the women's movement, as ploys by the bourgeoisie to break up the unity of the working class. Many critics have found fault with Marx for this, arguing that other kinds of exploitation, like discrimination against women, environmental degradation which usually impact minorities, or racial discrimination, also exist in advanced capitalist societies and need to be struggled against. These critics emphasize that these new social movements must be seen to be addressing issues other than class. For example, women are not merely exploited economically by men but face exploitation based on their sex, and caste is not just another form of class. For such critics, Marx is to be faulted for his economic and technological determinism.

With all the criticism, however, Marx's impact on the social sciences has been far reaching, with there having been as many attempts to refute his theories as there have been to further develop his insights. Much of 20th century sociology or political economy has been a response to Marx's questioning of class, and of the functioning of democracy in societies with sharp economic inequalities.

It also remains true that increasing wealth in the world has come at the cost of deepening inequalities. It is said, for example, that the amount of wealth possessed by half of the world's 587 billionaires, who are Americans, is the same as the combined gross domestic product of the world's poorest 170 countries. In the United States, the pay of chief executive officers of companies has increased by 300 per cent over the last 15 years, whereas wages have increased in the same period by only 5 per cent and minimum wage workers have seen their pay fall by 6 per cent.[17] Not only that, capitalism continues to sustain all kinds of retrograde labour regimes in the world, and it is these conditions governing the life of the working classes which make many individuals continue to 'make the case, if not for Marx and Marxism, then at the very least for some project to change the world'.[18]

## NOTES

1. A useful book for information on the details of Marx's life is David McLellan, *Karl Marx: His Life and Thought*, New York: HarperCollins, 1978.
2. Karl Marx, *Economic and Philosophical Manuscripts: Early Writings* translated by Rodney Livingstone, Harmondsworth: Penguin Books, 1975, p. 328.
3. Karl Marx, Theses on Feuerbach, *Early Writings*, p. 421.
4. Karl Marx, *Economic and Philosophical Manuscripts: Early Writings*, p. 324.
5. *Ibid.*, p. 326.
6. Karl Marx, *Economic and Philosophical Manuscripts:* Early Writings, p. 327.
7. *Ibid.*, p. 329.
8. Karl Marx, *Economic and Philosophical Manuscripts: Early Writings*, p. 331.
9. Karl Marx, *Capital: A Critique of Political Economy, Volume I*, Penguin Classics, p. 165.
10. Tom Bottomore, 'Surplus value', *A Dictionary of Marxist Thought*, pp. 472–73.
11. For this formula, and for this analysis, see Tom Bottomore, 'Surplus Value', p. 474.
12. Karl Marx, *Contribution to a Critique of Political Economy*, quoted in Gerald A. Cohen, *Karl Marx's Theory of History: A Defence*, Princeton: Princeton University Press, 2000.
13. *Ibid.*
14. Karl Marx and F. Engels, *The Manifesto of the Communist Party*, Moscow: Progress Publishers, 1952.
15. Karl Marx, *The Eighteenth Brumaire of Louis Bonaparte*, New York: Mondial, 2005.

16. Karl Marx and F. Engels, *Manifesto of the Communist Party*, Moscow: Progress Publishers, 1952, p. 44.
17. Paul D'Amato, *The Meaning of Marxism*, Chicago: Haymarket Books, 2006, p. 9.
18. Paul D'Amato, *The Meaning of Marxism*, p. 10.

## READING LIST

Cohen, Gerald A., *Karl Marx's Theory of History: A Defence*, Princeton: Princeton University Press, 2000.

D'Amato, Paul, *The Meaning of Marxism*, Chicago: Haymarket Books, 2006.

McLellan, David, *Karl Marx: His Life and Thought*, New York: HarperCollins, 1978.

Marx, Karl, *Economic and Philosophical Manuscripts: Early Writings*, translated by Rodney Livingstone, Harmondsworth: Penguin Books, 1975.

Marx, Karl, *The Manifesto of the Communist Party*, Moscow: Progress Publishers, 1952.

Marx, Karl, *The Eighteenth Brumaire of Louis Bonaparte*, New York: Mondial, 2005.

## CENTRAL THEMES

1. **Class struggle:** For Marx, 'the history of all hitherto existing society is the history of class struggles'. What does Marx mean by this statement? What is the meaning of the terms, 'class-in-itself' and 'class-for-itself'? Why does Marx call the proletariat the universal class?
2. **Historical materialism:** Marx is well known for his materialist conception of history as a succession of different modes of production. What is a mode of production? What does Marx have to say about the forces and relations of production? Why is Marx's conception of history called a materialist conception of history?
3. **Objectification and alienation:** The early Marx is said to have been influenced by the Hegelian idea of externalization or objectification. What is the difference between objectification and alienation? What are the different kinds of alienation discussed by Marx, alienation from the product of one's labour, alienation from one's labour and alienation from one's species being?
4. **Marx on the state:** Marxist theory is often presented as the opposite of the liberal conception of politics and of the state. What do the Marxist categories of base and superstructure refer to? How does Marx understand the relationship of the state to the different classes of society?

THIRTEEN

# Antonio Gramsci (1891–1937): Hegemony in Civil Society as a Basis of the Modern State

Gramsci was born in Sardinia in 1891 in a lower-middle-class family. Sardinia is an island in the Mediterranean Sea, located between Spain and Italy; at that time, Sardinia, as most of southern Italy, had a backward economy primarily based on agriculture. The Sard society has been described as 'superstitious' and 'fatalistic'; the largely peasant population of the island was looked down upon by the urban inhabitants of northern Italy. Gramsci himself suffered at the hands of his fellow Sardinians. He had an accident when he was four years old—he fell down from a maid's arms and as a result developed into a hunchback: for his Sardinian neighbours, "his handicap made him the object of fear and persecution."[1] He was teased mercilessly by other children in school and he reacted by becoming a solitary child. His school days anyway soon came to an end when his father was imprisoned for embezzlement when Gramsci was just eleven years old; Gramsci had to take up a job as an office boy to help with the family's finances. Gramsci resumed his schooling after a few years and eventually won a scholarship to the University of Turin in 1911. Turin was a modern industrial city in contrast to Sardinia. It was the home of the Fiat automobile, where this car was manufactured, and Gramsci came in contact with the Italian working class there. He studied language and literature at the University and also began to write journalistic pieces for socialist weeklies and dailies like *Il Grido del Popolo* and *Avanti!* Dissatisfied with the reformist line of these newspapers, Gramsci, along with Palmiro Togliatti and Angelo Tasca launched a new newspaper called the Ordine Nuovo in 1919. Gramsci probably joined the Italian Socialist Party (Partito Socialista Italiano—PSI) in 1913, but when the Italian Socialist Party split up in 1921 and a new Communist Party (Partito

Communista Italiano—PCI) was founded, Gramsci became a member of the Central Committee of this new party[2]. In 1926, Gramsci spoke at the national Congress of the Italian Communist Party at Lyons, and that November he was arrested in Rome. Gramsci's trial since late 1922 was turned into a show of force by the 'fascist leadership'—he was 'tried along with twenty-one other political prisoners' and all of them were sentenced to many years in prison. Benito Mussolini and the fascists had been in power in Italy since late 1921. In the general election of 1924, the National Fascist Party (Partito Nazionale Fascista–PNF) won a majority of seats in Parliament and by 1925, Mussolini began to crush all opposition, closing newspapers, and arresting those belonging to oppositional groups[3].

After his trial, Gramsci was condemned to twenty years in prison, and he died in 1937 while serving his sentence. It is in prison that he wrote his *Prison Notebooks* for which he is so famous. In prison, he filled twenty nine notebooks in all: seven notebooks between 1929 and 1931, ten notebooks between 1931 and 1933, and twelve more notebooks after 1933. Ten years had to pass after Gramsci's death for anything that he wrote in prison to appear in public; first, the letters he had written from prison were published in Italy in 1947[4]. Then, between 1948 and 1951, the notebooks he had filled were published in the form of six volumes[5].

## THE CENTRALITY OF THE POLITICAL

Gramsci has been called "the greatest of western Marxists"[6] because his thought has been considered to contain the most promise of moving away from a dogmatic and determinist Marxism. He objected to Bukharin's idea that natural science should be the pattern to which all forms of intellectual enquiry should conform[7]. Human beings unlike natural objects do not merely react to external pulls and pressures; their action is not an automatic response to material forces. Gramsci was critical of the positivism emanating from the development of sociology in the second half of the nineteenth century and he opposed the reduction of political science to sociology. He bemoaned the fact: "The rise of sociology is related to the decline of the concept of political science and the art of politics which took place in the nineteenth century (to be more accurate, in the second half of that century, with the success of evolutionary and positivist theories). [What was] initiated was an epoch of "natural" "evolution", that society had discovered its definitive, because rational foundations, etc. And, lo and behold, society can now be studied with the methods of the natural sciences!"[8] Gramsci admitted that "man cannot be conceived of except as historically determined man—i.e., man who has developed, and who lives, in certain conditions, in a particular social complex or totality of social relations."[9] Does this mean that historical materialism is to be interpreted as "a simple methodology of sociological research, separated from praxis?"[10] Gramsci's answer was firmly negative. "Since the will and initiative of men themselves cannot be left out of account, this notion must be false. The problem of what "science" itself is has to be posed. Is not science itself "political activity" and political thought in as much as it transforms men, and makes them different from what they were before?"[11]

Gramsci's characterization of the purpose of science as the gaining of knowledge followed by intervention on the basis of that knowledge signals that for him, the human ability to change things and to create something new—this is the political aspect of human life. Change does not only come about automatically—it is the result of some individuals wanting to bring about the change, planning to bring it about, and then giving direction to others in a collective attempt to change things. Gramsci's attraction for Marxism lay precisely in it being a call to bring about social transformation—it was a 'philosophy of praxis'. Marxist thought "sees as the dominant factor in history, not raw economic facts, but man, men in societies, men in relation to one another…men coming to understand economic facts, judging them and adapting them to their will until this becomes the driving force of the economy and moulds objective reality, which lives and moves and comes to resemble a current of volcanic lava that can be channeled wherever and in whatever way man's will determines."[12] Gramsci can be seen as concerned with providing us with a "political reading of Marxist theory,"[13] in which "it is not the economic structure which directly determines the political action, but it is the interpretation of it and of the so-called laws which rule its development."

For Gramsci, if the working class was to bring about a transformation in the social order, this was not just a reflex of economic conditions; the will of the workers had to be mobilized to act with respect to the objective social conditions. This brought to the foreground the importance of the question of leadership of the working class. Gramsci was clear from quite early on that the working class had to move beyond trade unionism. Trade unions could not go beyond an 'economic-corporate' perspective as their demands were limited to higher pay or better working conditions for the workers. The workers needed to realize that much more fundamental change was needed in society than better working conditions for the proletariat. Gramsci was pivotal in moving beyond trade unions to the establishment of factory councils in Turin in 1919. Factory councils were based on groups of 15 to 20 workers in a workshop with a mandated and recallable shop steward; these shop stewards would then elect their representatives who were recallable to them. The two years from 1919 to 1921 are known as the '*bienno rosso*' or the red years in Italy, because in this period there was an upsurge in the resistance of workers to their owners and managers. Inspired by the revolution in the Soviet Union and also radicalized because of World War I, many factory workers in the Turin factories organized themselves in Factory Councils. They then began a movement to occupy the factories and run them themselves. In April 1920, they attempted to occupy factories, and by September, this movement spread to Milan. Between 1 and 4 September, 1920, 300 factories were occupied in the Milan area, and some peasants also joined the movement and took over a few landed estates. Gramsci was at the forefront of running this movement, which unfortunately ran aground because the Italian Socialist Party refused to provide leadership. This led to the break in the PSI and the formation of the Italian Communist Party in January 1921 with Gramsci becoming a member of the new party.[14]

Gramsci always emphasized that transformation or the creation of something new could only come about through political organization. He often cited the role of the Jacobins during the French revolution as an example of the ability of the political to bring about change in society. Under the direction of the Jacobin party, all of French society had been transformed during the French revolution. "the Jacobins won their function of 'leading' (dirigente) party by a struggle to the death; they literally 'imposed' themselves on the French bourgeoisie, leading it into a far more advanced position than the originally strongest bourgeois nuclei would have spontaneously wished to take up. This feature, characteristic of Jacobinism, which consists in forcing the situation, in creating irreversible *faits accomplis,* and in a group of extremely energetic and determined men driving the bourgeois forward with kicks in the backside...the Jacobins opposed every 'intermediate' halt in the revolutionary process, and sent to the guillotine not only the elements of the old society...but also the revolutionaries of yesterday—today become reactionaries."[15] The Jacobins were able to stir up the great popular masses for their cause.

Gramsci believed that in the absence of a politically organized party, wide ranging revolutionary change cannot come about—what is possible then is only a passive revolution. If France had experienced revolutionary change because of the organization and action of the Jacobins, what the rest of Europe had experienced was a passive revolution. "The demands which in France found a Jacobin-Napoleonic expression were satisfied by small doses, legally, in a reformist manner—in such a way that it was possible to preserve the political and economic position of the old feudal classes, to avoid agrarian reform, and political experience such as occurred in France in the years of Jacobinism, in 1831, and in 1848."[16]

That is why Gramsci was attracted to the thought of his compatriot political thinker from the 15th century, Machiavelli. Machiavelli had spoken about the centrality and autonomy of the political. Whereas Machiavelli had given a new meaning to princely 'virtu' in his attempt to wean away political 'virtu' from its domination by the idea of moral virtue, Gramsci tried to rescue the idea of political action from its reduction to being an epiphenomenon of economic or historical forces.

Box 13.1

**THE CREATIVITY OF THE POLITICAL:**

The active politician is a creator, an initiator; but he neither creates from nothing nor does he move in the turbid void of his own desires and dreams. He bases himself on effective reality, but what is this effective reality? Is it something static and immobile, or is it not rather a relation of forces in continuous motion and shift of equilibrium? If one applies one's will to the creation of a new equilibrium among the forces which really exist and are operative—basing oneself on the particular force one believes to be progressive and strengthening it to help it to victory—one still moves on the terrain of effective reality, but does so in order to dominate and transcend it. What 'ought to be' is therefore concrete; indeed it is the only realistic and historicist interpretation of reality, it alone is history in the making and philosophy in the making, it alone is politics.

*The Prison Notebooks*

Of course, for Gramsci, the form of the Prince available to us in the 20th century was not an individual but a Party. "...the protagonist of the new Prince could not in the modern epoch be an individual hero, but only the political party."[17] The most important party for Gramsci's purposes was the party of the proletariat, the Communist Party. Just as the Jacobins had been a form of the modern Prince, so could the Communist Party be an embodiment of the modern Prince. Gramsci had been instrumental in the formation of the PCI in early 1921. Along with the Factory councils, it was necessary to form a workers' political party if the workers' revolution was to be successful. "Only the leadership provided by the party could give a permanent form and discipline to the disorderly and chaotic energies, the spontaneity, of the working classes." The political party, for Gramsci, is the convergence of three fundamental elements: first, "a mass element, composed of ordinary, average men, whose participation takes the form of discipline and loyalty, rather than any creative spirit or organizational ability", second, "the principal cohesive element, which centralizes nationally and renders effective and powerful a complex of forces which left to themselves would count for little or nothing. This element is endowed with great cohesive, centralizing and disciplinary powers; also—and indeed perhaps this is the basis for the others—with the power of innovation", and third, "an intermediate element, which articulates the first element with the second and maintains contact between them, not only physically but also morally and intellectually."[18]

It is ironic that according to some scholars, Gramsci's emphasis on the autonomy of the political can be explained by the backwardness of

Italy. The social and political conditions in Italy were so backward that no change could be brought about without political will. Historically, this had been the situation in Italy, so in the 15th century we find Machiavelli emphasizing the autonomy of the political versus the moral. Italy lagged behind the western European countries as they transformed themselves into modern nations, and the Italian Risorgimento or the process of Italian unification had to come about through the political effort of Italian leaders.[19] Similarly, now we find Gramsci who is often called the new Machiavelli emphasizing the autonomy of the political with respect to the economic.

## HEGEMONY AND CIVIL SOCIETY

Gramsci's emphasis on the political leads us to his concept of hegemony. Gramsci came to argue that the political leadership which is central to political transformation is effective not simply through command and domination but through consent and hegemony. Political leadership and political mobilization has to take the form of hegemony. According to Mouffe, "the concept of hegemony first appeared in Gramsci's work in 1926 in 'Notes on the Southern Question'" when Gramsci wrote, 'The Turin communists posed concretely the question of the 'hegemony of the proletariat': i.e. of the social basis of the proletarian dictatorship and the workers' State. The proletariat can become the leading (dirigente) and thedominant class to the extent that it succeeds in creating a system of alliances which allows it to mobilize the majority of the working population against capitalism and the bourgeois State.'[20] Gramsci's earliest use of the term hegemony was thus in reference to an alliance with other groups, mainly the peasantry, which the working class should move towards, in order to strengthen its position. The leadership of the working class could persuade other groups to become its allies only if the workers were willing to look beyond their own narrow economic interests. Any class which sought to establish its leadership in society had "to widen its class interests and to discover those interests which it had in common with the popular sectors."[21] What was this process of getting the consent of the other classes? Gramsci later took this idea of persuasion further when he began to use the term to refer to much more than a class alliance of the struggling workers; in the *Prison Notebooks* the term now began to mean the assertion of the intellectual and moral leadership of a ruling class over other subordinate or subaltern classes. For many commentators this meaning of the term hegemony is completely new; when it was reference to political leadership, one could say that Gramsci was influenced by Lenin's emphasis on leadership, but by shifting the focus of hegemony to 'moral and intellectual reform', Gramsci gave us a new concept, although this new concept does incorporate the earlier focus on the necessity of alliances. Mouffe and Bobbio have pointed out that Gramsci was aware that society would not just be the contradiction of two main classes—"a historical situation is never reducible to a pure and simple confrontation of two antagonistic classes"–several other groups were also a part of any society. There would always be a struggle between the two fundamental classes to exercise hegemony over these other groups, that is, to win them over to their side. A collective will representing the nation, not just a class, had to be formed, and this process has to be understood as the process of establishing hegemony through a moral and intellectual leadership.

A class exercises hegemony by being able to convince other groups in society that its interests are aligned with the interests of the other groups. The hegemonic class is seen as taking society forward in a direction which will benefit other sections of society as well. We have seen this often in a discussion of capitalism and the capitalist class—the capitalist class becomes hegemonic when many believe that with capitalism, social divisions based on caste, race, religion or gender will become less significant, or that capitalism will usher in a modernity which will be in everybody's interest.

## Box 13.2

**THE FUNDAMENTAL SOCIAL CLASS AND THE UNIVERSAL INTEREST:**

A third moment is that in which one becomes aware that one's own corporate interests, in their present and future development, transcend the corporate limits of the purely economic class, and can and must become the interests of other subordinate groups too. This is the most purely political phase, and marks the decisive passage from the structure to the sphere of the complex superstructures; it is the phase in which previously germinated ideologies become "party", come into confrontation and conflict, until only one of them, or at least a single combination of them, tends to prevail, to gain the upper hand, to propagate itself throughout society—bringing about not only a unison of economic and political aims, but also intellectual and moral unity, posing all the questions around which the struggle rages not on a corporate but on a "universal" plane, and thus creating the hegemony of a fundamental social group over a series of subordinate groups...the development and expansion of the particular group are conceived of, and presented, as being the motor force of a universal expansion, of a development of all the "national" energies.

*The Prison Notebooks*

If what is important is for the ruling class to convince the other groups in society that its interests are the universal interests, this means that for Gramsci, the ruling class maintains its rule not only by using the coercive powers of the state to establish its domination but also through establishing its hegemony. Hegemony means that the bourgeois class maintains its rule by manufacturing consent in civil society. This consent is not passive but active; it is not a result of 'administrative coercion' nor is it merely a form of ideological imposition. According to Buci-Glucksmann, we have to distinguish Gramsci's concept of hegemony both from the concept of ideology as well as from the idea of Weberian legitimacy. The process of the formation of hegemony is much more open ended precisely because it is a process of the formation of consent or agreement—it always leaves open the possibility of a subaltern class being able to overturn this hegemony: "The more authentically hegemonic a class really is, the more it leaves opposing classes the possibility of organizing and forming themselves into an autonomous political force." [22] The institutions and aspects of civil society such as schools, churches, the media, architecture and even the names of streets are used to establish hegemony. So the task before the communist party is not just to capture the coercive apparatus of state but to establish the hegemony of the working class in civil society. There is a constant struggle to establish hegemony—there is a "disarticulation-rearticulation of given ideological elements in a struggle between two hegemonic principles to appropriate these elements."[23]

**Box 13.3**

**CIVIL SOCIETY AND POLITICAL SOCIETY:**

What we can do, for the moment, is to fix two major superstructural 'levels': the one that can be called 'civil society', that is the ensemble of organisms commonly called 'private', and that of 'political society' or 'the State'. These two levels correspond on the one hand to the function of 'hegemony' which the dominant group exercises throughout society and on the other hand to that of 'direct domination' or command exercised through the State and 'juridical' government. These functions comprise: 1) The "spontaneous" consent given by the great masses of the population to the general direction imposed on social life by the dominant fundamental group. 2) The apparatus of state coercive power which "legally" enforces discipline on those groups which do not "consent" either actively or passively. This apparatus is, however, constituted for the whole of society in anticipation of moments of crisis of command and direction when spontaneous consent has failed.

*The Prison Notebooks*

Gramsci developed an expansive conception of the state, calling it 'the integral state', which included the two components of 'political society' and 'civil society'. Political society was the "juridical-administrative state: government, the military, the police, the judiciary", while civil society consisted of private organizations "such as trade unions, churches, cultural clubs, newspapers, publishers, political parties"[24] This institutional separation itself helped in establishing the hegemony of a particular class. Civil society was not, as in liberal thought, the domain of private freedom; it was the site where dominance of the ruling class was maintained. However this dominance in civil society was not enforced through coercive mechanisms, but through the manufacturing of consent. Civil society "operates without 'sanctions' or compulsory 'obligations', but nevertheless exerts a collective pressure and obtains objective results in the form of an evolution of customs, ways of thinking and acting, morality, etc."[25] For Gramsci, there was a major difference between the ancient and medieval state on the one hand, and the modern state, on the other. In the earlier forms of the state, subaltern groups were able to maintain "a life of their own"; the modern state, however, "substitutes for the mechanical bloc of social forces their subordination to the active hegemony of the leading and dominant group."[26] This is done through an internal distinction within the sphere of the state between the state strictly speaking, and civil society. In modern bourgeois liberal states, the conquest of power is complex because unlike in the case of Czarist Russia "where toppling the monarch ensured the seizure of power", in western capitalist states, "when the state tottered, a sturdy structure of civil society was immediately revealed."[27]

Under capitalism, the state is supposed to function only as a 'night watchman' responsible for maintaining law and order, and not interfering with the vast magnitude of social interactions that take place in the private sphere or in the voluntary sphere of civil society. For Gramsci, first, this non-interventionist state has never existed in actuality, and secondly, this division between the coercive state sphere and the voluntary civil society sphere is a division internal to the state under capitalism: "In this form of regime (which anyway has never existed except on paper, as a limiting hypothesis) hegemony over its historical development belongs to private forces, to civil society - which is 'State' too, indeed is the State itself."[28] The development of capitalism in the west took the form of the emergence of a strong civil society structure, and it is in this domain that the war against capitalism had to be fought. "The massive structures of the modern democracies, both as State organizations, and as complexes of associations in civil society, constitute for the art of politics as it were the 'trenches' and the permanent fortifications of the front in the war of position: they render merely 'partial' the element of movement which before used to be 'the whole' of the war."[29] This led Gramsci to argue that in order to win the battle in developed democracies, the leadership of the working class had to focus not on a frontal assault on the state (the war of manoeuvre), but to fight a protracted war of position in the trenches of civil society.

## PASSIVE REVOLUTION AND THE STATE

Apart from the concept of hegemony, another important idea that we find in the *Prison Notebooks* is that of 'passive revolution'. We have seen earlier that Gramsci contrasted the kind of far reaching change that was brought about by the Jacobins during the French revolution with the reformism that took place in other parts of Europe. For instance, "the Risorgimento, as a 'revolution without revolution', a passive revolution, is the opposite of the French Jacobin model, or the 'accomplished form' of revolutionary process."[30] Not only did Gramsci give us an analysis of specific instances of a passive revolution like the Italian Risorgimento and Fascism, but he also provided a general theory of it.

Passive revolution is a possibility in every moment of transition: "The passive revolution becomes a potential tendency intrinsic to every transitional process."[31] A period of transition can result either in far reaching transformation or it can be limited to piece meal reform. When class is replaced by state as the engine of change, what we have is a passive revolution where compromise is struck with erstwhile dominant classes, and the tendency is for the state to play an extremely large role.Instead of the participation of the masses in change, the initiative remains in the hands of the state, and this reduces the democratic potential which is implicit in phases of transition. "Every passive revolution develops a 'conservatism or moderate reformism'...and neutralizes and channels popular initiative in its, extremely partial, attempt to satisfy some of the latter's demand 'by small doses, legally, in a reformist manner', the passive revolution tends to resolve the problems of transformation in favour of the state... and the masses are ultimately treated as 'mass of manoeuvre'."[32] When the fundamental class is not able to establish its hegemony, and the state takes over leadership, society then heads in a conservative direction, because perhaps, the state as an institution has a conservative bent.

For Gramsci, during the passive revolution, the State becomes paramount as a dominant political structure as happened in the case of the Italian Risorgimento and Italian fascism. Writing about the process of the unification of Italy, Gramsci stated that "the Piedmontese State becomes the real motor of unity after 1848...in contrast to the French jacobins, the Italian liberals conceive unity as the extension of the Piedmontese State and of dynastic patrimony, not as a national movement of the base but as a conquest of rulership."[33] The State becomes the engine of reform in the absence of any mass participation. Even when there is mass mobilization, in a passive revolution, this mass participation is turned into a conservative direction as happened during Mussolini's fascism. The promise of radical change that is implicit in moments of transition, for instance, even in the transition marked by capitalism/liberalism, is dammed in a passive revolution, which stops short of extending the radical potential of periods of change—change is initiated but its radical implications are sought to be cut off.

Gramsci, like Marx, believed that a kind of fundamental social change was necessary if there was to be an improvement in the lives of the majority of the population. The driver of this transformation had to be the working class because its interests were in the direction of universal interests. The working class had however to convince other subaltern groups, like the peasantry, of this consonance. If the working class and its leadership did not take the initiative and if it was not able to get other groups to ally with it, there was the possibility of the state taking over the leading position in society. The state would only bring about incremental changes in society which would then leave the existing dominant groups in position. To overcome this eventuality, what was necessary, Gramsci argued, was the political organization and mobilization of the working class along with the other subaltern classes.

## NOTES

1. A.S. Sassoon, ed., *Approaches to Gramsci*, London: Writers and Readers Publishing, 1982, p. 150.
2. For some of these biographical details, see P. Ransome, *Antonio Gramsci—A New Introduction*, New York: Harvester Wheatsheaf, 1992, chapter 3.
3. For these details, see P. Ransome, *Antonio Gramsci—A New Introduction, op.cit.*, pp. 90–105.
4. See J. Buttigieg, 'Antonio Gramsci: liberation begins with critical thinking', in C.H. Zuckert, *Political Philosophy in the 20th Century—Authors and Arguments*, New York: Cambridge University Press, 2011.
5. For more details on how the *Prison Notebooks* are organized, see M.E. Green, ed., *Rethinking Gramsci*, London: Routledge Taylor and Francis Group, 2011, part IV.
6. A.S. Sassoon, op.cit., p. 161.
7. Gramsci was responding to Nikolai I. Bukharin's book, *Historical Materialism: A System of Sociology*, written in 1921.

8. Q. Hoare & G.N. Smith, ed. *Selections from the Prison Notebooks of Antonio Gramsci*, London: Lawrence and Wishart, 1971, pp. 243–244.
9. Q. Hoare & G.N. Smith, *op.cit.*, p. 244.
10. C. Mouffe, ed., *Gramsci and Marxist Theory*, London: Routledge & Kegan Paul, 1979, p. 6.
11. Q. Hoare & G.N. Smith, *op.cit.*, p. 244.
12. As quoted in P. Ransome, *op.cit.*, p. 74.
13. C. Mouffe, op.cit, p. 6.
14. For a description of the 'bienno rosso' and these details, see P. Ransome, *Antonio Gramsci—A New Introduction*, *op.cit.*, chapter 3.
15. Q. Hoare & G.N. Smith, *op.cit.*, pp. 77–78.
16. Q. Hoare & G.N. Smith, *op.cit.*, p. 119.
17. Q. Hoare & G.N. Smith, *op.cit.*, p. 147.
18. Q. Hoare & G.N. Smith, *op.cit.*, pp. 152–153.
19. See T. Nairn, 'Antonu Su Gobbu', in A.S. Sassoon, *op.cit.*
20. C. Mouffe, op.cit., p. 178.
21. C. Mouffe, *op.cit.*, p. 179
22. C. Buci-Glucksmann, *Gramsci and the State*, London: Lawrence &Wishart, 1980, p. 57.
23. C. Mouffe, *op.cit.*, p. 193.
24. M.E. Green, 'Gramsci cannot speak—Presentations and interpretations of Gramsci's concept of the subaltern', in M.E. Green, ed., *Rethinking Gramsci*, *op.cit.*, p. 72.
25. Q. Hoare & G.N. Smith, *op.cit.*, p. 242.
26. See C. Buci-Glucksmann, *Gramsci and the State*, *op.cit.*, p. 274.
27. See J. Francese, ed., *Perspectives on Gramsci: Politics, culture and social theory*, New York: Routledge, 2009, p. 26.
28. Q. Hoare & G.N. Smith, *op.cit.*, p. 261.
29. Q. Hoare & G.N. Smith, *op.cit.*, p. 243.
30. C. Buci-Glucksmann, *Gramsci and the State*, London: Lawrence &Wishart, 1980, p. 54.
31. C. Buci-Glucksmann, 'State, transition and passive revolution', in C. Mouffe, *op.cit.*, p. 208.
32. *Ibid.*, pp. 208–209.
33. *Ibid.*, p. 217.

## READING LIST

Francese, J., ed., *Perspectives on Gramsci—Politics, culture and social theory*, London: Routledge, 2009.

Green, M.E., ed., *Rethinking Gramsci*, London: Routledge, 2011.

Hoare, Q. & Smith G.N., ed., *Selections from the Prison Notebooks of Antonio Gramsci*, London: Lawrence and Wishart, 1971.

Mouffe, C., ed., *Gramsci and Marxist Theory*, London: Routledge & Kegan Paul, 1979.

Ransome, P., *Antonio Gramsci—A New Introduction*, New York: Harvester Wheatsheaf, 1992.

Sassoon, A.S., ed., *Approaches to Gramsci*, London: Writers and Readers Publishing Cooperative Society Ltd., 1982.

## CENTRAL THEMES

1. **Hegemony and Consent:** How does Gramsci's concept of hegemony develop from his pre-prison writings to the *Prison Notebooks*? Does the idea of hegemony have any implications for specifying the location of the site of class struggle?
2. **The Necessity of Political Intervention:** Why did Gramsci give so much importance to political initiative? What effect does political action have on the play of forces that make up a historical situation?
3. **Revolution-restoration or the Passive Revolution:** How does Gramsci use the idea of passive revolution to explain certain kinds of changes in society? Why does Gramsci believe that the passive revolution is a possibility that is implicit in every period of transition?
4. **Gramsci and Marx:** In your opinion, in what ways did Gramsci extend or modify certain important ideas of Marx?

# FOURTEEN

# John Rawls (1921–2002): A Liberal Egalitarian Theory of Justice

John Rawls was an American political philosopher, the publication of whose famous book, *A Theory of Justice*, in 1971, was an event of great significance because it almost single-handedly revived the disciplines of political philosophy and political theory. Rawls obtained both his undergraduate degree (1943) and his Ph.D. in philosophy (1950) from Princeton University. He joined the American army during the Second World War, and once the war was over, he finished his Ph.D. and began teaching. He taught at Harvard University for several decades from the 1960s to the 1990s[1], and became famous for writing several important books in political philosophy like *A Theory of Justice* (1971), *Political Liberalism* (1993), and *The Law of Peoples* (1999).

In an interview that he gave to the *Harvard Review of Philosophy* in March 1991, Rawls talked about writing *A Theory of Justice* in the context of the Vietnam War and the Civil Rights Movement in America. "...serious political conflict", he said, "shows the need for political philosophy and calls it forth". "For a long time there had been a relative dearth of political philosophy—both in political science and moral philosophy", and when the publication of *A Theory of Justice* filled this gap, it got an overwhelming response. In his interview, Rawls talked about the public role of political philosophy: "I see political philosophy as addressing the citizenry – not government, that's not who you are addressing... In a democratic society, political philosophy...can try to win the authority of human reason."[2]

Rawls's importance as a political philosopher lies not only in his success in making the doing of political philosophy respectable again. With his *A Theory of Justice* published in 1971, and translated into as many as twenty-seven languages[3], political theory, as it were, emerged from the attack by behavioralism. Behavioralism had castigated political philosophy as not worthy of being part of political science, with no relevance for empirical political questions. This was Rawls's answer in terms of presenting an analysis of one of the central moral and political problems as to how to establish just social and political institutions. In addition, what Rawls did was to lay out the elements of the position of liberal egalitarianism; by weakening the link between justice and moral desert, and presenting an argument for this uncoupling, Rawls introduced a position on justice which cut through the usual dividing lines on such questions, and thus generated fresh thinking not only on philosophical questions but also on a substantive question of politics and political theory.

Rawls's theory of justice, that is, justice as fairness, went through several revisions and recensions as he kept working on it; the later Rawls is known not only for his conception of justice as fairness, but also for how justice as fairness fits into his theory of political liberalism. It has been argued that Rawls's later work is marked by two breaks: first, in *Political Liberalism,* he veered away from his concern with reducing sharp economic inequalities as a matter of justice, to focusing more on issues of legitimacy and stability in liberal societies; and second, in *The Law of Peoples,* in his attempt to develop principles regulating just interaction between 'peoples', Rawls is supposed to have weakened even the 'liberal' component of his liberal egalitarianism.[4] In order to judge this issue for ourselves, we need an overview of the main themes of Rawls's work.

As we saw above, in his interview, Rawls had pointed out that his political philosophy was engaged with the politics of a democratic society: his project was to determine "the most appropriate conception of justice for specifying the fair terms of social cooperation between citizens regarded as free and equal and as fully cooperating members of society over a complete life, from one generation to the next."[5] Such free and equal, democratic citizens, if they had to choose a conception of justice, would they choose, Rawls asks, utilitarian, perfectionist, intuitionist, egoistic or liberal egalitarian principles of justice.

**Box 14.1**

**SOCIETY AS A FAIR SYSTEM OF COOPERATION:**

The most fundamental idea in this conception of justice is the idea of society as a fair system of social cooperation over time from one generation to the next... Social cooperation is distinct from merely socially coordinated activity – for example, activity coordinated by orders issued by an absolute central authority. Rather, social cooperation is guided by publicly recognized rules and procedures which those cooperating accept as appropriate to regulate their conduct. The idea of cooperation includes the idea of fair terms of cooperation... Fair terms of cooperation specify an idea of reciprocity, or mutuality: all who do their part as the recognized rules require are to benefit as specified by a public and agreed upon standard.

*Justice as Fairness—A Restatement*

As we observe Rawls highlighting the concept of justice for social cooperation, we remember that this idea is quite old in the western tradition of political philosophy. We are reminded of the classical Greek myth that humans were given the gift of justice so that they could live together and thus overcome the superior strength and speed of other animals.[6] Rawls makes a similar point about the importance of justice for social cooperation when he states: "Justice is the first virtue of social institutions."[7] What we have to do is to follow Rawls's argument not so much for the concept of justice but for his specific conception of justice, that is, justice as fairness and its link with political liberalism.

## JUSTICE AS FAIRNESS—ASSUMPTIONS

The idea of social cooperation, Rawls states, tells us first of all that justice is not a problem of allocation but one of distribution. We are concerned with allocation when we assume a readymade bundle of goods which are to be allocated fairly between several individuals. Distributive justice comes into play when this bundle of goods is taken to be produced through the cooperation of a number of individuals, and is then sought to be distributed amongst them. Cooperation is also different from coordination, as specified in Box 14.1.

Distributive justice assumes a certain kind of individual—not only one who will do his or her part, but also one who can do his part as a member of a cooperating collective. The implication is that these are able bodied, normal individuals who have the capacities to cooperate with each other: "we say that a person is...a normal and fully cooperating member of society over a complete life."[8] Questions of "illness and accident", of "these temporary disabilities and also permanent disabilities or mental disorders so severe as to prevent people from being cooperating members of society" are to be "put aside."[9] Justice as fairness begins with a situation of social choice: free and equal individuals have to decide about the principles of justice which will govern their interaction with each other. These Rawlsian individuals, free and equal, normal, able bodied, also have two moral powers: first, each of them has a sense of justice, that is, they are able to understand, to apply and to act from principles of justice; and second, each of them is able to form his or her own conception of the good. That means that each one of them is able to decide or choose the values or final ends according to which they want to live their lives. They can also revise and change their conception of the good. The two moral powers are connected with each other, in that these individuals see themselves as taking responsibility for their ends, that is, they can adjust their ends to fit into a fair system of cooperation. The two moral powers also make these individuals both reasonable as well as rational—their capacity to have a sense of justice allows us to define them as reasonable individuals who accept the idea of reciprocity; their ability to form a conception of their good allows us to name them as rational individuals who can place their several goals or goods into a coherent order.[10] Rawls places such individuals, before they make their choice, under certain conditions. In Rawls's terminology, they are in an 'original position' under the 'veil of ignorance'.

## The Original Position and the Veil of Ignorance

The original position is characterized by the circumstances of justice, both objective and subjective. This is an idea that Rawls takes from Hume. The objective circumstances of justice refer to the situation of moderate scarcity in which human beings live which leads to the "necessity of social cooperation for all to have a decent standard of life."[11] It is better for everybody that human beings cooperate with each other. Neither are human beings so hostile to one another that they cannot cooperate. The subjective circumstances of justice refer to the fact of reasonable pluralism. This means that the individuals of the original position know that they "affirm different, and indeed incommensurable and irreconcilable, though reasonable, comprehensive doctrines in the light of which they understand their conception of the good."[12] In addition, in *A Theory of Justice* the individuals who are to choose the principles of justice were "thought of as representing continuing lines of claims" or as "heads of families"[13]. This stipulation came from the idea of a society as a cooperative system 'over time from one generation to the next'. However, Rawls dropped this motivational assumption in his later work where the choice making parties in the original position are presented as just individuals.

These individuals, in the original position, do not know certain things: everyone is not only ignorant of their particular conception of the good, but also of their social attributes. No one knows whether they will be, in society, rich or poor, skilled or unskilled, black or white, or members of a majority or minority religious group: "It is assumed, then, that the parties do not know certain kinds of particular facts. First of all, no one knows his place in society, his class position or social status; nor does he know his fortune in the distribution of natural assets and abilities, his intelligence and strength, and the like. Nor, again, does anyone know his conception of the good, the particulars of his rational plan of life, or even the special features of his psychology such as his aversion to risk or liability to optimism or pessimism."[14] The veil of ignorance is a device that ensures that when deciding on principles of justice, everyone will be impartial, that is, everyone will choose those principles of justice which will be to the benefit of the worst off, since no one knows which position one will actually occupy in society. What everyone knows however, is that each one of them prefers more of the primary goods than less. Ignorant of their specific conception of the good, individuals know that whatever may be their particular conception of the good, more of the primary goods such as certain liberties, and income and wealth are preferable, rather than less. The individuals in the original position also know the general principles of the functioning of an economy.

Rawls's inspiration in using the intellectual devices of the original position and the veil of ignorance is the social contract tradition of the 17th and 18th centuries. We have already seen in the work of Locke and Rousseau that the hypothetical social contract was a way of replacing the hypothetical state of nature with a political society. Rawls's idea of the original position with its circumstances of justice mirrors the idea of the state of nature and his conception of the veil of ignorance ensures that when individuals choose the principles determining what a just democratic society looks like, they will make this choice impartially.

So, under these conditions, with their two moral powers which make them reasonable and rational, and ignorant of their social attributes, skills and specific conceptions of the good, these able-bodied, free and equal individuals will, according to Rawls, pick his two principles of justice. The first principle establishes the priority of liberty, and the second principle establishes fair equality of opportunity and allows only those inequalities which are to the benefit of the worst off group.

**Box 14.2**

**THE TWO PRINCIPLES OF JUSTICE:**

Each person has an equal claim to a fully adequate scheme of equal basic rights and liberties, which scheme is compatible with the same scheme for all; and in this scheme the equal political liberties, and only those liberties, are to be guaranteed their fair value.

Social and economic inequalities are to satisfy two conditions: first, they are to be attached to positions and offices open to all under conditions of fair equality of opportunity; and second, they are to be to the greatest benefit of the least advantaged members of society.

*Political Liberalism*

The two principles of justice apply to the 'basic structure' of society, which is Rawls's term for "a society's main political, social and economic institutions."[15] Since these institutions have a far reaching effect on how individual lives turn out, it is imperative that they be just. "The political constitution with an independent judiciary, the legally recognized forms of property, and the structure of the economy as well as the family in some form, all belong to the basic structure. The basic structure is the background social framework within which the activities of associations and individuals take place."[16] Rawls argues that so far as associations like universities and religious societies are concerned, their rules are a matter of local justice, whereas he is concerned with the principles of domestic justice, the subject of which then is the 'basic structure'. Questions of local and global justice are to be decided later at the constitutional, legislative and judicial stages.

Rawls arranges his principles of justice in a lexical or serial priority. The first principle is prior to the second principle and the principle of fair equality of opportunity is prior to the 'difference' principle. The first principle of liberty is about specific basic liberties which Rawls lists as follows: "freedom of thought and liberty of conscience; the political liberties and freedom of association, as well as the freedoms specified by the liberty and integrity of the person; and finally, the rights and liberties covered by the rule of law."[17] This principle is linked to Rawls's conception of the moral power of human beings to form their own conceptions of the good. Several of the particular liberties that Rawls specifies, like the freedom of thought and conscience and the liberty to form associations, enable individuals to form and revise their own conceptions of the good. These liberties are to be of the form that they are consistent with equal liberties for all. These liberties can only be regulated on the ground that the regulation is required for the sake of the moral powers. Rawls talks about the basic right to hold and to have the exclusive use of private property, for instance, in terms of allowing a sufficient material basis for personal independence and a sense of self-respect, both of which are essential for the adequate development and exercise of the moral powers. Wider conceptions of property such as the right to private property in natural resources and means of production generally, including rights of acquisition and bequest, are not taken as basic, because Rawls does not consider such a conception of property to be necessary for the adequate development and full exercise of the moral powers.

Another relevant example is provided by Rawls's discussion of the fair value of the political liberties. Rawls is critical of the American Supreme Court's decision in *Buckley v. Valeo* (1976), to strike down restrictions on campaign expenditure by political candidates in the name of free political speech; he argues instead, that private funding for political parties must be regulated to ensure the equal worth of the political liberties. As long as the content of the speech is not restricted, Rawls states, free speech cannot be used to prevent moving the political liberties beyond their formal status to a situation of their equal worth for all citizens.[18] Already we can see that questions of equality become relevant even as the first principle of liberty is being unpacked. The form of the basic liberties then is to be such that they fit together into a coherent scheme of equal liberties for all.

The basic liberties are one kind of primary goods, and justice in Rawls is about the distribution of primary goods. For Rawls, there are two kinds of primary goods—natural primary goods and social primary goods. The distribution of natural primary goods like health, vigour, intelligence and imagination is a matter of luck and chance. The social primary goods are five in number: they include "the basic liberties", "freedom of movement and free choice of occupation against a background of diverse opportunities", "powers and prerogatives of offices and positions of responsibility", "income and wealth" and "the social bases of self-respect."[19] These are called primary goods because of Rawls's belief that irrespective of whatever is one's conception of the good, and these will be very different for different individuals, one will wish for more primary goods than less. Rawls also points out that considering justice in terms of the distribution of primary goods rather than in terms of maximizing utility addresses the problem of adaptive preferences. In any society, individuals would be influenced by the constraints and opportunities of that society to adapt their preferences accordingly; therefore their calculation of their pleasure and pain, or their utilities would be subjective. In contrast, primary goods, Rawls argues, are objective in the sense that more or less of primary goods cannot be defined by an individual's preferences.

## THE DIFFERENCE PRINCIPLE

The second principle of justice has two components—fair equality of opportunity and the difference principle. For Rawls, fair equality of opportunity is not the same as formal equality of opportunity. The latter principle is satisfied as long as there is no discrimination, for instance, on the basis of sex, religion, race or caste, when individuals are chosen for different occupations. This is the idea, Rawls says, of 'careers open to talents'. But the principle of fair equality of opportunity goes beyond this: it requires "not merely that public offices and social positions be open in the formal sense, but that all should have a fair chance to attain them... [To this end,] Society must also establish, among other things, equal opportunities of education for all regardless of family income."[20] To take another example, formal equality of opportunity applies when, for instance, admission to a renowned medical school is open to anybody who cracks the entrance test; fair equality of opportunity, on the other hand ensures that those who pass the entrance test but do not have the material resources to pay the tuition fees are provided scholarships so that they can also gain admission in that medical school.

The difference principle acknowledges that a just society, even one based on the ideas of the fair value of the basic political liberties, and fair equality of opportunity, can contain social and economic inequalities. These social and political inequalities, Rawls states, can be permitted in a just society only if they can be shown to be to the benefit of that society's least advantaged individuals. In *A Theory of Justice,* Rawls points out that in the original position, under the veil of ignorance, individuals will choose the rule of *maximum minimorum,* that is, the maximin rule. Since in the original position, no individual knows which position they will finally occupy in society, it is rational to pick a rule maximizing the minimum, in case one turns out to be a member of the worst off group. So the difference principle permits only those economic inequalities which can be shown to be necessary in enhancing the prospects of the least advantaged groups.[21]

The justification of the difference principle does not lie merely in its being picked in the original position. Rawls develops a complex argument about regarding "as a common asset…the distribution of native endowments, that is, the differences among persons"[22] in order to defend the difference principle. Since nature follows the rule of diversity, it is natural that individuals differ in their natural endowments, some having more and others less. Here Rawls points out that since it is a truism that "we do not deserve (in the sense of moral desert) our place in the distribution of native endowments"[23], the idea of moral desert is inapplicable in a theory of justice. Just as we do not deserve our natural talents, similarly we do not deserve the social position we are born into. But for Rawls, a person's skills and capabilities are often the result of the opportunities available to that person because of his social position. One's capacity to work hard is also, for example, usually the result of having been born into a family where the value of hard work is inculcated: "The extent to which natural capacities develop and reach fruition is affected by all kinds of social conditions and class attitudes. Even the willingness to make an effort, to try, and so to be deserving in the ordinary sense is itself dependent upon happy family and social circumstances."[24] Therefore to claim more rewards on the basis of deserving them because of hard work is invalid because one did not deserve the ability to work hard in the first place. One gets one's abilities by chance, therefore it is not fair that one appropriates the returns that one gets for these abilities in one's society, solely for oneself.

In his later work, Rawls distinguishes three ideas of moral desert: "first, the idea of moral desert in the strict sense, that is, the moral worth of a person's character as a whole…second, the idea of legitimate expectations…[and] third, the ideas of deservingness as specified by a scheme of public rules designed to achieve certain purposes."[25] We have already shown above how Rawls refuses to make the idea of moral desert a part of his theory of justice. Justice as fairness does use "the second and third ideas of desert" in that it acknowledges "a deliberate effort of will, or acts intentionally done."[26] Yet justice as fairness is not so much a matter of matching economic rewards to willful effort as it is a matter of incentivizing individuals to attain occupational positions which require much effort. As Rawls puts it: the role "of inequalities in distributive shares in modern societies, is…to attract people to positions where they are most needed from a social point of view, to cover the costs of acquiring skills and educating abilities, to encourage them to accept the burdens of particular responsibilities, and to do all this in ways consistent with free choice of occupation and fair equality of opportunity."[27] So economic inequalities are only justified on the grounds that one cannot benefit unless one benefits others. Justice as fairness permits the variation in wages and salaries to be matched to the natural variation in endowments and the variation in social positions only in this manner, as specified by legitimate expectations. This is not really a desert-based view of justice because there is no claim that "treating a person in a certain way is made appropriate simply by what that person is like or has done, without reference to the good consequences of this treatment or to the fact that this treatment is licensed or required by justifiable institutions."[28]

So in spite of the criticism that Rawls leaves economic inequalities in place in his conception of justice, and that the usual strategy of progressive taxation is hardly sufficient to tackle economic disparity, one should note that he undermines the link between contribution and reward, or desert and justice. It is clear that, for Rawls, we do not deserve our capacities or even our capabilities; although Rawls points to the psychological and physical integrity of the person as guaranteed by the basic liberties, he also states that the distribution of native endowments is to be regarded as a common asset. Rawls's theory can be seen to advocate a specific kind of liberalism in that it attempts to locate individualism not in self-ownership but in our moral and rational capacities.

## Reasonable Pluralism and the Overlapping Consensus

Rawls's conception of an overlapping consensus is an attempt to answer the question with which he begins *Political Liberalism*: "how is it possible for there to exist over time a just and stable society of free and equal citizens, who remain profoundly divided by reasonable religious, philosophical and moral doctrines?"[29] When justice as fairness is chosen as the conception of justice according to which the basic structure of society is determined, the next question that arises for Rawls is that of ensuring the stability of this conception of justice. How is it to be brought about that citizens will continue to abide by the principles of justice as fairness?

While discussing the components of justice as fairness, we have already seen that Rawls characterizes the subjective circumstances of justice as those of reasonable pluralism. The original position is an idealization of certain aspects of a democratic society; such societies are characterized by a diversity of comprehensive doctrines. Of these doctrines, those which are irrational, unreasonable, and even mad, are to be contained, but those that are reasonable, that is those that 'acknowledge the freedom and equality of citizens' are to be considered to be a permanent feature of such societies. "A plurality of reasonable yet incompatible comprehensive doctrines is the normal result of the exercise of human reason within the framework of the free institutions of a constitutional regime."[30] Rawls goes on to explain this reasonable pluralism through the idea of burdens of judgement.

## Box 14.3

**THE BURDENS OF JUDGEMENT:**

a. The evidence-empirical and scientific-bearing on the case is conflicting and complex, and thus hard to assess and evaluate.
b. Even where we agree fully about the kinds of considerations that are relevant, we may disagree about their weight, and so arrive at different judgements.
c. To some extent, all our concepts, and not only moral and political concepts, are vague and subject to hard cases; and this indeterminacy means that we must rely on judgement and interpretation.
d. To some extent (how great we cannot tell), the way we assess evidence and weigh moral and political values is shaped by or total experience, our whole course of life up to now; and our total experiences must always differ.
e. Often, there are different kinds of normative considerations of different force on both sides of an issue and it is difficult to make an overall assessment.
f. Finally, any system of social institutions is limited in the values it can admit so that some selection must be made from the full range of moral and political values that might be realized.

*Political Liberalism*

Reasonable individuals, according to Rawls, also accept the burdens of judgement. When reasoning about an issue, so many factors bear on this reasoning, that it is very probable for reasonable individuals not to reach an agreement when they reason together. The empirical evidence bearing on the issue may be conflicting and complex; there may be too many facets to the issue; the individuals' reasoning about the issue may have been formed by different life experiences and their different social positions may give these individuals widely divergent perspectives on the issue. Such like burdens of judgement often lead to a situation of reasonable disagreement. Given that our judgements are burdened by so many factors, and in the context of life under free institutions, individuals will adhere to diverse and conflicting religious, philosophical and moral doctrines of what is good.

To come back now to the question of the stability of the conception of justice, the route to this stability cannot lie in the anchoring of the conception of justice in a particular comprehensive moral, philosophical or religious doctrine since modern societies are characterized by a plurality of such doctrines. Keeping in mind the burdens of judgement, reasonable individuals give up the expectation of convincing each other of the correctness of one comprehensive doctrine. Instead of that, while holding on to their incompatible comprehensive philosophical doctrines, they seek to find divergent ways to anchor the political conception of justice that they share, in their comprehensive doctrines. This leads to an overlapping consensus on justice, providing stability to the principles of justice.

**Box 14.4**

**THE OVERLAPPING CONSENSUS:**

[G]iven the historical conditions of the modern world, we do not say that its public political conception of justice is affirmed by citizens from within the same comprehensive doctrine... Citizens have conflicting religious, philosophical, and moral views and so they affirm the political conception from within different and opposing comprehensive doctrines, and so, in part, for different reasons... The fact of reasonable pluralism implies that there is no such doctrine, whether fully or partially comprehensive, on which all citizens do or can agree to settle the fundamental questions of political justice. Rather, we say that the political conception is affirmed by what we refer to as a reasonable overlapping consensus.

*Justice as Fairness—A Restatement*

We can pick up one of Rawls's examples of a comprehensive religious doctrine which holds, for instance, that 'outside the church there is no salvation'. When we reason with the adherents of this doctrine, we do not attempt to convince them of the falsity of their belief. We only seek agreement with them on the position that political power, which is by definition coercive power, should not be used to force individuals to abide with this belief. Neither should political power be used to compel individuals to follow comprehensive beliefs that we consider to be true. The domain of the political should be restricted to that which is necessary for individuals to be in a society together. As long as the conception of justice as fairness, which is a political conception of justice, is agreed to, individuals can live together with one another in a society.

So it is not necessary that there be a consensus on a comprehensive doctrine; it is sufficient that the consensus be confined to a political conception. Rawls also points out that only the political conception of justice should be the basis of public reason in a well-ordered society. The public reason of a society is public in being the reasoning of the public, that is, of the citizens; it is public in being concerned about the public good; and it is public in its nature and content, "being given by the ideals and principles expressed by society's conception of political justice, and conducted open to view on that basis."[31] When citizens reason about the public good in public forums, they are to be guided by the political conception of justice as fairness. Only then will their reasons count as part of public reason; they are not to bring in the non-public reasoning which they use in their associational life, into public reason. Public reason should not be, according to Rawls, metaphysical. Metaphysical doctrines, that is, the comprehensive moral, philosophical or religious views that are also part of us can be used to ground the political conception of justice. But we do not need to agree on the grounding; as long as we agree that our public reason is constituted by the conception of justice, we can establish stability for our political society. The limits imposed by public reason do not apply to all political questions but only to constitutional essentials and to questions of basic justice. The constitutional essentials include the fundamental principles that specify the general structure of government and the political process, that is, the powers of the legislature, executive and the judiciary and the scope of majority rule; and the equal basic rights and liberties of citizenship that legislative majorities are to respect. Questions of basic justice include some principle of opportunity and a social minimum providing for basic needs. When citizens and legislators are discussing these questions, their publicly stated advocacy and justification must not appeal to their comprehensive doctrines but must be based on public political values.

These ideas of justice as fairness, public reason, and an overlapping consensus are part of the reflective equilibrium of a modern democratic society. These ideas are already embedded in the public culture of this society, and form an equilibrium in the society. Our reflection on the requirements of justice adds to this equilibrium because it goes back to the ideas already present in the background culture of society.

## Principles of International Justice

We have, so far, seen Rawls at his strongest in framing a theory of domestic justice, that is, justice as it applies within a society. He did, however, also frame the principles of international justice by following the same method. In *A Theory of Justice*, he briefly discussed the extension of "the interpretation of the original position to parties as representatives of different nations who must choose together the fundamental principles to adjudicate conflicting claims among states."[32] Rawls stated that if the contracting parties, the representatives of states, were not permitted knowledge of the 'power and strength of their own society in comparison with other nations', these representatives would choose the principles of self-determination, of self-defense, of the right to form defensive alliances, of the binding nature of treaties, and of certain acts of violence being strictly inadmissible even in a just war, to regulate inter-state relations in the world.

By 1999, Rawls had written his long monograph on international justice, *The Law of Peoples*. No longer were the contracting parties representatives of states or nations; they represented 'peoples'. Now Rawls preferred to conceive of justice between peoples rather than between states because, whereas states are concerned predominantly with extending their power, peoples can be expected to "limit their basic interests as required by the reasonable." Rawls was more hopeful of a viable society of peoples than of peaceful interaction between states. Rawls classified domestic societies into five types: reasonable liberal peoples, decent hierarchical peoples, outlaw states, burdened societies and societies that are benevolent despotisms. Only the first two can be characterized as well-ordered societies, and the principles of international justice are a pact between the liberal and decent peoples.

Liberal peoples have "a reasonably just constitutional democratic government that serves their fundamental interests"[33]; they are united by 'common sympathies' even though they may belong to different linguistic and ethnic groups, and they have a moral nature in that they are willing to cooperate on fair terms with other peoples. Decent hierarchical peoples live under a dominant conception of the good, for instance, the conception of the good of a majority religion. Freedom of religion is allowed in such societies; however, members of minority religions are not permitted to hold political office. Rawls calls all decent hierarchical societies associationist in form: "the members of these societies are viewed in public life as members of different groups, and each group is represented in the legal system by a body in a decent consultation hierarchy."[34] Human rights such as the right to life (including subsistence and security), to liberty,(freedom from slavery, serfdom and forced occupation) including a limited right to conscience, to personal property, and to formal equality, are respected in these societies. Hence, such societies are decent but hierarchical because high political office is monopolized by members of one religious group. The political leadership does regularly consult with the representatives of other religious groups. Outlaw states are societies where human rights are not protected internally, and these societies also carry out aggressive policies against other peoples. Burdened societies are characterized by social conditions such as large-scale poverty and by other political and cultural conditions which prevent these societies from becoming well-ordered.

If the representatives of decent hierarchical peoples and liberal peoples meet in an original position behind a veil of ignorance where they do not know the population or the size of the territory of their peoples, or the extent or kind of natural resources they have access to, they will choose the principles of justice specified in Box 14.5.

**Box 14.5**

THE PRINCIPLES OF INTERNATIONAL JUSTICE:

1. Peoples are free and independent, and their freedom and independence are to be respected by other peoples.
2. Peoples are to observe treaties and undertakings.
3. Peoples are equal and are parties to the agreements that bind them.
4. Peoples are to observe a duty of non-intervention.
5. Peoples have the right of self-defense but no right to instigate war for reasons other than self-defense.
6. Peoples are to honor human rights.
7. Peoples are to observe certain specified restrictions in the conduct of war.
8. Peoples have a duty to assist other peoples living under unfavorable conditions that prevent their having a just or decent political and social regime.

*The Law of Peoples*

Rawls believed that when the representatives of different peoples met in an original position, they would not choose to establish a world government; instead, they would pick principles of international justice for a world divided into different 'peoples'. According to scholars, Rawls's conception of peoples does not merely mirror the reality of world divided into different political units. For Rawls, the concept of peoples has an ethical primacy in that, each people "take responsibility for their territory and the size of their population, as well as for maintaining the land's environmental integrity."[35]

Rawls's principles of international justice are for a world divided into different peoples. This conception has been characterized as social liberalism and contrasted with cosmopolitan liberalism. Rawls rejected a conception in which individuals living in different societies were taken as subjects of international justice; instead he chose to fix principles for different peoples. He did this not because that is how the world is...it is divided by several boundaries but also because he thinks that this division is a way of safeguarding and developing the world's resources. Given his understanding of private property... "As I see it the point of the institution of property is that, unless a definite agent is given responsibility for maintaining an asset and bears the loss for not doing so, that asset tends to deteriorate"[36] ...unless a people is made responsible for a territory in the sense that the territory belongs to them, the resources of the territory will not be looked after. "So it may be that a people should be treated as having special ethical significance because its flourishing as a people is essential to its capacity to manage its human, material, and cultural resources and, thus, to sustain its institutions, for the benefit of present and future members."[37]

This conception of international justice where the units of concern are taken to be 'peoples' is, as we have said above, defined as social liberalism in contrast to cosmopolitan liberalism where 'social arrangements are justified and assessed by their consequences for individuals'. For Rawls, his principles of international justice must protect the self-determination of both liberal peoples and decent, even if, hierarchical peoples. Intervention is permitted with respect to outlaw states which transgress the human rights of their own citizens. However, one reason for Rawls not adopting the perspective of cosmopolitan liberalism is that such a perspective will condone intervention even in decent societies in order to turn them into liberal societies. As against this, Rawls believes that "a decent hierarchical society meets moral and legal requirements sufficient to override the political reasons we might have for imposing sanctions on, or forcibly intervening with, its people and their institutions and culture." With reference to decent hierarchical societies, Rawls upholds the principle of toleration in order to 'maintain a stable peace among pluralistic societies'.

For peace in the international arena, Rawls also recommends a principle of aid to burdened societies. This duty of assistance is not to be confused with ideas of egalitarianism: Rawls explicitly rejects any version of the difference principle for the international arena. Burdened societies fail in being well ordered societies not only because of the lack of material resources, but also because of adverse political institutions and cultural traditions. Rawls uses the idea of a target to set a boundary to the duty of assistance. Once the goal of making the burdened society capable of managing its "own affairs reasonably and rationally" is reached, "further assistance is not required, even though the [assisted] society may still be relatively poor."[38]

Rawls rejects any global egalitarian principle without target, because he thinks such principles go against the political autonomy of well-ordered societies. "Once the duty of assistance is satisfied and all peoples have a working liberal or decent government, there is again no reason to narrow the gap between the average wealth of different people."[39]

## Critical Assessment

In having a far-reaching impact, Rawls's writings have also generated many critical responses.[40] Many critics have been very critical of Rawls's conception of the individual. Both the libertarians and the communitarians, for instance, reject the Rawlsian conception of the person, but from opposite ends. Nozick, for example, found fault with the Rawlsian idea that we do not deserve our skills because we are not solely responsible for the factors that lead to the development of these skills. Come to think of it, it is odd that Rawls insists on our responsibility for our conceptions of the good, which is one of our two moral powers, yet he also insists that we cannot take credit for our skills and capacities. Nozick comes up with his famous Wilt Chamberlain example to argue against Rawlsian type patterned theories of justice. In fact, his stronger claim is that Rawls's difference principle institutes a kind of slavery because it allows the state, as it were, to extract forced labor from individuals. For these reasons, Nozick rejects Rawls's theory of justice.[41]

Nozick also argues that if one is concerned with the just treatment of the worst off group in a society, one must first investigate why the group is in the worst off positon. A probable explanation could be that these individuals or their ancestors have been the victims of unjust treatment in earlier times, which has resulted in their worst off position in contemporary times. We must address the position of the worst off as a matter of rectificatory justice to compensate for the injustices that they suffered in the past. When we come to think of it, it certainly seems less patronizing to understand the situation of the worst off in terms of a history of past injustice, rather than in terms of the results of a natural lottery of native endowments.

In one way the communitarian critics of Rawls make just the opposite claim than Nozick. They focus on how Rawls considers each individual as responsible for his or her own conception of the good. The communitarians reject this idea of the 'unencumbered self' and argue that we are influenced by the communities we are born into, in our conceptions of the good. In addition they argue that since our conceptions of the good are so important for our identity, we cannot just relegate them to the private sphere, and ignore them in the public sphere.[42]

Egalitarians have also professed dissatisfaction with Rawlsian justice. Some have argued that justice should be seen as a matter of distributing capabilities and not just primary goods.

From a feminist perspective, much criticism has focused on Rawls's treatment of the family[43]. Rawls considers the family to be part of the basic structure since a child's treatment in the family has a far-reaching impact on her life prospects. Yet he argues that the principles of justice apply externally and not internally to the family. The family is also an important site for the formation of conceptions of the good and their transmission to the next generation. For this reason, Rawls does not advocate state interference in the family. As feminists have long pointed out, the family is also the institution where many women and children face abuse and unjust treatment. How can Rawls's conception of justice be complete unless the family itself is also governed by principles of justice?

Feminists have also pointed to Rawls's neglect of the ideas of dependency and care in his theory of justice. Rawls's assumption that the members of society are such as can cooperate with each other, and that questions of care for the dependent can be addressed later, is questioned on the ground that since human beings begin their lives with long periods of dependency, the issue of care cannot be left for later. This strategy of seeing care as a question for later has the effect of not providing justice for every society's care-workers who are primarily women. We have to consider incorporating care as a primary good in Rawls's theory, and in addition, design care work in such a way that it is not exploitative of care givers or care receivers. Feminists point out that a cooperative society is not only a productive society, but also a care giving and a care receiving society[44]. If one thinks of Indian families, in many of which we can find four generations living in the same house, questions of the sharing of resources and issues of care become central in the family itself.

Some feminists have also joined other critics of Rawls in rejecting his conception of human nature as envisioned in the original position. Human beings in the original position are assumed to be selfish and egoistic which is why the veil of ignorance is imposed on them: it ensures externally that their egoism does not have deleterious consequences. Because they are basically only concerned about their own interests but do not know who they will end up as, they choose the two principles of justice. Feminist critics have found this attempt to bring in benevolence through the external device of a veil of ignorance unacceptable.

Finally, Rawls has also been blamed for adopting a monological rather than a dialogical model of moral reasoning. Every individual in the original position reasons in essentially the same manner: 'what if I am in the worst off position, or what if I turn out to be in the minority'. Critics argue that adherence to principles of justice would be much more stable if reasoning about them was more in the form of a dialogue. "…exchanging claims and counterclaims in a dialogue in which different perspectives can be presented and investigated" or a process of "interpersonal dialogue where people can explain to one another their experiences and their diverse viewpoints"[45] contains more possibilities of coming up with a reasonable and acceptable conception of justice. Critics moving along this line do not agree with Rawls's stipulation of not allowing all the arguments that are available in civil society under diverse comprehensive doctrines an entry into public reason. Comprehensive doctrines, an integral component of which is sometimes gender hierarchy, must be debated in the spaces of public reason instead of, as in Rawls's view, being let alone as long as adherents of such gender hierarchy advocating comprehensive doctrines accept equal citizenship rights for all women. I can also add the criticism here that "liberal non-religious comprehensive perspectives are bound to suffer less and this establishes a kind of inequality".

There has also been criticism from a global justice perspective. Some thinkers have faulted Rawls for not extending his conception of justice to address the problem of global inequalities of wealth and resources. If it is partly a matter of luck and contingency how well-endowed some individuals are, surely it is even more a matter of contingency as to which countries are rich in natural resources and which are not. Even if we ignore for the moment the history, between countries, of conquest and plunder, we can still reject the idea of a country's deserving the natural resources within its boundaries. Thinkers like Beitz and Pogge have sought to address this issue by proposing mechanisms of redistribution; in Pogge's case, a Global Resources Dividend which is to be levied on the country using its natural resources, and collected into a Global Resources Fund.[46] This fund can then be redistributed to the poorer countries. These thinkers are critical of Rawls for not attempting to reduce global economic inequalities as part of his conception of international justice.

## NOTES

1. For these biographical details, see C. Belshaw & G. Kemp, eds., *12 Modern Philosophers*, Chichester: Wiley-Blackwell, 2009, pp. 34–35.
2. See 'John Rawls: For the Record', www.hcs.harvard.edu/hrp/issues/1991/Rawls.pdf.
3. See S. Freeman, ed., *The Cambridge Companion to Rawls*, Cambridge: Cambridge University Press, 2003, Introduction.
4. See L. Wenar, 'The Unity of Rawls's work', *The Journal of Moral Philosophy*, 1 (3), 2004, pp. 265–275.
5. J. Rawls, *Political Liberalism*, New York: Columbia University Press, 1993, p. 3.
6. Plato, *Protagoras* in E. Hamilton & H. Cairns, eds., *Plato - The Collected Dialogues*, Bollingen Series LXXI, Princeton: Princeton University Press, 1987.
7. John Rawls, *A Theory of Justice*, New Delhi: Universal, Fifth Indian Reprint, 2011, p. 3.
8. John Rawls, *Political Liberalism*, 1993, p. 18.
9. John Rawls, *Political Liberalism*, 1993, p. 20.
10. For more discussion of individuals as reasonable and rational, see John Rawls, *Political Liberalism*, pp. 48–54.
11. John Rawls, *Justice as Fairness–A Restatement*, edited by E. Kelly, Cambridge: The Belknap Press, 2001, p. 84.
12. *Ibid*.
13. John Rawls, *A Theory of Justice*, 1971, p. 128.
14. John Rawls, *A Theory of Justice*, 1971, p. 137.
15. John Rawls, *Political Liberalism*, p. 11.
16. John Rawls, *Justice as Fairness–A Restatement*, p.10.
17. John Rawls, *Political Liberalism*, p. 291.
18. For the details of this argument, see John Rawls, *Political Liberalism*, 1993, pp. 356–363.
19. John Rawls, *Political Liberalism*, p. 308.
20. John Rawls, *Justice as Fairness–A Restatement*, 2001, pp. 43–44.
21. John Rawls, *A Theory of Justice*, pp. 153–154.
22. John Rawls, *Justice as Fairness–A Restatement*, p. 75.
23. John Rawls, *Justice as Fairness–A Restatement*, p. 74.
24. John Rawls, *A Theory of Justice*, p. 74.
25. John Rawls, *Justice as Fairness–A Restatement*, p. 73.
26. John Rawls, *Justice as Fairness–A Restatement*, pp. 73–74.
27. John Rawls, *Justice as Fairness–A Restatement*, p. 78.
28. T.M. Scanlon, 'Giving desert its due', *Philosophical Explorations*, 16:2, 2013, p. 114.
29. John Rawls, *Political Liberalism*, p. 4.

30. John Rawls, *Political Liberalism*, p. xvi.
31. John Rawls, *Political Liberalism*, p. 213.
32. John Rawls, *A Theory of Justice*, p. 378.
33. John Rawls, *The Law of Peoples*, Cambridge, Massachusetts: Harvard University Press, 1999, p. 23.
34. John Rawls, *The Law of Peoples*, p. 64.
35. John Rawls, *The Law of Peoples*, p. 8.
36. John Rawls, *The Law of Peoples*, p. 39.
37. C. Beitz, 'Rawls's Law of Peoples', *Ethics*, Vol. 110, No. 4 (July 2000), p. 682.
38. John Rawls, *The Law of Peoples*, p. 111.
39. John Rawls, *The Law of Peoples*, p. 114.
40. For a basic sketch of these critical responses, see C. Audard, *John Rawls*, Stocksfield: Acumen, 2007.
41. See R. Nozick, *Anarchy, State, and Utopia*, Oxford: Basil Blackwell, 1974, Part II.
42. See Sandel's essay in M.J. Sandel, ed., *Liberalism and Its Critics*, New York: New York University Press, 1984.
43. See R. Abbey, *Feminist Interpretations of John Rawls*, University Park: The Pennsylvania State University Press, 2013.
44. See M.C. Nussbaum, 'Rawls and Feminism' in S. Freeman, *The Cambridge Companion to Rawls*, op. cit.
45. M.C. Nussbaum, 'Rawls and Feminism', op. cit., pp. 494–495.
46. T. Pogge, 'An Egalitarian Law of Peoples', *Philosophy and Public Affairs*, 23: 3, Summer 1994, 195–224.

## READING LIST

Abbey, Ruth (ed.), *Feminist Interpretations of John Rawls*, University Park: The Pennsylvania State University Press, 2013.

Daniels, Norman (ed.), *Reading Rawls: Critical Studies on Rawls' A Theory of Justice*, Stanford: Stanford University Press, 1989.

Freeman, Samuel (ed.), *The Cambridge Companion to Rawls*, Cambridge: Cambridge University Press, 2003.

Rawls, John, *Justice as Fairness—A Restatement*, ed. E. Kelly, Cambridge, Massachusetts: The Belknap Press of Harvard University Press, 2001.

Richardson, R., and Weithman, P. (eds.), *The Philosophy of Rawls: A Collection of Essays*, 5 vol., New York: Garland, 1999.

## CENTRAL THEMES

1. **Justice and equality:** Rawls claims that wide disparities in economic resources affect the equal basic liberties. Yet he permits some social and economic inequalities in his just society. What is his reasoning for this?
2. **Justice and difference:** Two kinds of differences that are salient in Rawls's theory are differences in natural endowments and differences in conceptions of

the good. How does Rawls approach these two types of differences in his theory of justice?

3. **National and international justice:** Rawls qualifies his principles of national justice when he applies them to the international arena. Is this because he is an advocate of social liberalism rather than of cosmopolitan liberalism?
4. **The idea of public reason:** For Rawls, the public reason of a society is constituted by the political conception of justice. Is such a political conception sufficient to hold a society together?

FIFTEEN

# Carole Pateman, Martha C. Nussbaum, Judith Butler: Contemporary Feminist Theory

In the tradition of western political thought, we have found political philosophers examining the productive and coercive play of political power as it regulates the relations between individuals interacting with each other in the public sphere. Who are these individuals? Are they men or women? The demand that we pay attention to the gender identity of these individuals set off an explosion of writing in political thought and theory. How differently from male individuals are female individuals incorporated in social life and in the public domain, and what are the implications of this differential incorporation in the lives of men and women?

The first wave of the women's movement in the 1840s in the Anglo-American world began with the demand for women's entry into the public political sphere. Women wanted to know why they were being denied the vote: when the suffrage was being extended to all white men, irrespective of wealth and educational levels, why did the categories of sex and race remain as the basis for the exclusion of many from the vote? What was the justification for women's exclusion from the public world of employment, and why were they denied ownership and control over property? The argument that women were more emotional and less rational than men, that they were also physically weaker than men and had to be protected, was contested on many grounds. The claim that woman's main role was to take care of domestic affairs and family members was also debated. If women were taken to be making their own contribution to society by looking after the family, why did they suffer domination and sexual violence at the hands of men? If the category of modern political thought was that of the individual, why did this category not apply to half of the human race, which was female? Finally, if women nourished the values of care and interdependence in the domestic sphere, then why were they denied a role in the public sphere that would benefit from the same values?

Questions such as these began to be addressed specifically during the second wave of the women's movement after the 1960s. By now, there has been so much writing in political theory on women, and by women, that the literature has begun to be divided into categories like liberal feminism, radical feminism, socialist feminism, black feminism, queer feminism and post-colonial feminism. Some feminist theorists reject these divisions and point out that looking at social processes from a feminist perspective changes the contours of whichever theory one is using; so, for example, the shape of liberal or socialist political theory changes once feminism is added to it. In this chapter, we look at the work of three important feminist thinkers from the late 20th century, Carole Pateman, Martha C. Nussbaum and Judith Butler, who differ significantly from each other, even as they share an overriding concern with investigating the effects of gender. Pateman and Nussbaum accept the identity, women, and seek to understand how women get treated in society; Pateman examines the political exclusion of women, and why the work they do in looking after family members at home, often does not get acknowledged as work. She also analyses the sexual subordination of women through the modern marriage contract, and the practices of prostitution and surrogacy contracts. Her emphasis is on the categories of domination and subordination as structuring the lives of women. Nussbaum looks at the lack of material resources that women suffer from, in many parts of the world, and asks what political theory must do, in order to address this lack. However, apart from focusing on issues of redistribution, she also raises the question of how our idea of the individual will change once we include the activity that women have traditionally been engaged in, in our picture of how societies function. Butler points out that since the effects of the sex/gender system are so pernicious, our efforts should not be limited to intervening at the level of these effects, but we must attempt to destabilize the sex/gender system. She examines the process of the formation of one's sexual and gender identity, and focuses on the mechanisms of repression that are part of identity formation. In that sense, feminism has come full circle. It began by focusing on the gender identity, women, and now one variant of feminist theory wants to do more than just acknowledge a woman's intersecting identities—one could be a middle class, upper caste, Hindu, Indian, middle-aged, lesbian woman. This feminist theory instead advocates a move away from identity politics in the name of freedom: "The positions of resistance recommended are thus, those that are involved in 'queering' identity, in preference to merely promoting oppositional categories like 'lesbian'."[1]

## CAROLE PATEMAN (1940–)

Carole Pateman did not begin her scholarly career as a feminist. She came to feminist theory through her interest in democratic theory. Pateman began her writing career as a democratic theorist with her 1970 book, *Participation and Democratic Theory,* in which she critiqued liberal democracy for its reduction of political participation to the mere act of periodic voting. In contrast, Pateman talked about models of economic democracy where workplaces and not just formal political institutions were democratically organized, with workers having a say in decisions about what to produce and how to produce it. Pateman's interest in the meaning of democracy and in processes of democratization has remained a central concern of all her work.

In her next book, *The Problem of Political Obligation* (1979), Pateman took her critique of liberal democracy further by going back to the origin of the theory of liberal democracy in the social contract tradition. She argued that since thinkers of this tradition began with the assumption of equal and free individuals by nature, it would follow that political authority could only be established on the basis of self-assumed obligations of these free and equal individuals. They began with the subversive ideal of voluntarism but Hobbes and Locke did not follow through to the consequences of this voluntarism. Instead, they advocated the position of hypothetical voluntarism—if citizens benefited from the existence of the liberal democratic state, they could be said to have consented to the policies of the state, and hence they were obliged to obey the state. This derivation of obligation from consent and of hypothetical or tacit consent from benefits was done because the theorists did not want to disturb the authority of the state. They wanted to show that citizens had an obligation to obey the state, because they had accepted or assumed this obligation voluntarily, but they were not able to show any evidence of self-assumed obligation. Voluntarism remained just an idea. The social contract tradition was actually a theory of the exchange of protection for obedience, and in this, the social contract mirrored the other contracts of society, like the marriage contract and the employment contract. The social contract tradition, and the liberal democracies based on it, did not give us, according to her, so much a theory of political obligation as a theory of political obedience. "The dilemma for liberal theory is that it cannot afford to abandon hypothetical voluntarism, and talk merely of political obedience, or the liberal state is deprived of major ideological support. But nor can it really afford to retain voluntarism, because the concept of 'obligation' is a standing reminder that the liberal state is being presented as something other than it really is, and that there is a democratic alternative to liberal theory and practice."[2]

The reference to the homologous structure of the social contract, the marriage contract and the employment contract points to her next book. In her 'Afterword' (written in 1985) *to The Problem of Political Obligation*, she mentions how she has realized that liberal theory does not only emphasize the obedience of citizens to the state, but also that of women to men. Not the inequality between the state and citizens, but that between men and women in liberal democratic societies then becomes the theme of her most famous work, *The Sexual Contract*.

Pateman took her critique of the social contract and its contribution (or lack of it) to democracy, further to make the far-reaching claim that the social contract was simultaneously a sexual contract. In her 1988 work, *The Sexual Contract*, Pateman argues that the social contract was not only an agreement between individuals to obey the laws of the government; it was also at the same time, an agreement between male individuals to allow each other an orderly access to, and control over women. Thus the social contract is actually the basis of modern patriarchy. The original social-sexual contract not only masks the subordination of the citizens to the state, it also masks the domination of women by men. Thus women's inequality becomes a significant aspect of the lack of democracy in modern societies.

**Box 15.1**

**THE SOCIAL-SEXUAL CONTRACT:**

The original contract is a sexual-social pact, but the story of the sexual contract has been repressed... Men's domination over women, and the right of men to enjoy equal sexual access to women, is at issue in the making of the original pact. The social contract is a story of freedom; the sexual contract is a story of subjection. The original contract constitutes both freedom and domination. Men's freedom and women's subjection are created through the original contract—and the character of civil freedom cannot be understood without the missing half of the story that reveals how men's patriarchal right over women is established through contract. Civil freedom is not universal. Civil freedom is a masculine attribute and depends upon patriarchal right. The original contract is a sexual as well as a social contract: it is sexual in the sense of patriarchal—that is, the contract establishes men's political right over women—and also sexual in the sense of establishing orderly access by men to women's bodies... Contract is far from being opposed to patriarchy; contract is the means through which modern patriarchy is constituted.

*The Sexual Contract*

## Domination through Contract in Modern Society

By referring to modern patriarchy, Pateman is clearly asking us not to understand patriarchy as some kind of 'feudal relic' or 'feudal remnant';[3]

for her, it is a modern institution like contract that establishes inequality in contemporary societies, including the inequality between men and women. Pateman argues that it is not the principle of contract but the principle of democratization that increases freedom in a society. The road to freedom lies not through contract but through democratization, and contract is actually a principle antithetical to democratization. We have already seen how for Pateman, the social contract creates not free but obedient male citizens who acquire the right to dominate over women. Modern societies are organized as systems of domination and subordination through a series of contracts and Pateman shows this by analyzing not only the original social-sexual contract, but also the employment contract, the marriage contract, the prostitution contract and the surrogacy contract.

For Pateman, the employment contract, like the other contracts is about property in the person. This means that it assumes that the individual owns himself and his mental and physical attributes, like his capacity to labour, or his talent at playing basketball well. Since he owns these capacities, he can contract the use of them to some other agency and in return he gets a wage or a salary. This is a free exchange. For Pateman, since the individual cannot separate himself from his physical or mental attributes, when he contracts with someone for the use of these attributes, he puts himself under the control of that someone. The idea of property in the person is a political fiction in that unlike property in the form of a house or a car, property in the form of an individual's mental and physical faculties cannot be separated from him. So the employment contract is not a free exchange; instead, it places the employee under the control of the employer. Pateman points out that we must not forget that what is at issue in the labor contract is not just the exploitation of the person who has contracted out his labour but also the domination of the worker. The employer is able to extract surplus value from the worker (exploitation) because the employment contract places the worker under the employer's control (domination). Pateman wants us to see that what is wrong with this relationship of inequality is not so much an inequality in access to material resources, but rather an inequality in who can exercise command over another.

The marriage contract works similarly. In her discussion of the marriage contract, Pateman shows how historically, married women were seen as a kind of property of their husbands and there is a legacy of that time left over in that in many jurisdictions the wrong of 'marital rape' does not exist. To replace that situation by seeing marriage as a mutual contract is something Pateman questions. She analyzes Kant's position on this and points out that for Kant, what saves contractual marriage from being a kind of mutual cannibalism is that in marriage the two partners contract for the use of each other's bodies not for a short period but for an extended period. It is Hegel who shows that marriage cannot be reduced to a contract. Nevertheless, what is interesting, as Pateman points out, is that in the tradition of western political thought, although women are not seen as party to the social contract, yet they are seen as entering marriage through contract, since contract has become the legitimating principle of modern society. Here Pateman takes on those liberal feminists who think that the institution of marriage will be reformed in the interests of women by making it truly contractual.

Pateman is against using neutral terms like sex-work to refer to prostitution. The prostitution contract, like all labor contracts, places the prostitute/worker under the control of the client/employer. Pateman argues that in the prostitution contract, given that the majority of individuals who work as prostitutes are women, the client's interest is in exercising control over the female body: "Prostitution is now part of an international sex industry that includes mass marketing of pornographic books and films, widespread supply of strip-clubs, peep-shows and the like and marketing of sex-tours for men to poor Third World countries. The general display of women's bodies and sexual parts, either in representation or as live bodies, is central to the sex industry and continually reminds men and women—that men exercise the law of male sex-right, that they have patriarchal right of access to women's bodies."[4] This male sex-right is occluded when prostitution is referred to as sex work, an occupation that is available to women just as any other occupation or form of employment.

## For Democratization and Against Contract

In her larger argument, Pateman unpacks the linkages between employment, contract and modern citizenship. In contemporary societies, the pact of citizenship assumes that the citizen will be a respectably employed taxpaying individual. Employment is supposed to give one the status of an independent citizen. Pateman's whole effort, however, is to show that both contract and employment create not relations of independence but those of subordination. Not only does paid employment "not promote or develop abilities needed for democratic citizenship", the citizen has been reduced to a voter in modern democracies. The emphasis on universal employment takes our focus away from the necessity of social reproduction for democratization. Social reproduction includes not only the care-work that is performed at home, but also the work that goes into meeting the educational and health care needs of a society. It is through the meeting of these needs that the citizens of a democracy are created. "...if a society is not merely to continue but to flourish, and flourish as a democracy, social reproduction extends far beyond parenting. Each new generation has to be kept healthy, educated in appropriate ways, and exposed to cultural life... To be concerned with democratization, that is, with the creation of a more democratic society in which citizenship is of equal worth to all so that every citizen enjoys full standing, necessarily involves an interest in welfare and the requirements for social reproduction."[5]

Pateman's feminism gives us an alternative vision of how a society is to be organized—in which the citizen is not just a voter, in which work is not equated with paid employment alone; in which contract is not allowed to mask domination as freedom; and in which 'free women and men' 'agree to uphold limits' since 'freedom requires order and order requires limits'[6]. As a feminist, Pateman is able to flesh out her project of showing how liberal democracy establishes only a minimal form of democratization (universal adult suffrage) that she began with, and to paint in the many other salient elements of democratization. If liberal democracy offers its citizens, both male and female, the promise of paid employment, contractual relations, and voting, Pateman's democratization replaces these, for both men and women, with the ideas of a basic income, a focus of the state on social reproduction, and forms of agreement between citizens that are non-contractual.

## MARTHA C. NUSSBAUM (1947–)

Like Carole Pateman, Martha C. Nussbaum also did not begin her academic career as a feminist. Her initial interest and training was in classical Greek philosophy and her prolific writings include many books and articles on Greek and Hellenistic philosophers like Plato, Aristotle and the Stoics. The works that immediately spring to mind are *The Fragility of Goodness: Luck and Ethics in Greek Tragedy and Philosophy* (1986) and *The Therapy of Desire: Theory and Practice in Hellenistic Ethics* (1994). Aristotle's deep influence on Nussbaum shows up in much of her work, whether she is writing about the human capabilities, or about the importance of the emotions for human beings, or about seeing individuals as both dependent and rational creatures.

Nussbaum's turn towards a focus on the rights of women came not because of her philosophical work, but when she became involved in the projects of the World Institute for Development Economics Research (WIDER), which was set up under U.N. auspices in Helsinki in 1985.[7] Nussbaum became a Research Adviser at WIDER and from 1987 to 1993 spent a month there each summer. Participation in the interdisciplinary conferences organized there spurred Nussbaum to argue that the best way forward to achieve women's rights was to strengthen Rawlsian liberalism with Aristotelian features. Instead of abandoning liberalism, feminism required modifying liberalism in specific directions: so Nussbaum began to develop a position of feminist liberalism, which can be seen in her books such as *Sex and Social Justice* (1999), *Women and Human Development—The Capabilities Approach* (2000), and *The Frontiers of Justice: Disability, Nationality, Species Membership* (2006).

One of the tenets of feminist liberalism is to, while acknowledging that women were often concerned about the welfare of family members and sometimes put the interests of others well before their own, insist that women should also be seen as individuals with their own needs. Women require more of individualism, rather than less, so that they are able to see themselves as separate individuals with separate needs rather than always attached to family members.

This focus on individualism goes together, in Nussbaum, with an analysis of how the independent individual of liberalism only becomes possible because of the 'care' provided by female family members. The invisibilizing of care denies the contribution of women to social reproduction and at the same time presents the myth of the independent individual. It is no wonder that many feminists have argued that the independent individual of liberal political theory is a male category—only men get their needs for a clean home environment and healthy food, for example, fulfilled by unacknowledged others so that one gets the impression that they are independent of these needs. Nussbaum shows how feminist liberalism begins with the idea of dependence, given that human animals go through long periods of dependency not only at the beginning and end of their life, but also for periods during their adult life due to illness or an accident.[8] Political theory must find a place for this dependence by recognizing that both men and women require care, and that some kind of balance must be found between the needs of care receivers and care givers. The work of care must not be shouldered only by women, or be passed on to the women of a certain race, caste, or class.

**Box 15.2**

**HUMAN BEINGS AS BOTH CAPABLE AND NEEDY:**

...we need to adopt a political conception of the person that is more Aristotelian than Kantian, one that sees the person from the start as both capable and needy—"in need of a rich plurality of life activities," to use Marx's phrase, whose availability will be the measure of well-being. Such a conception of the person, which builds growth and decline into the trajectory of human life, will put us on the road to thinking well about what society should design. We don't have to contract for what we need by producing; we have a claim to support in the dignity of our human need itself.

*The Future of Feminist Liberalism*

While recognizing that dependence is part of human nature, and therefore care is an essential component of an ongoing society, Nussbaum also claims that justice requires that all individuals be enabled to contribute to society in their own individual way. Following Aristotle, Nussbaum believes that a human life must be understood on the basis of certain capacities that most human beings possess. She actually lists out ten capabilities that human beings have the possibility of. These capabilities are those of life, bodily health, bodily integrity, the senses, imagination and thought, the emotions, practical reason, affiliation, other species, play and control over one's environment, political and material. If we unpack this list, we see that a recognizably human life assumes that human beings have the ability to live "to the end of a complete human life,…not dying prematurely"; that they are "able to have good health and adequate nourishment and shelter"; that they are able to "avoid unnecessary pain"; that they are "able to use the five senses and are able to imagine, think and reason"; that they are "able to form a conception of the good and to engage in critical reflection about the planning of their life"; that they are "able to live for and with others, to recognize and show concern for other human beings in various forms of familial and social interaction"; that they are "able to live with concern for and in relation to animals, plants, and the world of nature"; that they are "able to laugh, to play and to enjoy recreational activities"; and that they are "able to live their own lives in their own surroundings and context."[9] She calls this list a thick vague theory of the good: it is thick because it specifies different aspects of human functioning instead of just listing five primary goods as Rawls' did; and it is vague "because it admits of much multiple specification in accordance with varied local and personal conceptions."[10] Once such a list has been specified, we can ask whether social and political institutions are giving people what they need in order to be capable of functioning in all these human ways.

Society and state are to be held responsible for enabling individuals, both male and female, including differently abled individuals, to achieve these capabilities. The quality of care that human beings receive can be judged by seeing the extent to which the cared for individual is enabled to act as like an independent person as far as possible. Nussbaum's commitment to liberalism is apparent here: even though she focuses on dependence and criticizes Kant and Rawls for ignoring this aspect of human beings, she still seems insistent on the transcendence of dependence as a mark of humanity. In one of her articles she points out that it was her field visit with poor women in a developing country like India that brought her to recognize how important it was for women to be independent. The other aspect of her liberalism is that she leaves it up to an individual to make the transition from capabilities to functioning.[11]

When we think about the transformation of human capacities into human capabilities, we realize that this is affected by the different social institutions of which we are part. The families we are part of, the kind of educational institutions we go to, all of them affect the development of our capacities. Nussbaum takes up the issue of the family from the perspective of how it affects the interests of women. Criticizing Rawls for making the family a part of the basic structure, yet applying the principles of justice to it externally, Nussbaum argues that since the family has such an important effect on our capabilities, and since most families are structured according to patriarchal norms, justice requires intervention by the state to restructure the family. Under modern patriarchal conditions, women and children in the nuclear family are subordinate to the male head of the family, and feminists have long talked of the need to establish equality in the family. As a feminist, Nussbaum goes beyond liberalism when, although she accepts that families are where individuals learn to form their conceptions of the good, she also agrees that families cannot be treated as purely private spaces. The family is defined by the laws of the state, that is, the state constitutes a set of individuals into a family; therefore, the state must be able to reorganize the family on more egalitarian lines.[12]

We saw earlier how Nussbaum had tried to combine her admiration for Aristotle with her advocacy of a Rawlsian liberalism. We have also been examining her attempt to combine liberalism with feminism. Just like Nussbaum's Aristotelian leanings have led her to hold the state responsible for individuals' lack of capabilities, similarly her feminist position demands state action with respect to inequities in the family. At the same time, however, Nussbaum's commitment to liberalism leads her to take certain positions on sex work, pornography and free speech which have a bearing on women. Nussbaum does not see anything wrong with prostitution as long as it is an occupation freely chosen. She argues that prostitutes work with their bodies just as many others do in their professions, for example, in teaching and in medicine, and as long as the contracts that regulate sex work are valid, prostitution should be considered as just another viable occupation for women.[13] Her position on free speech is also wary of the attempt to constrain freedom of speech on grounds of causing offence, as is allowed by the laws of many countries, including India. She makes a distinction between causing offence and causing harm and only in the latter case should free speech be regulated. This distinction between offence and harm applies in the case of pornography. Nussbaum agrees that pornography can be said to harm women because it reduces women to sexual objects, yet she is wary of the fact as to how the harm of pornography will be addressed by the law.

The kind of feminist liberalism advocated by Nussbaum is very critical of certain positions taken by post-modern thinkers which have a bearing on women's position in society. Nussbaum completely rejects the post-modern claim that local traditions cannot be held up to universal human values because all universal values are a masquerade for some group's parochial way of life. Nussbaum's attempt is to intervene and reform local practices, like dowry, which hamper the human capabilities of women, determined according to a universal perspective. Nussbaum contrasts her historically grounded empirical essentialism (in other words, an internalist essentialism) to a local tradition relativism: her list of universal human capabilities is a way of moving beyond local traditions and preferences to attack patriarchal practices.[14]

Those who are critical of liberal feminism however, turn around and ask whether patriarchal practices which restrict women's capabilities can be addressed primarily by state policies on the redistribution of resources. Liberal feminists are criticized for not moving the focus of gender justice beyond questions of distributional inequality to issues of relational inequality. Injustice arises not merely because of a skewed distribution of resources such as income or education between individuals; relations of domination and subordination also structure human capabilities. 'Hierarchies of command' exist in many societies, "where members of one group monopolize positions of authority, which they exercise over members of other groups". Such hierarchies are consolidated through unjust social practices or social interaction including 'violence, exploitation, segregation and discrimination'.[15]

This hierarchy is not only the result of a skewed distribution of material resources: many individual members of the dominant group may lack access to sufficient material resources, yet as members of the dominant group, they are able to treat better resourced individuals of the subordinate group in unjust ways. Unless specific social practices and social interactions which create this injustice are changed, the dominant group will stay dominant.

In contemporary societies, for example, despite some progress, remedies against sexual violence by men are still weak, and in this situation, women as a group are in a relation of subordination to men. This is not a question of distributional inequality but of relational inequality. To take another example, racist ideology constructs black people as inferior to white people, and as not as good in their work, or more prone to crime and disturbance. This sets up practices of discrimination and exploitation that cannot be addressed primarily through a redistribution of material resources in society.

It could be said that Nussbaum's focus on capabilities will take her theory beyond distributional equality. The idea behind replacing the list of primary goods with a set of capabilities was to see that the fair distribution of capabilities would require more than a sharing of resources. For human beings to be 'able to live their own lives in their own surroundings and context' needs an equal standing between groups in society. In her later work on *Frontiers of Justice* and *The Political Emotions,* Nussbaum does address these issues of equal standing.

## JUDITH BUTLER (1956–)

Whereas Pateman has shown us how modern institutions like contract and citizenship are built on the exclusion of women, and Nussbaum has highlighted the lack of resources like adequate nutrition and health care of women in many parts of the world, Butler's work has focused on the process of acquiring a gender identity. Butler studied at Yale University both as an undergraduate and a graduate student. Before she joined graduate studies at Yale's philosophy department, she was a Fulbright scholar studying Hegel and German Idealism at Heidelberg University. At Yale, she received her Ph.D in 1984 for writing a dissertation on the concept of desire in Hegel's *Phenomenology of Spirit* and its appropriations in 20th century French philosophy. She revised her dissertation in 1985–86 and published it as *Subjects of Desire: Hegelian Reflections in Twentieth-Century France* (1987). Her most famous work, *Gender Trouble: Feminism and the Subversion of Identity,* was published in 1990, followed by *Bodies That Matter: On the Discursive Limits of "Sex"* (1993) and *Undoing Gender* (2004). She has also written *Antigone's Claim: Kinship Between Life and Death* (2000), *Excitable Speech: A Politics of the Performative* (1997), and many other works. Since 1993, she has taught at the University of California, Berkeley. In 1998, she became the Maxine Elliot Professor in the Department of Comparative Literature and the Program of Critical Theory at Berkeley.

### Gender as Performativity

For Butler, gender is a role scripted by social norms. Societies divide human beings into two main genders, male and female and expect these men and women to fulfil different roles. Human individuals come to identify with a particular gender as they perform their gender role repeatedly. The older feminist distinction between sex and gender, where sex was anatomical and gender was social, was given a new interpretation by Butler. She points out that both one's gender identity as well as one's sexual identity are a result of social processes. When a human baby is born, or a human fetus appears on an ultra sound machine, and is greeted by the words, "It's a girl!", the process of forming a sexual and a gender identity begins. Social norms about how a girl behaves show the person who has been named a girl what she is expected to do, and by behaving in the expected way, the person becomes a girl: "There is no gender identity behind the expressions of gender; that identity is performatively constituted by the very "expressions" that are said to be its results."[16]

In *Gender Trouble*, Butler had tried to explain her idea of gender identity through the example of drag, that is, men dressing up as women. While discussing a book on female impersonation in America, Butler talks about how, by dressing up and putting on make-up as women do, and acting as women, these men were seen to be women with their mannerisms. Similarly, Butler argued, women and men normally acquired their gender identity by behaving as women and men were expected to in society. "…the performance of gender that the drag queen offers is no less real and no less true than the performance of gender that any ordinary man or woman might perform,…it gives us a kind of allegory of the mundane performance of gender, and…we are all, all the time, as it were, performing gender. The drag show is a moment in which that performance is rendered explicit. It's not an aberration from the norm; it shows us how the norm actually functions, how the norm is instituted through our bodies, through our stylistics, through our bodily gestures."[17]

Butler reveals how she saw a link between gender performativity and drag when she was younger, and visited gay bars in the evenings. At these bars, she occasionally encountered men dressed up as women, which made her think that since "these so-called men could do the feminine turn much better than I ever could", this showed "the transferability of the attribute of femininity"[18]. It is as if femininity is something that is put on. Butler developed this idea further in *Bodies That Matter* by discussing the 1991 film, *Paris is Burning*, about drag balls in New York City, in Harlem, attended by, performed by "men" who are either African-American or Latino[19].

This does not however mean that gender is choice that we consciously make as we get up each day. We do begin to identify with many of these gender norms. But the congealing of a gender identity requires the constant repetition of the requirements of the role. However, because gender is an endlessly repeated performance, rather than an identity ascribed by one's nature or by one's body, this opens up a space for a refusal to perform according to the script given by society. The result is that one experiences one's gender identity as more open: one can be a man or a woman in ways different from that expected by one's society, and one can even try and move away from the rigidity of the sexual binary in understanding things. For Butler, the whole process of subject formation is both opaque and open ended: since subjectivity is also a form of subjection, when we struggle with our self-hood, we should not set ourselves the aim of a unified subjectivity or identity.

Box 15.3

THE SOCIAL PRACTICE OF GENDER:

Gender performativity is not a matter of choosing which gender one will be today. Performativity is a matter of reiterating or repeating the norms by which one is constituted: it is not a radical fabrication of a gendered self. It is a compulsory repetition of prior and subjectivating norms, ones which cannot be thrown off at will but which work, animate, and constrain the gendered subject, and which are also the resources from which resistance, subversion, displacement are to be forged. The practice by which gendering occurs, the embodying of norms, is a compulsory practice, a forcible production, but not for that reason fully determining. To the extent that gender is an assignment, it is an assignment which is never quite carried out according to expectation, whose addressee never quite inhabits the ideal s/he is compelled to approximate.

*Critically Queer*

## Gender and the Heterosexual Matrix

According to Butler, the social norms that bring gender into being, do so by instituting a code of compulsory heterosexuality. Women and men are beings who desire the opposite sex. Taking up the Freudian analysis of early childhood sexual development, Butler describes how in his discussion of the Oedipus complex, Freud has shown children learning to sublimate or displace their desire for a parent. Butler points out that Freud had explained the boy child's fixation on the mother sometimes through the Oedipus complex and sometimes through the resolution of a disposition to bisexuality: "That the boy usually chooses the heterosexual would, then, be the result, not of fear of castration by the father, but of the fear of castration—that is, the fear of "feminization" associated within heterosexual cultures with male homosexuality. In effect, it is not primarily the heterosexual lust for the mother that must be punished and sublimated, but the homosexual cathexis that must be subordinated to a culturally sanctioned heterosexuality."[20] It is through this heterosexual framework that gender consolidation takes place. That is why Butler is dismayed at what she says is feminism's holding on to the sexual binary even as it attempts to question gender based inequalities.

## From Identity Politics to Queer Politics

Butler is considered a 'queer' theorist, not so much because she is critical of heteronormativity, and considers homosexuality to be an acceptable way of expressing one's sexuality (Butler had a "tempestuous coming out at the age of 16"[21]), but more because she advocates an understanding of sexual identity as much more fluid than limited to either the binary of male or female or heterosexual and homosexual. Queer theorists do not want to replace one set of identity terms with another set of identity terms; the point is not to valorize 'womanly' attributes instead of male qualities, or to celebrate gay and lesbian identities instead of, or along with, heterosexual ones. Butler discusses the Barry Winchell case to make her point: Winchell, a U.S. army soldier, was bludgeoned to death by another soldier for going out with Calpernia Addams, a pre-operative transsexual, who was anatomically male but who identified as female. When some gay rights groups responded by suing the U.S. army, they built up a case of discrimination against gays by presenting Winchell as being in a relationship with another man, even though Addams identified as a woman. Butler is wary of this fixing of identity in the name of rights. She is disturbed to find a group that has struggled with exclusion for so long making the same move of being willing to fight for Addams only by reconstituting her as a man, "reduc[ing] her as it were to her anatomy and therefore violat[ing] her self-understanding and her self-naming practice."[22]

Butler uses this example to warn us that "the assertion of identity can never become the end of politics itself"[23] because as she points out, "What happens when identity politics gets instituted in the law and becomes a very rigid structure so that the capacity for making a claim or seeking redress becomes effectively dictated by very narrow identity terms."[24] As a queer theorist, Butler is not about demanding inclusion for the homosexual identity in the structures of the world as they are today, but about queering identity itself.

As a queer theorist, Butler is also critical of the idea of the unitary and the sovereign subject, the subject in 'possession' of himself. She offers us the conception of a "dispossessed subject", a subject who does not own property in her person, and who becomes a subject in relation to others. Her dilemma is how to contest the forms of dispossession from their land or from their natural resources that the displaced and colonized have suffered under capitalism, on the basis of a "dispossessed subject": she wants "to find ethical and political ways of objecting to forcible and coercive dispossession that do not depend upon a valourization of possessive individualism."[25] She wants to replace the liberal idea of a possessive self with the idea of a dispossessed self, a self who is not in control of her identity; yet at the same time she wants to be able to criticize the dispossession that many people suffer of their lands and resources. Her politics is about being able to criticize this kind of dispossession while at the same time holding on to a conception of a dispossessed self.

Box 15.4

**CHALLENGING A SOVEREIGN AND UNITARY SUBJECTIVITY:**

The idea of the unitary subject serves as a form of power that must be challenged and undone...ethical and political responsibility emerges only when a sovereign and unitary subject can be effectively challenged...Yet as much as we prize the forms of responsibility and resistance that emerge from a "dispossessed" subject...we were also keenly aware that dispossession constitutes a form of suffering for those displaced and colonized and so could not remain an unambivalent political ideal.

*Dispossession: The Performative in the Political*

## CONCLUSION

What feminist theory does is not only to shine a light on the several kinds of inequalities that women as a group are subject to, as compared to men, but feminist theory also attempts to explain the causes of this discrepancy in power and resources. In undertaking this analysis, although feminist theory began with a focus on the inequality between men and women, it soon began to also discuss the differences between women, on grounds of their class, caste, and race. The experience of a woman can be deeply inflected by her class position, for example; hence feminist theory has to be careful to raise issues which are common to women of different classes. The women's movement, as well as feminist theory, has to address the subordination of all women, and not just look at the problems of middle class women or of upper caste women. When feminist theorists write about the sexual violence, and the sexual domination that women are subject to, or about the discrepancy in the amount of work that women do, both at home, and outside the home, and the material resources they have ownership or control over, these theorists also look at how belonging to different castes, or classes, or races, impacts the position of women in these respects.

## NOTES

1. C. Beasley, *Gender & Sexuality—Critical Theories, Critical Thinkers*, London: Sage Publications, 2005, pp. 109–110.
2. C. Pateman, *The Problem of Political Obligation: A Critique of Liberal Theory*, Cambridge: Polity Press, 1985, p. 169.

3. See A. Phillips, J. Medearis & D.I. O'Neill, 'The Political Theory of Carole Pateman', *PS: Political Science and Politics*, Vol. 43, Issue 4, Cambridge University Press, October 2010, p. 816.
4. Carole Pateman, *The Sexual Contract*, Stanford: Stanford University Press, 1988, p. 199.
5. Carole Pateman, 'Another Way Forward—Welfare, social reproduction, and a basic income' in T. Carver & S.A. Chambers, *Carole Pateman—Democracy, feminism, welfare*, London: Routledge Taylor & Francis Group, 2011, pp. 181–182.
6. Carole Pateman, *The Sexual Contract*, *op.cit.*, p. 232.
7. See Ruth Abbey, *The Return of Feminist Liberalism*, Durham: Acumen, 2011, p. 152.
8. Martha C. Nussbaum, 'The Future of Feminist Liberalism', *Proceedings and Address of the APA*, Vol. 74, Issue 2, November 2000, pp. 49–59.
9. Martha C. Nussbaum, 'Human Functioning and Social Justice: In Defense of Aristotelian Essentialism', *Political Theory*, Vol. 20, No. 2, May 1992, p. 222.
10. *Ibid.*, p. 215.
11. Martha C. Nussbaum, *Frontiers of Justice—Disability, Nationality, Species Membership*, New Delhi: Oxford University Press, 2006, ch. 3.
12. Martha C. Nussbaum, 'Rawls and Feminism' in S. Freeman, ed., *The Cambridge Companion to Rawls*, Cambridge: Cambridge University Press, 2003, pp. 499–507.
13. See Martha C. Nussbaum, 'Whether From Reason or Prejudice: Taking Money for Bodily Services', *The Journal of Legal Studies*, Vol. 27, No. S2, June 1998.
14. See Martha C. Nussbaum, 'Public Philosophy and International Feminism', *Ethics*, Vol. 108, No. 4, July 1998.
15. E. Anderson, 'Towards a Non-Ideal, Relational Methodology for Political Philosophy: Comments on Schwartzman's *Challenging Liberalism*', *Hypatia*, Vol. 24, No. 4, Fall 2009, p. 132.
16. J. Butler, *Gender Trouble*, New York: Routledge, 1990, First Indian Reprint, 2012, p. 34.
17. S. Salih, ed., *The Judith Butler Reader*, Malden: Blackwell Publishing, 2004, p. 344.
18. E. Beck-Gernsheim, J. Butler and L. Puigvert, *Women and Social Transformation*, New York: Peter Lang, 2003, p. 10.
19. J. Butler, *Bodies That Matter—on the discursive limits of "sex"*, New York: Routledge, 1993, p. 128.
20. J. Butler, *Gender Trouble*, *op.cit.*, p. 80.
21. J. Butler, *Gender Trouble*, *op.cit.*, (Preface).
22. S. Salih, ed., *The Judith Butler Reader*, *op.cit.*, p. 346.
23. *Ibid.*, p. 337.
24. *Ibid.*, p. 347.
25. J. Butler & A. Athanasiou, *Dispossession: The Performative in the Political*, Polity Press: Cambridge, 2013, p. 7.

## READING LIST

Abbey, Ruth, *The Return of Feminist Liberalism*, Durham: Acumen, 2011.

Beasley, Chris, *Gender & Sexuality—Critical Theories, Critical Thinkers*, London: Sage Publications, 2005.

Butler, Judith, *Gender Trouble*, New York: Routledge, 1990.
Nussbaum, Martha C., *Sex and Social Justice*, Oxford University Press, 2000.
O'Neill, Daniel I., et. al. eds., *Illusion of Consent: Engaging with Carole Pateman*, Pennsylvania State University Press, 2008.
Pateman, Carole, *The Sexual Contract*, Stanford: Stanford University Press, 1988.

## CENTRAL THEMES

1. **Liberal feminism and its limits:** Nussbaum argues that liberalism has the resources to address the injustice of women's inequality as long as it remains open to some important modifications. How can we combine feminism and liberalism and what are the limits of this alliance, from the perspective of women's equality?
2. **Contract and freedom:** Instead of accepting the link between contract and freedom, Pateman instead claims that contract masks domination. How does she show that contract establishes relations of subordination through her analysis of the employment contract or the marriage contract or the social contract?
3. **The gender binary and heteronormativity:** According to Butler, since the social practice of gender does not have any natural basis, gender identity is reinforced only if the heteronormative social norms that define gender are followed repeatedly. Can this idea of 'gender as performativity' help us address the discrimination that women face in society?
4. **Marriage, the family and justice:** A large part of our life is lived in the family, which often begins with a marriage. The family is the site where a large amount of domestic work, mostly unpaid, is performed by women. The economy and the state benefit from this work, yet it is rendered invisible in the public discourse. What kind of interventions would be required to establish justice in the family for women, and with respect to the work they do?

# AFTERWORD

Human history is about change. We have seen, in our study of Western political thought, a number of changes taking place in political institutions, social practices and ideas. How is the change in ideas implicated in political and social change? When new social practices emerge, do new ideas arise in order to legitimize these emerging social practices, or do earlier social practices begin to fade as they succumb to intellectual challenges?

A series of changes that turned the course of human history has been given the name of modernity. In the tradition of Western political thought, we have seen modern political institutions being defended on the grounds that they enlarge human freedom. We have also come across the argument (pace Rousseau and Marx) that these institutions need to be modified, or extended if their claim of bringing about freedom is to be substantiated.

More recently, new subjects of political action have emerged, such as women. New goals for politics have arisen, such as protecting the environment. These new subjects and goals of politics must affect our conceptions of politics. Do the conceptions of politics that we have become familiar with, in our reading of Western political thought, have space for these new subjects and goals of politics? Contemporary political theorists, debating the issue of women's equality, or of political ecology, continue to take their bearings from some of the thinkers we have discussed so far. Today, as we discuss different facets of deliberative democracy, or the waxing and waning of the nation state, or the extension of the idea of human rights to include various new rights, we also decide whether a conversation with the past, or with some of our past, is useful as a resource in this discussion.

# Index

**B**

## Q



## R

T



U



V



W



Z